God's Mercies

For Anne and Bill

O LORD, how long shall I cry, and thou wilt not hear! even
cry out unto thee of violence, and thou wilt not save!

Why dost thou shew me iniquity, and cause me to behold
grievance? for spoiling and violence are before me: and there
are that raise up strife and contention.

Therefore the law is slacked, and judgment doth never go
forth: for the wicked doth compass about the righteous;
therefore wrong judgment proceedeth.

—HABAKKUK 1:2-4, KING JAMES BIBLE

CONTENTS

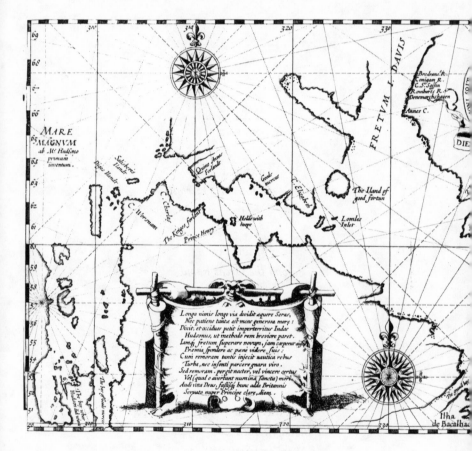

MARE
MAGNVM
ab Mr Hudsono
primum
inventum.

FRETVM I. DAVIS

Brodeus R.
Conigam R.
C. S. Suffin
Rombarts R.
Denemarchhaven

Annes C.

DIE

The Iland of
good fortun

Salisberie
Iland

Digs Iland.

C. Charles

Weer-man

C. Charles

The Kinges fortland

Quine Anne
Fortlund

Goods
mercer

C. Elizabeth

Holde with
hoope

Lomles
Inlet

Prince Henry

Longa nimis longo via diuidit æquore Seras,
Nec patiens tantæ est mens generosa moræ:
Dixit, et occiduas petit imperterritus Indos
Hudsonus, ut methodo rem breviore paret.
Iamq́; fretum superare nouum, iam cœperat audax
Præmia spondere ac pæne videre suæ:
Cum remoram tantis injecit nautica rebus
Turba, nec insonti parcere gnara viro.
Sed remoram: pergit noster, vel vincere certus
Vel (quod o avertant numinâ sanctâ) mori.
Audi vota Deus, fassíq́; hunc adde Britannis
Seruato nuper Principe clare, diem.

If The bay where
Hudson did winter

The bay of Gods mercie

Ilha
de Bacalha

The good he

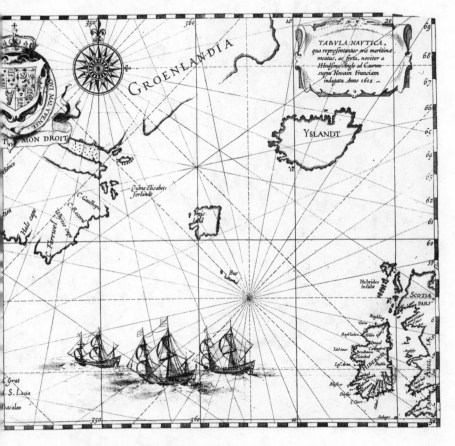

Hessel Gerritsz. *Tabula Nautica*. 1612. Library Archives Canada,
National Map Collection 16174

Samuel de Champlain. *Carte geographique de la Nouelle franse en sonnvraymeridiein.* 1613.
Library Archives Canada, National Map Collection 6329.

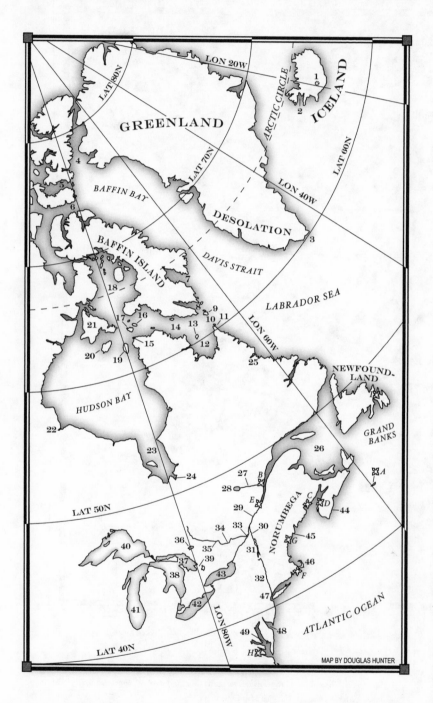

MAP BY DOUGLAS HUNTER

1. MOUNT HEKLA
2. BREIDA FJORD
3. CAPE FAREWELL
4. SMITH SOUND
5. ALDERMAN JONES SOUND
6. LANCASTER SOUND
7. CUMBERLAND SOUND
8. FROBISHER BAY (FROBISHER STRAIT; LUMLEY'S INLET)
9. RESOLUTION ISLAND
10. THE FURIOUS OVERFALL
11. CHIDLEY CAPE
12. UNGAVA BAY
13. AKPATOK ISLAND
14. HUDSON STRAIT (MISTAKEN STRAIT)
15. CAPE WOLSTENHOLME AND THE DIGGES ISLANDS
16. SALISBURY ISLAND
17. NOTTINGHAM ISLAND
18. FOXE BASIN (MARE MAGNUM)
19. MANSEL ISLAND
20. COATS ISLAND
21. SOUTHAMPTON ISLAND
22. MOUTH OF NELSON RIVER
23. JAMES BAY
24. RUPERT BAY
25. NAIN
26. GULF OF ST. LAWRENCE
27. SAGUENAY RIVER
28. LAC ST-JEAN
29. ST. LAWRENCE RIVER
30. RICHELIEU RIVER
31. LAKE CHAMPLAIN AND LAKE GEORGE
32. HUDSON RIVER
33. THE GREAT RAPID
34. OTTAWA RIVER
35. SUMMER CAMP OF TESSÖUAT
36. LAKE NIPISSING
37. GEORGIAN BAY
38. LAKE HURON
39. HURONIA
40. LAKE SUPERIOR
41. LAKE MICHIGAN
42. LAKE ERIE
43. LAKE ONTARIO
44. LAHAVE (PORT DE LA HÈVE)
45. GEORGES RIVER
46. CAPE COD
47. NEW YORK BAY
48. DELAWARE BAY
49. CHESAPEAKE BAY

EUROPEAN SETTLEMENTS
(WITH YEARS OF OCCUPATION)

FRENCH
A. ÎLE DE BOURBON (SABLE ISLAND) 1598-1603
B. TADOUSSAC 1600-01
C. STE-CROIX 1604-05
D. PORT ROYAL 1605-07, 1610-13
E. QUEBEC 1608-PRESENT

ENGLISH
F. ELIZABETH'S ISLE 1602
G. SAGADAHOC 1607-08
H. JAMESTOWN 1607-PRESENT
I. CUPERS COVE 1610-?

PART I

—

Beyond the Furious Overfall

One

—

O N SEPTEMBER 6, 1611, a veritable ghost ship—sails flapping seemingly untended, the hull gnawed by pack ice and gouged by groundings, her course speaking more of accident than intent—drifted from the western horizon into the reluctant company of fishermen setting seines for mackerel off Dursey Island, on Ireland's south coast. The eight emaciated Englishmen aboard the bark *Discovery* had all but given up hope of ever reaching a friendly shore.

It had been a mistake not to steer for Newfoundland when they'd had the chance, and instead to trust that a favourable new breeze could carry them all the way home. The wind had failed them. First, the grain supply ran out, followed by the stock of wild birds they had killed. After exhausting their individual daily ration of salt broth and half a bird, they resorted to eating tallow candles—and, as a special treat, the marrow of gnawed bird bones fried in candle grease and dressed with vinegar. They were so weakened that they sat rather than stood at the whipstaff to steer the ship, and they steered her badly. As one survivor, Habakkuk Prickett, wrote of his skeletal shipmates, they "cared not which end went forward . . . some of them would sit and see the foresail or mainsail fly up to the tops, the sheets being either flown or broken, and would not help it themselves, nor call to others for help."

Their last hope had been to make Ireland, and they had begun to fear that they had missed it altogether. With a few more careless turns at the whipstaff, they might well have blundered too far south to spy their intended landfall. They then could have missed Land's End, or even strayed south of Brest and into the Bay of Biscay, by which point the *Discovery* would have become a ghost ship in fact.

Instead, there was salvation. "A sail! A sail!" they cried. Then more sails appeared: an entire fishing fleet. They steered for the nearest vessel, a bark at anchor.

They had no guarantee of a warm reception. The idea of a common duty of the sea, of sailors of all nations coming to one another's aid in times of distress, was unknown to the times. That same summer, Jonas Poole narrowly escaped the capsizing of his ship while loading aboard the oil boiled down at a land station after a High Arctic whale and walrus hunt at Spitsbergen. When he and his crew rowed to a nearby ship from Hull, the *Marmaduke,* the men from the Humber broke out pikes and took to boats to prevent them from boarding. The *Marmaduke* was considered to be poaching on the commercial territory of Poole's employers, the Muscovy Company, and the *Marmaduke*'s crew was entirely prepared to prod fellow Englishmen to certain deaths in open boats in Arctic waters. The *Marmaduke*'s master had to be talked into rescuing his own countrymen.

The *Discovery*'s men, however, had approached the right ship. She was out of the Cornwall port of Fowey. Her master, John Weymouth, took stock of the misery aboard the hulk and made the charitable decision to weigh anchor and guide these poor starving souls into nearby Bearhaven, on the north shore of Bantry Bay.

Weymouth delivered the men into one of the most virulently anti-Anglo fissures of the Irish coast. Ten years earlier, Spanish forces had landed at Bearhaven and assumed command of Dunboyne Castle from Daniel O'Sullivan, of the O'Sullivan Beara clan. O'Sullivan was the chieftain of the Irish Catholic Congress, and his baronies for centuries had earned most of their income from leasing local fishing rights to the Spanish. When the English defeated invading Spaniards at Kinsale in 1602, O'Sullivan was undeterred by the Spanish withdrawal and chose to fight on as the last Irish chieftain not to recognize the rule of the English crown. And when the English under Sir George Carew, Lord President of Munster, arrived by sea and land to deal with the insurrection, the customary atrocities followed.

On Dursey Island, all two hundred inhabitants were killed—some by the sword, others burned to death in a church, others tied in pairs and tossed from the island's cliffs into the ocean. After Dunboyne Castle was overrun, an untold number of defenders were killed as they tried to swim to Bear Island; those pulled from the water by the English probably became the twenty-seven men Carew hanged as traitors in the market square of Bearhaven. It was in this harbour, so recently bloodied by English soldiers slaughtering Irish patriots like walrus in the Greenland Sea, that the *Discovery*'s famished men sought mercy.

If enlightened mariners had learned anything from their wildly unpredictable encounters with indigenous populations in this age of exploration and conquest, it was that they could never be sure of how the people on the shore had been treated by previous visitors—and how, as a result, these people would choose to treat those who followed. In Bearhaven, the eight people aboard the *Discovery* were about to reap the consequences of Carew's atrocities.

The locals did not harm the *Discovery*'s men. Neither did they want anything to do with them. They were advised to deal with their own kind—the English who were fishing offshore. And so the starving eight were turned away. But their countrymen in the fishing fleet were no more charitable. The *Discovery*'s men "found them so cold in kindness that they would do nothing without present money, whereof we had none in the ship," wrote Prickett.

They were rescued a second time by John Weymouth, who agreed to let them pawn their best anchor and cable. They used the proceeds to buy beer, bread, and beef from the other fishing boats. They also needed seamen and a pilot to get home, for the *Discovery*'s complement was down to eight greatly weakened hands. Another English ship's sympathetic captain, a man named Taylor, agreed to accept a note from Weymouth for the value of the anchor and cable so that Taylor could guarantee the wages that the *Discovery*'s crew promised to the men they hired from the fishing fleet. So angry was Taylor with the men who had otherwise refused to help the *Discovery* home that, according to Prickett, "Taylor swore he would press them, and then, if they would not go, he would hang them."

And so the *Discovery*'s small circle of survivors were able to strike a bargain with the necessary hands: three pounds ten shillings for every man who could help them reach Plymouth or Dartmouth, and five pounds for the pilot. And what if the weather forced them instead into Bristol? Another pound for each of them, then. It was at Plymouth, about twenty miles west of Weymouth's home port of Fowey, that the *Discovery* regained England proper after a seventeen-month absence.

No one knows what the survivors volunteered of their ordeal between their hailing Weymouth's bark off Dursey Island and dropping anchor off Plymouth Castle. Prickett allowed that men in the fishing fleet had "made show that they were not willing to go with us for any wages." Taylor's anger with their reluctance suggests their unwillingness was based on nothing stronger than revulsion with the state of the ship and crew. But the questions would have been inevitable: Where had they been? How had they come into such desperate straits? And most pointedly: Where was the rest of the crew? There had been fourteen other men aboard on the outbound journey in April 1610, as well as a youth, the captain's son. What of them all?

No one, English or Irish, likely would have offered their charity or services had even the most basic details of the *Discovery*'s voyage been surrendered. The extra hands may have noticed the darkened splotches of blood in some of the berths; in explanation, the survivors may have been compelled to produce the clothing, bloodstained and torn by weapons, of missing men, which they had so carefully preserved. From there, a story of sorts would have tumbled forth. The survivors may have learned from these initial experiences of being questioned what to emphasize, how to parry the skepticism. Far more educated and worldly men would be demanding more specific answers once the ship was back in England. And the consequences of not providing an entirely credible answer would be so much greater.

However close-lipped the survivors managed to remain on the final leg home, there would have been no suppressing their awful tale once they touched Plymouth. They would hurry on to London, to explain themselves. And if explanations were not enough, then promises would be made—enough, hopefully, to save them all from the hangman.

Two

—

THERE WOULD BE NO SINGLE, coherent account of
what had occurred aboard the *Discovery* on her voyage of
1610–11: of how the explorer Henry Hudson, his son
John, and seven companions had disappeared on this expedition
in search of the Northwest Passage; of how five more men then
perished on the voyage home.

After the *Discovery* regained England in September 1611, the
survivors delivered Hudson's papers to one of the voyage's key
investors, Sir Thomas Smythe. Hudson had concluded his journal
entry for August 3, 1610, with: "Then I observed and found the
ship at noon in 61 degrees 20 minutes with a sea to the westward."
Hudson was about to steer the *Discovery* into a vast subarctic bay.
It was a cul-de-sac from which he would not escape with his life.

Once Hudson turned south into the great bay that would eventually bear his name, he ceased to exist in flesh and blood. The
pages of his journal beyond August 3, like the man himself, would
go missing. Their publication was likely prevented by censorship
imposed while the passage search continued. The suppressed pages
were then lost altogether, robbing him of his own voice and reduc-
ing his final months to hearsay and anecdote, difficult to define
against the scheming and pleading of the voyage's conspirators and

apologists and the self-serving statements of the survivors. The story of how and why Hudson and his companions were lost would never be his to tell. And those who did do the telling had much to answer for.

The story of the *Discovery*'s final voyage is also one of storytelling. Different people attempted to preserve observations for posterity. But words were discarded, destroyed, suppressed, selectively edited, and lost. Not everyone who lived would be heard from in the end. Not everyone who died would be kept silent.

The story of Hudson's final, fateful voyage might fittingly start not with the *Discovery*'s departure from London in April 1610 but with words set down on paper, written months beforehand. They captured Henry Hudson en route from the unfathomable to the unknowable, with both life and career in the balance.

Three

—

ONE NEVER QUITE KNEW WHAT would creep into, or slip out of, a port like Dartmouth. This major centre of the English cod fishery was a hub of activity on a span of the English Channel that was notorious for bad behaviour. Foreign agents could move in and out of the country through the coast's myriad bays, coves, creeks, and estuaries. West Country ports like Dartmouth also had a disreputable standing among London's merchant adventurers. They were places beyond their administrative reach, havens for pirates, who were a threat not only to ships but also to ship's masters as they lured crewmembers away with promises of easy riches. The letter of commission to Sir Henry Middleton, the general, or commander, of the sixth voyage of the East India Company, which would sail from London in April 1610, firmly directed: "To prevent disorder either on the outward or homeward voyages, the General is forbidden (unless compelled by necessity) to allow any of his ships to touch at Falmouth, Plymouth, or Dartmouth."

The arrival that Dartmouth's mayor, Thomas Holland, observed in the lower reaches of the river Dart on November 7, 1609, was a genuine curiosity, and he promptly placed her under his personal surveillance.

The ship was under the flag of the Verenigde Nedelansche Geoetroyeerde Oostindische Compagnie—the United Netherlands Chartered East India Company, better known by its initials as the VOC, and to the English as the Dutch East India Company. However one referred to it, the VOC was the most powerful and profitable commercial entity in the world, the main engine of prosperity for the Dutch Republic.

A typical VOC merchant vessel, a plodding hauler of trade wares that might have wandered into Dartmouth's riverine harbour on a return voyage from Java, would have been of passing interest to Holland. But this VOC ship was a special case. She was a small, well-armed, nimble vessel: a *jaght*, or hunter, designed for chasing down pirates and capable of conducting piracy of her own. As the crew came ashore, Holland determined that sixteen people were aboard. Most were, predictably, Dutch, and some of them were ill, battling the onset of scurvy after six months away from home. But Holland discovered that her captain, or master, and two other crewmembers were English. Holland did not know that there had been a fourth Englishman, whose life had been cut short two months earlier by an arrow through the throat.

The ship wasn't going anywhere soon. There were fresh provisions to secure, sick men needing rest and recuperation, and doubtless some odds-and-ends repairs to effect after a long ocean passage. Holland had the opportunity to chat up the ship's master about where he had been and what he was intending to do next with this wayward Dutch vessel. The mayor was then compelled to set down what he had learned in a letter.

Holland explained that this ship out of Amsterdam called the *Half Moon,* "of 70 tons or thereabouts," had just arrived, "whereof one Henry Hudson, an Englishman late of London, is master." English masters and pilots in the service of the Dutch were not unusual, but the voyage Hudson was close to concluding with this penultimate stop in Dartmouth was without precedent, and in many aspects seemingly without logic.

Hudson had informed Holland "that in March last he was set forth out of Amsterdam by the East Indian Company there for the discovery of the North-East passage." The mayor was taken with the *Half Moon*'s English master, "finding him also in my understanding to be a man of experience and fit for such employment." After more than a summer's worth of epic wandering across the Northern Hemisphere, Hudson would have been considerably more burnished, considerably less spit and polish, than the man who appeared in later speculative portraits with a neat beard, close-cropped dark hair, and a pleated ruff collar almost as wide as his shoulders. In 1609 Hudson was perhaps forty, married with three boys, who ranged in age from a toddler, Richard, to a young adult. His eldest, Oliver, had made him a grandfather the previous September. His middle child, the teenaged John, was with him aboard the *Half Moon*.

The mayor was in the presence of one of the most accomplished and experienced explorers of northern waters. Hudson might have told Holland, by way of impressing him with his skills, that he had previously attempted the passage over the top of Asia for English investors in 1608, and that this earlier attempt was preceded by a 1607 effort to reach China by the audacious strategy of sailing directly over the North Pole. However much Henry Hudson chose to share with Thomas Holland about his past and his present circumstances, he did not confide to the mayor that the swift, well-armed Dutch vessel he had just guided into the river Dart had effectively been stolen. By him.

Never mind the filched *Half Moon*. There was more to Henry Hudson's most recent escapades than he would let on to an inquisitive functionary like Holland.

For the past few years, Hudson had been the leading figure in international efforts to find a northerly passage to the Orient. Interest in the passage had been falling in and out of fashion among merchant adventurers for decades. A viable route would reduce a round-trip trading voyage to the Far East from two years or more to about six months. Returns on investment capital would be far quicker, and risks could be greatly reduced. About one ship in five tended not to come back from the round-Africa route. A northern passage could avoid, among other hazards, battles with the Spanish and Portuguese, devastating diseases, hulls that rotted out from under their commanders during lengthy stays in tropical waters, and the mysterious, debilitating scourge of scurvy, which cut down men by the score on lengthy ocean passages.

It was up to merchant adventurers and wealthy nobles to risk their own money, men, and ships to find such a passage, and for fifteen years the English gave up looking in any northerly direction after John Davis's third and final voyage of 1587 to the northwest. Davis had gained a sidelong glance at a possible passage entrance as he sailed by it in 1587: a strait beyond a tidal rip around latitude 62 that became known as the Furious Overfall. Interest in investigating Davis's observations resumed in 1602, when a West Country shipwright and mariner named George Waymouth was sent out by two of London's foremost chartered trading companies. The East India Company, formed in late 1600, held the exclusive English right to the Oriental trade on southern ocean routes. The Muscovy Company, which dated back to 1553, had been formed to find the Northeast Passage above Asia, and had long enjoyed an exclusive English right to exploiting any viable northern route. Until such a route could be proved, its investors were satisfied to profit from a monopoly on the Arctic whale and walrus fisheries and the Russia trade.

Waymouth claimed to have pressed one hundred leagues, or three hundred nautical miles, beyond the Furious Overfall. But his failure to sail clear through to China and hand-deliver a letter of greeting to the emperor from Elizabeth I cooled English ambitions to prove any Arctic route for another four years. John Knight was then sent out in 1606 by the same two companies as Waymouth. After a disastrous arrival on the Labrador shore that cost Knight his life, the venture capitalists again swore off any further efforts to the northwest. But their interest in discovering some kind of northerly route persisted, and the Muscovy Company, perhaps again in conjunction with the East India Company, turned to Henry Hudson.

Nothing is known about Hudson's life before then. No birth or marriage records for him survive. No details of previous voyages have been preserved. While men named Hudson occasionally appeared in the earlier history of the Muscovy Company, there is no proof he was related to any of them. The most that can be said is that he was a professional seaman, as the positions of master and pilot, claimed for him by his own journals and by observers, were licensed by Trinity House at Deptford Strand.

Hudson was to attempt the transpolar route in 1607 and then the northeast route in 1608. When neither effort produced anything like a promising passage-making result, Hudson's brief career as an Arctic explorer appeared in jeopardy.

A man was fortunate to reach forty in this day and age. After attending the christening of his granddaughter in London in September 1608, with no immediate prospects of passage-seeking employment, Hudson could well have seen his moment in the exploratory limelight pass.

Then the VOC had come calling, enquiring about his availability to make another attempt on the Northeast Passage.

English navigators had been serving the Dutch on major ocean passages since at least the 1590s, as the little nation transformed itself into a global power in trade, finance, and seafaring. English pilots were hired to teach at the navigation academy founded at Enkhuisen in 1593 by cosmographer Petrus Plancius, while John Davis served as chief pilot on the first Dutch trading voyage to the Orient, in 1596. English and Dutch interests had become further entwined by English military support of their fellow Protestants in the northern provinces of the Netherlands, who had thrown off the yoke of Catholic Spain to found the Dutch Republic in a rebellion that had begun in 1572.

Hudson crossed the channel around October 1608, to discuss the offer of employment by the VOC's Amsterdam chamber, which was the single largest group of VOC investors, controlling eight directors' votes on the ruling Council of Seventeen. Its overture to Hudson came at a critical moment in a multinational effort to broker a peace between the Spanish and Dutch. Talks at The Hague had just collapsed, Spain having insisted that the Dutch give up trade to the Orient as a condition of peace. After Spanish negotiators went home, the VOC was left to consider the financial impact of outright war with Spain on the southern trade routes. It made sense to the Amsterdam chamber to have a fresh look at the possibility of a northeast passage route that could avoid entirely the galleons of Philip III, and it was able to persuade at least the Zeeland chamber to join it in having the Council of Seventeen authorize by majority vote a VOC voyage under Hudson's command.

Hudson was only too happy to express his enthusiasm for the feasibility of a high-latitude passage above Novaya Zemlya—the "belt of stone" of the Russian Arctic—despite the discouraging conclusions he recorded in his journal for the 1608 voyage to the northeast. He had confessed in his entry of June 25, "our hope of passage was gone this way," persistent pack ice having forced him well below the course he needed to steer to clear the northern tip of the scythe-like archipelago. In turning back on July 6, he had pronounced the expedition "void of hope of a north-east passage," the route over the top of Novaya Zemlya being the only course he considered feasible in that direction. It was the northwest route, as last tested by George Waymouth, that Hudson now wished to investigate. Hudson accordingly tried to convince his crew to make for the Furious Overfall rather than return home in failure from Novaya Zemlya, but he was forced to heed their demand to steer for London. Deftly concealing his entirely sensible conviction that the northeast route was folly, a few months later Hudson accepted the VOC's money and the use of its ship for another attempt in 1609.

Negotiations to hire Hudson had fallen chiefly to Petrus Plancius, chief cartographer of the VOC. The fifty-seven-year-old cosmographer (and firebrand theologian and minister in the Dutch Reformed Church) was indefatigably enthusiastic about the possibilities of the Northeast Passage. He had championed the particular route over top of Novaya Zemlya when the Dutch dispatched three expeditions to the north and northeast in the 1590s. The multivoyage effort had died along with its chief pilot, and Plancius's protégé, Willem Barentsz, on the final voyage, in 1597.

Hudson's voyages of 1607 and 1608, to the north and northeast, had been English fact-checking missions of the exploits of Barentsz, and Hudson knew how to play to Plancius's interests. Hudson told the aging VOC cartographer things he already knew and believed about the possibilities of the northeast route, and tailored his findings to suit his audience. For Plancius, he blamed his failure in 1608 on inexperience, that instead of keeping to the open sea, which was supposedly ice-free because of its great depths and the action of waves and currents, he had clung to the shoreline. But his voyage journal indicated otherwise. He had tried to approach Novaya Zemlya from higher latitudes, and was persistently forced southward by pack ice in the open ocean. Only when the high-latitude course was denied him did he find himself coasting the archipelago, working southward in search of an alternative route. As for the climate, in his voyage journal Novaya Zemlya abounded with evidence of its temperate nature and plant and animal life: "Generally, all the land of Nova Zembla that yet we have seen, is to man's eye a pleasant land . . . looking in some places green, and deer feeding thereon." But in his discussions with Plancius, Hudson stated that the archipelago was "barren," and populated only by "carnivorous animals." The deer and greenery, Hudson avowed, were to be found much farther north, at Spitsbergen, thereby agreeing with Plancius that the world became warmer as one travelled closer to the pole.

At the same time, Hudson was able to secure copies of precious items from the collections of Plancius and fellow cartographer Jodocus Hondius, who translated for Hudson during the VOC negotiations and witnessed the contract he signed. These items had nothing to do with the task at hand but had everything to do with Hudson's unshakable ambition to seek a passage elsewhere.

Hudson carried away a set of sailing directions for Iceland and the east coast of Greenland, originally written by a native Greenlander named Ivor Boty and first translated out of Norse into High Dutch in 1560. A merchant named William Stere (according to Hudson's own annotation) translated it into English for him, from a Low Dutch version possessed by Hondius, "which I have seen." Hudson had no need for Boty's instructions on the VOC voyage, unless he planned to actually head for the Northwest Passage.

Foremost in Plancius's collection were journals of George Waymouth, which the Dutch cartographer and chronicler Hessel

Gerritsz stated Plancius had acquired from his own incomparable sources. Gerritsz assumed the journals were from the 1602 voyage to the Furious Overfall, but he was entirely unaware of Waymouth's 1605 voyage to the coast of what is now Maine, where he had assessed the potential for a colony on a site at latitude 44, at the mouth of the Georges River. Gerritsz's description of Hudson's acquisition of the Waymouth journals (he used the plural *diaria*) was sufficiently confused to make it possible that he also acquired materials relating to the 1605 voyage.

A Waymouth journal from 1605 (which otherwise has never been found) would not have been without interest to a passage-seeker. Left out of the voyage account published in late 1605 was a crucial sentence in author James Rosier's manuscript, doubtless struck out by censors: "And our Captain verily thought (though he concealed it) [that the Georges River] might possibly make a passage into (or very nigh) the South Sea; which he neither had commission nor time now to search."

The idea of a midcontinental route to the Pacific Ocean—the South Sea—had particular currency among the English at the time. And for all Hudson was prepared to agree with Plancius that a High Arctic route to the Orient was feasible, he was understandably intrigued by the notion that there might be a route to the Orient far from the icy privations of Novaya Zemlya, Spitsbergen, and the Furious Overfall. Given the opportunity, if not the permission, Hudson was determined to find it.

The contract Hudson signed with the Amsterdam chamber in January 1609 was, in modern parlance, back loaded. The fee of only 800 guilders (about $11,000 U.S. today) not only compensated Hudson for his services and provided for his wife and children but was also to fund "his outfit of the said voyage." If he didn't return within a year, the VOC would pay Hudson's widow,

Katherine, 200 guilders. It was an inexpensive venture for the VOC, since the voyage of a single ship in the Asia trade required an investment of about 100,000 guilders, or about $1.4 million U.S. today. For Hudson there were promises of unspecified financial rewards from the VOC should he be successful, and the possibility of long-term employment with the great trading firm.

The VOC's problems with Henry Hudson came to a head long before the *Half Moon* left the dock. After signing him to the contract, his Dutch backers quickly realized that Hudson was all but impossible to control. Hudson momentarily left the project in a huff in March 1609, after arguing with the VOC's chief boatswain, Dirck Gerritsz, about who knows what, and being dissatisfied with the wages offered to the select group of Englishmen he intended to take with him: his own son, John; John Colman, a veteran of his 1607 voyage; and Robert Juet, a skilled navigator who had been with him in 1608. The Zeeland chamber of the VOC, writing their counterparts in Amsterdam, presciently stated, "We are much surprised at Mr. Hudson's strange behaviour and consider it inadvisable to let him undertake the voyage, for if he begins to rebel here under our eyes what will he do if he is away from us?"

The Zeelanders, who had reluctantly approved of the voyage in the first place, provided the Amsterdam chamber with firm advice: "that whereas the said Hutson has taken his departure he shall remain dismissed; and even if he came to change his mind with respect to performing the journey Your Honours shall in no wise engage him but leave him dismissed. And whereas there was advanced to him certain monies to the amount of twenty-five pounds more or less, Your Honours shall compel the said Hutson, by law or arrest, to repay the aforesaid monies which the Company has advanced him." Petrus Plancius should then find a "competent and sensible person" to replace Hudson so that the voyage could proceed as planned at the end of the month.

But the company, with its decision-making dominated by the Amsterdam chamber, chose not to heed the Zeeland advice. With the *Half Moon*'s scheduled departure only a few weeks away when Hudson stormed off, the VOC may have run out of time in finding a suitable replacement for him. Instead, the VOC strove to rein in the returned Hudson with a severe set of sailing directions, which Plancius would have drafted.

Hudson's contract had called upon him to return within a year with proof of a viable northeast route if he wished to collect further rewards from the company. He was now to undertake a basic investigation of the northeast and be back before winter set in. The sailing directions ordered him explicitly "to think of discovering no other routes or passages, except the route around by the North and North-east above Nova Zembla; with this additional provision, that if it could not be accomplished at that time, another route would be the subject of consideration for another voyage."

On April 4, 1609, Hudson sailed from Amsterdam up the inland sea, the Zuiderzee, negotiating the shifting sands at The Texel to gain the North Sea on April 6. He dutifully sailed for Norway's North Cape, clearing it on May 5. Having every expectation of failure for this assignment, he did not disappoint himself. Novaya Zemlya stood as emphatically in his way as it had in 1608. He needed to sail above latitude 77 to clear the north tip of the archipelago, but didn't come anywhere close. The familiar obstacles of ice and fog were compounded by the fears of sailors accustomed to the sweltering heat of the proven route to the Orient, around Africa's Cape of Good Hope.

As Dartmouth's mayor, Thomas Holland, related in his letter, Hudson had "proceeded as far as the coast of Nova Zembla and was in 72 degrees [latitude], and that his company (who are all

Flemings besides himself and two others), being unable to endure the cold, he altered his voyage, and passing by the northern parts of Scotland directed his course for the coast of America."

Holland's quick recounting of Hudson's altogether strange and extraordinary voyage for the VOC continued. Hudson came "to the Banks on the coast of Newfoundland, from whence by stormy weather he was forced to put into Nova Francia, where he new masted his ship and so passed to a place called Cape Codd." Hudson then "sailed to the southward of the London Colony in Virginia, and trended that coast till he came to Cape Henry, and so sailed up into the bay of Chicepeiake, and there having viewed the coast and the fashion and trending of the land, he came forth out of that bay to the northward."

Holland had just described one of the most eccentric passages in seafaring history. Hudson had gone all the way from Amsterdam to the Arctic waters of Russia, to the Georges River ("Nova Francia"), on to Cape Cod, then south to Chesapeake Bay, where the London wing of the Virginia Company had established the Jamestown settlement in 1607. This was all true enough, as far as it went, which by the raw measure of the voyage was a terribly long way. But Hudson would not have let Holland know that in turning the *Half Moon* around at Novaya Zemlya and steering instead for North America, he had been in blatant violation of his sailing orders.

Henry Hudson's success in achieving the astonishing course reversal with the *Half Moon* was a tribute to his personal powers of persuasion. The crew, especially the Dutch majority (which included the master's mate), had no real reason to agree to this unauthorized and radical change in plans. Some of them probably had experience as "sea beggars"—Dutch pirates who had gained folk-hero status for attacks on Spanish shipping. The sea beggars could be unscrupulous, helping themselves to whatever struck their fancy on land and at sea. The fact that the *Half Moon* was named for the good-luck medallion worn by sea beggars underscored the ship's essential capabilities. Hudson surely understood what the men aboard her were capable of, what sort of dark bargain he could strike with them.

After being rebuffed by Novaya Zemlya, Hudson had presented his Dutch charges with two options: to probe the Northwest Passage, or to seek a passage through the middle of North America. It might be the Georges River, as Waymouth suggested, or it might be a river in the Chesapeake. Hudson's friend Capt. John Smith of the Jamestown venture had written Hudson on the matter, and even sent him a chart. The James River had initially been chosen as the colony site because it was thought it might lead toward the Pacific, but exploration had proven this idea wrong. Smith was beginning to suspect that the Potomac, at the head of the bay, might provide a way through, although he could never have imagined that Hudson might show up in a VOC *jaght* to have a look for himself.

Having had their fill of the ice, fog, and cold of the northeast, the Dutch sailors chose Hudson's option of seeking the passage through North America. In return, they must have anticipated opportunities to pursue some casual piracy against Spanish and Portuguese shipping. They were conveniently ignorant of the fact that the Dutch Republic and Spain (whose House of Castile also ruled Portugal) had at last struck a truce, the day after the *Half Moon* cleared The Texel.

It was all Hudson could do for the next few months to keep these hungry dogs pulling for him as the promise of swag eluded them. Approaching North America, they about-faced and chased a ship for six hours eastward, in what must have been an unsuccessful attempt at high-seas robbery, though they were on their best behaviour when they subsequently spoke with a French vessel off Nova Scotia. The voyage was also persistently unproductive as an exercise in discovery. They made their first landfall at the Georges River, but Hudson had no opportunity to investigate its passage potential. After they stopped to cut and fit a replacement for a broken forespar, their brief visit ended with an assault on a native village by Dutch sailors who were tired of having nothing to show for their time at sea, far from home.

Turning south for the Chesapeake, Hudson was extraordinarily fortunate not to be killed by the Spanish or imprisoned in one of their slave galleys. Even though Spain was at peace with England and France, and the truce had just been struck with the breakaway Dutch Republic, the Spanish remained adamant that eastern North America was the exclusive territory of Philip III. A small warship, *La Asunción de Cristo,* had been dispatched with a company of soldiers from San Agustín in Florida on June 21 to locate and eradicate the Jamestown colony, and to then cruise north, beyond the Georges River, to deal with any other interlopers at sea or on land. *La Asunción* arrived at the entrance to the Chesapeake on July 24, but was chased away by an unknown vessel—it might have been Samuel Argall's *Mary & John*—the next day. The *Half Moon*'s men at that moment were overrunning the native village at the Georges River, and Hudson was about to return to sea, onto a collision course with the Spaniards. But he was saved by a show of hands aboard *La Asunción.* After fleeing the Chesapeake, the senior officers decided to return to San Agustín rather than continue their search-and-destroy cruise any farther north.

Hudson's visit to the Chesapeake was even briefer than his stop at the Georges. He was scarcely into the bay on August 18 before bolting from it, with Robert Juet blaming a stiff northerly for compelling them to head back out to sea, where they would have room to manoeuvre without risk of being blown aground. Hudson then would have stayed well clear when he saw the first four ships in the Virginia Company's storm-battered relief flotilla approaching. They reached the bay on the twenty-first, though their approaching sails would have been spotted on the nineteenth or twentieth. Hudson would not have been welcomed in a VOC ship transgressing on the company's territory—territory that not only included the Chesapeake but stretched under its charter from latitude 34, in the Carolinas, all the way north to latitude 45, along modern Nova Scotia.

Hudson loitered out at sea for several days, enduring rough weather. ("This night," Juet wrote of the twenty-first, "our cat ran crying from one side of the ship to the other, looking over-board, which made us wonder; but we saw nothing.") After reaching the latitude of the Carolina Banks to the south, the *Half Moon* returned to the Chesapeake, sighting the entrance again on the morning of the twenty-seventh, but went no farther. Another ship in the storm-wracked supply fleet—the *Diamond,* the flag-ship of the flotilla's vice-admiral—had stumbled into the Chesapeake without a mainmast a few days after the arrival of the first four, according to a letter written by Gabriel Archer, who had been aboard one of the first ships to reach the colony; still another ship, the *Swallow,* followed three or four days after the *Diamond.* These arrivals would have interrupted Hudson's plans a second time. The possibility of exploring unchallenged any river in the bay had vanished, now that Virginia Company ships were on hand in such number.

Rarely has someone sailed so far to accomplish so little, in so many far-flung locations, on a single voyage. But then Hudson began to make genuine contributions to cartography as he returned north, along the Atlantic seaboard. He made a cursory inspection of Delaware Bay, a possible first for Europeans. Then, as he revealed to Thomas Holland, "he discovered a goodly river, into which he sailed with his ship 50 leagues up and found by his sounding there that the same is navigable with any ships whatsoever."

The river was no passage to the Orient, but it was a major transportation corridor, and it would come to bear Hudson's name. By
the time he had finished exploring its navigable length as far north
as modern-day Albany, though, Hudson's grip on command was
fingernail deep. While he could neither read nor write Dutch, he
must have known enough of the spoken language to understand
the increasing verbal abuse and threats of violence that came his
way from the restless sea beggars.

On October 4, 1609, when the *Half Moon* returned to sea
where New York City now sprawls, the crew was on the edge of
revolt. According to Emmanuel van Meteren, the Dutch consul in
London, who relied on Hudson for his account, the Dutch mate
said they should overwinter in Newfoundland and search for the
Northwest Passage the next season. But Hudson was opposed:
"He was afraid of his mutinous crew, who had sometimes savagely
threatened him, and he feared that during the cold season they
would entirely consume their provisions, and would then be
obliged to return. Many of the crew also were ill and sickly."
Hudson's suspicions were raised when, as they discussed their
options, nobody in the crew suggested returning to Holland. If he
agreed to the overwintering scheme, the Dutch crew, bent on full-
time piracy, more than likely would wrest the ship from him and
his handful of English companions—now down to two, as a
native American arrow had cut down John Colman soon after
their initial arrival at the mouth of the great river.

Hudson persuaded the crew to sail home. Or, at least, in its
general direction. Initially they agreed to make landfall in Ireland.
For some reason the *Half Moon* steered instead from the Hudson
River directly to Dartmouth, neither seeing nor touching land
along the way during a month of sailing.

For Hudson, calling on Dartmouth was infinitely preferable to
an immediate return to Amsterdam, where he would face the

wrath of powerful, wealthy, and litigious merchants. The VOC had already begun to wonder what had become of him. At a meeting of the Council of Seventeen on September 1, the Amsterdam chamber's directors were asked to produce Hudson's sailing instructions. Copies of them, along with the contract, were made and distributed. The council would have hoped that the *Half Moon* had not been crushed in Arctic ice approaching Asia's Cape of Tartaria, with death benefits to Katherine Hudson soon to be added to the company ledgers. The ship's true position at that moment—steering north-northwest, the lead line tickling the plunge of the continental shelf off present-day Atlantic City as Robert Juet took note of "fair weather, the wind variable between east and south"—would have infuriated them to the cores of their pragmatic Calvinist souls.

The Dutch sailors may have been no more eager than Hudson was to show their faces in Amsterdam any time soon. Holing up in Dartmouth's slightly disreputable comforts gave Hudson time to plot his next move in this rogue voyage of discovery. To Thomas Holland he explained that he planned to stay in the port for ten days, "and upon advice, which he expects from a Dutchman in London, being furnished with some necessaries here, intends to return again to the coast of America."

Dartmouth's mayor felt it critical that this news be conveyed before Hudson set out again. His letter arrived at Hatfield House in Hertfordshire on November 13, after a four-day delivery across southern England. The massive estate was home to Sir Robert Cecil, Earl of Salisbury, who had acquired it in a land swap with his king, James I, in 1607. James was wont to call the diminutive, hunchbacked earl "my little beagle," and Elizabeth before him had teased Cecil with "my elf." Holland included the title Lord High Treasurer of England in the letter's address. It would have been more to the missive's purpose had Holland addressed it to Sir Robert in his other, more longstanding capacity, as Secretary of State, a position that made him the kingdom's chief spymaster.

"My duties to your Honour humbly acknowledged," Holland had begun the letter, as he shifted from mayor to state informant. The mayor was a member of Cecil's domestic intelligence network, and he had learned enough from the freespeaking Hudson to consider his imminent departure from Dartmouth a matter of national security.

Four

—

HENRY HUDSON WAS NO FOOL, and yet on his arrival in Dartmouth he had behaved in what appeared to be a recklessly foolish way. He had spoken all too candidly with Thomas Holland about where he had been and what he had in mind next. By admitting that he planned to return to the "coast of America," Hudson suggested an intention to take the VOC ship right back into the territory of the Virginia Company. This threatened intrusion on English territory raised concerns at the state level. What is more, the Virginia Company was financed by the leading political and commercial figures of James's realm. And similarities between the surviving 1609 voyage journal of pilot Robert Juet and an unpublished account of Gabriel Archer from the 1602 voyage of Bartholomew Gosnold showed that Hudson had employed confidential English information in guiding a VOC ship into the territory of the Virginia Company.

Hudson's carelessness with Holland was shocking, coming from someone so well connected in political and commercial circles. The discovery business was just that, a matter of business, of seeking new trade opportunities and profitable resources. And in England (as most everywhere), matters of business were deeply entwined with matters of state, to the point of insidious corruption

among men like Sir Robert Cecil who could not always differentiate between the nation's interests and their own feathernesting.
Since his debut in exploration's annals in 1607, Hudson had come
to know merchants and statesmen in the most senior ranks of
court life, the Privy Council, and the major London trading companies. Indeed, as Thomas Holland related in the letter to Cecil,
Hudson was "well known (as he told me) to Sir Walter Cope and
Sir Thomas Challener."

Hudson chose carefully the two names he mentioned to
Holland. Challener (or Challoner) was a close adviser to Prince
Henry, encouraging his enthusiasm for scientific matters, which
included the search for the Northwest Passage. Cope was none
other than Cecil's right-hand man, a longstanding associate both
in affairs of state and personal business ventures. By January 1609,
when Hudson signed his VOC contract, it was common knowledge that Cope would soon secure the second highest financial
position in the realm, Chancellor of the Exchequer. The appointment was confirmed in June, while the *Half Moon* was crossing
the Atlantic. And the private interests of Cecil, Cope, and
Challener converged within the Virginia Company, in which they
were all investors.

Hudson could not have been oblivious to how his actions
would affect powerful men he knew personally. England was
aboil with subterfuge: domestic turncoats and foreign spies,
murderous intrigues against the crown, and fierce factional
rivalries within the corridors of political and commercial power.
Hudson knew too many high-ranking people not to appreciate
that the wrong words said to the wrong person could prove
ruinous, sometimes even fatal. He must have known too that in
this veritable police state, someone like Holland would write
down everything he was telling him and get it to Cecil in the
shortest possible time.

That Hudson dangled the weighty names of Sir Walter Cope and Sir Thomas Challener before Cecil's informant suggests that he knew what he was doing in speaking so unguardedly with Dartmouth's solicitous mayor. Hudson may well have been letting major political players associated with the Virginia initiative and other overseas ventures know that he was back among them. Not only did he have a Dutch ship he had to return somehow; he had information from his North American meanderings that they might want to hear before he moved on to Amsterdam. For all that Hudson had told him, Holland suspected the ship's master was holding something back: "it seems to me, by conferring with him, that he has discovered some especial matters of greater consequence which he would not impart."

Hudson had persuaded the Dutch crew to rest, recuperate, and replenish in Dartmouth before striking out for Amsterdam. Ten days was all Cecil's people had to get some word back to him, and perhaps to make him a counter-offer he couldn't refuse.

Hudson had vowed to Dartmouth's mayor that he was going to sail for the "coast of America" as soon as he had received word from a Dutchman in London. For a cartographer, *America pars* was a Latin label that could apply to a vast range of coastal geography. It would have been understandable if Cecil, digesting Holland's urgent letter, concluded that Hudson was referring to the Virginia Company's territory. But the label extended all the way to the Northwest Passage, and this was unquestionably where Hudson intended to sail next.

Hudson's "Dutchman in London" could only have been the Dutch consul, Emmanuel van Meteren, who had lived in the English capital since he was a youth and knew virtually everyone who was worth knowing there. It was assuredly van Meteren who had brought Hudson to the attention of the VOC in late 1608. He would write authoritatively about Hudson's communications with the VOC, as well as the events of the 1609 voyage, without ever acknowledging his own role in Hudson's employment.

When Hudson reached Dartmouth, he sent word of his return to the VOC through van Meteren. "A long time elapsed through contrary winds before the Company could be informed of the arrival of the ship in England," van Meteren would write.

According to van Meteren, Hudson had made a rather forward proposal to the VOC. He wanted to exchange six or seven of his crew, presumably men who were ill, or had been making as much trouble for him as he was for the VOC, and increase the ship's complement to twenty. In the London consul's account, there was no urgency on Hudson's part to quit Dartmouth so soon after arriving in early November. Hudson's plan, according to van Meteren, was to sail again from Dartmouth on March 1, 1610. He proposed spending April and half of May fishing and whaling, to relieve the investors' expenses, before trying the Northwest Passage.

Hudson had in mind a basic, fair-weather reconnaissance: he would investigate the passage until mid-September, then return to Holland after sailing over the north of Scotland, a curiously specific assurance of the final course, which may have been a promise that he wouldn't again be tempted by West Country refuges on the return trip. Hudson demanded 1,500 florins (as the Dutch guilder was also known) for supplies, above and beyond the crew's wages, for the new voyage.

The VOC had other ideas. When word at last reached the directors of Hudson's return from an entirely unapproved direction, and of his presumptuous request for further funding for a Northwest Passage attempt they had never been interested in making, they ordered Hudson back to Holland with the *Half Moon*. But as Hudson prepared to leave Dartmouth in January, he and the other Englishmen, according to van Meteren, "were commanded by the government there not to leave England but to serve their own country."

The *Half Moon* eventually made it back to Amsterdam, in early 1610, but Hudson himself did not return with her to face the ire of the VOC. As for the ship's papers, including the log and Hudson's journal, they seem to have been collected from him in London by van Meteren and forwarded to the VOC, but only after being carefully inspected by men of import in London. "Many persons thought it rather unfair that these sailors should thus be prevented from laying their accounts and reports before their employers, chiefly as the enterprise in which they had been engaged was such as to benefit navigation in general," van Meteren groused of the delay in the return of the ship's papers to Amsterdam.

Van Meteren insisted that Hudson would have sailed for the Northwest Passage in 1609 if his crew had been agreeable when he first turned the *Half Moon* around off Novaya Zemlya, and if he wasn't in such fear of them by the time he left the Hudson River. Van Meteren also believed Hudson had been fully prepared to seek the northwest route for the VOC in 1610, as his proposal indicated. Yet Dutch cartographer and historiographer Hessel Gerritsz, writing about Hudson in 1613, would express the broadly held suspicion that Hudson had duped the Dutch on the *Half Moon* voyage: "He seems . . . according to the opinion of our countrymen, purposely to have missed the right road to the western passage, unwilling to benefit Holland and the Directors of the Dutch East India Company by such a discovery."

It remains far from clear what Hudson's true intentions ever were. The English order not to sail again for the VOC, which is presumed to have come from the Privy Council, might have been made against Hudson's will, or with his conniving cooperation.

Van Meteren wrote that when Hudson was detained in January 1610, "it was then thought probable that the English themselves would send ships to Virginia, to explore the river found by Hudson." But the Virginia Company showed no interest at this time in the Hudson River, leaving it open for independent Dutch fur traders to rapidly exploit.

Far from being punished by the English state after he was allegedly forbidden to return to work for the Dutch, Hudson was able to attract a wonderful commission for a Northwest Passage search from his country's leading figures. Indeed, men who had seemingly little interest in his ambitions just a year before now demanded that he sail in their service in 1610.

For all its outwardly quixotic, seemingly pointless wanderings, the 1609 voyage had helped transform Hudson into an omnibus of his era's passage-making quests. Men like Petrus Plancius and the English historiographer Richard Hakluyt could say they had read original manuscripts, interviewed voyage participants, and formulated cosmographic views that posited routes awaiting exploitation. But by the time Henry Hudson brought the *Half Moon* into Dartmouth, Hudson had become peerless in his depth of experience. Others might have seen more than he had in some directions, but no one else could claim to have commanded searches for passages to the northeast, the north, and the west. Only the northwest remained untested by him.

The experience he had gained through this VOC voyage (and, perhaps, the secret knowledge he hinted at to Holland) was enough to see him rewarded in a way he could not have hoped to exceed. London's leading merchant adventurers, statesmen, and parliamentarians—including Sir Robert Cecil, Sir Walter Cope, and Charles Howard, Lord High Admiral, as well as the Muscovy and East India companies—hired him to pick up in the northwest where George Waymouth had left off in 1602, using Waymouth's old ship, the *Discovery*. And young Henry, newly minted as Prince of Wales—with Sir Thomas Challener his adviser and governor of his household—signed on as royal patron.

Hudson would at last be able to make good on the ambition he had stated near the conclusion of the journal from his 1608 voyage to Novaya Zemlya: "to make trial of that place called Lumleys Inlet, and the furious over-fall by Captain Davis, hoping to run into it an hundred leagues, and to return as God should enable me."

Five

—

WHILE SIR ROBERT CECIL, Sir Thomas Challener, and Sir Walter Cope were vital to Henry Hudson's success in securing the *Discovery* commission, no one would have been more important to Hudson's career than Sir Thomas Smythe. Some fifty years of age when Hudson was given command of the *Discovery*, Smythe was a merchant adventurer who oversaw the main avenues of opportunity in every noteworthy overseas initiative. The great hall of his home on Philpot Lane in London's east end was where trade companies that Smythe led conducted their business. It was also a point of convergence for sailors seeking work and a resolution to wage disputes. While ships sent out by Smythe's various ventures were at sea for months, even years, wives like Katherine Hudson gathered there awaiting some news, for good or for ill, of a voyage's outcome.

Smythe was a member of the Skinner's and Haberdasher's companies, two of the great livery companies of London. He had narrowly escaped ruin when he was implicated in the Essex plot against Queen Elizabeth in 1601. He was fined heavily and incarcerated in the Tower of London, which was where James I found him when he came to power in 1603.

Liberated by James, Smythe flourished. Parliamentarian, favourite of the king, financier extraordinaire, and member of the Company of Merchant Adventurers, as "customer" of the port of London he had oversight of 90 percent of the nation's foreign trade. Smythe also personified England's commerce-driven exploration in the early years of James's reign. A past governor of the Levant Company, which traded in the eastern Mediterranean, Smythe was governor of the Muscovy and East India companies during Hudson's exploration career. His various activities placed him at the forefront of trade in the northeast to Russia, through the Mediterranean to the Middle East, and around Africa to the Orient.

Smythe was one of four patentees of the London wing of the original Virginia Company of 1606, and his duties would include taking in a young native girl who contracted tuberculosis when she came to London with Pocahontas in 1616. Smythe had ambitiously re-engineered the Virginia venture as Hudson prepared to sail for the VOC. A new company charter, issued on May 23, 1609, transferred oversight of the colony (now focused on Jamestown) from the crown to private investors. As treasurer, Smythe was the company's de facto governor. When the Virginia Company spun off the Somers Islands Company in 1612, to oversee the Bermuda colony, he would assume its governorship as well.

Henry Hudson would have known Sir Thomas Smythe well. The Muscovy and East India companies almost certainly had co-sponsored Hudson's voyages of 1607 and 1608, and Smythe was the leading figure not only in financing such voyages but in promoting navigational literacy and accuracy in exploration results. Richard Hakluyt's published praise for Smythe gave fair measure of his importance and esteem: "Your erecting of the Lecture of Navigation at your own Expenses, for the better instructing of our Mariners in that most needful art: your setting down of better orders in dispatching forth our East Indian [flotillas]: your employment with extraordinary entertainment of skilfull Mathematicians and Geographers in the South and North parts of the world: This your providence and liberality is like, in time, to work many special good effects."

Smythe's London, a city of some 200,000 people, was beginning to spill beyond its medieval walls. Henry Hudson lived in one of the emerging suburbs, St. Katherine precinct, in the east end, home to the bustling St. Katherine's Docks and the associated anchorage, the Pool. Immediately downriver was Wapping, "the usual place of execution for pirates and sea rovers," as John Stowe remarked circa 1600. Moving upriver from St. Katherine, a visitor encountered the looming Tower of London, marking the waterside limit of the old city gates. Then came the custom house, where Smythe held sway. Next was Billingsgate, described by Stowe as "a large watergate, port or harbour for ships and boats, commonly arriving there with fish, both fresh and salt, shell fishes, salt, oranges, onions, and other fruits and roots, wheat, rye, and grain of divers sorts for service of the City, and the parts of this Realm adjoining." The prominent landing point gave its name to the city ward, and just ahead, before river navigation was interrupted by London Bridge and its gruesome, ever replenishing display of the decapitated heads and other severed body parts of convicted criminals and traitors, was a more modest landing point, Butolph Wharf. Butolph Lane ran north from here, turning into Smythe's Philpot Lane after crossing Little East Cheap.

Hudson would have called on Smythe after each of the 1607 and 1608 voyages, meeting perhaps in his home's great hall, where an Inuit kayak was suspended from the ceiling. The 1607 voyage had failed to find a transpolar passage, but delivered the bonus of identifying a new whale fishery off Spitsbergen that could enrich the Muscovy Company. The 1608 voyage's benefits were far less obvious. Straining to prove that the endeavour hadn't been a complete waste of time and money, Hudson would have proffered to Smythe the grubby evidence his crew had collected of Novaya Zemlya's resources and alleged temperate climate: a severed walrus head (by then hopefully boiled down to bone or reduced to a pair of tusks); scavenged whalebone; reindeer hair, antlers, and dung; and (as Hudson's voyage journal recorded) "flowers and green things."

Walrus at Novaya Zemlya was old news, and the other items were hardly inspiring. Hudson in any event wasn't interested in returning to the northeast. It was the Northwest Passage that was drawing him in. But Smythe and his fellow investors (all 650 of them) were preoccupied with pulling together the new Virginia Company and had enough to concern them without entertaining another Hudson quest for a northern passage.

The ensuing VOC voyage turned out to be a brilliant interim assignment for Hudson. The information "of some especial matters of greater consequence" on which Hudson would not elaborate for Thomas Holland would never be revealed. It might have been a promise of minerals or precious metals, any hint of which from the New World wetted the lips of men like Smythe. Hudson had scarcely set the *Half Moon*'s anchor off the Georges Islands when he began grilling the native greeting party (which spoke French) about possible riches. Robert Juet's journal for the voyage would recount that the natives "told us that there were gold, silver and copper mines hard by us."

Whatever their motivation, Smythe and his like-minded merchant adventurers and members of James's court were persuaded to reward Hudson with the command of a renewed Northwest Passage expedition. It fell to Smythe, who had more experience than anyone in London with sending out voyages of discovery and trade, to produce the man who would keep an eye on Hudson for the investors in the *Discovery* venture.

———

That Habakkuk Prickett was assigned to the *Discovery* voyage was not in itself a sign of investor distrust. The backers would not have known the full story of the *Half Moon* voyage, especially that Hudson had so egregiously defied his sailing directions. It was true, however, that his previous English voyages, of 1607 and 1608, had problematic endings.

In both cases, he had attempted to salvage his expedition by making a dash for the Northwest Passage, to the displeasure of his crew. With the first voyage, the evidence was circumstantial but persuasive. Hudson sailed above Spitsbergen and beyond latitude 80, farther north than anyone to date, but carrying on over the North Pole to China was impossible. On the return leg he took the *Hopewell* about five hundred miles off course to the west before correcting back toward London. He was so far off course that he discovered a new landfall, a volcanic speck north of Iceland, which he named Hudson's Touches. But Hudson gutted his journal account of the details of the return leg, thus costing himself the credit for discovering the landfall. Whalers out of Hull called it Trinity Island in 1611; the Dutch who found it in 1614 gave it the name that would endure, Jan Mayen Island. The best explanation for Hudson's peculiar decision was that he was loathe to address a crew insurrection that would have erupted when the men realized where he was trying to take them, for his course, in delivering him to Jan Mayen Island, had been pointed at southern Greenland, and ultimately at the approaches to the Northwest Passage.

The incident at the end of the 1608 *Hopewell* voyage was more clear-cut. When the crew rejected Hudson's suggestion that they sail for the Northwest Passage after failing to overcome Novaya Zemlya, he was compelled to formally absolve them of any responsibility for the termination of the voyage. As he recorded in his journal: "I gave my company a certificate under my hand, of my free and willing return, without persuasion or force of any one or more of them . . . I thought it my duty to save victual, wages, and tackle, by my speedy return, and not by foolish rashness, the time being wasted, to lay more charge upon the action than necessity should compel."

Yet neither of these incidents necessarily would have given pause to Hudson's backers, provided his sailing directions, which often included a panoply of secondary goals, had not been as restrictive as the ones issued by the VOC in 1609. (Only the sailing directions for this third voyage survive.) Previous English explorers like John Davis felt compelled to press for every possible success, so that their investors' money was not wasted on a fruitless voyage. It was up to an expedition's commander to judge when his perseverance was wasting capital through "foolish rashness."

Hudson might have invited criticism for trying to deceive his crew into making a run at the Northwest Passage in 1607, but a master's success or failure in convincing mariners to go along with alternative plans, at the wages they had agreed to on departure, was a labour-relations issue, nothing more. Neither of the revolts Hudson had experienced—or incited—could even be called a mutiny, as the concept didn't exist in English maritime law at the time for commercial voyages. If the crew forcibly took control of the ship, then it was a case of spoliation, or piracy. If lives were lost in the process, then there was murder besides. But a dispute over where to sail next, and for how many pounds and pence? That was a workaday grievance that could be addressed, once home, by taking the case to the elder brothers of Trinity House at Deptford Strand, which held legal sway over employment issues in English commercial shipping out of London.

In any event, when the master himself did not have an equity interest in the enterprise, commercial voyages of any sort had someone on board to represent the interest of the shipowners or financiers. This representative was usually referred to as the super-cargo, although literally this was someone who was along to watch over the trade goods aboard.

Beyond the fact that he was a member of the Haberdasher's Company, Habakkuk Prickett's background would remain unknown. But Smythe was the one who would have placed him aboard. Sir Thomas had served as master of the Haberdasher's Company, and it was to Smythe that Prickett would directly report at the end of the voyage.

An investment group as august as the one behind the 1610 *Discovery* voyage would not have agreed to place with Hudson someone young and inexperienced as their representative. When George Waymouth sailed for the Furious Overfall in the *Discovery* in 1602, the Reverend John Cartwright was chosen as the super-cargo. More than a man of the cloth, Cartwright had the experience of an epic Muscovy Company expedition that had travelled all the way from the subarctic White Sea to Persia by hopscotching from one Russian river to another before finally gaining the Caspian Sea.

Prickett must have been at least of early middle age, close enough in age to be able to later claim Hudson as a friend on the voyage, yet young enough to call Robert Juet (whose precise age is not known) an "ancient man." And Prickett must have been to sea before, even if he was officially a landsman. Given that this was an Arctic voyage, Smythe would have selected a man who had made a Muscovy Company trade passage to the port of Arkhangels'k on the White Sea. It was important to have someone who would not recoil in shock and horror at the first sign of sea ice, the first bite of cold northern air and chilling salt spray. And Smythe needed someone who could be trusted to monitor the voyage but not actively interfere in it, the way the Reverend Cartwright unfortu-nately had in Waymouth's 1602 assignment.

Waymouth had been expected to overwinter in the Arctic, between latitudes 60 and 70. His sailing instructions ordered him not to think of returning until he had been away for a year, and he was victualled for eighteen months. But as the crew of the *Discovery* felt the chilling embrace of Davis Strait at the height of summer, as they took note of the ice forming in the rigging and on the sails, ropes, and blocks, as they watched the sea heave frozen slabs against and around them, the thought of spending a *winter* in these latitudes stirred them to a respectful but firm uprising. As one, they compelled Waymouth to wrap up his explorations in less than a single season. When Waymouth returned home after only three months, having probed the strait beyond the Furious Overfall for as long and as far as his crew would permit him, his sponsors concluded that Cartwright had been largely responsible for inciting the mass insubordination.

Prickett may have been entirely aware of Cartwright's misstep, even lectured on it by Smythe and others. *Do not interfere with the master's business,* he would have been told.

In one aspect of the voyage, at least, Prickett's task would be much easier than that of the much-maligned Reverend Cartwright. Although no sailing directions would survive, it was plain that Hudson was not expected to overwinter in the Arctic. His voyage was to be fundamentally as he had proposed to the VOC from Dartmouth: a single-season reconnaissance mission, which would attempt to sort out the confused and confusing geography of the northwest in preparation for a more concerted push into the presumed passage. He could enter the strait guarded by the Furious Overfall, but he would have to return to England before exhausting an eight-month supply of provisions.

Significantly, Hudson was given only one ship, where Waymouth had had two: the sixty-ton *Godspeed,* to deliver home an interim report on the expedition's progress, and the seventy-ton *Discovery* in which Waymouth would be frozen in for the winter. That is, if the Reverend Cartwright hadn't queered the entire plan with his well-mannered insurrection. Nor was Hudson provided with a pinnace, a small bark that explorers routinely took with them, unassembled in the hold. A pinnace could be knocked together on a distant shore and was sufficiently seaworthy to make a messenger voyage home. Instead, Hudson had only the usual ship's boat and a larger craft, which the English called a shallop, from the Basque *chaloupe*.

Hudson did not have a shallop on his first voyage of discovery, in the transpolar effort of 1607, and it was almost the end of him. West of Spitsbergen, the *Hopewell* was becalmed while a large sea left over from an earlier blow pushed the little ship toward an ice field. Hudson heard "a great rut or noise with the ice and sea." The waves were tossing about floes, working the multi-ton slabs against each other like teeth in a grinder. He launched the ship's boat and attempted to have the *Hopewell* rowed clear, but the boat was too small and the tow ineffective. Had the waves flung the ship in among the crashing floes, the hull would have been crushed in moments. Instead, Hudson and his men were rescued by Providence: an unexpected wind arose from the northeast. With this favouring breeze in his sails, Hudson gave his thanks to God and steered away, to live and explore another day.

Hudson made sure he had a shallop on every voyage that followed. As on previous expeditions, the *Discovery*'s shallop would travel with him unassembled. Hudson would have it nailed together ashore when he was ready to use it. The craft was twenty to thirty feet long, with a rudder and oars, and probably sported a two-masted rig on which square sails were hoisted. The shallop was perfect for coastal exploration, and they could fish from it, to relieve the tedium of rations: dried pork and peas, ship's biscuit—brick-hard bread—and a porridge-like meal. In a crisis, the shallop could be used to tow the *Discovery*. And if things became truly desperate, it could serve as a lifeboat for some—but not all—of the ship's complement. The only drawback of a shallop was the prospect it held for mutiny, or more accurately for desertion. Men determined to abandon the voyage could conspire to steal away in it, and hope it could deliver them to a friendly shore. But on balance, the shallop was a tremendous asset. Hudson would have been glad to have it along.

—

Six

ON APRIL 17, 1610, the *Discovery* departed St. Katherine's Pool below London Bridge, in the shadow of the Tower of London. Hudson's new command was a water beetle compared to the *Trade's Increase,* which had left London about two weeks earlier, at the head of a three-ship flotilla of the East India Company. At 1,100 tons, she was the largest merchant ship yet to sail in England. After she was launched by Sir Thomas Smythe in 1609, James I held a celebratory banquet and personally hung a gold medal around the merchant adventurer's neck.

Compared to the challenges Sir Henry Middleton faced in managing a crew of several hundred aboard the *Trade's Increase* on a multi-year voyage to the Orient, those confronting Hudson in leading fewer than two dozen men for several months aboard the *Discovery* might have seemed trivial. But the challenges of command, of maintaining discipline and cohesive purpose, increased geometrically as any crew grew in number. And the 1610 voyage was by far Henry Hudson's largest command.

Only twelve men had been aboard the little *Hopewell* in 1607, fourteen when he then sailed her to Novaya Zemlya in 1608. The complement then increased to about sixteen on the *Half Moon* in 1609. With the *Discovery,* the head count swelled to twenty-three. The demands on Hudson's management skills had never been greater. There were more opportunities for cliques, more quiet whisperings, and more pronounced divisions among the senior ranks, the specialists, and the common hands.

The *Discovery* was scarcely clear of London when Hudson began to tamper with the roster.

A few of the men had been to sea with Hudson before. There was his son John, of course, and Robert Juet, who was making his third voyage with the master. Hudson also took along from 1608 Arnold Ludlow, as well as Michael Perce, who probably had been with him (as "Feirce") in 1608. But the rest were new faces to Hudson's seagoing world. Among them were a carpenter, Philip Staffe; a twenty-year-old barber-surgeon, Hudson's first-ever medical man, from Portsmouth, Edward Wilson; and a master's mate, William Cobreth (whose name was alternately spelled Coolbrand, Colbert, and Coleburne). Cobreth had served as George Waymouth's mate aboard the *Discovery,* and as second-in-command on that two-ship expedition to the northwest, in 1602. Cobreth lasted less than a week with Hudson.

He was placed aboard the *Discovery* in 1610 at the behest of the investors. And why not? Cobreth knew the ship, which Waymouth in 1602 had described as a flyboat, a Dutch design that was beamy, shallow in draft, with a high stern structure. Cobreth also knew the route Hudson was about to sail. And he was well praised, even by Waymouth, who held him partly responsible for the 1602 insurrection yet still called him, in the voyage journal, "a skillful man in his profession." The explorer Luke Foxe, who followed in Hudson's wake in the northwest in 1631, went so far as to write that Cobreth "was every way held to be a better man" than Hudson.

On April 22, five days after departing London, the *Discovery* paused at Sheppey Isle in Kent. The tidal shallows offshore, where the lower river broadens into the Mouth of the Thames, are known as the Cant. "Cant" in nautical slang meant to toss or throw. And that is what Hudson did here with Cobreth.

As Hudson explained in the surviving abstract of his journal, "I caused Master Coleburne to be put in a pink bound for London, with my letter to the Adventurers, importing the reason wherefore I so put him out of the ship, and so plied forth." Which was not an explanation at all, as the contents of that letter would never become known.

Ships were routinely guided down the Thames as far as Tilbury Hope by a delivery crew before a voyage's final complement came aboard. Hudson may have used this convention as a pretense for dismissing Cobreth at Sheppey Isle, informing the investors that Cobreth's services thereon were no longer required.

This change in the *Discovery*'s second-in-command might have raised alarms with any supercargo who was well informed about Hudson's behaviour on earlier voyages. The 1607 and 1608 expeditions had been marked by curious shufflings in the ranks that Hudson never bothered to explain in his journal accounts.

In 1608, Robert Juet and Arnold Ludlow both served as Hudson's mate. Hudson listed Juet as the mate in the opening roll call of the journal, but then alternated between Juet and Ludlow in the narrative, without any pattern or reason. Both were now aboard the *Discovery*, so neither appeared to bear a grudge against Hudson, although how they might have felt about each other went unexplored.

And there was the strange precedent of the 1607 expedition. By mid-voyage, Hudson had demoted his mate, James Collins, to boatswain, and James Young from boatswain to common sailor, while promoting the fourth-ranked man, John Colman, to mate.

It was a seismic change in such a small crew, involving three of the ten participants other than Hudson and his son. Hudson left no clue as to what had provoked it, any more than his journal abstract for the *Discovery* voyage would explain why William Cobreth was shipped back upriver to the investors.

And Habakkuk Prickett was no help to posterity, or to Cobreth. He watched as Cobreth was dismissed, and raised no apparent objection. Prickett addressed the matter succinctly in the second sentence of his voyage account: "Thwart of Shepey, our master sent Master Colbert back to the owners with his letter." And that was that. Prickett failed to even mention who was now the second-in-command.

In Cobreth's place, Hudson had promoted a man with a long, at times productive, and at other times worrying, history with the master.

June 20, 1608: Henry Hudson was almost two months out of London and steering the *Hopewell* eastward, well above and beyond Norway's North Cape, continuing to hold a course roughly along latitude 74 degrees toward Novaya Zemlya. It was the height of summer, and the Arctic world was alive around him. Hudson saw "an incredible number of seals" and heard "bears roar" on the ice floes. He was, he hoped, on his way to the Orient. No Englishman had attempted the Northeast Passage in a quarter century. No Englishman had ever attempted the Northeast Passage by sailing above Novaya Zemlya. And no one of any nationality, other than Willem Barentsz and his Dutch companions in 1594 and 1596, had ever succeeded in clearing the north tip of the archipelago.

Unable to calculate his longitude by any practical observation, Hudson had to make daily estimates of his easterly progress. But on the twenty-second, he was flummoxed by an inability to reconcile his dead reckoning with his observed latitude as he attempted to plot his position.

Robert Juet knew the reason, even if Hudson, his master and pilot, did not. Juet was maintaining his own journal of observations, as good practice recommended of a master's mate, and he took note of a sudden change in compass variation—the difference between true and magnetic north—that would have skewed Hudson's dead reckoning.

Already, Hudson had left behind a clue in his 1607 voyage journal that his navigating was not the best. A confused description of a latitude fix using the midnight (rather than the noon) sun would be cited as evidence of Hudson's sophistication. But it was no great accomplishment. The required mathematics and geometry were straightforward and plainly described in Edward Wright's standard navigation treatise. And Hudson's account indicated he was using an archaic form of the cross staff, more than twenty years after John Davis had invented a far more accurate and useful instrument for northern navigation, the backstaff. Juet's correction of Hudson's dead reckoning in 1608 was one of several accumulating suggestions that this new face in Hudson's world was the more skilled man at wayfinding. And it was a firm indication that, at this early stage of their relationship, Hudson's second voyage of exploration, they were making observations independent of one another—two men in one ship, calculating their own particular places and destinations in the world.

Robert Juet had come, by ways unknown, to form a seagoing partnership with Henry Hudson in 1608. Although Prickett's qualification of Juet as "ancient" suggested someone in his fifties or sixties, Juet was still a robust man, with the journals of the 1608 *Hopewell* and 1609 *Half Moon* voyages capturing him leading shore parties, climbing the rigging to sight land, taking to a ship's boat to make soundings, and handling weapons.

There was no designated pilot aboard the *Hopewell* in 1607, and in the 1608 journal's crew ranks, Henry Hudson reserved the role for himself, as Juet served for at least part of the voyage as mate. Most of Juet's journal from the 1608 voyage would not survive, but his 1609 journal would provide evidence of his skills in taking soundings, securing latitude fixes, and determining compass variation, and of his knowledge of the latest theory, by William Gilbert, on the nature of the earth's magnetic field. Rudimentary navigators did well to take latitude fixes using the noon sun and Polaris, the Pole Star. Juet's 1609 journal revealed him at one point determining the *Half Moon*'s position with a midnight measurement of both the Pole Star and "the scorpion's heart," the red star Antares in the constellation Scorpio. He consistently exhibited skills at the forefront of both pure and applied science.

Juet lived in Limehouse, the east London address favoured by seafarers, although he was probably a Scot, or a "borderer" from the Anglo-Scot frontier. At one point in Hudson's 1608 journal, Juet was called Everet, and his "real" name might have been something close to Ewart, a good borderer surname. When Juet described a smear or blemish on the sun in May 1609 as a "slake"—which might have been the world's first recorded observation of a sunspot—he penned a dialectic clue to his northern roots.

Given his breadth of navigational knowledge, he might have arrived in London as part of the sprawling entourage of court figures introduced by James VI of Scotland when he succeeded Elizabeth as James I of England in 1603. Juet's familiarity with Gilbert's work suggested an academic streak. Navigation had been made a fashionable subject among gentlemen by the slew of new works on mathematics and method published in England, and by the popularity of Hakluyt's recent multiple-volume second edition of *Principal Navigations.* Perhaps Juet came to Hudson's attention through Sir Thomas Challener, who encouraged an interest in scientific enquiry in Prince Henry and an enthusiasm for proving a northern passage to the Orient. But a Limehouse address hardly suggested a privileged life, and the familiarity Juet would demonstrate with a ship's weapons showed that he was no armchair theorist or dabbler from the gentry. He was a seasoned and sophisticated mariner, and he may have been put aboard the *Hopewell* in 1608 at the insistence of one of the voyage's senior investors, to serve as mate as well as a personal observer.

Being well versed in navigation practice and advanced theory, Juet would have instructed the young John Hudson in the latest knowledge of stars and compass needles and magnetism. By the time the fourth voyage came along, there would have been a ready familiarity between Juet and John Hudson.

Henry Hudson and Robert Juet were an odd couple, in the inversion of their ages, seniority, and knowledge. Hudson, the younger man by perhaps ten to twenty years, was an advocate of the pseudoscientific and quasi-mystical ideas that supported arguments for northern passage-making schemes and which were preserved in the uncritical amber of Richard Hakluyt's popular compendia of exploration literature. The older Juet was a deft navigator who embraced the latest tools and concepts of an increasingly scientific art. Hudson came to rely on Juet, making sure he was with him when he signed on with the VOC for the *Half Moon* voyage in 1609. And now Hudson had discarded the experienced and skilled Cobreth to install Juet as his second-in-command.

Hudson would have had in mind replacing Cobreth with Juet even before the *Discovery* left St. Katherine's Pool. The breadth of Juet's experience, and the confidence Hudson showed in him, must have satisfied Prickett that the change was all for the good.

In any event, by the time Cobreth had been dismissed, Habakkuk Prickett's attention was on an unauthorized arrival on board.

When Henry Greene joined the ship at Tilbury Hope in the Thames's lower reaches, he was not, as protocol required, "set down in the owner's book, nor any wages made for him," as Prickett would observe. Prickett also noted cryptically that Greene should have gone ashore at Harwich with another man, by the name of Wilkinson. Did Prickett mean that Greene, like this Wilkinson, was supposed to be a temporary guest of Hudson who should have departed at Harwich? Or did he mean that everything would have turned out far better for everyone if he had been disposed of there? However he had come to be among the crew, Greene remained aboard as the *Discovery* sailed on, up the North Sea.

Greene was, in Prickett's judgment, a problematic sort, "born in Kent, of worshipful parents, but by his lewd life and conversation he lost the good will of all his friends, and had spent all that he had." He was not entirely bad. Prickett would allow that he "stood upright, and very inward with the master, and was a serviceable man every way for manhood; but for religion he would say, he was a clean paper whereon he might write what he would."

Greene seems to have been taken under Hudson's wing after the 1609 *Half Moon* voyage. In Prickett's telling, Hudson gave him "meat, drink and lodging" in his London home. A man named Venson, Prickett would explain, had secured four pounds from Greene's mother to buy him some clothes. Greene was so untrustworthy with money that Venson insisted on spending it himself on Greene rather than handing it over to the young man.

Greene's joining of the *Discovery* may have been as premeditated as Juet's replacement of Cobreth. Prickett would not speculate on what paternal impulse inspired Hudson, a father of three boys, to take the wayward Greene not only into his home but into his career at sea, although this did not appear to be the first time Hudson had brought along young men from prominent families. In 1608, Hudson had aboard the *Hopewell* John Barnes, Thomas Hilles, and Humfrey Gilby, any or all of whom could have been high-born passengers. Prickett did offer of Greene: "our master would have to sea with him, because he could write well."

This was a new, literate age of exploration, emerging in lock-step with the blossoming of the commercial publishing industry. Publishers had moved from producing chronicles of past travels to flogging (where censorship permitted) first-hand accounts of commercially sponsored voyages. These voyages were scarcely over when pages lush with the hyperbole of new discoveries and colonizing possibilities were issued, in as many thousands of copies as would sell.

Ships' masters often assigned a crewmember the task of work-ing up the daily log into a summary journal of the voyage. Some or all of the sole surviving account of Hudson's 1607 voyage, for example, was written by a participant named John Playse, although Playse might have drawn on a journal written by Hudson himself. As voyages of exploration became blatantly commercial, scouting out possibilities for passages or colony sites, it dawned on some expeditions to take along someone who could write up the adventure with sufficient flair to captivate the ven-ture capitalists necessary for underwriting follow-up voyages or settlement schemes.

Hudson was perfectly literate. But he must have seen in Greene an educated young man whose gift with words could turn this straightforward reconnaissance mission to the northwest into a passage-seeking triumph that would ensure Hudson a properly funded commission for another, larger voyage. James Rosier had done the same job for George Waymouth in 1605. Even though

Waymouth had already penned an accomplished nautical treatise, *The Jewell of Artes,* he understood the need for a writer who could package an account of his 1605 voyage to the Georges River in a way that would attract investors for the colony that was to follow. Although nothing came of Waymouth's ambitions for the Georges River, the expedition was well recorded for posterity in Rosier's *A True Relation.*

Henry Greene was to be Henry Hudson's Rosier: that was as much as Habakkuk Prickett would have gathered about his unofficial presence. And in a way, the addition of Greene was no concern of Prickett's. The young man did not officially exist, never having been entered in the ship's roll. Greene would not even appear in the admittedly heavily edited abstract of Hudson's journal when it was eventually published. Greene's care and feeding were Hudson's concern, not the investors'. And he was answerable exclusively to Hudson.

But Greene could not remain ignored by Prickett. His sheer force of personality would ensure that.

The letter, dated May 30, 1610, was the sort of chatty, cheerful note any young man on an exotic holiday might pen. Thomas Woodhouse, a "student of mathematics," as historiographer Samuel Purchas would describe him, was on a grand adventure, the fourth voyage of Henry Hudson, and he jotted his news and observations at the *Discovery*'s first landfall.

The ship had passed the Orkneys and then the Faeroes before reaching Iceland on May 11, twenty-four days after departing London. "We kept our Whitsunday in the northeast end of Iceland," wrote Woodhouse, "and I think I never fared better in England than I feasted there. They of the country are very poor, and live miserably, yet we found therein store of fresh fish and dainty fowl."

Woodhouse was detained in and around Iceland with the *Discovery* for three weeks. She skirted the south coast, taking in the sight of the well-known landmark of Mount Hekla. Local tradition said the volcano's fissure cauldron was a portal through which the souls of the damned descended to Hell. At least, it was a tradition that outsiders liked to ascribe to locals. The writings of European historians on his people and their land, which amounted to so many libels and fictions, so exercised the Icelandic scholar Arngrimus Ionas that he wrote a lengthy rebuttal that Richard Hakluyt very decently included in his first edition of *Principal Navigations* in 1589. Much of Ionas's far-from-brief "brief commentary" was concerned with the mythology surrounding Hekla. Ionas wondered why learned Europeans would think specifically of his Hekla, and not erupting mountains in their own backyards, as a "prison of unclean souls." But he also strove to dissuade Hakluyt's readers of the notions that Icelanders sold their children; or lay together, men and women, upwards of ten at a time, in the same bed, eating meat while doing so; and that when they were not doing so, "do nothing but play at dice or at tables"; or, most egregiously for a Danish outpost of devoted Lutherans, that they "wash their hands or their faces in piss."

The better-read members of the *Discovery* crew who knew their Hakluyt presumably took Ionas's diatribe under advisement as they found themselves around Iceland and its people for weeks on end. But Prickett would assert that Hekla was "a famous hill . . . which cast out much fire, a sure sign of foul weather to come in short time." As a voyage chronicler, Prickett wasn't much up on popular chronicles. He missed Ionas's complaint that writers wrongly described Hekla being in a regular state of smoke and flame, with Ionas noting that at the time of his writing, there had not been an eruption in thirty-four years. Hekla had been entirely well behaved for almost three decades when the *Discovery* sailed by.

Whether it was Prickett or Hudson who turned to Hekla for some forewarning of the weather, they would have seen only unblemished snow on the ridgeline on the day of their passing . . . and on any other day on which they might have chosen to look during the next twenty-six years. Satisfied perhaps by the volcano's milk-white benevolence, Hudson attempted to make for Greenland. But sea ice forced him to turn back and take refuge in Dyre Fjord on Iceland's northwest coast.

The crew restocked the larder there with wild birds. "I myself," Woodhouse boasted, "in an afternoon killed so much fowl as feasted all our company, being three and twenty persons, at one time, only with partridges, besides curlews, plover, mallard, teal and goose."

A second attempt to sail west also failed, as contrary weather drove Hudson into the broad expanse of Breida Fjord. The men went ashore and enjoyed the hotsprings. "I have seen two hot baths in Iceland, and have been in one of them," wrote Woodhouse, while Prickett would attest that the water in the baths "was so hot that it would scald a fowl."

As a mathematics student, Woodhouse could have been one of the wards of Christ's Hospital in London, where navigation was taught to youths who were then apprenticed for seven years to ship's masters like Henry Hudson to learn the piloting trade. But there was something about Woodhouse's way with words and general manner that made it more likely he had come to the voyage through a more privileged route. The Woodhouse name was prominent in English society as well as in naval and colonization circles. The brothers Sir William and Sir Thomas Woodhouse, and Sir William's son, Sir Henry, all served as vice-admirals during Elizabeth's reign. Sir Henry's son, Captain Henry Woodhouse, was a member of the London wing of the 1606 Virginia Company as well as the company reorganized by Sir Thomas Smythe in 1609, and would be named governor of Bermuda in 1623.

Thomas Woodhouse sounded very much like one of the young gentlemen enthusiasts of advanced navigation arts who attended university lectures by the acclaimed expert Thomas Hood, which Smythe underwrote. These keen students of spherical trigonometry and cartographic projection tended to gather around St. Paul's, whose churchyard was home to the retail arm of the London publishing trade, which drew much vitality from a stream of first-class navigation manuals as well as travelogues like Rosier's account of the 1605 Waymouth voyage.

As it happened, Woodhouse's letter was addressed to Samuel Macham, an Ashby printer who sold books in a stall under the sign of the Bull's Head in the churchyard. Macham had most conspicuously published *Nova Britannia* in 1609, a slice of propaganda written in support of the rejuvenated Virginia venture by Smythe's son-in-law in the form of an address to Smythe himself.

And so Woodhouse, in addition to having a possible association with Smythe as well as blood ties to Captain Henry of the Virginia Company, more than likely had signed on for the voyage with a plan in hand to write a book for Macham about the *Discovery* adventure, whether Hudson knew it or not.

Woodhouse was already immersing himself in the chronicler's role, reading the past accounts of the pioneering efforts to the northwest. The published journals of the Frobisher voyages of the 1570s were plainly close at hand, as he lifted, consciously or not, from Dionise Settle's description of the second Frobisher voyage, published by Hakluyt. Of the Icelanders, Settle had written: "The fishermen of England can better declare the dispositions of those people than I, wherefore I remit other their usages to their reports." Biding his time in Iceland, Woodhouse twenty-three years later allowed: "I can write unto you no news, though I have seen much, but such as every English fisherman haunting these coasts can write better than myself."

Thus it was that no fewer than five people on the *Discovery* were making some account of the voyage. There was Hudson himself, maintaining the master's log and journal, and Robert Juet, doing the same as the mate. Greene was supposed to be doing Hudson's bidding in writing well about the master's triumph-in-progress. The young Thomas Woodhouse, publisher already secured, was adding his literary aspirations to the output of this unusually fecund crew. Finally, there was Prickett, the supercargo, who would find himself penning an explanation for the voyage's terrible events.

"We are resolved to try the uttermost," Woodhouse concluded his letter to Macham, with an all-for-one, one-for-all optimism, "and lie [waiting] only expecting a fair wind, and to refresh ourselves to avoid the ice, which is now come off the west coasts, of which we have seen whole islands, but God be thanked, have not been in danger of any. Thus I desire all your prayers for us."

The day after the letter was written, June 1, the *Discovery* was able to depart Breida Fjord, as Hudson at last took his leave of the storied island and its slandered people. The English who fished Iceland's rich waters knew the fjord as Louise Bay, and Woodhouse's letter was delivered home to Macham by one of the many English vessels he mentioned seeing.

Nothing more was heard of Hudson's fourth and final voyage until the tattered *Discovery* reappeared off Dursey Island on Ireland's south coast on September 6, 1611.

Seven

—

WHEN THOMAS WOODHOUSE WROTE to Samuel Macham from Iceland, the increasing strangeness of his circumstances may already have begun to sink in. But he pressed on with his brief, enthusiastic letter, saying nothing of a serious row that had just broken out.

Unsurprisingly, no mention of the brawl was made in the heavily edited abstract of Hudson's journal that was eventually published by Purchas. The task of addressing it would fall to Prickett. Henry Greene had argued aboard the *Discovery* with the surgeon, Edward Wilson, about some unknown matter while at sea off Iceland. Greene then gave the surgeon a beating ashore, "which set all the company in a rage," according to Prickett. Wilson tried to quit the voyage at that point, and "we had much ado to get the surgeon aboard."

Now that Greene had assaulted a senior member of the ship's crew, Prickett felt his duties to the owners stir. He reported Greene's attack to Hudson; what he expected Hudson to do about it he never said. The master, Prickett avowed, waved off the incident, clearly favouring the troubled, and troublesome, high-born young man. Hudson "bade me let it alone, for (said he) the surgeon had a tongue that would wrong the best friend he had." And so no disciplinary action was taken. The *Discovery* continued west-ward from Iceland with Greene still aboard. Soon thereafter, Robert Juet's tongue would be wronging the best friend he had.

How baffling it must have seemed to the men aboard the *Discovery* that the man on whom Hudson had so relied on his two previous voyages, and who had been promoted to mate after Cobreth was shipped back up the Thames to the investors, sud-denly turned so unguardedly insubordinate.

Hudson's journal abstract had nothing to say about the inci-dent involving Robert Juet, and in Prickett's hands, the tale was as much about Henry Greene as it was about the mate. After depart-ing Iceland, loaded with drink, Juet told the carpenter, Philip Staffe, that Hudson had brought aboard Greene "to crack his credit that should displease him." Greene's main role, then, was not as a chronicler but as a snitch. Hudson must have told the ship's company that Greene was to write the voyage account in part as a cover for his more essential duty, which could not be filled by Hudson's son John.

John was berthed on the starboard side of the ship, in the same cabin as five other men: the barber-surgeon, Edward Wilson; Woodhouse; and three common hands, Sydrack Faner, William Wilson, and Arnold Ludlow, a veteran of the 1608 *Hopewell* expe-dition to the northeast. Hudson would have hoped his son could keep him apprised of any dissent in the crew ranks, but he could hardly expect would-be conspirators to confide in John. Greene, who could roam at will, not having any official place in the crew, was better positioned to overhear unguarded conversation. And he had been berthed amidships with the ship's boy, Nicholas Sims, who could have passed along to Greene whatever he might learn of dark plottings.

Most likely Juet had been in on Greene's clandestine role from the beginning, and only spilled the news to Staffe when he became disgusted with Hudson's refusal to control the man, after the fight with the barber-surgeon. Staffe must have wondered aloud to Juet why this arrogant young man remained among them after almost causing the loss of their barber-surgeon. In reply, he received the full story from Juet. It was a "long tale" in Prickett's telling, spilled while Juet was deep in his cups, and it stripped away Greene's cover as a voyage chronicler.

Juet "would needs burn his finger in the embers," according to the haberdasher. Staffe may have taken the revelation directly to Hudson for an explanation. The news of Greene's subterfuge otherwise would have spread quickly through the crew and found its way back to the master.

They were forty leagues west of Iceland, making for Greenland's east coast, when Hudson learned of Juet's revelations about Greene. Enraged at the exposure of his shipboard spy by no less than his second-in-command, Hudson considered turning back to Iceland, so that he could send Juet home with a fisherman. "But being otherwise persuaded," Prickett allowed, "all was well."

But things were far from well. As the *Discovery* left Iceland, no onboard relationship would have been more critical than the one between Henry Hudson and Robert Juet. Certainly Juet would have seen it that way. He would have been privy to Hudson's conniving in 1609, when the sailing directions of the VOC were so blithely discarded in favour of Hudson's own agenda. He would also have been privy to what Hudson truly had in mind for this mission to the northwest. But a different subterfuge had come between them. While Greene's role had been to crack the credit of crewmembers, Hudson's handling of his spy had cracked Hudson's credit with the mate.

When the *Discovery* departed Breida Fjord, she was only a few miles south of the Arctic Circle, which bands the earth at approximately latitude 66 degrees, 30 minutes. The latitudes to the north were known as the Frozen Zone, a cap on the world that Ptolemy had pronounced uninhabitable by man. Henry Hudson had long begged to differ. He subscribed to—even perpetuated—the theory of the temperate Arctic. Just as a small fire burning constantly would warm a room more effectively than a larger fire lit for shorter periods, the perpetual sun of the Arctic summer would create an ice-free zone, somewhere above latitude 72, that would open the top of the world to navigation.

Fundamentally Hudson was a disciple of John Davis in his pursuit of northern passage-making opportunities. Davis (who was murdered by Japanese pirates off Borneo in 1605) had set down his ideas in *The World's Hydrological Description* in 1595. The veteran Arctic explorer had assured his readers that "under the pole is the place of greatest dignity," where "the whole year is but one day and one night." Davis advised that "the sea freezeth not," and that "the air in cold regions was tolerable."

Hudson had counted on the sun's low, weak, warming rays to allow him to sail over the North Pole in 1607. Not even persistent encounters with massive ice fields and bitter cold on that first voyage could dissuade Hudson from upholding the temperate Arctic theory. It was impossible to know how much he sincerely believed, and how much of his reportage was torqued to satisfy the theoretical biases of his audience so that further commissions would come his way. Hudson regularly commented on a favourable climate in one of the world's most inhospitable environments. After passing along the Greenland shore above latitude 70 in the *Hopewell* in 1607, he observed that the land "was very temperate to our feeling." Such a conviction also required Spitsbergen to be warm and welcoming. And so when the *Hopewell* first came upon this high-latitude archipelago, Hudson proposed: "Here it is to be noted, that although we ran along near the shore, we found no great cold; which made us think that if we had been on shore the place is temperate." When Hudson's crewmembers did go ashore at the top of Spitsbergen, above latitude 80, he insisted "we found it hot," and further emphasized, "Here they found it hot on the shore, and drank water to cool their thirst." And at Novaya Zemlya in 1608, Hudson claimed that crewmembers who were sent ashore also reported the land to be "hot."

A temperate, ice-free Arctic was one element in a disorderly assemblage of first-hand experiences, hoary evidence, and imaginative theories that fuelled the all-encompassing fever dream of northern passage-making opportunities. With the *Hopewell* voyage of 1607, Hudson had intended to penetrate the great polar landmass of Septentrion, charted by Gerhard Mercator. King Arthur had conquered it; a wandering Oxford friar named Nicholas de Linna had taken measure of it with an astrolabe in the late fourteenth century. The pole, as Mercator had illustrated, was a cone of lodestone thirty-three leagues—some one hundred miles—in diameter. Four passages, spaced equidistant around the circumference of the globe, divided the polar landmass like spokes in a wheel and drew the surrounding oceans toward the pole. At the mouth of the spoke aligned with Spitsbergen was what Hudson called the Great Indraught, into which a "sucking sea," a tide of all tides, coursed into the polar land through the passage leading to the pole itself.

Around the cone of magnetic rock, the inrushing sea plunged into the earth.

Hudson had fled to the open ocean when this sucking sea tried to take hold of the *Hopewell* on the west coast of Spitsbergen, as a flooding tide filled one of its western fjords. He eventually retreated from Septentrion and never returned to this fantasy landscape. Nor did he ever indicate that he had relinquished his faith in this portion of the larger fever dream. Although he was capable of tailoring his findings to suit a particular audience, the temperate Arctic remained a defensible fact for him. Being rebuffed at Novaya Zemlya in his attempt to prove the Northeast Passage in 1608 only led him to conclude that ice produced by rivers, filling the ocean with conveyor-like monotony, had blocked his way and made the passage over Asia impossible. No one believed that sea ice, being made almost entirely of fresh water, was created by a freezing ocean. No one could manage the simple experiment of freezing seawater and noting how the salt precipitated out of the ice, increasing the salinity of the surrounding water.

In coming at last to the northwest with the *Discovery,* Hudson was to confront an especially nightmarish strain of the fever dream. No two navigators appeared capable of visiting the world west of Iceland and reporting the same arrangements of land and sea. The reports could brush up against the hallucinatory: Waymouth in 1602 saw water that flowed like black pudding. But then, both Hudson and Juet had reported without question in their 1608 voyage journals the sighting of a pair of mermaids by crewmembers. Wrote Hudson: "from the navel upward, her back and breasts were like a woman's, as they say that saw her; her body was as big as one of us; her skin very white; and long hair hanging down behind, of colour black: in her going down they saw her tail, which was like the tail of a porpoise, and speckled like a mackerel."

The most trying and confusing aspects of the northwest experience were rooted in the sheer difficulty of navigation. The early seventeenth-century mariner was already severely disadvantaged, having no effective way to measure longitude, his location along the north–south lines of the grid of the globe. Distances travelled east or west could be determined only by dead reckoning, a best-guess system based on a ship's speed, course steered, and latitude observed. Speed was a rough estimate. Course steered depended on the compass, and in Hudson's time no one properly understood the relationship (or sometimes even the difference) between the north magnetic pole and the north geographic one, or the fact that the north magnetic pole's location wandered over time. The closer a ship sailed toward the Furious Overfall, the greater the angular difference became between the directions of the two poles. At the same time, the magnetic pole's influence on the compass needle weakened as the lines of force became increasingly vertical. The compass wandered, and struggled with local anomalies, and otherwise pointed in directions in profound disagreement with the direction of north as indicated by the sun's meridian and the location of the Pole Star in the night sky.

As for determining latitude, navigators like Hudson and Juet were capable of reasonably accurate results, by measuring the angular altitude of the noon sun or certain stars. But in the Arctic, atmospheric distortions could cause pronounced measurement errors. A mistake of half a degree of celestial elevation, already well within the margin of error of observations made at sea, produced a position error of some thirty miles. Moreover, on four days out of five the sky was overcast in this realm, denying a clear view of the heavenly bodies. And when the weather was clear, the perpetual daylight of the summer sky defeated the glimmer of the navigator's most reliable stars.

Little wonder that men came to the northwest and stepped off the face of the earth.

Eight

—

As mid-June 1610 approached, Henry Hudson worked his way south along the east coast of Greenland. Behind him was Robert Juet's eruption over Henry Greene's shipboard role. Waiting for him, when he reached Cape Farewell at Greenland's southern tip, was Davis Strait, leading north from the Labrador Sea, between western Greenland and what would become known as Baffin Island. Beyond Davis Strait, to the west, was an almost incoherent geography. And beyond the Labrador Sea was the last known position of the man whose disappearance had launched Hudson's career as an explorer.

In assuming command of the *Hopewell* in 1607, Henry Hudson inherited a dead man's ship, quite possibly took command of at least part of the dead man's crew and may also have signed on one of the dead man's relatives. He could not have helped but share in the disquiet surrounding his predecessor's fate before taking up his quest. For his first three voyages, Hudson plotted courses at least initially contrary to the one that described John Knight's final days. But there was something about the northwest route, which had drawn in and swallowed Knight, that also irresistibly attracted Hudson. With the *Discovery* in 1610, Hudson could at last steer his own course toward and then, hopefully, beyond the awfulness of that loss.

The appearance of the *Hopewell* in Dartmouth on September 24, 1606, had announced the disappearance of her captain, John Knight, on the Labrador shore, some 560 nautical miles west of Hudson's present position off Cape Farewell. The *Hopewell's* departure from London under a new commander, seven months later, had then marked Hudson's appearance in exploration's annals.

John Knight was the first Englishman assigned to follow up on George Waymouth's discoveries beyond the Furious Overfall, four years after Waymouth tried and failed to reach China. Knight was absolutely determined to reach the passage, and he kept pressing his own luck, and that of his crew, as he confronted a mass of floes choking the Labrador Sea. The *Hopewell* was very nearly lost around latitude 58 on June 14, 1606, when Knight ordered the little ship rowed through the ice field. Knight escaped, but with a ship that could scarcely sail toward the wind, he was steadily outmanoeuvred. The longer he jousted with the wind, waves, and current that persistently rearranged and reshaped the ice, refusing to retreat before an endlessly inventive and overwhelmingly superior enemy, the more perilous his situation became. Knight's options were steadily reduced as he was forced toward a dangerous lee shore.

When he sighted Labrador on June 19, two long months after clearing Gravesend, he was somewhere just north of the modern settlement of Nain. He had squeezed himself between the open water along the rocky, undulating coast and the drifting, shifting floes in the Labrador Sea. There was no longer a clean avenue of retreat.

Knight experienced a heart-in-mouth moment on the twenty-first when he ran aground, clearing himself without damage. But at one o'clock in the morning on the twenty-third, the wind freshened and drove toward the *Hopewell* what Knight's journal described as "a mighty island of ice." Knight steered into a cove "to save our ship and lives."

There, the *Hopewell* "rode very dangerously all this day and night following," with sea ice marching toward Knight and the unyielding granite of the shoreline at his back. A storm with stiff northerly winds of cold, dense arctic air then drove before it the heaving floes, which spun and slammed in the surf that broke against and around the ship. The lines securing the *Hopewell* to shore snapped, a large floe smashed away the rudder, and Knight was driven aground. Leaks were pounded into the hull. Only by settling onto the shallow, rocky bottom did the *Hopewell,* half full of water, not actually sink. Two thousand miles from home, these Englishmen were a hair's breadth from entering exploration's annals of fatal misadventures.

Giovanni Caboto, the Venetian exploring under the English flag as John Cabot, probably saw this coast in 1497—and, for that matter, again in 1498, when he disappeared on his follow-up voyage. In 1501, Gaspar Cortereál passed along the coast. How far north and west his Portuguese expedition probed no one can say. Like Cabot, he vanished in his flagship. Gaspar's brother Miguel took up the cause with an expedition of his own to these waters in 1502. He too disappeared, along with his flagship and one other vessel.

Knight needed to move the *Hopewell* to a safer anchorage to effect repairs. On June 25 he had the crew begin assembling their shallop, while his mate, Edward Gorrell, and three other men set out in the ship's boat to see if there was a better anchorage at an island about one mile away. But the sea was so choked with ice that they returned without having come near it.

The next morning, Knight began a fresh entry in his journal— "Thursday the 26th being fair weather"—but then put down his quill without completing the first sentence. He had resolved to seek the better anchorage himself, without wasting time on a journal entry. He could finish it later when he had results to report. He would take with him in the ship's boat Gorrell, his own brother, Gabriel, and three other men. In addition to carrying navigation instruments, they were as armed to the teeth as any corsairs. For his six-man shore party, Knight laid aboard the boat four pistols, three muskets, five swords, and two half-pikes.

When they reached the island at ten o'clock in the morning, Knight had a trumpeter and another crewmember named Oliver Browne stay with the boat, leaving with them a few weapons for their protection. Knight and his brother, along with Gorrell and another man, then strode away. The sun had been up since three-thirty. The weather was fair.

After cresting the island's rise and walking out of view, Knight's party was simply swallowed by the landscape.

The northwest had witnessed yet another vanishing.

Three months later, the *Hopewell* reappeared in England. On the arrival of the Knight expedition's survivors, according to Purchas, "they wrote to the owners at London, of the loss of the master and his three companions, and of the doleful success of the voyage."

The survivors told a harrowing tale, not only of the mysterious loss of Knight and the other men but also of their struggle to refloat and make seaworthy the half-sunk ship and escape the hostile shore. After Knight's disappearance, they suffered an attack by the "country people"—"about 50 little people, tawny, [with] thin beards and flat noses," as Purchas would relate, based on a statement by Oliver Browne. They were most likely Inuit, and had arrived in the night, loosing a shower of arrows as they swarmed the half-built shallop to scavenge its components, above all the iron fastenings. The ten surviving members of the *Hopewell* crew mounted a counterattack with muskets and the ship's great dog, driving the Inuit back to their large open boats, or umiaks. When the umiaks became trapped in the ice, the English stood over them on the shore and poured a dozen volleys into the struggling Inuit, "which made them cry out bitterly."

The Inuit withdrew into the night with their untold dead and wounded. The *Hopewell's* men had escaped the assault without a loss, but they now well suspected what had become of their captain and his companions. They hurried along the repairs to the ship, all the while fearing another attack. The *Hopewell* was refloated, moved offshore and moored for a spell to an island of ice.

By early July they were "worn out with watching and hard work" and ready to limp to Fogo Bay in Newfoundland. There, several weeks were spent preparing the ship for the transatlantic passage, aided by the fishermen who took pity on them.

It was a compelling story, and the return of the *Hopewell* was a tribute to the resourcefulness of the crew, who tore strapping from Knight's sea chest to fashion repairs to the rudder. But it is still not clear that they could entirely be believed.

It would have been possible to accept that Knight's party had vanished without a single shot being heard, if they had been taken utterly by surprise. John Davis had lost four men along this very coast in 1586, cut down without warning by arrows as they collected fish they had set to dry on a rack. But in the *Hopewell* voyage's case the four lost men had been heavily armed, and Knight had gained plenty of experience with hostile Inuit in Greenland, when he sailed there for the Danish crown. More troubling was why the *Hopewell's* survivors had made what seemed to be so little effort to discover what had become of Knight's party.

The voyage's journal, continued by Oliver Browne, stated that Browne had waited on the shore in the ship's boat with the trumpeter for some sign of Knight until eleven at night on the day he disappeared, when Knight himself had instructed him to wait no longer than three in the afternoon. Browne also mentioned an attempt by a search party to return to the island the next morning, which was prevented from landing by ice. Once the Country People had attacked the *Hopewell* in force, a reluctance to divide their strength would have excused the survivors from sending out another search party, as they became wholly concerned with refloating the *Hopewell* and leaving this terrible shore as soon as possible.

Nevertheless, there was no shortage of examples of insubordination on Arctic voyages when John Knight went missing and Henry Hudson took charge of the *Hopewell*. These were commercial ships, not naval vessels. Discipline began and ended with the captain's ability to persuade the crew to follow him into the unknown. Sebastian Cabot would claim that he had reached latitude 68 in what would become known as Davis Strait, and would have reached China had his crew not forced him to turn back. On his second voyage to the northwest, in 1586, John Davis was able to ignore without incident entreaties from his crew to turn back— "that I ought to respect the preservation of my own life and theirs, and that I should not through my overboldness leave their widows and fatherless children to give me bitter curses"—but in making his three celebrated searches for the passage in the 1580s, he was disobeyed by the companies of ships in his little fleets at least twice. And George Waymouth of course had been forced to cut short his explorations in 1602 by an uncooperative crew aboard the *Discovery.*

It was in full knowledge of routine occurrences of insubordination that the investors in Knight's voyage from the Muscovy and East India companies could well have wondered about an alternate narrative for *Hopewell* misadventure. No one would have questioned the story of the survivors more than Sir James

Lancaster. A director of the East India Company, he had led that company's inaugural voyage in 1601, gathering intelligence in the Orient that "the passage to the East India lieth in 62 ½ degrees by the north-west on the American side," thus spurring the conviction that the Furious Overfall represented the eastern gateway. Returning from an earlier, protracted voyage to the East Indies in November 1593, Lancaster had made the mistake of going ashore on Mona Island, west of Puerto Rico, in a party of nineteen men, leaving the *Edward Bonaventure* in the care of a skeleton crew of five men and a boy. The ship's boat delivered Lancaster and his party ashore, but rough seas then prevented it from retrieving them. As Lancaster waited for the weather to improve and the boat to return for him, the carpenter, who had been left aboard the ship, cut the anchor cable in the middle of the night. The *Edward Bonaventure* sailed away, marooning Lancaster and his companions on the little island. It was almost a month before Lancaster and ten others finally were rescued by a French ship, before the Spanish could hunt them down to the last man.

No one familiar with the experience of Lancaster at Mona in 1593—above all Lancaster himself, now a director of one of the companies that had sponsored the 1606 *Hopewell* voyage and was about to send out Henry Hudson in 1607—could have avoided wondering if Knight and his companions truly had been lost to some unwitnessed ambush by the Country People.

Henry Hudson would have taken the time to read the *Hopewell's* 1606 journal before taking command of the little ship. While Knight's was a voice that Hudson in particular dearly would have wished to hear, it could not be heard, beyond his final entry in the ship's journal, made after being cast up on the Labrador shore.

After Knight put the pen down, to strike out for the island and his unknowable fate, the quill was next taken up by the hand of

Oliver Browne, who had returned to the *Hopewell* from the island without Knight and had overseen the ship's return to England. Hudson would have observed how the journal's handwriting changed, how Knight's existence slid from the page with the word *weather*. It was an effect as striking to a ship's master as a shift in the ocean's hue from the blue-black of deep waters that consumed hundreds of fathoms of lead line to the abrupt greygreen of rising shoals.

Never turn your back on your own men. Was this too obvious a lesson for someone like Henry Hudson? Armed to the teeth against what might lie in wait ahead of you, failing to take note of what treachery might be gathering shape and strength behind you.

There is no way to know for certain if the anecdotal evidence from the survivors of the 1606 *Hopewell* voyage was truth, halftruth, or lies. And even if everything happened exactly as related, Browne would not have conceded that no one yet alive aboard the *Hopewell,* after Knight vanished, wanted badly enough to find him and his companions. If the crew were to have saved Knight (and not been killed trying), their captain's jousting with the ice in the Labrador Sea probably would have resumed, as he refused to retreat from his mission of probing the Furious Overfall. Traumatized by ice and shipwreck, and by an Inuit attack, the *Hopewell* survivors would have wished only to go home.

Back home, it was accepted that the Country People had more than likely dispatched Knight and the others. There was no concrete reason to disbelieve the survivors. The *Hopewell* was prepared for a new voyage, which was to investigate the feasibility of a transpolar route to China, under her new master, Henry Hudson. No one would attempt what Knight had in the northwest until Hudson returned Waymouth's *Discovery* to these waters in 1610.

Nine

—

As much as Martin Frobisher's three voyages to the northwest of the 1570s unveiled new lands and waters, they compounded longstanding cartographic confusion. Maps arising from the Frobisher expeditions showed Frobisher Strait leading through a sieve of islands called Meta Incognita and westward across the top of North America to the Orient. The land bordering the strait was actually one solid mass, eastern Baffin Island, and the strait was in truth a bay that led nowhere, as Frobisher himself would have realized had he sailed but twenty miles farther west, close enough to accept that a mountain range blocked the route. To aggravate matters, the Frobisher cartography dismissed the waters leading west, to the south of Baffin Island, as the "Mistaken Strait." Even though a 1578 map published by Frobisher associate George Best showed this Mistaken Strait linking with Frobisher Strait in the west, with "the way trendin[g] to Cathaia," it had been pronounced impassable after a cursory investigation of about sixty miles.

The cartographic image of the northwest was further muddled by the persistent fictions of the fabulous Zeno brothers. The findings attributed to these supposed late-fourteenth-century Venetians became fixed to charts like conceptual barnacles. Some of the Zeno placenames, like Estotiland, were attached to genuine landfalls. Their island of Friesland, said to be as large as Ireland, persisted in part because it was confidently sighted by the homeward-bound *Busse of Bridgewater* on Frobisher's final expedition in 1578, en route to discovering a fresh, nonexistent landfall of her own, Busse Island, which Henry Hudson attempted to locate during the 1609 *Half Moon* voyage.

John Davis's voyages of the 1580s created further chaos from Frobisher's findings. On his third and final Arctic expedition, in 1587, Davis "sailed by a great bank or inlet." It was the opening to Frobisher's so-called strait, and Davis correctly concluded that this bay would not pass through. He did not realize, however, that this was the same place Frobisher had frequented only a decade earlier, mining fool's gold and bankrupting investors. Davis gave this deep indentation in eastern Baffin Island an entirely new name: Lumley's Inlet.

Because Davis never did positively identify Frobisher Strait in all his Arctic meanderings, the leading cartographic minds of England who gathered to aid Emery Molyneux in creating the nation's first globe, in 1592, were faced with the vexing problem of where to place it. William Sanderson, who had financed Davis's voyages, was funding the globe project, and Davis no doubt had considerable influence on the mapping decisions. With longitude so difficult to determine by explorers, there was little to prevent these esteemed men from plucking Frobisher Strait from where Frobisher thought it was, and piercing through southern Greenland with it. And so the strait that was actually a bay in eastern Baffin Island was relocated fully six hundred miles east. Friesland, clinging stubbornly to the planet's surface—it had to go somewhere, once the *Busse of Bridgewater* had actually sighted it—was placed to the east of Greenland and southwest of Iceland.

Edward Wright, who advised on the Molyneux globe, repeated this interpretation of the location of Frobisher Strait in his famous 1599 world map, which was included in the final volume of Hakluyt's second edition of *Principal Navigations* in 1600. Other cartographers followed the examples of Molyneux and Wright, agreeably drawing Frobisher Strait right through the glacier and granite of Greenland, transporting with it the islands of Meta Incognita, which purportedly formed the south shore of the strait.

The gores for the Molyneux globe had been engraved by Jodocus Hondius, who later witnessed Hudson's 1609 contract with the VOC and provided translation help. Hondius likely had access to some of Davis's cartography from the globe project, which otherwise has been lost to us, and he might have been the source of an unknown chart based on Davis's northwest visions that Hudson carried aboard the *Discovery.*

Not surprisingly, Hudson expectantly sailed directly for the wayward Frobisher Strait after departing Iceland, and on June 9, 1610, as he skirted the east Greenland shore, his journal confidently recorded that "we were off Frobishers Straits." But thick pack ice thwarted his approach. He had then sailed southwest until he was off what we know to be Cape Farewell, the southern tip of Greenland.

"The fifteenth day," Hudson recorded, "we were in sight of the land, in latitude 59 degrees, 27 minutes, which was called by Captain John Davis Desolation." Prickett described how, after rounding Cape Farewell, "our course for the most part was between the west and north-west, till we raised the Desolations, which is a great island in the west part of Groneland."

A great island called Desolation did not exist. Cartographers, loyal to the Zeno vision, had placed Greenland too far north, leaving it to Davis to give the actual west coast of Greenland an entirely new identity. Desolation was another misnamed landfall in an Arctic tableau populated by Zeno fictions and ice fields masquerading as solid ground.

Hudson devoted two weeks to surveying the Greenland coast, hoping to clarify the location of both entrances to the strait. He then sailed on, against storm and ice, across Davis Strait, to turn his attention to Lumley's Inlet and the Furious Overfall.

The *Discovery*'s little shipboard world was a place of regimented piety. Hudson regularly gave thanks to God, in particular for the mercy he showed, in journal entries for his voyages. Back on land, failure to attend the weekly Mass of the Church of England was a criminal offence, and Hudson's debut in the historical record had been a visit on April 19, 1607, to London's St. Ethelburga's Church, near Bishopsgate, to take communion with his crew before setting sail in the *Hopewell*. At sea, ship's masters were expected to hold morning and evening prayers and common services. And as Cabot's thirteenth ordinance to the inaugural sailing of the Muscovy Company in 1553 put it, "the Bible or paraphrases [are] to be read devoutly and Christianly in God's honour, and for his grace to be obtained, and had by the humble and hearty praise of the Navigants accordingly." Cabot's ordinances, which were the template for shipboard order well into Hudson's time, also prescribed "that no blaspheming of God, or detestable swearing be used in any ship, nor communication of ribaldry, filthy tales, or ungodly talk to be suffered in the company of any ship, neither dicing, carding, tabling, nor other devilish games to be frequented, whereby ensueth not only poverty to the players, but also strife, variance, brawling, fighting, and oftentimes murder to the utter destruction of the parties."

Picture what twenty-two men and a ship's boy might endure in such a rude barrel of a vessel, in such a place: perpetual dampness, each crewmember exhaling his own stale fog from the mean comfort of his wooden berth, then drawing in with his next breath whatever miasma of misery his companions had just expelled. Heavy, loose coughs. The creaking of the rigging's cordage, rimed with ice from salt spray, braiding with occasional strains of mournful whalesong resonating through the hull's timbers. Men sporting leather hoods, cassocks and breeches lined with lambswool, gowns lined with frieze (a lightly twisted yarn that would have given the linings the texture of looped carpet pile), linen shirts, cotton waistcoats, woollen hose, and fur-lined cloth mittens. Freezing feet shod in uninsulated leather shoes and boots. Quietly muttered curses, and an impromptu prayer for the weather to improve enough for the stove to be safely lit.

In late June, Hudson raised land to the north, "which our master took to be that island which Master Davis setteth down in his chart," wrote Prickett. Some twenty-four miles wide and fifteen hundred feet at its highest point, this bleak landmark would be named Resolution Island (after the *Resolution* in the Thomas Button expedition of 1612–13). It was the largest island in a group marking both the southeastern approach to Frobisher Bay/Lumley's Inlet and the north side of the entrance to the strait beyond the Furious Overfall.

Davis had sailed south, past this island cluster, on his final Arctic voyage of 1587. "We had oftentimes, as we sailed alongst the coast, great ruts, the water as it were whirling and overfalling, as if it were the fall of some great water through a bridge." So John Janes, a gentleman participant in the voyage, would remark of their traversing the mouth of what Davis called Lumley's Inlet. "This day and night [July 31]," Janes added, they then "passed by a very great gulf, the water whirling and roaring as it were the meetings of tides."

Waymouth reported that on the afternoon of July 26, 1602, "I did reckon my self to be in the entering of an inlet, which standeth in the latitude of 61 degrees and 40 minutes." He had passed through the Furious Overfall at Janes's "very great gulf," with still more open water to be tested. He sailed on into this strait (the one Frobisher had called Mistaken) until July 30, when a stiff wind out of the west-northwest forced him back. "Now because the time of the year was far spent, and many of our men in both ships sick, we thought it good to return with great hope of this inlet." Waymouth pronounced it to be "a passage of more possibility than through the Strait of Davis: because I found it not much pestered with ice, and to be a strait of forty leagues broad." There would be good reason to doubt Waymouth's claim that he had managed to sail one hundred leagues into the strait in only four days. Apart from the extraordinary progress, he wrote that the strait trended southwest, when it actually leads northwest, and so he may have done nothing more than enter the dead end of Ungava Bay.

As the incoming sea meets the rise of the continental shelf at the Furious Overfall, both the range of the tide and the speed of its flow are greatly amplified. The full range from high to low tide along the strait can reach thirty to fifty feet, with peak flow at the eastern entrance of around five knots. That was about as fast as the *Discovery* could sail in ideal conditions. The only place in the world with higher tides was the Bay of Fundy, whose mouth Hudson had grazed on the way to the Georges River during the *Half Moon* voyage of 1609.

Hudson at last was about to make good on the ambition he had committed to paper at the end of his 1608 voyage: "to make trial of that place called Lumleys Inlet, and the furious over-fall by Captain Davis, hoping to run into it an hundred leagues, and to return as God should enable me." To that end, Hudson planned to sail first to the north of Resolution Island, to inspect Lumley's Inlet. But, as Prickett told it, "the wind would not suffer him: so we fell to the south of it, into a great rippling or overfall of current, the which setteth to the west. Into the current we went."

It was around June 25. The incoming tide swept the *Discovery* along. A Great Indraught, as it were, had taken hold of Hudson and dragged him into his destiny. He was borne bodily by this sucking sea into the strait that would one day bear his name.

Ten

—

BEYOND THE FURIOUS OVERFALL, Henry Hudson's journal abstract continued for some six weeks, then fell silent altogether. Habakkuk Prickett's words were left as the sole version of events for almost a year of shipboard activity. The story became his alone to shape and tell, except for one startling moment, when a fuller narrative suddenly resurfaced.

After overcoming the Furious Overfall, Hudson ran into serious difficulties. Despite Waymouth's assurances that he found the strait "not much pestered with ice," pack ice thwarted Hudson's efforts to keep to the north side of the strait. He may have been comforted nevertheless by Waymouth's misleading advice that the strait led to the southwest. The powerful incoming tidal flow also trends southward, and Hudson could have been swept along by it. Hudson soon found himself in Ungava Bay, on the south shore of Hudson Strait, nearly embayed by ice, and his crew on the verge of revolt.

"Here our master was in despair," wrote Prickett, "and (as he told me after) he thought he should never have got out of this ice, but there have perished. Therefore he brought forth his card [chart] and shewed all the company, that he was entered above an hundred leagues further than ever any English was: and left it to their choice, whether they would proceed any further; yea, or nay."

Hudson's claim of having sailed a hundred leagues farther than any Englishman was hardly credible, even if by now he had good reason to doubt that George Waymouth had ever been much beyond Ungava Bay. Frobisher's people, after all, had made some twenty leagues of progress beyond the Furious Overfall. The best that could be said in Hudson's defence was that the *Discovery*'s course, in his recent wanderings in the eastern end of the strait and Ungava Bay, might have totalled one hundred leagues. But Akpatok Island, which Hudson was approaching when the ice hemmed him in, was only about thirty leagues from the tidal chokepoint at the eastern end of the strait.

Prickett wrote that "some were of one mind and some of another, some wishing themselves at home and some not caring where, so they were out of the ice: but there was some who then spake words, which were remembered a great while after." Prickett never identified the dissenting voices: "There was one who told the master, that if he had an hundred pounds, he would give four-score and ten to be home." One suspects this was Juet, and that the talk of money had been prompted by promises from Hudson of some wage bonus for carrying on or proving the passage. According to Prickett, Staffe, the carpenter, replied "that if he had an hundred, he would not give ten upon such condition, but would think it to be as good money as ever he had any, and to bring it as well home, by the leave of God."

The issue of whether to continue or turn back may not have been settled—as Prickett put it, there were "many words to no purpose." Saving themselves from the ice was the greater priority. The men pulled together and brought *Discovery* clear of Ungava Bay. Hudson gave Akpatok Island the name Hold With Hope, and was able to continue the voyage westward, along the strait.

Hudson dispensed favours of nomenclature as he pressed on, recognizing members of the royal family and key investors with immortalizing placenames. These included Salisbury's Island, for Sir Robert Cecil, and Hudson concluded his labelling of the strait's features by naming the promontory marking the western-most point of its south coast for Sir John Wolstenholme, and the small pair of islands a few miles offshore for Sir Dudley Digges.

At this point, Hudson was 350 nautical miles west of the Furious Overfall. If Waymouth truly had penetrated the strait one hundred leagues, this was about as far as he took the *Discovery* before turning back. But the idea must have struck Hudson as absurd. It had taken Hudson more than a month to sail the *Discovery* a distance that Waymouth claimed to have covered with her in four days.

At the beginning of August, Hudson paused at the northeast coast of East Digges Island, to send ashore the ship's boat under Prickett's command. Included in the party were Henry Greene, Philip Staffe, and a sailor named Robert Bylot. They were to scout from the island's high ground the possible courses to the north-west, west, and southwest, and to observe the strength and direc-tion of the tide, as these were thought to provide important clues to the location of the Northwest Passage.

Raked by a violent thunderstorm, Prickett's party made it ashore and began the ascent of the island's steep granite terrain. Some six miles in length, east to west, and about two from north to south where they landed, East Digges Island rises to a height of more than nine hundred feet. Reaching "plain ground" about seven hundred feet above the ocean, they found a herd of a dozen or more caribou, but could not approach within musket range. To the west, the land rose abruptly several hundred feet to its highest ground, and was too steep for them to climb, denying them an unimpeded view in the direction they were supposedly headed.

Restricted to the island's east end, they were pleased to find "sorrel" and "scurvy grass" in "great abundance." Prickett may have been referring to a single plant, a member of the *Cochlearia* family known as scurvy-grass. The low, creeping plant, with white flowers, has leaves rich in vitamin C, and was valued by sailors for its antiscorbutic properties.

They also spied what, at a distance, appeared to be evidence of Europeans: low mounds that suggested haystacks. They turned out to be rock cairns. More were found as they approached the southern limits of the island. The men lifted away the top stone of one and inside they found birds hanging by the neck. The cairns were caches of game, fashioned by unknown and unseen hands. And the game was close at hand, in astonishing abundance.

A lake-fed stream, coursing with enough force "to drive an overshot mill," plunged over the edge of the shore's steep granite cliffs, which rose five hundred feet or more directly from the sea. The cliffs of Cape Digges were a riot of seabirds, mostly thick-billed murres, a staple of sailors across the Northern Hemisphere. Then as now, there were probably nearly 300,000 breeding pairs at this colony, divided between Cape Digges and Cape Wolstenholme, a few miles across Digges Sound. After visiting the island in 1615, William Baffin would proclaim that "in this place is the greatest quantity of these fowl . . . that in few places else the like is to be seen: for if need were we might have killed many thousands, almost incredible to those which have not seen it." The *Discovery* had come upon one of the murre's most important breeding colonies in the world, and an ample supply of scurvy-grass besides.

Fog began to roll in. Hudson, who had moved the *Discovery* around to the island's south coast, had a signal cannon fired.

Prickett and Greene went back to the north shore, to fetch the ship's boat, while Bylot (and probably Staffe) found their way down a valley to the south shore, where they were retrieved by the boat. It was most certainly Bylot who at this point took tide measurements, noting (as Hudson's journal abstract recorded) a flood from the north, into Digges Sound.

Prickett's party returned to the ship with breathless news of the abundant scurvy-grass and bounty of murres. They pressed Hudson to remain a day or two, so they could harvest the grass and birds, "but by no means would he stay," wrote Prickett. Hudson was "not pleased with the motion" of the ship in this shoal-strewn sound, where anchoring was difficult, and was determined to press on.

To that end, he made a striking decision. Rather than carry on farther west, or northwest, where there was ample open water, he chose to steer south, into the great bay that would be named for him. The shore party's inability to scale the island's highest ground for a clear view to the west may have influenced his decision. But the course he chose took him away from the purported strait, somewhere along latitude 62 and a half. He may have been influenced by Sebastian Cabot's claim to have sailed into a strait beyond Labrador in 1508. After progressing westward through twelve degrees of longitude, Cabot avowed, the way forward trended south, and Hudson had just covered almost exactly those number of degrees.

It was August 3, Hudson's journal observed, when the *Discovery* "put through the narrow passage, after our men had been on land." He continued southwest, along Digges Sound. "Then I observed and found the ship at noon in 61 degrees, 20 minutes, and a sea to the westward," his journal entry concluded for August 3. His result was a full degree south of the true position of East Digges Island, a considerable error amounting to sixty nautical miles. Those were Hudson's last preserved written words. For a navigator, it was a decidedly low note on which to take leave of the world.

Over the next month, Hudson sailed the length of the bay, with no surviving journal abstract or comment to explain precisely where he went or what he saw. This portion of Prickett's account, as published by Samuel Purchas in 1625, was terse and confused. Hudson's course may have trended toward the western shore, before the land's persistent curve delivered him southeastward, into James Bay. He had covered some seven hundred miles of latitude in this push south. Despite the apparent dead end in which he then found himself, he would not give up the search for whatever he was searching for. It was then that the final break came with Robert Juet.

Prickett made surprisingly little of the dramatic confrontation aboard the *Discovery* on September 10. After they took aboard water and ballast at an island around latitude 53 and began another surveying jaunt north, Prickett noted that Hudson had decided "to displace Robert Juet from being his mate, and the boatswain from his place, for the words spoken in the first great bay of ice."

There was no explanation of why, these many miles and many weeks later, the distress in Ungava Bay was of sudden urgency. Prickett suggested that Juet's downfall was due to Hudson's decision to unnecessarily revisit past tensions, noting "our master took occasion to revive old matters." But there had been so much more to Juet's dismissal as mate.

The task of telling it fell to Thomas Woodhouse, the young gentleman adventurer. After writing his cheerful note to Samuel Macham at Iceland, Woodhouse had, on this tumultuous occasion, found the sense and the duty to write down the details of the most dangerous moments on the ship to date. His account, when it finally surfaced, would put Prickett's reportage to shame.

In Woodhouse's telling, Juet demanded the hearing. He argued for it as an opportunity for the entire ship's company "to hear and bear witness of the abuse of some of the company . . . that [Hudson] should redress some abuses and slanders, as [Juet] called them, against this Juet."

What unfolded was a litany of disturbing allegations, stretching back to before the *Discovery* had even reached Iceland. If Hudson wrote down the hearing's details, they were lost with the disappearance of the balance of his journal after the entry of August 3. Only Woodhouse's record of them would endure. Prickett—his pen concentrated on tracing the malevolent shape of the man who became his particular villain, Henry Greene—never bothered.

Hudson called the crew together after dinner on September 10, to have Juet's accusers confront him, as he had requested. They were unflinching and damning. Bennet Mathew, the cook, testified that when the *Discovery* came within sight of Iceland, he heard Juet intimate an uprising: Juet "confessed, that he supposed that in the action"—by which Woodhouse meant the voyage—"would be manslaughter, and prove bloody to some." It was next alleged (by whom, Woodhouse didn't say) that after departing Iceland, within hearing of the ship's company, Juet "did threaten to turn the head of the ship home from the action."

Mathew's testimony that Juet promised manslaughter on the approach to Iceland roughly aligned with the timing of Greene's fight with Edward Wilson in Prickett's narrative. Juet's disgust with Greene at this point, and Hudson's refusal to do anything about it, could have motivated his promises of insurrection. And the allegation that Juet threatened to turn the ship around after departing Iceland also seemed to coincide with the confrontation

Prickett reported between Hudson and Juet, after Juet told Philip Staffe of Greene's snitch's role. But in Prickett's telling, it had been Hudson who was tempted to turn the *Discovery* around, to leave Juet in Iceland, and not Juet who threatened to turn the vessel back.

And however much Prickett assured his readers that all was well between Hudson and Juet after their differences flared shortly after departing Iceland, all most certainly was not. Juet had been noticeably absent from Prickett's account of the shore party at East Digges Island. A reconnaissance that should have been given to Juet to command had instead been entrusted by Hudson to Prickett, with Juet apparently remaining aboard the *Discovery.*

What was most striking about Woodhouse's account of the hearing was that there was no mention of Henry Greene at all. As a cause of Juet's anger and insubordination, Greene existed solely in Prickett's rendering. Woodhouse might have had his own inscrutable reasons for ignoring Greene, but it was more likely that no one who gave testimony against Juet raised the underlying behaviour of Greene, and that Woodhouse wrote down only what he heard in the Bible-sworn testimony.

Greene did not number among the ship's company, and that made him a man apart. Even if crewmembers understood that he was a source of Juet's vexation, he was on a different plane of existence. And there may have been a measure of fear of Greene among those giving testimony, because of his special relationship with Hudson. The master had looked the other way as Greene had laid a beating on the barber-surgeon at Iceland. And now, not even Juet attempted to make an issue of Greene as part of his own defence.

But something well beyond Greene was gnawing at Juet, something that had been causing him to threaten to turn the entire ship around, with violence if necessary, for the longest time.

According to Woodhouse, Juet had been talked out of his rashness by Hudson himself after the uproar that followed the Iceland departure: "which at that time was by our master wisely pacified, hoping of amendment." But there was no amending Juet's behaviour. The carpenter, Philip Staffe, and the sailor Arnold Ludlow testified "to [Juet's] face upon the holy bible, that he persuaded them to keep muskets charged, and swords in ready in their cabins, for they should be charged with shot ere the voyage were over."

The final allegation recorded by Woodhouse was that Juet had twice incited the crew to mutiny, and had nearly succeeded. The first occasion was in July, in Ungava Bay. As Woodhouse noted, "we being pestered in the ice, [Juet] had used words tending to mutiny, discouragement, and slander of the action, which easily took effect in those that were timorous; and had not the master in time prevented, it might easily have overthrown the voyage."

The next uprising incited by Juet was recent, and doubtless precipitated the hearing he demanded.

Woodhouse related how "now lately being embayed in a deep bay, which the master had desire to see, for some reasons to himself known, [Juet's] word tended altogether to put the company into a fray of extremity, by wintering in cold."

An insurrection had already broken out aboard the *Discovery* over the prospect of "wintering in cold"—back in 1602, when George Waymouth's men forced him to abandon his instructions to overwinter somewhere between latitudes 60 and 70. But if ever Juet thought this hearing would clear his name, or could be bent toward persuading the crew to join him in turning the ship around, he was gravely disappointed. As Woodhouse put it, after Hudson had listened to the testimony of the crew and "heard with equity what [Juet] could say for himself, there were proved so many and great abuses, and mutinous matters against the master, and action by Juet, that there was danger to have suffered them longer: and it was fit time to punish and cut off farther occasions of the like mutinies."

In the Royal Navy, mutiny was a serious offence, subject to martial law. If the *Discovery* had been a warship, Juet could easily have been strung up, given all the Bible-sworn testimony to his promises of violence. But with insubordination on an English merchant ship, Hudson's hands, legally speaking, were fairly tied when it came to punishment. If Hudson locked up Juet and took him home, the disgraced mate could not be tried before a jury on a "mutiny" charge. Unless some dire act of violence was committed in the course of an insurrection, there was nothing worthy of a criminal indictment. And Juet had not actually led a mutiny, only attempted to incite one.

In the worst cases, a master like Hudson could rid himself of a disobedient employee by putting him ashore, provided this didn't constitute an unwarranted severe punishment. According to Prickett, this had been Hudson's initial instinct, when Juet's insubordination first surfaced. He would turn the *Discovery* around and leave Juet in Iceland, to find his way home with an English fishing boat. But they had made their peace, and Juet had kept his mate's position. Abandoning Juet now, on a godforsaken shore, was unthinkable and indefensible.

When George Waymouth was defied by his crew in Davis Strait in 1602, he reacted with fury. He called forward the ringleaders and (in his own words) "punished them severely, that this punishment might be a warning to them afterward for falling into the like mutiny." The Reverend Cartwright and William Cobreth were among the recipients of this unelaborated severe discipline, although Waymouth allowed, "upon their submission, I remitted some part of their punishment." The explorer Luke Foxe, commenting on Waymouth's behaviour in 1635, was shocked by it.

"This doth not appear [reasonable] that he could punish, and yet suffer them to carry the ship back," he observed.

Hudson took no such vengeance on Juet after the *Discovery* skirted a far more dangerous insurrection than the one that had overcome Waymouth on the very same deck. Hudson simply demoted his mate, replacing him with Robert Bylot. He also demoted the boatswain, Francis Clement. "This man had basely carried himself to our master and to the action," wrote Woodhouse. In his stead, Hudson promoted William Wilson, "a man thought more fit." He also elevated to boatswain's mate a sailor named Adrian Moter. Juet's master's mate wages were to go to Bylot, and the "overplus" wage that Clement enjoyed as boatswain was to be divided going forward between two crewmembers, William Wilson and John King, who "had very well carried themselves to the furtherance of the business." Woodhouse singled out King as well for mention as a quartermaster who was "to the owners good liking."

After the September 10 hearing, the surviving narrative returned to the exclusive care of Habakkuk Prickett for more than ten months. Henry Hudson's behaviour after Juet's demotion was, according to Prickett, without apparent reason. He sailed back and forth in James Bay ("Up to the north we stood till we raised land, then down to the south, and up to the north again, and down again to the south . . .") Hudson would not give up the bay, and Prickett had no idea why not. He was not alone, as Woodhouse, in his account of Juet's hearing, described Hudson's desire to see James Bay "for some reasons to himself known." Some expectation was holding Hudson there, down toward latitude 51, far south of where the Northwest Passage was meant to lie.

The expectation must have been a passage from the Northern Sea to a Protean Great Lakes, called Lake Tadouac, as drawn by

Edward Wright in his well-known 1599 chart of the world. Lake Tadouac in turn was shown as the source of the St. Lawrence River, flowing eastward out of the continent. Wright's portrait was conjectural, based not on first-hand exploration but on anecdotal evidence gathered from French and Basque sources in the late sixteenth century.

James Bay would have been particularly persuasive of imminent success in finding the passage south into Lake Tadouac. Despite its expanse—some two hundred miles long and a hundred wide—it represented a considerable narrowing from Hudson Bay. It was also quite shallow, and the many rivers feeding it noticeably diluted its salt water. Hudson would have detected water that became increasingly fresh the farther south he progressed. A major freshwater passage into the continent would have seemed close at hand.

But if proving this passage was Hudson's goal, why was Juet in the dark? The disgraced mate would have understood from the beginning of the voyage that Hudson did not intend to return after eight months and a basic reconnaissance of the northwest, that he had a grander scheme to pursue. But rather than showing Wright to be correct in his rendering of the passage from the Northern Sea to the St. Lawrence via Lake Tadouac, in Juet's telling Hudson was intent on making it all the way to the East Indies. As Woodhouse related in his account of Juet's hearing, Juet lately had been deriding Hudson's ambitions to reach the Orient—"Jesting at our master's hope to see Bantam by Candlemas [February 2]."

Did Hudson indeed intend to be in Java in five months, or was this Juet's bitter mockery, made in ignorance of his actual plans? The latter seems possible, but Juet had been too close to Hudson for too many voyages, and too valuable and skilled a pilot, not to know what Hudson truly had in mind for the voyage from the moment of sailing.

Hudson may have been hoping that the way south as depicted in Wright's chart in fact would turn out to be a gateway to the Orient, and not just to the St. Lawrence. In 1603, the French explorer Samuel de Champlain had travelled to the height of navigation on the St. Lawrence, to the broad sheet of rapids at present-day Montréal. After interviewing native guides, Champlain concluded that the way upstream led west, through one or more large lakes, to the Pacific. Champlain published his conclusions in late 1603, in a book called *Des Sauvages*. Richard Hakluyt had it translated, and would have gladly shared this English manuscript with someone as well connected and as interested in passage-seeking as Hudson.

Hakluyt's translation unfortunately botched some of Champlain's key findings. Champlain's references to fresh water upstream of the rapids, which he called "wholesome" (*salubre*), were misread as salty (*salé*), making an even more forceful case than Champlain did for a passage to the Pacific. All ambiguity in Champlain's evidence as a result was eliminated in the English version.

Hudson would have hoped that the vision contained in Edward Wright's 1599 map would intersect with the fresh intelligence generously published by Champlain in 1603. A passage south, from the Northern Sea, would enter the lake that Wright's map called Tadouac. This lake, in turn, would be one of Champlain's great lakes, and a further passage would lead westward, to the Pacific, as Champlain claimed. Hudson just might be in Bantam by February. And by September 10, Hudson was probably as weary of Juet's doubting mockery as he was of his violent threats of turning the whole enterprise around.

Henry Hudson's refusal to sail back north must have distressed Robert Juet beyond sensibility. For all the simmering violence beneath Juet's words, he was a sophisticated navigator. He must have come to realize that the pursuit he had been making with Hudson for the past three voyages of some kind of passage to the Orient was an exquisitely crafted delusion that would ultimately see them all killed, locked in ice without hope of salvation.

Hudson's genuine discoveries, like the Hudson River, had been few and far between. He had based his exploration career on investigating what others thought, on revisiting places others had been. He never went anywhere that he didn't already understand at some fundamental level. His perspective was burdened by the arcana of the efforts of earlier explorers, these figures and their accomplishments a mix of real and imagined, and by almost hallucinatory visions of cosmographers and cartographers of the shape and nature of northern lands and seas. And the sincerity of Hudson's convictions was muddied by his propensity to shape results to satisfy whoever was in a position to employ him. It was a practice to which explorers hungry for the next assignment, the next cash infusion, were prone. The fever dream, however, could blur the line between self-promotion and self-delusion. A man desperate for success could begin to convince himself that hypothesis was reality.

To avoid this trap, Hudson needed the expertise of Juet, who could provide dispassionate observations based on the most advanced methods. But Juet's faith in his own navigational skills also must have been shaken. On the 1609 voyage, a single reference in his journal while off New Jersey demonstrated his allegiance to William Gilbert's theory of magnetism: "That night I found the land to haul the compass 8 degrees. For to the northward of us we saw high hills."

Gilbert's experiments with a spherical magnet led him to reject the notion that a lodestone mountain at the top of the world attracted compass needles. Gilbert argued that the earth itself was an enormous magnet. He concluded that compass variation was due to local distortions in the earth's magnetic field, which were caused by unevenness in the height of the earth's surface. Continental land masses, mountains, and ocean depths were the cause of aberrations in compass direction.

Gilbert, who had been Queen Elizabeth's physician, succumbed to the plague in London in 1603. The influential Edward Wright championed his work, and impressed upon navigators that they should heed it. Gilbert's results, expressed in the six-volume *De Magnete* of 1600, were in Latin so dense as to discourage actual reading, and Juet's understanding of Gilbert probably was based on some distillation delivered in a pamphlet or a lecture. But as much as Gilbert's investigation was a great leap forward in modelling the earth's magnetic field, and a landmark advance in scientific method, it was still dangerously wrong when it came to navigating ships. Continental land masses and ocean depths were not responsible for local differences in magnetic bearings, and the geographic pole and the northern magnetic pole were not, as Gilbert insisted, one and the same place.

Gilbert's predicted results would have fallen apart completely as the *Discovery* entered Hudson Strait, where variation grew dramatically as the ship drew closer to the magnetic pole, and where compass readings were also harried by weakness in the horizontal magnetic force and areas of significant magnetic anomalies. The failure of Gilbert's system would have left Juet directionless. And with persistently overcast skies thwarting efforts to take latitude fixes with the sun or stars, Juet would have become increasingly at odds with Hudson over where they were located, where they were headed, and what if any chance they might have of finding a passage. Juet's systematic and carefully observed world would have collapsed around him. The one-degree error in Hudson's position for the waters around East Digges Island—secured perhaps with an archaic cross-staff that Hudson would not give up for force of habit—was a lingering clue to persistent and serious disputes, as they compared independent and irreconcilable observations.

For Juet, Hudson's fever dream had inevitably transmogrified into a nightmare.

Hudson was conspicuously tolerant of Juet's insubordination. There had been enough testimony to Juet's promises of violent action to tempt another captain to at least clap him in irons for the balance of the voyage. Hudson had merely demoted him, and then held out the possibility of forgiving him entirely. According to Woodhouse, Hudson "promised, if the offenders yet behaved themselves henceforth honestly, he would be a means for their good, and that he would forget injuries, with other admonitions."

There may have been some pity for an old ally whom Hudson could have considered a genuine friend. The pity was laced perhaps with fear that Juet was in fact right, that the cause of finding a passage through to the Orient down toward latitude 51 was utterly hopeless. Hudson could not bring himself to deliver stern justice to someone whose doubts might prove to be well founded. But neither could Hudson bring himself to abandon the search for a passage in the south. He refused to turn north and return to England.

Hudson probably never counted on having to overwinter in a place where there was actual winter. But summer was turning to autumn, and Juet's warnings about the dangers of "wintering in cold" went unheeded.

Eleven

—

WAITING OUT FOUL WEATHER, Hudson anchored for eight long and difficult days in James Bay soon after the hearing into Juet's behaviour. The anchor was constantly reset, never holding for more than an hour. "But the eight[h] day, the wind beginning to cease," Prickett would assert, "our master would have the anchor up, against the mind of all who knew what belonged thereunto."

Hudson's decision to raise anchor "against the mind" of everyone aboard who knew the business of seafaring had a predictable result. The *Discovery* was tossed by great seas before the anchor was completely shipped. As it ran free, the flailing handles of the spinning capstan injured a number of the crew. Only the quick action of Philip Staffe, anticipating trouble and axe at the ready, saved the anchor cable: the carpenter cut away the anchor itself.

Prickett would blame the mishap for enfeebling two crewmembers, Michael Bute and Adrian Moore, who never fully recovered. But the accident did not mean Hudson was unusually headstrong or at all incompetent, and a landsman like Prickett was the last person to be relied on for a learned judgment of the sea sense of the *Discovery*'s commander. In four voyages of exploration in remote, hazardous waters, there were precious few instances in which a ship of Hudson's was at risk of being lost.

And in James Bay, Hudson was tackling some of the most dangerous uncharted waters in the world. He sailed on south after the capstan incident, approaching the land as close as he could in shoaling waters. Most of the bay was less than fifty feet deep, and within ten miles of shore it was generally less than twenty. In addition to shoals, glacial erratics—enormous granite boulders, deposited on the bay's bottom some ten thousand years earlier by retreating ice at the end of the Wisconsin glaciation—lay in wait for a passing keel. Mud flats that extended a half mile or more from shore at low tide thwarted approaches to land.

At the shoreline the taiga began, a transitional environment between the stark subarctic tundra of Hudson Bay and upper James Bay and the dense mixed coniferous forest of the Laurentian Shield's boreal zone. The taiga was a sodden world, of salt marsh, peat bog, and tidal and freshwater ponds, and of grasslands tufted green and grey and dappled with bright wildflower blooms. Wading shorebirds—sandpipers, godwits, and yellowlegs among them—probed the wetlands and tidal flats and moved in low, flickering flocks. The horizon's sweep was scarcely challenged. Marching inland were successive ridgelines of old beachhead, where the sea once reached, and where black spruce, tamarack, and dwarf birch provided much of the thin forest cover. In some places this forest was close by the shore; in others, it lay beyond the half-drowned land a half mile or more, clinging to the first ridgeline.

The terrain sloped imperceptibly and incongruously downhill, away from the shore, a consequence of the fact that the bay's bottom was rising at a geologically astonishing rate, almost four feet per century, as the earth's crust rebounded from the crushing weight of the last glaciation. James Bay's contours as a result were changing markedly with every passing decade, so much so that, four hundred years after Hudson visited, with the land having risen a full sixteen feet, it would be impossible to say exactly where in this shallow, shrinking corner of the northern sea Hudson sailed. Some of the waters he explored would become dry land; new ridgelines would form as the land rose and the water receded.

Hudson could not know that the world was rising beneath him as he probed the bay. But he had experienced a terrain of beach ridgelines and low growth very much like this at Novaya Zemlya, which was also recovering from the ice age's crush. Lower James Bay was a strange, remarkably flat and windswept place, but in summer it was also teeming with life, positively lush after the severity of Hudson Strait and Hudson Bay. The taiga must have provided reassurance of a return to the temperate zone as the *Discovery* moved deeper into James Bay. The expectation of gaining the heart of the continent and a passage westward would not have seemed so far-fetched as the lowlands made the most of a brief summer.

But the longer Hudson remained in James Bay, the more isolated he would have felt as the air sharpened and high cirrus wisps foretold the arrival of cumulus fronts leaden with snow. It was now October. The shorebirds moved on south; lesser snow geese, flocking in profuse waves high overhead, arrived from their Arctic breeding grounds to stage for the final migratory push for the Gulf of Mexico. When the geese left, the taiga's waiting for winter was all but over. The *Discovery* needed sanctuary.

Hudson dispatched a shore party, which found footprints of two divergent creatures: a duck, and a man. It was the first sign of any human life the expedition had recorded since encountering the strange cairns at East Digges Island.

Something about his ship's present location dissatisfied Hudson. The weather might have been turning, with storm tracks raising anxiety that the *Discovery* might founder on tidal flats or be torn open on a shoal or a glacial erratic. At midnight on October 30, Hudson ordered the ship moved. Juet's account followed the old Julian calendar still in use in England, which lagged behind the modern Gregorian calendar by ten days. The Gregorian date, of November 9, meant that the equinox was almost three weeks behind them; night was becoming steadily longer than day. Staffe warned Hudson that there were shoals ahead. Hudson, wrote Prickett, "conceived that he was passed them." On cue, the *Discovery* slammed hard aground.

The sun rose about 7:20, revealing the *Discovery* to be suspended on the outcrop. Hudson probably waited for high tide to shift the vessel clear, and by noon the *Discovery* was on her way again. Prickett related how "(by the mercy of God) we got off unhurt, though not unscarred." The felicity of their escape may well have encouraged the name "Bay of gods merces" preserved in the chart later published by Hessel Gerritsz.

As autumn progressed, Hudson's determination to overwinter in James Bay became apparent. A passage south had not been found, and there was little time for them to escape the bay and make their way back north to Hudson Strait and then east to the Furious Overfall. It might be November by the time they gained the Labrador Sea, not a month in which a seventeenth-century mariner would choose to negotiate malevolent ice fields. The *Discovery* was soon anchored again, as Staffe and Prickett together set off in the ship's boat to find a wintering place. Prickett wrote that "it was time, for the nights were long and cold, and the earth covered with snow." They had "spent three months in a labyrinth without end."

The next day, they sailed "to the south and the south-west, and found a place, whereunto we brought our ship, and hauled her aground: and this was the first of November." It was likely Rupert

Bay, or a location close by. Wherever Hudson had chosen to wait out the ice, ten days later, the *Discovery* was frozen in.

It should have been clear by then that Hudson had never intended to be back in England after eight months and a basic reconnaissance. He was seizing the *Discovery* voyage as if it were his last chance at a grand success. He would only return home in triumph. Perhaps now, some of the crewmembers understood why Hudson had disposed of William Cobreth before the *Discovery* had left England.

Luke Foxe would attribute Cobreth's dismissal to envy on Hudson's part, suggesting that Hudson could not tolerate the service of a better man as his subordinate. But Hudson's motivations assuredly were more complex. Cobreth had gone along with the insurrection that prevented George Waymouth from overwintering. With the investors not even expecting Hudson to overwinter, Cobreth would have demanded that the *Discovery* return to England before 1610 was out. Had Hudson kept him aboard, Cobreth never would have allowed him to press so far beyond the Furious Overfall and place the enterprise and its men in their present predicament. If he was as capable a mariner as Waymouth attested, Cobreth would have had little difficulty in getting the crew to support him.

That Robert Juet, Hudson's hand-picked replacement for Cobreth, turned out to be so vexatiously opposed to his plans, and so contemptuous of his judgment, must have been a startling and disheartening surprise. But Hudson had been able to keep the crew on his side, and away from Juet's. The men could not have been enthusiastic about the overwintering, but as their master had left them in the dark about what he had been looking for in James Bay, there was no way for them to be disappointed when he failed to find a way through. If they had become disillusioned with his leadership, with winter setting in there was nothing they could do about it.

Hudson would have reminded them of his near-unblemished record. Only one of Hudson's men, John Colman, with an arrow in his throat, had ever been lost, and the *Discovery* voyage continued to be free of fatalities. Hudson's record was extraordinary, and any crewmember who had survived a lengthy voyage before signing on with the *Discovery* would have known it.

But still he had to overcome the sailor's elemental fear of over-wintering in an icebound northern location. It had been attempted only once by the English, and it was such a disaster that the memory of it continued to haunt mariners. In 1553, three ships were sent out on the inaugural expedition of what was to become the Muscovy Company, to prove the Northeast Passage over Asia. Only one ship returned. The flagship *Bona Esperanza,* commanded by the expedition's captain-general, Sir Hugh Willoughby, sought refuge for the winter, along with the *Bona Confidentia,* in the estuary of Russia's Varsina River, on the Kola Peninsula. All aboard them perished—thirty-eight on the *Bona Esperanza,* twenty-eight on the *Bona Confidentia.* Both vessels, still hosting their frozen crews, were discovered the next year by Russian fishermen. It would be said that Sir Hugh's corpse was found sitting in a chair, his logbook and a fresh will nearby.

Hudson was perfectly capable of quelling the fears the ship's company would have had of dying the terrible deaths of Willoughby and his men. He talked money men into backing his voyages. He had talked a dozen Dutchmen, mate included, into defying the VOC and sailing away with him to North America. He had already talked this crew into pressing westward, along Hudson Strait, after almost being trapped by ice in Ungava Bay. And when Juet tried repeatedly to turn them against him, Hudson had prevailed.

There is no chance of going the way of Willoughby, he would have assured them. *This is not the Arctic. Look around you at the temperate climate. Consider the latitude of the wintering place: 52 degrees. Farther south than Liverpool and Hull.*

And we shall not be running out of victuals in January, as Willoughby did, Hudson would have promised. The new mate, Robert Bylot, could support his assertion. It would have been standard shipboard practice for Hudson to take a weekly inventory of provisions with Bylot and the cook, Bennet Mathew. Hudson had done exceptionally well in managing the food supply. When the *Discovery* was beached for the winter, after more than six months away from England on a voyage that had been provisioned for only eight months, there was enough food to hold out for six months more, according to Prickett. Hudson had been able to stretch the rations tremendously by living off the land and sea. The fresh meat from fish and birds had boosted the overall health of the crew and greatly improved their chances of survival. Barring spoilage, the food supply would last through the following April, without any supplement from hunting and fishing, which had served them so well to date. Hudson set the rations for the coming winter, and further proposed to replenish the larder by instituting a reward system for those who "killed either beast, fish or fowl."

There was reason aplenty to be optimistic about their chances, if they could endure whatever cold this sanctuary would experience, stay healthy, and hold the *Discovery* together. And then? Prickett expected that, when the ice was gone in the spring, they would return north, to where they had seen the thick-billed murres in their massive summer colony at Cape Digges and Cape Wolstenholme. After overwintering in James Bay, reaching the murres "was all the hope we had to bring us home," Prickett would allege.

The *Discovery*'s men, Hudson included, doubtless were surprised by the intensity of winter's onset. Despite the temperate reassurances of the latitude and the verdant taiga, snow routinely accumulated three feet deep. Blizzards blasted across a terrain that offered no resistance, beyond the drift catches of the ridgelines. Ice would dominate the bay for nine long months, lingering into July.

Hudson's decision to remove the *Discovery*'s ballast, so that she could be hauled as close to shore as possible, clear of shifting pack ice, showed sound preparation and some expectation of a harsh trial. But the crises rapidly accumulated. In mid-November, only a few days after the bay froze around the beached *Discovery*, the expedition suffered its first death. The gunner, John Williams, was lost to an unknown cause. Williams could have succumbed to some miscellaneous malady that circa 1610 could be called "natural causes." But his death was, in Prickett's telling, the beginning of the end for Hudson.

"God pardon the master's uncharitable dealing with this man," Prickett avowed, without elaborating. He may not have meant that Hudson had dealt uncharitably with Williams himself but rather with his death. For it was the way Hudson handled the consequences of Williams's passing that Prickett blamed for sowing the fatal discord on board. Prickett intoned that he had now come "to speak of him [Williams], out of whose ashes (as it were) that unhappy deed grew which brought a scandal upon all that are returned home, and upon the action itself."

Word of Prickett's culpability in the loss of Henry Hudson and his companions was circulating in England as he composed his journal account. He paused in the narrative where Williams died, to charge that "the multitude (like the dog) [is] running after the stone, but not at the caster." The critics of the survivors, in Prickett's telling, had fallen victim to misdirection, and Prickett was stung by having been struck by the stone, and fearful of the pack nipping at his heels. Prickett pledged: "therefore, not to wrong the living nor slander the dead, I will (by the leave of God) deliver the truth as near as I can."

And it all began, he insisted, with the dead gunner's grey cloth gown.

A dead seaman left behind more than a body to be buried or dumped overboard. His wages had to be accounted for up to the day of his death and provided to his next of kin at the voyage's end. His personal effects on board—and on his back—which could amount to the entirety of his earthly possessions, also had to be inventoried and dealt with in an orderly fashion. The rabble of the crew were not allowed to pick their way through the man's effects and pull off his boots. These possessions were either returned home to his heirs or auctioned at the mast.

"Now, when our gunner was dead," Prickett explained, "and (as the order is in such cases) if the company stand in need of anything that belonged to the man deceased, then it is brought to the main mast, and there sold to them that will give most for the same." A cloth gown would have been a treasured possession as winter set in, and there was interest in owning it. But according to Prickett, Henry Greene went to Hudson and offered to pay as much for it as any man. Hudson, who was paying Greene out of his own pocket, agreed, handing it over to him. When other crewmembers approached Hudson about acquiring it in a main-mast auction, they were told "that Greene should have it, and no one else, and so it rested."

It is unclear how the price was set, and if or when Greene would ever have to pay it. Hudson had subordinated a shipboard policy affecting the entire crew to a private arrangement with a man who wasn't even in the company roll. Surely there was com-plaining belowdecks, not only about the missed opportunity to own the gown but also about the possibility of Greene's ending up with the choicest personal effects when the next of their number expired.

The issue of the gown made a profound difference in Greene's relationship to the shipboard world. The fight with Edward Wilson already had been an unhappy intrusion, but it was more a matter of a personal spat. Hudson had made it clear with the way he handled the Wilson fight that Greene stood apart. But in allowing Greene to defile the conventions of a dead man's effects, Hudson had caused Greene to enter into that shipboard world. And the transgression was as much Hudson's as it was Greene's.

Still, the incident may well have rested there, with some small but not terribly serious disgruntlement, had not shipboard cohesion rapidly begun to unravel as another thread was pulled from another corner of this tattered fabric.

As winter took hold more severely than imagined, the limited precedents for an overwintering in the ice would have been a pressing concern. Beyond the Willoughby expedition's disastrous attempt of 1553–54, there was only the example of the Barentsz expedition of 1596–97, which had managed to bring most of its members through the privations of a high-latitude winter encampment at the tip of Novaya Zemlya. A survivor, Gerrit de Veer, wrote a bestseller about the ordeal, which had just been translated into English in 1609. The Barentsz expedition distinguished itself from the doomed English venture of 1553 by building a cabin on shore—a strategy forced upon it when ice crushed its ship. There was even a drawing of it in de Veer's book.

Philip Staffe, the *Discovery*'s carpenter, perhaps following the Barentsz strategy, proposed to Hudson that they build a cabin. Many illnesses, including scurvy, were thought to be caused by harmful fumes. A ship locked in ice, with a nauseating stew of dead rats, spoiling food (particularly cheese), and bilge water, was rank with such vapours. Moving into a cabin would have spared the men from breathing them.

Hudson initially rejected Staffe's proposal. But at some point after the death of the gunner, he changed his mind. The ferocity of even late-autumn weather, with ice thickening around the ship and snow gathering in wind-whipped drifts, was more than he had bargained for, or had asked the men to endure. Hudson ordered the carpenter to begin the cabin's construction.

The master's tardy agreement angered Staffe. The carpenter let it be known among the crew that there was now too much snow and ice for him to be able to follow Hudson's orders: "he neither could nor would go in hand with such work." When Hudson heard of his refusal, Prickett reported, "he ferreted him out of his cabin to strike him, calling him by many foul names, and threatening to hang him."

It was an astonishing outburst against a man whom Prickett otherwise portrayed as being steadfastly loyal to Hudson. The threat of execution was all the more extreme, considering the leniency Hudson had shown to the mutinous behaviour of Juet. If the cabin was meant to alleviate the suffering of the sick, Hudson's anger at Staffe's insubordination at least underlined his concern for the welfare of his men. But Staffe stood his ground, telling his captain that he knew his job better than Hudson, and that Hudson "was no house carpenter." Still, on Hudson's insistence, the cabin was built, "with much labour, but to no end," Prickett charged. The building was either unserviceable or deemed unnecessary as the *Discovery* continued to provide a safe refuge.

A day after the altercation between Hudson and Staffe, the carpenter went ashore with a musket, taking Henry Greene with him. Prickett did not say what they were up to. They were probably hunting, but it was not impossible that Staffe was determined to search for help. A surviving page from Willoughby's journal, transcribed and published by Hakluyt, had captured the 1553–54 expedition in almost the same circumstances as Hudson's crew now found themselves. Willoughby had chosen a haven for his two ships on September 18: "seeing the year far spent, & also very evil weather, as frost, snow, and hail, as though it had been the deep of winter, we thought it best to enter there." A week later, the journal scrap explained, "we sent out three men." Nothing more of the account survived.

Prickett wrote that Staffe was following the orders Hudson had set down for forays ashore: at least two men were to travel in company, one with a gun, the other with a pike. But Staffe seems not to have secured Hudson's permission to make the reconnaissance.

When Hudson heard that it was Greene who had gone ashore with Staffe, in Prickett's telling the captain turned against his shipboard informant and would-be chronicler in a capricious fit of pique. Hudson decided that the gunner's gown should now belong to Robert Bylot, who had earlier replaced Juet as master's mate.

When Greene returned and learned that Hudson had delivered the gown to Bylot, he reminded Hudson of how it had already been promised to him. At which Hudson exploded.

"The master did so rile on Greene," Prickett wrote, "with so many words of disgrace, telling him, that all his friends would not trust him with twenty shillings, and therefore why should he." By Prickett's account, Hudson not only had promised to pay Greene a wage equal to other crewmembers' but also to secure him a position in the guard of the Prince of Wales when they returned, a position that would have come through Sir Thomas Challener. With Greene wholly dependent on Hudson for his pay, he was suddenly vulnerable to being cut off without a cent and denied his princely sinecure once home. "As for wages he had none, nor none should have, if he did not please him well," Prickett had Hudson threaten.

Hudson had broken with Greene seemingly as abruptly and as violently as Juet had with Hudson. For the misstep of joining the out-of-favour Staffe on an unauthorized shore party, Greene had tumbled precipitously from his position of privilege. The margins of error Hudson had set for the problematic young man were narrow, and Greene may have tested them more over the course of the voyage than even Prickett knew.

More than the loss of the gown or even the thought of lost wages, the public disgrace would have cut Greene most deeply. Hudson's harangue in that small ship would have been loud enough for Prickett, and most anyone else, to feel as it reverberated within the hull's close-set wooden walls. Hudson had now fallen out with Juet, with Staffe, and with Greene. For that matter, he had long ago dismissed William Cobreth, and had also demoted his boatswain, Francis Clement. It was Greene who was most affected by a fall from Hudson's grace. He could no longer expect a place of privilege above the ship's common herd. But rather than being beaten down, Greene now forged his own particular role among the men.

"But you shall see," Prickett promised, "how the devil out of this so wrought with Greene, that he did the master what mischief he could in seeking to discredit him."

Twelve

—

F OR THE TIME BEING, with the ship beached and the sea frozen, there was nowhere for any would-be mutineers to go. The winter was brutal, but beyond Prickett's enthusiasm to recall. "To speak of all our trouble in this time of winter (which was so cold, as it lamed the most of our company, and myself do yet feel it) would be too tedious."

Yet Hudson's men endured, blessed by a bounty of fresh meat. Willow ptarmigan flocked in the hundreds, and the waters around the *Discovery* yielded plenty of fish, which they would have jigged for through a fire hole chopped in the ice. There must have been worrisome moments with the ship, but Prickett did not cite any significant repair having to be made when summer finally returned. Staffe and the new boatswain, William Wilson, held their wooden world in one piece. A carpenter could work his way back into a master's favour, and Hudson's enmity toward Staffe apparently abated.

Only in the spring, with the *Discovery* still frozen in, did circumstances become desperate. For three months, they had been able to feast on the ptarmigan, of which they killed more than "a hundred dozen," according to Prickett. But then the flocks were either hunted out locally by Hudson's men or had moved on.

Still, Hudson had calculated six months of rations being on hand even before the ptarmigan harvest and the fishing began. Rationing should have seen them through in good shape at least until April, with reserves still on hand. And in early April, the first chevron flocks of Canada geese would have descended, the advance brigade in a massive spring migration.

Indeed, after the ptarmigan disappeared, "in their places came diverse sorts of other fowl, as swan, geese, duck and teal, but hard to come by," wrote Prickett. "Our master hoped they would have bred in those broken grounds, but they do not; but came from the south and flew to the north, further than we were this voyage; yet if they be taken short with the wind at north, or northwest, or northeast, then they fall and stay till the wind served them and then fly to the north. Now in time these fowls are gone, and few or none to be seen."

The failure of the *Discovery*'s men to take advantage of the steady parade of millions of waterfowl descending on the James Bay shore during the spring migration on this major flyway was a serious blow to their survival prospects. The birds may not have stopped to breed, as Hudson hoped, but the supply of meat was constant for several months as the flocks rested and fed in the wetlands. After Canada geese began the parade, their main wave arriving around mid-April, the ducks—black and mallard especially—winged in around the third week of the month and lingered until mid-May. Around the first week of May, the snow geese appeared in such quantities as to blanket the saltwater marshes near the *Discovery* in a downy frost, well over one million of them pausing in James Bay on the return to their Arctic breeding grounds.

The crew faced starvation amid this ridiculous plenty because the waterfowl were not the sorts of birds sailors were accustomed to harvesting. They sought out colonies of diving birds like murres and auks, which could be readily clubbed in their densely packed rookeries, or shot at close range as they congregated on a cliff face. At the first report of a musket, the geese and ducks would have exploded into the air and settled out of range of the inaccurate powder weapons of the English. Thomas James, commanding an expedition that overwintered—with far more trauma than Hudson's—in roughly the same corner of James Bay two decades later, would report his own frustrations in hunting geese and duck: "never did I see such wild fowl; they would not endure to see anything move." Little wonder men like Prickett yearned to be back among the murres. A few men with clubs and muskets loaded with multiple shot could harvest enough meat in a single afternoon to keep a ship's crew fed for weeks on end.

The men began combing the landscape for any morsel of sustenance. They gathered moss, and overcame their revulsion (and fear of mistakenly eating poisonous toads) to feed on frogs that emerged in the spring melt. Scurvy was beginning to take hold, weakening Prickett's limbs, and others suffered with him.

Typically the first signs of scurvy were discoloration of the skin and swollen, dying gums, from which Edward Wilson, the barber-surgeon, would have carved away the dead flesh. Another telltale sign would have been the "flexed frog" posture that sufferers assumed in their berths—knees pulled up and hips flexed outwards as the vitamin-C deficiency broke down their body's tissues. As the illness progressed, old wounds would open and bleed afresh.

Hudson's ability to bring his crews through four extended voyages without any losses attributed to illness of any kind was nothing short of incredible, as any more than three months at sea generally brought out the scurvy cases. After the death of the gunner John Williams in November, not a single person aboard the *Discovery* perished in the winter of 1610–11.

Voyages that followed Hudson into the Arctic lost dozens to scurvy. Hudson's success was such a singular achievement that he must have been privy to the rarefied knowledge that citrus juice was an effective remedy. Only James Lancaster had demonstrated this understanding in surviving records of previous English ocean voyages. Lancaster seems to have gained the knowledge on his return from the Far East in 1593, when he stopped at St. Helena Island in the south Atlantic and found "great store of very wholesome and excellent good green figs, oranges and limons very fair." The voyage chronicler noted: "Here two of our men, whereof the one was diseased with scurvy, and the other had been nine months sick of the flux, in short time while they were on the island recovered their perfect health."

When Lancaster set out in command of the first East India Company voyage in 1601, he alone among the fleet's captains brought along bottles of "limon" juice—by which the chronicler probably meant lime—and dispensed three spoonfuls of it every morning to his men. But knowledge of the antiscorbutic properties of citrus fruit was surprisingly slow to spread, and the East India Company rapidly forgot Lancaster's example: many men died on the very next voyage, of 1604–05. The journals of the 1601–03 Lancaster expedition were not published until 1625, and in the meantime, calamitous losses continued for decades. The deaths extended all the way to Sir Robert Cecil, the most powerful politician in England. When he expired in 1612, he was most likely battling scurvy, without any idea of how to treat it. His last earthly act was to travel to Bath to take the curative waters. Some daily teaspoons of lime juice could have saved the life of the country's spymaster.

Hudson must have known of Lancaster's success with lime juice, and brought some along on all of his voyages. Its presence aboard the *Discovery* would explain why he was so disinterested in pausing at East Digges Island to harvest scurvy-grass. The disease would only have begun to take hold among the *Discovery*'s crew during the winter, when the juice spoiled or the supply ran out. Hudson's men still came through the winter intact, in no small part because of the actions of the barber-surgeon, Edward Wilson.

Prickett related that Thomas Woodhouse went out into the country and "brought home a bud of a tree full of a turpentine substance. Of this our surgeon made a decoction to drink, and applied the buds hot to them that were troubled with ache in any part of their bodies; and for my part I confess, I received great and present ease of my pain."

Woodhouse most likely had been dispatched to collect the buds on Wilson's direction. For a young saw man from Portsmouth, Wilson's knowledge of the antiscorbutic properties of what was probably black spruce was exceptional, the only recorded use of such a treatment at this point in history. It recalled how Jacques Cartier, suffering through an overwintering at Quebec in 1535–36 that devastated the ranks of his men, was provided by the Montagnais people with a tea he reported to have come from a tree called the anneda. Long after Cartier was gone, and well into Hudson's time, Frenchmen in the New World, despite being in regular contact with native people, succumbed in droves to the vitamin deficiency, never having determined the identity of Cartier's anneda.

The decoction that Prickett and others drank was a lifesaver. Wilson evidently knew to steep the buds in water so as not to destroy the ascorbic acid through boiling. This knowledge may have been gained first- or second-hand by Wilson from English encounters with natives on the Eastern Seaboard, although there is no record of Europeans after Cartier understanding this treatment. Another possible source was the Sami, or Lapps, of what is now northern Scandinavia and Russia. These nomadic reindeer herders were part of the Muscovy Company trade network. Their medicine was rich in herbs, but poorly documented. No mention of a spruce treatment for scurvy survived. Blood, rather, was used as a ritualized Sami treatment of an illness thought to be caused by sorcery.

It just may have been the case that the lifesaving remedy walked to the *Discovery* across the frozen taiga. For coincidentally, Wilson had just begun applying the remedy in Prickett's account when Hudson and his crew had their first encounter on this entire voyage with the indigenous people.

As the ice began to break up, the *Discovery* was visited by a lone "savage." No white man had ever been seen in these parts, so far as anyone knows. But the Cree visitor's willingness to trade, and the determination he would show to receive a particular value for furs in European goods, suggests that the barter system had already delivered French trade items deep into the country, from one tribe to another. And with the trade items may have come knowledge of the spruce treatment. The Cree themselves were not affected by scurvy, though poultices of the sort described by Prickett ("applied the buds") in treating wounds and sores were part of Cree medicine. Their diet was rich in berries, which they continued to eat through the winter as the fruit was added to their main staple, the bread-like pemmican they made from pounded meat. But the man who visited Hudson might have learned of the spruce treatment through the trade network. The people immediately to the south, who controlled the trade route through what is now Quebec to the main trading post at Tadoussac on the St. Lawrence, were Naskapi. And it was the coastal Naskapi, whom the French called the Montagnais, who had shown Cartier how to save his men some eight decades earlier.

Prickett did not describe the visitor in any way. He would have been fully fortified against the cold in tanned leather clothing, including a fur-lined parka. Snowshoes fashioned from steamed birch and hide lashings would have buoyed his weight in the drifts. The man had come to the *Discovery* from within a day's journey, but Hudson's people, in all their wanderings in search of game, never saw a camp, nor was any mention made by Prickett of telltale smoke.

The Cree were nomadic hunters and trappers, and the visitor may have been from a hunting party, with the main group of wigwams several days away. With the *Discovery*'s masts visible from a great distance, the Cree would have monitored Hudson's progress for months as the bark reconnoitred the bay. As Hudson settled into winter quarters, the ship's canvas clouds would have dissipated to reveal a stand of spindly trunks and branches.

It is impressive that the man was willing to approach this strange vessel and its strange men alone. He would have heard about the Europeans who visited the great river to the southeast, and he would have traded personally with native middlemen for some of the goods the strangers offered for furs. And he alone, among his people, may have studied the Hudson party long enough to decide that contact was a risk worth taking.

What would have seemed at a distance like a floating island was now like some massive creature of the sea, scarred and encrusted and cast upon the shore, suffocating slowly under its own crushing weight. The ice and snow around the *Discovery* would have been stained with human filth. It was a wonder he even agreed to go aboard.

Hudson treated the visitor well, and promised him a bounty of goods. But the *Discovery* had not been fitted out for trade. Hudson turned to the crew to volunteer some of their own possessions. Only Prickett, quartermaster John King, and Philip Staffe complied.

They would have gathered in Hudson's stern cabin. A few members of the ship's company might have been permitted to attend and gaze upon the stranger. Figures shambled into heavily shadowed view in woollen cloaks: faces coarsely bearded, skin discoloured, teeth loosened by scurvy, and breath foul. The *Discovery* would have been a dark and distressed place. None of the sweetness of cedar and spruce of a Cree camp. No women or children.

Hudson gave the man a knife, a mirror, and some buttons. The visitor "received them thankfully," wrote Prickett, "and made signs that after he had slept he could come again, which he did."

When the Cree returned as promised the following day, he was pulling a sled across the snowy ground laden with two beaver pelts and two "deerskin," which would have been caribou. Perhaps he produced the spruce buds at this time, and made Edward Wilson understand how to prepare them. From a satchel under his arm he withdrew the items Hudson had given him. He placed the knife on one beaver skin and the mirror and beads on the other, and then handed them over to Hudson.

The man had every intention of paying for the gifts Hudson had made. Hudson understood the near-universal method of establishing the rate of exchange. He accepted the furs, and the trade goods returned to the man's satchel.

Hudson then produced an iron hatchet. The man was willing to surrender one caribou skin in return. Hudson insisted on having both of them. His behaviour brought to mind the attitude shown by East India Company sailors. Indigenous people at landfalls in the Indian Ocean were mistrusted, always suspected of attempting to hoodwink the English, and the company's men bargained hard. While Hudson had considerable experience with North American natives from his 1609 voyage, like other Englishmen he may also have failed to appreciate that a first exchange in the New World was often a ritualized gift giving.

The man agreed to Hudson's demand for the additional skin, "although not willingly," Prickett recalled. Through signs, he then made Hudson understand that people lived to the north and south of the *Discovery,* and that he would return "after so many sleeps." He took his sled in tow and disappeared into the landscape.

They never saw him again. Perhaps his own people implored or ordered him to stay away from the *Discovery* and its sickly crew. Perhaps he was insulted by the grasping behaviour of these strangers. But for one caribou skin's difference in the price of a simple hatchet, the next few months might have unfolded very differently for Henry Hudson and his men.

Thirteen

—

T HE ICE AT LAST BEGAN TO WITHDRAW FROM THE BAY
in which the grounded *Discovery* had been frozen into
place. Now that there was à measure of open water,
Hudson moved to replenish stores, sending out some of the company's members, including Henry Greene, in the ship's boat with
a seine. They reaped a marvellous catch on their first day: "five
hundred fish, as big as good herrings and some trouts," according
to Prickett. But they never again had a catch quite so bountiful,
and there were twenty-two famished mouths to feed.

Meanwhile, Philip Staffe assembled the shallop, which had
remained in pieces aboard the *Discovery* since their departure
from London. Emboldened by the survival of his company,
Hudson was not about to abandon his secretive surveying.
Refastening the shallop's planks to ribs and keel, hanging its
rudder, laying aboard its oars, and rigging its sails and spars was
a signal from Hudson that he was not through with his unex-
plained probing of James Bay. He now had a separate vessel,
seaworthy, capacious, and with a much shallower draft than the
Discovery, for scouting the coast.

The sight of the little vessel taking shape under Staffe's expert
direction would have been both disheartening and tempting to

the crewmembers who had had enough of Hudson's passage-seeking. According to Prickett's account, Henry Greene had been able to forge alliances within the crew. He began plotting with William Wilson, whom Hudson had promoted to boatswain the previous September, "and some others" to take the shallop and the fishing net and strike out for themselves.

It might have seemed a rash plan. But the men who survived Barentsz's overwintering at the tip of Novaya Zemlya had successfully made their escape in two open boats. While Barentsz had perished on the return journey, most of the men were able to complete an exceptional passage of hundreds of miles down the west coast of Novaya Zemlya and then across the White Sea to the Kola Peninsula, where they were at last rescued and transported back to Amsterdam. With luck and good seamanship, the shallop's thieves might make it to the Labrador coast or Newfoundland and find a passage home with fishermen or whalers.

With the ice receding, his men going hungry, and the plague of scurvy (somewhat attenuated by the spruce drink) still among them, Hudson was balanced on a thin edge of opportunity. Although he could not have known of the plan hatched by Greene and Wilson, he well understood his own vulnerability in an expedition with such a history of dissension. He was back aboard the *Hopewell* at Novaya Zemlya, carefully calculating his own security.

June 30, 1608: Henry Hudson was behaving as a gentleman would in a disreputable Southwark tavern, choosing a seat that placed his back safely to the wall and afforded a view of everyone in the room. Henry and his son John remained together, alone, aboard the *Hopewell* as she swung at anchor while the rest of their shipmates—all accounted for, all in plain view—stroked for Novaya Zemlya in the shallop.

"At the island where we rode lieth a little rock," Hudson noted in the voyage journal, "whereon were forty or fifty morses [walruses] lying asleep, being all that it could hold, it being so full and little. I sent my company ashore to them, leaving none aboard but my boy with me."

Hudson consistently made a point of staying aboard the *Hopewell,* and otherwise never wandering far from it for any length of time. He made no mention of having left the *Hopewell* during the 1607 voyage, and the 1608 expedition was no different. The ship was both his command and his sanctuary. He would not permit himself to be separated from it. The shore party of June 30 was the third he had dispatched to the western shores of the Russian archipelago, and the third that he had declined to join. And, as on this occasion, he might always have kept John close by him.

Two years earlier, sailors aboard this same ship had watched a very similar scene, of John Knight and his companions rowing away to an island. Hudson could not have taken more care not to repeat John Knight's possible error.

The assignment of leading this party was given to Robert Juet, and the shallop drew up to the rock where the walruses were sleeping, warming themselves in the summer's never-setting sun, which coaxed their hides to a cinnamon brown as blood engorged their skin. These animals were massive enough to justify the name "sea oxen": the males were upwards of ten feet long and three thousand pounds, the females still formidable at perhaps half their size. Calving would have ended in June; females would have been nursing pups they bore only every two to three years.

Walruses are wary animals, easy to startle. Slow and lumbering on shore, the beasts scattered into the sea at the arrival of the shallop, heaving their bodies in panic over the rocks. Henry and John Hudson, maintaining a secure distance on the deck of the *Hopewell*, would have heard the thunderous splashes, the squealing of the pups, the barking of the adults, the shouting of the men, the flailing oars smacking on stone as blades sought to bite water, the clatter of pikes seeking a mark, the percussion of muskets.

The single killing was, as Hudson related, a male. Walrus hunters never brought the whole animal back aboard their ship but rather butchered them ashore, their tusks sawn off and their blubber rendered into train oil in kettles at land stations.

While some of the men went off to bludgeon nesting murres and gather eggs to replenish the ship's larder, others would have begun to work on the walrus, slicing through the tough hide of the neck, which could be more than an inch thick, then quickly through several inches of blubber and down into powerful muscle.

When Juet returned to the *Hopewell*, the shallop and the men in it would have been slathered and speckled with blood, the very picture of dark deeds, bearing sacks full of birds that would provide fresh meat. They came aboard, Hudson noted, with the severed head, a grisly trophy of the shore party. Its ivory tusks, and the implicit promise of more of them, were about the only things of any value that Hudson took back to his sponsors. But the sight of the cruel competence of Robert Juet must have stayed with Hudson to the end of his days.

The shallop was assembled, but the *Discovery* was still beached. Only after the ship was refloated could she be readied for sea. If Hudson permitted a large portion of the ship's company to go fishing with the shallop, with the *Discovery* not yet prepared to sail, they might not come back, leaving him stranded with a handful of companions and a ship they could not put to sea. But so long as the *Discovery* was not ready to sail, he could seize the opportunity to command the shallop himself, to ends that were not entirely understood.

Prickett thought that Hudson wanted to make contact with the people their lone Cree visitor had told them lived nearby, in hope of securing fresh meat. Yet Hudson provided no firm date for his return—and what is more, he took the extraordinary step of ordering the men who remained behind actually to prepare the *Discovery* to sail: "They that remained aboard were to take in water, wood and ballast, and to have all things in a readiness against [i.e., for when] he came back," Prickett related. The *Discovery* would be fully operational, fully capable of being sailed home, while Hudson was off in the shallop.

Perhaps there was still enough pack ice in James Bay that Hudson felt assured the *Discovery* could not leave before he returned. But no aspect of the *Discovery* voyage was stranger, and would be less appreciated for its strangeness, than this single, seemingly reckless decision by Hudson. He provided would-be mutineers with an unparalleled opportunity to sail away without him. And not in the shallop, but in the main ship.

Hudson was proposing to take an unknown number of the ship's crew with him in the shallop. Prickett wrote that the master took out of the *Discovery* enough food to last the men in the shallop for "eight or nine days." Hudson could have intended to stay away from the *Discovery* much longer, by fishing and hunting, as he also took the seine with him. He could not count on the men left with the *Discovery* waiting for him to return. But he also could not help himself: he was absolutely determined to make the journey in the shallop.

If Hudson's sole intention was to contact the Cree to secure food from them, it would have been far less risky for him, and for the venture overall, if others were sent, in a smaller party, to accomplish the same thing. As both Prickett and Woodhouse independently asserted an essential air of mystery around Hudson's persistent interest in the southern extreme of the bay, they appear not to have appreciated what Hudson surely was up to: a last-gasp attempt to find the passage south. For it was not without coincidence that, given the choice between steering north or south to find the Cree camps, Hudson went south.

Why did Hudson not just continue to investigate with the relaunched *Discovery?* After the grounding the ship suffered before the overwintering, Hudson must have known that any further coastal surveying should be done in the shallow-draft shallop. And he probably had held the crew together by assuring them (as Prickett understood) that as soon as the ice was clear, they would sail north, to replenish their stores at the murre colony. Using the *Discovery* to explore south now could have ignited the mutiny he had thus far held at bay. If he were to make one last attempt to find the passage south to Lake Tadouac, which would then connect to the one Champlain avowed led to the Pacific, it would have to be on his own, in the shallop, while the *Discovery* was being prepared to sail for the murre colony. Hudson might never again get the chance to find the route, and he was more than likely prepared to die trying if necessary.

The decision as to who should stay with the *Discovery* and who should come with him in the shallop must have sorely tried Hudson. He would have wished to take every able-bodied and dutifully subordinate hand he thought he could draw away from the *Discovery.* But if he left behind too few loyal men, the likelihood of a mutiny was all the higher, and the *Discovery* could be lost. He could try to divide up the known troublemakers, taking a potential ringleader or two with him, but he had to be sure they would not then be in a position to wrest command of the shallop.

Prickett, who apparently remained with the *Discovery*, did not say how the crew was divided or how many accompanied Hudson. The mate, Robert Bylot, also would have stayed behind, overseeing the outfitting of the ship. Hudson would never have parted willingly with his son John; perhaps he also took along the trusted quartermaster, John King. The carpenter, Philip Staffe, was an especially valued hand, but Hudson may not have been able to spare him from his primary duty of ensuring the *Discovery* was fit to return to sea. The boatswain, William Wilson, who was responsible for the physical state of the ship, also would have stayed behind to supervise her refitting. And the barber-surgeon, Edward Wilson, would have remained with the *Discovery*, to tend to the dead weight of the lame like Prickett.

Those whom Hudson left behind could be forgiven for thinking that they might not ever see their master again. It was not only because he might come to harm, or because mutineers in the shallop might abandon him, or because mutineers left aboard the *Discovery* would seize the chance to make off with the ship. It was because, in pursuing an unknown and possibly illusive goal, he simply might never turn around. They were the first crew in the history of seafaring to bear witness to a master who, in sailing away from his main command in a shallop, was quite possibly leading his own mutiny.

An untold number of days passed without any sign of Hudson. How far he went, and what he saw, is unknowable. If he was wintering in the vicinity of whatever constituted Rupert Bay in 1611, he may have steered deeper into it, hoping one of several feeder rivers could provide the passage south. Then as now, he would have found rapids blocking his way on every one of them.

Alternatively, he may have left the shelter of his wintering place and steered farther south, to Hannah Bay, where the Harricanaw River enters James Bay at its (now) southernmost point, or searched farther west, gaining the mouth of the Moose River. Neither one of these rivers, their outflows cutting through extensive mud flats, their lower courses impassable by a ship at low tide, would have provided the passage he was hoping for.

This was how and where Hudson's quest to find a passage out of the Northern Sea and on to the Pacific may well have ended: in a shallop anchored in mud flats against an outflowing tide that was draining a river's lower reaches dry, with yellowlegs striding delicately across the slick, exposed bay bottom, and clouds of mosquitoes tormenting him and his men.

The chart published by Hessel Gerritsz in 1612, based on Hudson's own cartography, would show the lower reaches of James Bay ending at latitude 50. Four hundred years later, the bay would not quite reach latitude 51. Even with the land some sixteen feet lower at the time of Hudson's visit, he could not have reached that lower measure. But he still would have progressed much farther south than anyone who would follow him, than anyone possibly could in the coming centuries. With the bay shrinking and retreating north, Hudson retreated with it.

In Hudson's absence, the able-bodied hands under Bylot readied the *Discovery* for her return to sea and, as all likely prayed, a speedy return to England. A few aboard her may have been prepared to take the *Discovery* now, if the bay's ice cover permitted, but the balance of power must have rested still with men who were willing to wait for Hudson's return in the shallop and allow him to make good on his understood promise to sail for the murre colony.

Hudson "returned worse than he went forth," according to Prickett. He had been unable to make any contact with the native people. Prickett reported that they set the woods alight whenever the shallop approached. The ridgeline of spruce was transformed into a bonfire of fear and hostility.

Nothing further was ever reported on what Hudson had seen or done.

Fourteen

—

THE CREWS OF THE *Discovery* and the shallop were reunited, along with their fortunes. Hudson must have known he was facing a potential crisis. Despite the spruce treatments, scurvy threatened the survival of some of the crew. There was also frostbite—Francis Clement had lost all his fingernails—and Michael Bute and Adrian Moore had never fully recovered from their injuries in the capstan incident. And rations were running low.

Hudson drew up what Prickett called a "bill of return," a document that would have spelled out the command structure for the voyage home, including the order of succession should he not survive. Robert Bylot or Habakkuk Prickett would have taken possession of the bill. It probably included a certificate much like the one he had issued to his crew near the end of the 1608 voyage, absolving them of any responsibility for his decision not to press any further in his explorations. For as Prickett put it, Hudson drafted it "willing them to have that to show, if it pleased God that they came home; and he wept when he gave it to them."

In the crew's mind, the voyage at this point would have been over as a venture of discovery. Hudson had not found a passage through to the Orient, and his decision to linger in James Bay, searching for evidence of the passage south to Lake Tadouac, and then westward as Champlain had proposed, had been a waste of almost a year of his life and of his backers' capital. Smythe, Digges, Cecil, and the rest—the Prince of Wales even—would want to know why he had defied his instructions to make a single-season reconnaissance. They might well be unsatisfied with whatever explanation he had provided for dismissing his appointed mate, William Cobreth, particularly when the man he chose to replace him then had to be dismissed for repeatedly inciting mutiny. And they would want to know why had he pressed on so far to the south when he was supposed to investigate a Northwest Passage believed to lie somewhere along latitude 62. Why had he not pursued the open water he had seen to the west of the Digges Islands? Why had he not made a proper investigation of Lumley's Inlet?

Hudson was sailing home to a difficult reception. His discoveries deep into Hudson Bay and James Bay were not without interest, and he surely did a better job of charting Hudson Strait than Waymouth, who may not actually have seen much of it. But even if his results were considered sufficiently promising to warrant a follow-up expedition, Hudson would not have been assured of its command. His disobedience was becoming pathological, and he was getting on in age: younger to be sure than Robert Juet, but most certainly older than Robert Bylot. And Bylot, whom he had sent ashore at East Digges Island to observe the tide, may have been responsible for much of the expedition's surveying work. If there was to be a follow-up voyage, Bylot might well end up being chosen over Hudson to lead it. The end of Hudson's explorations of James Bay could have struck him as the end of his career. The bill he gave the crew to show when they reached home as much as said: there is no one to blame for the outcome of this voyage except the master. And so the tears had flowed unashamedly.

It was early June when Hudson returned in the shallop, to a ship that was running low on food. Hudson had all the "bread," or ship's biscuit, removed from the storeroom and divided so that there was a pound for every man. At a little more than an ounce a day, the biscuits were expected to last two weeks. Hudson delayed their departure to send out the ship's boat (not, conspicuously, the shallop, which could have provided an escape vehicle for deserters) with the seine, to spend three full days fishing. The men left on Friday the thirteenth, and they fished through Sunday, but with little result: "fourscore small fish, a poor relief for so many hungry bellies," according to Prickett. Hudson moved the Discovery away from shore and anchored in the mouth of the wintering bay, then shifted her again to an anchorage in open water.

With the fishing expedition having produced so little nourishment, Hudson now turned to the other main staple, the cheese. According to Prickett, some "grudged" about the cheese; there were five blocks, and they thought there should have been nine. Hudson insisted on distributing the cheese equally, as he had the biscuits, even though some counselled that an equitable distribution of rations wasn't necessary. Higher ranks might have laid claim to a greater share, and sailors expected to work the ship arguably deserved a bonus, to maintain their strength. Hudson moreover wanted everyone to share alike in all of what remained, edible or not, "that they should see that they had no wrong done to them: but every man should have alike the best and worst together, which was three pounds and a half [of cheese] for seven days," Prickett remarked. The cheese would run out in a week.

Hudson's decision was a disaster in the making. The men, as Prickett told it, could not be depended on to manage their personal supply, and hunger got the better of some of them. For the readers of his journal account, Prickett held up for scorn the two would-be thieves of the shallop, boatswain William Wilson and Henry Greene. Wilson had wolfed down his entire supply of biscuit in a single day, "and hath been two or three days' sick for his labour." Greene had the sense to give the second week of his bread ration to someone trusted, who was not to return it until Monday the six-teenth. But by Wednesday the eleventh, Greene had taken it back and consumed it all.

Before sailing, Hudson made yet another change in the ship's command structure, replacing Robert Bylot as his mate. John King, the quartermaster, became the fourth person to serve as master's mate on the voyage, after Cobreth, Juet, and Bylot.

With the switch from Bylot to King, Hudson erased the command structure that existed under the bill of return he had recently drafted. Appointing someone other than Bylot as mate sabotaged the succession conditions of the bill. A new bill most certainly was created with King's promotion, although Prickett did not mention it.

Hudson's reasons for the switch from Bylot to King probably were many. One reason was self-preservation. By promoting King and issuing a new bill of return, Hudson would have ensured that anyone with notions of seizing command could not do so now without disrupting the formal succession plan for the ship. If some accidental loss were contrived for Hudson, Bylot would have been the one to take over under the succession plan under the first bill. Back in England, some excuse could be made for Hudson's loss, and the bill of return would leave them free and clear. Now, the command would shift to King. If any would-be mutineers were considering seizing control with a simple shift to Bylot, King was in the way. Perhaps Hudson's odd shufflings in senior ranks during the 1607 and 1608 *Hopewell* voyages had the same purpose: to extinguish the succession order of a bill of return.

Hudson's actions suggested he had serious concerns about Bylot as the food ran low and the *Discovery* prepared to sail. He may have been less concerned with Bylot's absolute loyalty than with his own ability to persuade Bylot to abandon a direct course home. In Prickett's telling, the switch to King was Hudson's way of consolidating absolute control over the *Discovery*'s course. King could neither read nor write, Prickett avowed, which meant he was no navigator. And at the same time, all navigational devices except Hudson's own were confiscated. Denying men like Bylot and Juet their navigational tools while promoting someone as ignorant as King to second-in-command meant that only Hudson would know where the *Discovery* was, and where he was steering her.

On the eve of sailing, Hudson appeared to have decided that he could not return home without some measurable success. His course south from the Digges Islands the previous August had most likely been to the west side of the bay. Perhaps he now wished to head back that way, to see if the set of the tide there gave any further clues to the location of a passage. He also may have wished to press to the north and west once the murre colony had been reached, rather than turn east, back down Hudson Strait to the Furious Overall. To do so, he would have to keep the crew in the dark about how far north they had sailed. Anyone taking a latitude fix would know when he had overshot the turn down Hudson Strait.

Demoting Bylot was a final gambit to maintain control of the *Discovery* and dictate her course. But mariners who were sorely tried by his secrecy in probing James Bay would not abide any further clandestine explorations. Hudson's strategy was more than secretive: not having a mate who could make his own observations and compare them with those of the master was poor seamanship.

And the idea that a man as ill schooled as King would be in charge should Hudson die would have fuelled considerable disquiet. The promotion of King over Bylot, with the food almost expended, was too much to bear for too many hungry men.

After setting sail, the *Discovery* immediately encountered pack ice. Hudson anchored the next day, Tuesday the seventeenth, and waited for a lead to open. The anniversary of their passage through the Furious Overfall was only days away. They were still at anchor on Saturday the twenty-first when Habakkuk Prickett claimed he first learned directly from Henry Greene of the plan to consign Hudson, King, and the weakest members of the crew to the shallop, and to make off with the *Discovery*.

Fifteen

—

A T THE MOMENT HENRY GREENE came to Habakkuk
Prickett with his plan to seize control of the *Discovery,* the
haberdasher was destined to lose the control of the voyage
account, which he had enjoyed since Henry Hudson's journal
abstract fell silent after August 3, 1610. Until the point of Greene's
revelation, Prickett's exclusive narrative was interrupted only once,
by the note written by Thomas Woodhouse that detailed Robert
Juet's hearing of September 10. Prickett's narrative would now be
joined by a chorus of new voices. Crewmembers not yet heard
from became eyewitnesses to the insurrection, with perspectives
and agendas of their own. They were no longer simply names in
Prickett's narrative whose actions, characters, and motivations the
supercargo could choose to reveal, distort, or ignore.

The chorus began to assemble three months after the *Discovery*'s
return to England, as the High Court of the Admiralty took its first
step toward understanding how Henry and John Hudson and
seven companions were cast adrift in a shallop, and toward deciding who if anyone should be tried, and on what grounds.

While mutiny per se was missing from its list of felonious
crimes, the Offences at Sea Act of 1536 permitted the admiralty
to prosecute "traitors, pirates, thieves, robbers, murderers and

confederates upon the sea" with the same standards of evidence and testimony that applied to offences committed on land. The Lord High Admiral's "full power and authority" under the act included the right "to enquire of such offences," which meant locking people up in a dismal place like Marshalsea Prison in Southwark and subjecting them to interrogation. And so six of the eight *Discovery* survivors were compelled by the High Court of the Admiralty to make depositions on January 25, 1612. After a lengthy period of scandalous legal disinterest, the court resumed its questioning of survivors in February 1617. The insights afforded by these depositions often hinted at the fuller story, as only the answers, and not the questions, were preserved. Much was left to be inferred from the evident line of interrogation, and from how that line changed over a five-year period.

Men who were likely imprisoned at the time of their depositions, who justifiably feared for their lives, who in some cases were hauled more than once before the High Court of the Admiralty to answer increasingly pointed questions, produced accounts of the mutiny that were predictably self-serving, and often at odds. Prickett outdid all by giving three versions of the events: his written narrative, which he would have provided to Sir Thomas Smythe on his return (and may have refined over the ensuing years), and two court depositions, in 1612 and 1617. The longer that Prickett was given to answer for himself, the more contradictory, the less credible (and in some ways more revealing) many aspects of his answers became.

Not all of the men who avoided sharing Henry Hudson's unknowable fate in the shallop were heard from, because not all of them lived to see England again. And some of those who survived the passage home remained silent: their own writings disappeared, or the admiralty court was unable to interrogate them before they melted back into anonymity. The surviving perspectives, then, were selective, almost arbitrarily so. And Henry Hudson himself was not only bound by the mutineers but gagged by those who took possession of his log and journal and decided it was best to silence him forever after August 3, 1610.

In time, many aspects of the survivors' accounts were dismissed by historians as so many lies. To be sure, there were elements of the mutiny that seemed too strange to be believable. And men facing the prospect of death on conviction for their crimes were notorious for spinning most any fiction, short of alleging that their king was a secret Papist and necromancer. But sometimes the strangeness conveyed by the *Discovery*'s men was what made their collectively uneven and occasionally absurd recounting believable. More had been going on than they were prepared to admit, and not having admitted it created seeming incongruities. Even with significant questions left unanswered, it was remarkable how a consistent and credible story could still be stitched together from their at times discordant recollections.

This much, in any event, may have happened.

Sixteen

—

HABAKKUK PRICKETT WAS LYING IN HIS CABIN, his weakened legs aching from scurvy, when Henry Greene, accompanied by the boatswain, William Wilson, approached him on Saturday, June 21, with the plan to overthrow Henry Hudson.

Prickett would have been among the last men they spoke to. If he were as close to Hudson as he claimed, it would have been a tremendous risk for the mutineers to involve him in advance. Surely he would tip off the master, the way he had already informed on Greene when he had his fight with the barber-surgeon at Iceland.

Greene and Wilson must have been confident of enjoying the support of enough able-bodied seamen both to seize control and to steer the ship home. And their idea of shoving the weakest crewmembers into the shallop with Hudson would have terrified Prickett, who was by his own account bedridden. He was surely older than Greene and Wilson, who even in their famished state would have been physically imposing. The threat to the haberdasher was baldly stated, according to Prickett. Greene told him that if he did not side with them, "I must take my fortune in the shallop."

Prickett was given a chance to save himself because the mutineers needed him. He was the supercargo, the investors' representative. The men who went along with Greene and Wilson would not have relished spending the rest of their lives as outlaws. If control of the ship was to be seized, it was best if it were done in a defensible legal fashion. Prickett's cooperation was the surest way to save themselves from the gallows.

By the time Greene and Wilson came to Prickett with a crude scheme to wrest control of the ship, both were starving. They had already consumed their bread rations far ahead of schedule, and informed Prickett that there was only enough food aboard to last another two weeks. Greene in Prickett's telling was violent and head-strong, a gambler, a spoiled young man with a poor record of self-restraint. Prickett wrote that Greene initially stormed out of his cabin in a rage when he would not agree to join him, leaving him alone with William Wilson, to attempt to talk Wilson out of the plan. Greene then stormed back in, demanding to know what Prickett had said. Wilson replied: "He is in his old song, still patient."

Prickett tried to have Greene and Wilson agree "to stay three days, in which time I would so deal with the master that all should be well." Prickett never said how he intended to deal with Hudson. He could have proposed to seek a promise from Hudson to sail directly home, and to involve a capable man like Bylot— even Juet—in the navigation. But the conspirators would not hear of three days, or two days, or twelve hours, Prickett claimed. They were determined to act as soon as possible: that night.

Prickett then offered a striking option: "if they would stay till Monday, I would join with them to share all the victuals in the ship, and would justify it when I came home." While Prickett immediately related that "this would not serve their turns," in attempting to defend himself from the cast stones by presenting evidence of all of his efforts to discourage Greene and Wilson, he touched on the very heart of the matter. Greene and Wilson had no real plan, except offloading Hudson, his most loyal men, and the weakest crewmembers in order to stretch the rations. That would not do. The action needed a more coherent rationale for Prickett to take home with him. And by saving unsavoury men like Greene and Wilson, who would gladly see him to his death if he opposed them, Prickett in turn could save himself.

Ironically, the precedent evidently chosen on which to build the insurrection involved none other than Henry Hudson's own friend, Captain John Smith. To seize the *Discovery* and rid themselves of Henry Hudson, the mutineers would follow carefully how Smith had helped seize control of the Jamestown colony in September 1607, deposing its first president, Sir Edward Maria Wingfield. Leading men of the Virginia Company like Sir Thomas Smythe, Sir Dudley Digges, Sir John Wolstenholme, and Sir Robert Cecil, all of whom now backed the Hudson expedition, had been satisfied with the legality of the action against Wingfield. To persuade Smythe and his fellow investors of the legality of Hudson's overthrow, the mutineers needed to adapt the basic script of the Wingfield action. And to persuade some members of the crew to go along with their insurrection, they would have to be convinced that what they were planning to do was no different than how Wingfield had been dealt with by Smith at Jamestown.

The mutiny scheme was far from perfect. In fact, in most ways it was terribly clumsy, and burdened by incongruities that pressed its logic beyond breaking strength. But it had an essential, cohesive shape. And in the end, it may have worked because the people who should have been casting the most critical eye over its uneven, even indefensible details after the *Discovery*'s return chose to go along with its rationale.

———

Anyone attuned to England's overseas colonial ambitions would have been aware of the Edward Maria Wingfield case. Wingfield, who mercifully survived the coup unharmed, demanded a hearing on his return to England so he could refute the allegations made by John Smith and others in deposing him at Jamestown. There is no surviving record of the hearing, which may never have been held. But a lengthy draft defence by Wingfield, which he seems to have drawn up to guide him through the hearing, dates from around May 1608.

How many people aboard the *Discovery* would have known the details of how Wingfield was brought down is unanswerable, although Prickett more than anyone was in a position to know. Regardless, there is no more compelling echo of Wingfield's unseating at Jamestown in September 1607 than Hudson's overthrow aboard the *Discovery* in June 1611.

The many charges against Wingfield were tedious, and quite possibly not without cause, but among them were two basic ones germane to the *Discovery* mutiny: he played favourites to the detriment of the colony, and he hoarded and squandered food in a time of desperate need. The charges against Wingfield struck someone among the Hudson mutineers as eminently portable to a ship far from home and locked in shifting ice. Especially portable was how Wingfield was dealt with during the investigation into his conduct at Jamestown. On September 10, 1607, Wingfield was seized and placed in a pinnace, anchored off the fort in the river James, while his accommodations were searched for evidence.

The Wingfield-like elements of favouritism and food hoarding would be presented in the *Discovery* survivors' High Court of the Admiralty depositions as the main case for having overthrown

Hudson, and would also figure in Prickett's voyage narrative. But none of these elements had been part of the case Greene and Wilson first made to Prickett on the eve of the mutiny. All that mattered to the duo was that they had eaten their rations long before everyone else had, and they wanted to wrest control of the ship to get their hands on the food belonging to the people they would put in the shallop. The ravenous pair also complained of Hudson's lack of forward motion—"that there they lay, the master not caring to go one way or other." But it was the ice cover on James Bay, which typically does not clear until July, that limited their progress, as the mutineers themselves would discover.

Desperation was Wilson and Greene's primary motive. When Prickett asked why they, married men with children, would risk an action that would "banish them from their native country," Greene "bade me hold my peace, for he knew the worst, which was, to be hanged when he came home, and therefore of the two he would rather be hanged at home than starved abroad."

When Greene refused to divert from the plan to proceed that very night, Prickett told Greene that he suspected "it was blood and revenge he sought, or else he would not at such a time of night undertake such a deed." At that, Prickett alleged, Greene took up Prickett's Bible "and swore that he would do no man no harm, and what he did was for the good of the voyage, and for nothing else, and that all the rest should do the like."

Prickett did not explain how he was persuaded that no man would be harmed once cast adrift in an open boat among ice floes thousands of miles from home. Or how a man like Greene—who in Prickett's own words with respect to religion considered himself "an open book" on which Prickett could write whatever he wished—could be relied on to swear to anything on a Bible, particularly when he and Wilson had already made clear to Prickett their intention to cast away Hudson, those most loyal to him, and the sick. But swear Greene did, to Prickett's satisfaction, as did Wilson. And so, Prickett claimed, did the rest of the conspirators, who filed that night into Prickett's cabin: John Thomas, Michael Perce, Adrian Moter, Bennet Mathew, and Robert Juet.

Juet was the first to enter Prickett's cabin to join Greene and Wilson in taking the oath. Prickett found Juet "worse than Henry Greene, for he swore plainly that he would justify this deed when he came home." It was the only moment in Prickett's narrative when Juet undeniably was a ringleader.

Prickett acknowledged that the basis of the case against himself, which might yet see him hanged, was his administering of the oath: "I am much condemned for this oath, as one of them that plotted with them, and that by an oath I should bind them together to perform what they had begun." He was careful not to allow that he ever took his own oath. His case was rather that he had organized the conspirators along Christian lines. He made a point of including the actual oath in his account: "You shall swear truth to God, your prince and country: you shall do nothing, but to the glory of God and the good of the action in hand, and harm to no man."

The oath-taking was the core of Prickett's bid for exculpation: he had made every man involved swear to do no harm. Whatever followed that veered from that sacred promise was the sin of the oath-takers, not of Prickett. But at that point, Prickett also became an active co-conspirator, because whoever ended up in the shallop, whatever the pieties of Prickett's precious oath, received a death sentence. The men who were persuaded to take seats in the shallop (just as Wingfield had been held in the pinnace) were supposed to be allowed back aboard once the "evidence" for Hudson's alleged hoarding of food was gathered. But Prickett expected these men to die, and he wished that one of the more useful ones remain with the mutineers to get the ship—and himself—home.

The mutiny, according to the list of oath-takers in Prickett's journal account, enjoyed the participation of six members of the able-bodied crew and the cooperation of Prickett. Of the remaining men, Thomas Woodhouse, Sydrack Faner, Michael Bute, and Adrian Moore were all unwell and confined to bunks, and so were prime candidates for the shallop. The former boatswain, Francis Clement, was also expendable. Although he had suffered a demotion at the same time as Juet and was criticized in Woodhouse's note for having "basely carried himself to our master and to the action," he had lost his fingernails to frostbite and may have been too lame to work the ship. Henry and John Hudson were doomed to be cut loose, as was the new first mate, John King. But that still left a significant group of skilled and mobile men: the recently demoted first mate, Robert Bylot; the carpenter, Philip Staffe; the barber-surgeon, Edward Wilson; the cooper, Silvanus Bond; the veteran Hudson sailor Arnold Ludlow; and the ship's boy, Nicholas Sims. This list of highly capable hands who were not among Prickett's oath-takers revealed that the insurrection fomented by Greene, Wilson, and Juet, at least in its formative stages, was a creature of the lower ranks and marginal (or marginalized) voyage participants. And among the co-conspirators was potential instability, for Bennet Mathew had provided some of the most damning testimony against Juet at the September 1610 hearing.

In the hours leading up to the action, there would have been selective bargaining with men considered key to carrying off the uprising and then getting the ship home. When it came time to act, some of the men who had not taken the alleged oath would have to go in the shallop. Others would be allowed, persuaded, or forced to stay.

Greene told Prickett that, along with Henry Hudson (and, it went without saying, his son), they intended to put in the shallop King, Staffe, and "the sick men." To this Prickett helpfully replied that "they should not do well to part with the carpenter." In a wooden ship that had already experienced a tough overwintering and shuddering groundings, Staffe was a crucial crewmember, and Prickett urged them to keep him. But they disliked Staffe, Prickett alleged, for the same reason they disliked King. The pair was "condemned for wrong done in the victual."

Edward Wilson, the barber-surgeon, in his testimony before the High Court of the Admiralty in January 1612, would provide the most complete rationale for the conspirators' actions. He alleged that at the time of the mutiny "their victuals were so scant that they had but two quarts of meal allowed to serve 22 men for a day, and that the master had bread and cheese and aquavit in his cabin, and called some of the company whom he favoured to eat and drink with him in his cabin, whereupon those that had nothing did grudge and mutiny both against the master and those that he gave bread and drink unto."

The mutiny began, the barber-surgeon would attest, when the boatswain, William Wilson, approached Philip Staffe and asked "the reason why the master should so favour to give meat to some of the company, and not the rest." Staffe supposedly replied "that it was necessary that some of them should be kept up," at which Wilson told Greene what he had learned from Staffe. Greene and the boatswain Wilson then hatched a plan to put Hudson and King in the shallop, but to keep Staffe aboard.

According to Prickett, King was also disliked for having displaced Bylot as master's mate. The conspirators had alleged to Prickett that "the master and his ignorant mate would carry the ship whither the master pleased: the master forbidding any man to keep account or reckoning, having taken from all men whatsoever served for that purpose." Juet, for one, would have been deeply offended at an illiterate man without apparent navigation skills ultimately having come to serve in his place as master, and further being denied the right to make navigation observations himself.

Prickett, and some of the others who would go along with the mutiny, were trapped between two extremes of insurrection. On the one hand, there was the legitimate concern that Hudson was withdrawing into a scheming shell as the fever dream of discovery overcame him, cutting off all reasonable communication on the ship's location, course, and ultimate destination. Not having others share in the navigation duties was discreditably dangerous. On the other hand, at the head of the plot were violent, starving men who wanted nothing more than to stretch the rations by getting rid of about one third of the crew. Where they thought the ship should go next was another matter.

There was a reasonable course for Prickett to pursue, and it had been provided to him by the Reverend Cartwright's action against George Waymouth on the deck of this very ship in 1602. As the supercargo, Cartwright marshalled a civilized and respectful insurrection, with the crew's objections to an overwintering written down for Waymouth and an alternative plan proposed, of helping him spend the rest of the season searching for possible passages, which led to the probing of the strait beyond the Furious Overfall. Prickett could have followed Cartwright's example—his position being even more advantageous, as Hudson had already disobeyed his sailing directions. Instead, Prickett allied himself with Greene and his henchmen, racking his brain for some way to make the action they had in mind seem defensible, while saving his own skin.

Prickett wrote that he was successful in persuading Greene and Wilson to keep Staffe, but naturally he claimed noble motives. It was Prickett's stated hope that after the conspirators "had satisfied themselves" by getting their hands on the ship's rations, Staffe could work to convince them to allow Hudson and the sick men to come back aboard from the shallop. "Or, I hoped, that someone or other would give some notice, either to the carpenter, John King, or the master; for it so might have come to pass by some of them that were the most forward." But Prickett could have raised the alarm himself by hollering blue murder, even if he was too ill to get out of his berth. By his own accounts, he would prove himself perfectly capable of communicating by shouting, and of venturing onto deck.

Already, his account of the mutiny's unfolding was suspect. The idea of a line of conspirators on that small ship, parading unnoticed into Prickett's cabin, to swear to his noble words on a Bible, strains credulity. Prickett's berthmates in the cabin outside the gunroom were King, Bylot, and Clement, none of whom took the oath. They all must have been elsewhere in the ship that night, if Prickett were to be believed.

But there would be ample reason for Prickett not to be entirely believed. His main version of events, set down in his journal narrative, was contradicted by Bylot, who in a court deposition admitted to having foreknowledge of the mutiny. Bylot maintained that he was not involved in planning, but he did allow that he was aware on the night before the coup "that Hudson and the rest were [to be] put into the shallop the next day." Still, Bylot asserted that he and Prickett together attempted to talk the mutineers out of going through with their plan, but that "Greene answered the master was resolved to overthrow all, and therefore [Hudson] and his friends would shift for themselves."

Greene's reasoning was plain. He expected Hudson to obey the conventions of a commercial voyage, in which any deviation from the agreed course required the approval of the crew. With Bylot's demotion, King's promotion, and Hudson's seizure of navigation instruments, the master was suspected of having secret plans for their course. If Hudson intended to operate without the approval of his men—if he was "resolved to overthrow all"—then he and the men he favoured should "shift for themselves." The statement was as close as anyone came to acknowledging what remained unspoken. In getting their hands on the remaining foodstores and making with all haste for the murre colony, the core conspirators may have been determined to return the expedition to its recent state, when Hudson departed in the shallop for points and purposes unknown with what must have been a hand-picked crew of loyal people.

Prickett would avow that Hudson and Staffe were his closest friends on the ship. If so, he sorely betrayed that friendship. Both he and Bylot knew something was coming, and found themselves a safe role in the coup, without making any effort to warn Hudson or his closest associates of the malice that was closing around them.

Something alerted the *Discovery's* captain to the movements against him. Perhaps it was the shuffling of too many feet on the poop deck, above his cabin, or the sound of ice-hardened ropes moving jerkily through blocks as the trim of the sails was changed and course was altered. Whatever it was, George Waymouth was brought fully alert on the night of July 19, 1602, in the waters of Davis Strait, to the east of Baffin Island.

All of Waymouth's men had "conspired secretly together, to bear up the helm for England, while I was asleep in my cabin, and there to have kept me by force, until I had sworn unto them, that I would not offer any violence unto them for so doing. And indeed they had drawn in writing, the causes of their bearing up of the helm, and thereunto set their hands, and would have left them in my cabin: but by good chance I understood their pretense, and prevented them for that time."

Waymouth's fortune was shortlived: at eleven the next morning the crew "bare up the helm, being all so bent that there was no means to persuade them to the contrary." When he came out of his cabin to ask them who had changed the ship's course, "they answered, One and All. So they hoisted up all the sail they could and directed their course south and by west." He managed to reassert his command, and even punish the ringleaders, while acceding to the crew's demands. And not only did these mutineers spare his life: by refusing to overwinter in the Arctic, north of latitude 60, they may well have saved it.

Nothing caused Henry Hudson to stir in the darkness of the *Discovery*'s cabin, nine years later, as another crew planned another, far more malevolent insurrection.

As the conspirators waited for the right moment to act on the night of June 21, King's whereabouts were a concern, as he was the key person after Hudson that they were determined to cast away. They at first thought he was with Hudson, although Greene kept Hudson company for some time, despite their estrangement. King turned out to be up on the poop deck with the carpenter, probably enjoying a summer night under a half moon, breathing in fresh air that was chilled by an ice-strewn sea. Bylot must have been on watch in the early-morning hours. Clement, who was Prickett's bunkmate, was who knows where.

King returned to the cabin, apparently with Bylot. The current and former first mates were bunkmates, and Bylot had given nothing away. This was around four in the morning, at the changing of the four-hour watch, as Prickett attested "it was not long ere it was day" and the sun rose around 4:45.

Bennet Mathew, the cook, arose to fetch water for the kettle. King also awoke and went into the hold—lured there probably by Mathew for a discussion of the stores. King was trapped as the hatch was shut down on him. Who kept it closed Prickett claimed not to know, but Prickett said Mathew was quickly on deck. Meanwhile, Greene and "another" went to Staffe and occupied the carpenter in conversation while Hudson was taken.

Prickett's journal described how John Thomas—a bunkmate of Juet's in the gunroom—and Mathew led Hudson onto deck, while William Wilson pinioned his arms behind him. But Prickett would testify in February 1617 that he never witnessed any of this, or that he ever saw Hudson pinioned. And the barber-surgeon, Edward Wilson, remembered the sequence differently.

The first that the barber-surgeon knew of a mutiny, he insisted in his court deposition in January 1612, was when Hudson "was brought down pinioned and set down before this examinant's cabin." Wilson looked out the door and saw men he declined to name struggling to force Hudson onto the floor and secure his arms behind his back, by passing a length of pole through the crook of his elbows and tying his arms in place.

Edward Wilson offered up a surreal exchange: like a solicitous physician he "asked Hudson what he ailed, and he said that he was pinioned." The barber-surgeon then apparently hoped to come out of his cabin to share in the victuals he would have known the mutineers were after, but those who had pinioned Hudson told him "if he were well he should keep himself so."

Hudson, according to Prickett, asked his captors "what they meant." And "they told him he should know when he was in the shallop." But since Prickett wasn't even on hand, this was entirely hearsay.

Down in the hold, with the hatch slammed shut over him and held in place, John King would have known immediately that something was terribly wrong. Bennet Mathew had suddenly disappeared, and by Prickett's telling had rushed to help roust and pinion Hudson. An otherwise quiet morning, which should have given way to another laconic day of waiting for the ice to shift out of the anchored *Discovery*'s way, was alive with urgent activity.

The hold was a cramped, frigid prison. Cold air sank into it; the subarctic sea on the other side of the hull kept it refrigerated. The bilge water fouled its air, and condensation made the beams and planking slimy. Different levels of deck above him transmitted staccato shocks of scurrying feet. Some percussions were distant and muffled and moving with urgency. Others were crisp and sharp and purposeful and directly overhead.

The hatch was being lifted. Descending into view was the man who had promised Bennet Mathew there would be "manslaughter" and "action that proved bloody to some" before the voyage was over. Robert Juet was coming for him.

Seventeen

—

ON THE *Discovery* VOYAGE, Robert Juet existed only in the words and perceptions of others. The log and journal he kept as mate was probably taken from him after he was demoted at the September 1610 hearing. As an official part of the ship's papers, they would have been given to the next mate, Robert Bylot, to maintain. And because the mate to replace Bylot, John King, was illiterate, the record was probably reclaimed by Hudson. Where the mate's papers ultimately ended up, no one would ever say. Whatever thoughts and observations Juet—or Bylot, for that matter—wrote down were lost forever.

Juet was cursed by the vicissitudes of the documentary record. His mate's journal for the 1608 *Hopewell* voyage was acquired by the historiographer Samuel Purchas when he bought the unpublished papers of the late Richard Hakluyt. But when Purchas went to include the 1608 voyage in *Purchas His Pilgrimes* of 1625, he decided he had more than enough to go on in Hudson's journal. Apart from including in the Hudson narrative a few margin notes drawn from the mate's painstaking effort, Purchas set aside Juet's account, and it did not survive his caretaking.

Only with the 1609 voyage of the *Half Moon* did Robert Juet's observations manage to be preserved. Hudson's log and journal passed to the Dutch, with fragmentary journal quotes and para-phrases eventually published but the rest of the papers ultimately lost. But Juet's *Half Moon* journal endured in England in its entirety, and was used by Purchas to tell the story of the strange voyage for the VOC. The journal related more than basic navi-gational facts. As the only document that survived in Juet's voice, it also conveyed much about what he was capable of, and not just as a navigator.

Travelling along the Hudson River in September 1609, Henry Hudson began to feel most keenly his isolation from much of his crew. The Dutch and English were already in two solitudes, and native relations were at the heart of the shipboard antagonisms. At the Georges River earlier in the voyage, the Dutch crew had launched a raid on a native village that had turned into something of a massacre. Juet likely participated, as some of the ship's guns were unmounted and taken ashore, and his explanation for the atrocity was brief and feeble. The *Half Moon*'s men "took the spoil of them, as they would have done of us." But Juet could not offer up a single incident that would have justified their concerns or warranted the ferocious assault by the European visitors. George Waymouth had kidnapped five men in this very area, four years earlier, in order to take them home and train them as interpreters, but there was no indication from the natives that vengeance was ever on their minds.

Hudson appears to have opposed the action. Emmanuel van Meteren, who evidently examined Hudson's journal, recounted that Hudson found the Georges River area to be "a good place for cod fishing, as also for traffic in skins and furs, which were to be got there at a very low price. But the crew behaved badly towards the people of the country, taking their property by force; out of which there arose quarrels among them. The English fearing that they would be outnumbered and worsted, were therefore afraid to make any further attempt [at trade]."

Juet operated on the primary assumption that people they met, whatever their outward appearances of goodwill, meant them ill. Hudson, on the other hand, was tolerant and understanding, if cautious. "They appear to be a friendly people," he related in a surviving scrap of his 1609 journal, "but have a great propensity to steal, and are exceedingly adroit in carrying away whatever they take a fancy to." Most every explorer in eastern North America came to a similar conclusion. What set men like Juet apart from men like Hudson was how they reacted to this light-fingeredness. Hudson found that, while the natives "are very changeable, and of the same general character as all the savages in the north," nevertheless they "are well disposed, if they are only well treated." It followed that the only times Hudson found them ill disposed toward the *Half Moon* was when his men treated them badly.

The journey up the Hudson River had suffered the worst possible beginning. While anchored somewhere in the approaches to Upper New York Bay, Hudson sent out five men in the shallop, to sound a river about four leagues away. During their return they encountered two great canoes, carrying more than two dozen men.

What happened next is impossible to know for certain. Juet said there was an ambush by the natives. Two men were wounded, and John Colman, the veteran of the 1608 Novaya Zemlya voyage, was killed by an arrow in his throat. The survivors spent a terrible night in rain and darkness, unable to find the ship or to set a grapnel against the coursing tidal stream.

The attackers must have been from an entirely different tribe than the one that had so enthusiastically welcomed Hudson on previous days. The large number of men in the canoes suggested a raiding party, but they could have been as surprised by the Europeans as the Europeans were by them. Whatever had actually occurred, Colman was dead, and his loss helped firm Juet's stance against the local people.

Even Juet had to admit that the native people living where the *Half Moon* was anchored showed no knowledge of the attack made against the shallop. But that didn't prevent the *Half Moon*'s crew from kidnapping two men who had come to trade.

The natives seemed bewildered by this aggression, and sent two emissaries to the *Half Moon*. Hudson's men responded by deciding to keep one of them as well. This third captive leapt overboard. The *Half Moon*'s anchor was weighed, and the ship was moved out into the river channel for the night, still holding its two abductees.

More visitors arrived the next day, "making show of love," wrote Juet. They gave Hudson's men tobacco and corn, but as Juet related in a monotone of suspicion, "we durst not trust them." The death of Colman would have fuelled an understandable apprehension, yet the men of the *Half Moon* could not differentiate between Colman's killers, who by this time even Juet must have understood were from an entirely different tribe or nation, and the people who were so persistently determined to establish friendly and profitable relations. Juet's hostility reached absurd levels when he recounted how on the morning of the twelfth "there came eight and twenty canoes full of men, women and children to betray us." They were refused permission to come aboard, as were more visitors the next day.

On the morning of September 15, with the *Half Moon* at anchor, the two captives escaped through a porthole and swam away. "After we were under sail," wrote Juet, "they called to us in scorn." Hudson may have sanctioned or tolerated their capture so they could be taken home to train as interpreters. He may have even considered them hostages that would ensure good behaviour

from other natives during trading. Whatever Hudson's intentions, the *Half Moon* left behind the people of the river's lower
reaches, having sewn distrust and distaste among them for the
European newcomers.

As the *Half Moon* proceeded upriver in the vicinity of present-day
Albany, Hudson would have hoped that he was following the passage shown on Edward Wright's 1599 world map leading from the
Atlantic to the St. Lawrence, a speculative waterway inspired by
Jacques Cartier's explorations. But around ten o'clock on the
evening of September 22, 1609, his ship's boat returned in rain
and darkness from sounding the course ahead to report (as Juet
related) that they "found it to be at an end for shipping to go in.
For they had been up eight or nine leagues, and found but seven
foot water, and unconstant soundings." There was nothing else to
do but turn back.

On October 1, the *Half Moon* was close to regaining the
Atlantic. As the tide turned to flood, the ship anchored at noon,
and "the people of the mountains," as Robert Juet described them,
"came aboard us, wondering at our ship and weapons." Both sides
were new to each other; the natives must have been a tribe that
ventured down to the river from the Catskills.

Some small skins were purchased from them "for trifles," and
that should have been the end of the encounter. But one man in
a canoe loitered under the stern, despite efforts by the crew to
keep him clear. He scrambled up the rudder and reached the open
window of the stern cabin, plucking away a selection of Juet's
property: a pillow, two shirts, and two bandoliers, which were
small, leather-covered wooden containers that each held a single
musket charge.

The Dutch mate levelled a musket and shot the escaping tres-
passer in the chest, killing him.

The thief had already tossed Juet's belongings to his companions, who began paddling away in their canoes, some of them jumping into the water to swim to safety. The *Half Moon's* men took to their own boat to retrieve Juet's possessions. One of the swimmers grabbed hold of the boat's gunwale, attempting to capsize it, according to Juet. The ship's cook swung a sword, cleaving away the man's hand, and they watched him fall away from the boat and drown.

Juet wrote nothing about getting back his possessions. The *Half Moon* was moved downriver two leagues—they were now somewhere off Manhattan Island—and anchored in darkness.

The natives returned the next day, after the *Half Moon* had moved another seven leagues downriver before setting anchor as the tide again turned to flood. And they came in strength.

Juet claimed to recognize one of the previous day's swimmers "going up the river with many other, thinking to betray us." His assertion was questionable, since by then the *Half Moon* had moved about thirty miles downriver, and this alleged miscreant was approaching from farther downstream. Some of those arriving could have been the "mountain people," but it was also possible that the natives now turning out to intercept Hudson were motivated by the *Half Moon's* kidnapping of several men on the way upriver. Had Wright's chart been correct, the *Half Moon's* men would never have had to deal with them again, as by continuing upriver they would have gained the upper St. Lawrence and then been able to sail east, into the Atlantic. But if Hudson had ever imagined he could leave these angered people astern, they knew he had to return, eventually, and waited patiently to remake his acquaintance.

The natives in the approaching canoes were refused permission to come aboard, and this time for good reason; two more canoes appeared, and arrows flew from them at the *Half Moon*. Six muskets erupted in reply, and "three or four" natives were struck down. Then Juet saw a mass of warriors on the nearby point. More than one hundred, he claimed, had emerged from the trees to fire arrows at the ship.

Juet took command of a small cannon called a falconer, swivelling the weapon in the direction of stone-age adversaries. It erupted at the touch of the fuse: a four-pound ball tore apart two of the archers. As the other attackers withdrew into the woods, the gun was reloaded in time for Juet to swing it toward an approaching canoe carrying about ten archers. The shot blew through its hull and killed two occupants. Musket fire from Juet's shipmates finished off another three or four.

In all, about a dozen natives were killed in the actions of October 1–2, with no casualties reported among the *Half Moon*'s men. And at the centre of it all had been Juet.

While other co-conspirators were hauling Henry Hudson out of his cabin and pinioning him, Juet took it upon himself to deal with John King, the man who only days previous had received the mate's assignment that had earlier belonged to Juet. Juet could not have thought less of Hudson for ultimately promoting an illiterate man in his literate and learned stead. King was a lackey who had to go. Juet descended into the hold to personally get him off the ship.

King groped in the dark hold for some means to defend himself. His hand settled on a sword. Juet wasn't expecting this, and King had no intention of going quietly.

It was never recorded what weapon Juet had taken along with him, but King was more than he could handle. He called to the other mutineers for help, and three of them rushed to his aid. They would have been appropriately and overwhelmingly armed, levelling a musket or two in King's direction.

King was hopelessly outnumbered, cornered in the bowels of the ship. His was the last and only meaningful resistance. King's appearance on deck under escort from Juet—the current mate in the custody of the disgraced mate—was a sure sign that the mutineers had succeeded.

Eighteen

—

NOT EVERYTHING HAD BEEN THOUGHT THROUGH. Not everyone involved was following the same script. There would have been a maelstrom of shouting, with angry orders given by the mutineers, and threats backed up by brandished weapons. Some of the victims gave as good as they got in the verbal lashings. The mutineers argued amongst themselves. One crewmember they intended to take along wanted nothing to do with them. And some of the crew they consigned to the shallop tragically may have wanted nothing to do with Hudson.

The survivors insisted in their testimony that the first rush to seize control was made without any general signal, as if the action had somehow erupted spontaneously around sunrise. It went quickly and well, except for the part where John King found himself a sword in the hold and almost diced up Robert Juet. But in very rapid order the mutineers had achieved their main objectives. Hudson was pinioned and King was under control. Prickett wrote that he heard Hudson call out to Staffe that he was bound, but heard no reply from the carpenter.

They now had to bring alongside the shallop, which was moored astern, and get into it Hudson and King, along with the others they planned to dispose of. And here the action began to lose its coherence, while maintaining its brutal momentum.

Prickett wrote, "The poor, sick and lame men were called upon to get them out of their cabins into the shallop." It might have been five in the morning when these miserable cases were rousted out of their berths and forced shivering across the deck and into the shallop. Bennet Mathew would testify in 1617 that the people ordered into the shallop went "with out any violence offered, saving that the master was pinioned."

According to Robert Bylot and Edward Wilson, Hudson, King, and seven other crewmembers were not being cast away. Rather, the shallop was to be used as a temporary holding pen. Bylot would testify that he thought the men were put in the shallop "only to [allow the mutineers to] search the master's cabin and ship for victuals, which the said Greene and others thought the master concealed from the company to serve his own turn." Wilson similarly would attest that six men "who thinking that they were only put into the shallop to keep the said Hudson the master and King [company] till the victuals were a sharing went out willingly."

This was precisely what had happened with Edward Maria Wingfield at Jamestown: consigned to a pinnace anchored off the fort while his quarters were ransacked for evidence of hoarding during a time of famine, then brought back into the fort to answer charges. Among other allegations, Wingfield was said to have buried a secret trove, and his accusers needed him out of the way while they looked for it. The main *Discovery* conspirators, Greene, Juet, and William Wilson, clearly had gotten a number of fence-sitting bystanders to abide by their action, and the victims to cooperate with their transfer to the shallop, by assuring all that the relocation was only temporary.

Had the mutineers been serious about proceeding with a proper case against Hudson and those said to benefit from his food hoarding and favouritism, the ship would have been thoroughly searched, the evidence gathered, and then Hudson and the others brought back aboard. Documenting this evidence, gathering testimony, and providing the Hudson faction with an opportunity to refute the allegations would have been the safest legal course. Hudson at the least deserved the hearing Wingfield did at Jamestown, or that Juet had been granted by Hudson the previous September over his mutinous behaviour.

The problem would have been how to proceed once the evidence against Hudson was in hand. Legally speaking, the mutineers were entirely at sea. A written protocol for deposing a ship's master simply did not exist, being anathema to the principles of command hierarchy. The most that the crewmembers opposed to Hudson could safely attempt was to place him under ad hoc arrest and proceed home, where they could all answer to the investors, the elder brothers of Trinity House, and, if need be, the High Court of the Admiralty.

But no such thing was going to happen. Greene and his partners only wished to have Hudson, his closest associates, and the sick men off the vessel. Once they had been persuaded to enter the shallop, they were not going to be allowed back. Any pretense of due process was abandoned. No search was even made of the ship for victuals before the shallop was cut loose.

It is impossible to be certain who among the mutineers had truly believed that the transfer of Hudson and the others to the shallop was only to be temporary while food was searched out. Few of the oath-takers likely had any intention of allowing these men back on board. Whatever his claims to the contrary, Bylot, like Prickett, well knew the temporary relocation to the shallop was a ruse, as he would rather carelessly testify that Greene had already told him on the night before the mutiny that he intended for Hudson and his friends to shift for themselves. Bylot, trying to look as much the innocent bystander as possible, did not even stand by. He, Edward Wilson, and Prickett would all aver that they were belowdecks when the sorry events transpired.

Prickett alleged that he heard Hudson call out to him, and that he managed to come out of his cabin far enough to plead with the mutineers through the hatch: "on my knees, I besought them, for the love of God, to remember themselves, and to do as they would be done unto. They bade me keep myself well, and get me into my cabin; not suffering the master to speak with me." But once back in his cabin, Prickett said that Hudson shouted to him through the "horn," which allowed light into his cabin. Hudson told him "that Juet would overthrow us all; nay (said I) it is that villain Henry Greene, and I spake it not softly."

Prickett would give a different version of this exchange in his 1617 deposition. Prickett (who would also allege that Greene wanted him in the shallop but was overruled) was now on deck and able to see and speak directly with Hudson, whom he said was no longer pinioned but "at liberty" in the shallop, wearing "a motley gown." Prickett now recalled Hudson saying, "It is that villain Juet that hath undone us; and [Prickett] answered: No, it is Greene that hath done all this villainy."

No one else recalled any exchange between Prickett and Hudson, or any words from Hudson at all. But the ruckus raised by Philip Staffe made a vivid impression.

Staffe, despite his apparent loyalty to Hudson, was free on the *Discovery*'s deck as his master was put aboard the shallop. The mutineers had accepted Prickett's helpful advice and decided to keep the carpenter. But Staffe, several survivors testified, was not having any of it. Edward Wilson stated in 1617 that he heard the carpenter say that the mutineers "were all dead men when Hudson forsook the ship because he thought there was no man left able to carry the ship home." Prickett wrote and then later testified that

Staffe asked them "if they would be hanged when they came into England." But Bylot, in his 1617 testimony, stated that the carpenter "never used such speeches, to his knowledge."

It was widely agreed that Staffe ended up in the shallop because he absolutely refused to remain with the mutineers aboard the *Discovery.* Mathew recalled Staffe's threats to jump on the first ice floe that passed by if they made him stay. As Bylot put it, "He went into the shallop of his own accord, without any compulsion." Edward Wilson noted that Staffe "might have stayed still in the ship, but he would voluntarily go into the said shallop for love of the master."

By the time Staffe mutinied at the thought of remaining with the mutineers, it would have been clear to the men who had consented to board the shallop that they were not going to be allowed to return. The true intentions of the core conspirators caused immediate anguish. John Thomas, who had been one of the oath-takers, was distressed to see his friend Francis Clement ordered into the shallop. Bennet Mathew was similarly stricken by the sight of his cook-room bunkmate, the cooper Silvanus Bond, being cast away. Mathew would testify that he was "weak and sick" when the shallop was being filled, and he fully expected "that he should have been put into the shallop also." But he wasn't, of course, and he was already deeply complicit, beyond his oath-taking, in having helped lure John King into the hold and then hauled Henry Hudson out of his cabin and likely restrained him while he was pinioned.

The best that could be said of Mathew was that he had staunchly testified against Juet in September 1610, and that he probably had been threatened with disposal in the shallop, as Prickett was, if he didn't cooperate. The threat would have occurred before his oath-taking, not on the morning of the mutiny, as he alleged. As the cook, the ringleaders must have seen him as essential to the seizure of power. They needed him to lure John King into the hold, on the pretext of deciding what of the remaining stores should be prepared for breakfast. And after the mutiny, if he was well, he could help work the ship, not to mention do the cooking and mind the foodstores. Mathew must have been scared to death of Juet, but would have been persuaded to cooperate by being assured that the men transferred to the shallop would be allowed back. Now, in the moment of the action, he could see that he had been conned, and that his closest friend aboard, Silvanus Bond, was about to be cut loose.

Prickett wrote that John Thomas and Bennet Mathew pleaded with Greene to allow their friends to clamber back aboard the *Discovery*. Greene relented and decided to spare them. But others would have to go in their stead.

Prickett would recall how, after Hudson was brought onto the deck, Arnold Ludlow and Michael Bute "railed at [the mutineers], and told them their knavery would show itself." And Ludlow, who had alternated with Juet as master's mate on the 1608 voyage to Novaya Zemlya, had testified against Juet at the hearing that saw him stripped of the mate's position.

Bute and Ludlow were now ordered into the shallop, to take the places of Clement and Bond.

The composition of the shallop's crew was settled: Henry and John Hudson, Philip Staffe, John King, Adrian Moore, Arnold Ludlow, Michael Bute, Sydrack Faner, and Thomas Woodhouse.

This was not the ending Thomas Woodhouse had imagined to his story of the *Discovery* voyage. Although he was ill, Woodhouse was probably condemned to the shallop for a more pressing reason. The expedition had too many writers, too many witnesses with ink and paper. Woodhouse's ambitions to create his own account with the publisher Samuel Macham may have become known.

Woodhouse was accustomed to exercising privilege, and he was not going to go quietly. He raised hell over his ejection, and began to try to buy his way back aboard the *Discovery.*

Trinity House's terse accounting of the *Discovery* voyage on October 24, 1611, singled out Woodhouse for comment, saying he was "put away in great distress." In 1617, the admiralty court would question the survivors about the rumour that Woodhouse made a last, desperate bid to stay aboard the ship. But no one would agree that he did so. Bennet Mathew testified that Woodhouse "never offered the keys of his chest to save his life to his knowledge." Prickett similarly allowed: "whether he willed them to take his keys and share his goods to save his life as is articulate he knoweth not."

The court may not have entirely understood Woodhouse's frantic effort to save himself by turning over the keys to his chest. Nothing was going to prevent the mutineers from breaking into the chest at their leisure once he was gone. Woodhouse probably was offering to open the chest and destroy all of his writings.

But the mutineers weren't interested in trading Woodhouse's life for the most precious thing Woodhouse could offer: his silence. There would be no controlling his future testimony, no preventing him from writing his account afresh once home, to their possible damnation.

While Woodhouse ultimately was lost, not all of his writings were. The letter written in Iceland reached Samuel Macham. It shed no light on the impending fate of the expedition. But one extraordinarily significant item survived, awaiting retrieval from his "desk" or chest when the *Discovery* reached home.

The item was Woodhouse's account of the hearing on September 10, 1610, when all the allegations against Juet were aired in Bible-sworn testimony. Without this small sample of Woodhouse's shipboard writing, Juet's increasingly mutinous behaviour would have gone forever unrecognized. That it survived and resurfaced was almost miraculous. Woodhouse's chest would have been broken into and ransacked along with the rest of the possessions of the men sent off in the shallop. It was as if someone had sifted through all of Woodhouse's notes and discarded everything but this important account. The one item to survive that emphatically argued: *not Greene, but Juet.*

Once the mutineers led by Greene, Juet, and William Wilson made clear their intention to evict nine members of the company from the *Discovery,* and once a final roll call for the ship was arrived at, the mutiny quite possibly evolved into something like an orderly parting of ways, as if they were repeating the division of the crew between the two vessels made a few weeks earlier, when Hudson voluntarily sailed off in the shallop. Staffe may have introduced the strained air of normalcy by offering to join the rest of the men in the shallop if he was allowed to take his clothes, which Edward Wilson said was agreed to. The others in the shallop, said the barber-surgeon, also requested their clothing, "and so part of it was delivered them."

Prickett's written account alleged that considerably more was provided to Staffe, and gathered by him for the shallop. The haberdasher claimed Staffe requested and received his entire chest, and that after it was put in the shallop for him, Staffe was allowed to go below in the *Discovery,* to speak with Prickett. Staffe then returned to the shallop with some supplies: a musket, with powder and shot, as well as some pikes; an iron pot, with some meal; "and other things." Bennet Mathew further alleged that "after the master was put out of the shallop he came on board again to warm him & went away again into the shallop after he had warmed himself, & many of the rest came also on board & fetched such things as they had, and went again into the shallop."

A sendoff so cozy and congenial might seem absurd, but the confusion of the parting was not restricted to motivation and action. Minds were bending to accommodate a horror that was somehow deniable because the consequences were not immediately at hand. No one was being shot, hanged, run through, or forced to jump into the sea. Woodhouse's pleadings would have been disconcerting, but were the castaways not being provided with clothing, equipment, and a bit of food to help them on their way? Bylot even suggested to the court that Hudson and his companions *chose* to leave certain possessions behind on the *Discovery:* "Such beds and clothes as were left in the *Discovery,* and not taken by Hudson and the rest into the shallop, were brought into England, because they left them behind in the ship."

When all were aboard the shallop, the tow line was paid out again, according to Prickett. The *Discovery* was steered out of the ice that had gathered around her, and when the shallop had fallen astern—"when they were nigh out, for I cannot say they were clean out," Prickett recalled—an axe cut the tow line.

On the morning of Sunday, June 22, 1611, Henry Hudson, his son John, and seven others, four of whom were known to be in poor health, were turned loose on James Bay, some twenty English leagues—sixty nautical miles—north of the overwintering bay.

Only after Hudson's party was cast away, and after the *Discovery* momentarily had sailed clear of the ice, did the search for the purported missing food begin. Topsails were furled, the helm was put down, and the foresails were trimmed to keep the *Discovery* idle while the mutineers "ransacked and searched all places in the ship," according to Prickett.

They broke open the chests of the evicted men. Some of their clothing was sold at the mainmast and would be worn on the voyage. The rest was shut back up and carried home.

Edward Wilson would claim that only the clothing items the castaways didn't choose to take with them were sold at the mast, "and an inventory of every man's particular goods was made and their money was paid by Mr. Allin Cary to their friends here in England and deducted out of their wages that so bought them when they came into England." The entire affair in the barber-surgeon's telling could not have been more fair-minded or by the book.

Into the hold the mutineers went, to assess the remaining foodstores. It was a misconception to think that the ship's crew had been down to meagre rations of biscuit and cheese. Hudson had divvied only the stores that could be managed by individual sailors and eaten as is. Belowdecks were still the stores that Mathew would cook up in a communal kettle. Prickett reported that there were two barrels of porridge meal, one full, the other half empty. There also were two firkins—wooden pails that each held about fifty-five pounds—of butter, twenty-seven pieces of dried pork, and half a bushel of dried peas. There was nothing in Prickett's commentary that suggested these remaining stores were anything like a surprise: no more or less than should have been there.

The butter, more than a year after departing London, was well past its prime—six months was optimistic—and may not have been edible. Prickett noted that they had left England with two barrels of meal, which meant they had yet to consume three-quarters of their supply. Perhaps porridge was an unpopular menu item, but they would have to learn to like it. And with so much meal on hand, there may have been no immediate danger of starvation.

Even so, it was in Hudson's cabin that Prickett's narrative alleged the true hoard was found: two hundred biscuits, a butt, or cask, of beer that would have amounted to about 126 gallons, and a peck (a quarter-bushel) of meal. Prickett did not explain how Hudson was supposed to cook up meal on his own, unde-tected. Bylot spoke to the court only of how the mutineers "thought" Hudson was hoarding food, and conspicuously failed to offer supporting evidence or agree with the allegation. In his admiralty court depositions, Prickett never referred to the stores allegedly found in Hudson's cabin or the provisions itemized in the hold after the mutiny. Nor did anyone else. No hard evidence was ever produced that Hudson was showing favouritism in the dispensing of rations. And Prickett's itemizing of what was found in Hudson's cabin said nothing about the aquavit Edward Wilson alleged Hudson had been dispensing to his inner circle. (Splashing aquavit about, however, was a charge that had been brought against Wingfield.)

Only a summary of the testimony given to the admiralty court in January 1612 by Prickett, Edward Wilson, Clement, Moter, and Mathew addressed the essential allegation: "They all charge the master with wasting the victuals by a scuttle made out of his cabin into the hold, and it appears that he fed his favourites, as the sur-geon, etc., and kept other at only ordinary allowance."

The source of food, then, was not a private store to which Hudson, as master, would have been entitled but a secret hatch permitting access to the hold, through which Hudson would have replenished his personal cache and built a hoard to the benefit of favourites.

But Wilson and Prickett in their individual testimony that January made no such claim, as the court interrogations' summary suggested. And the barber-surgeon, Wilson, certainly would not have accused himself of having benefited from Hudson's favouritism. If anyone made these allegations, it was likely Moter or Mathew, both of whom Prickett identified as conspirators who took the oath. And Mathew's self-serving testimony was some of the least credible.

The allegations against Hudson in any event sounded suspiciously familiar. Wingfield in his draft defence had stated that Captain John Smith, "in the time of our hunger, had spread a rumour in the Colony, that I did feast myself and my servants out of the common store, with intent (as I gathered) to have stirred the discontented company against me." Hudson never had the chance to answer the allegations made against him, the way Wingfield did at Jamestown. One of Wingfield's defences was that he was perfectly entitled to his own personal supply of provisions, distinct from the general supplies of the colony. Hudson too probably could have made the same claim with perfect reason, provided he was not living large while his men starved around him. But this was not the Hudson that Prickett elsewhere described, the master with the remarkably high survival rate of crews on his four voyages.

Hudson had taken pains after the shallop expedition to bring out the remaining biscuit and cheese, so everyone could see how much was left, both edible and spoiled, and then divided it equally. And Hudson's decision to distribute those rations among the crew for their own management and safekeeping was a clear attempt to further demonstrate that nothing was being held back, that no one would be favoured or shortchanged. For this fairmindedness, Hudson paid with his life. And after his vanishing, he suffered a slander of his character, as survivors alleged whatever they had to, to save themselves from justice.

By the time Prickett was called upon a second time to answer questions before the admiralty court, in February 1617, he testified that Hudson and his companions had been forced into the shallop because, with victuals critically short, the mutineers "should starve for want of food, if all the company should return home in the ship." There was nothing from Prickett now about hoarding or unwarranted privilege.

It was just after the search of the *Discovery* for food was concluded that the mutineers proved themselves new to the logistics of abandoning fellow sailors on the open sea. It must have been a dry-mouthed moment for them, as they realized that Henry Hudson was in determined pursuit, refusing to go quietly to his death, the persistent shape of the shallop's sails growing like a damned spot on the horizon astern.

The shallop was behaving precisely as Prickett at least expected, according to his account. In recalling his conversation with Staffe belowdeck before the shallop was cast off, Prickett said he tried to persuade Staffe to stay aboard the ship with him, "which if he did, he might so work that all should be well: he said, he did not think but they would be glad to take them in again. For he was so persuaded by the master, that there was not one in all the ship that could tell how to carry her home; but (saith he) if we must part (which we will not willingly do, for they would follow the ship) he prayed me, if we came to the Capes before them, that I would leave some token that we had been there, near to the place where the fowls bred, and he would do the like for us: and so (with tears) we parted."

The shallop, like the *Discovery*, was making for the murre colony.

While this must not have been entirely surprising, the mutineers would have expected the larger *Discovery* to outstrip the shallop and leave Hudson and his companions astern. But pausing to search for food had allowed the shallop to close quickly with them. In the right conditions, the smaller, nimble shallop could keep pace with the ship. And with ice fields otherwise slowing them down, the mutineers could now find themselves in the constant company of the castaways. The mutineers must have shuddered at the prospect of the shallop shadowing them to the murre colony, some six hundred nautical miles north; of the two vessels sailing in absurd company or sharing the same prison of sea ice; of the crews exchanging insults and threats across the water; of howls of promised damnation from the shallop turning to pleadings for mercy and salvation; even of confrontations on land when they stopped at the capes, and wherever they might pause to take on fresh water.

The passage to the murres was certainly feasible in the shallop. Consider what the Barentsz expedition had managed in open boats in escaping Novaya Zemlya. Prickett had already noted that Greene and William Wilson had considered stealing away with the shallop at the overwintering bay. And it was an interesting coincidence that Wingfield, in the course of his draft defence, mentioned that a member of the Jamestown colony had conspired to steal the settlement's shallop and sail it all the way from the Chesapeake to Newfoundland—a straight-line Atlantic passage of about twelve hundred nautical miles.

The prospect of the *Discovery*'s being shadowed all the way to the murre colony—and beyond it—was very real. How long could the mutineers endure this manifestation of their own guilt? How many nights could they spend sleepless, waiting for it to draw near them in darkness and claw at the side of their hull?

The survivors reinterrogated in 1617 were asked if any shots were fired at the men in the shallop. All answered to the negative, with Bylot adamant that "no man, drunk or sober" could say such a thing.

According to Prickett, after half an hour of being chased by Hudson, the men aboard the *Discovery* piled on canvas, setting the mainsail and topsails, and were able to leave the shallop astern.

The *Discovery*, Habakkuk Prickett wrote, flew "as from an enemy."

———

At the initial interrogation of survivors by the High Court of the Admiralty on January 25, 1612, the presiding judge, Richard Trevor, had to ask: What became of Henry and John Hudson, and the seven men accompanying them, after they were cast away in the shallop in a field of ice?

None of the men questioned could say. Edward Wilson volunteered that, after the *Discovery* began to draw away from the shallop on June 22, the little open boat "put in for shore and so [the *Discovery*] lost sight of them and never heard of them since." Thus did the nine shunned souls vanish.

Except, it would seem, for John Hudson.

PART II

—

Beyond the Great Rapid

Nineteen

—

I N THE LATE SUMMER OR EARLY AUTUMN OF 1612, Nicolas
de Vignau lighted onto the pier at Honfleur, the seaport of
Paris, with the weight of Samuel de Champlain's entire world
on his shoulders. It was a burden supported by a scaffolding of
revelatory language.

MITASWI ASIDJ NIJWASWI. *Dix-sept.* Seventeen.
AKAM. *Bord de l'eau.* The water's edge; the seashore.

The translator was a young man, probably not even out of his
teens. He was employed by Champlain, the navigator, explorer,
cartographer, artist, soldier, mariner, and colonial visionary, who
was determined to make something of the precarious French presence in North America, and of himself in the process. In 1611,
Champlain had given de Vignau the task of living among the
Kichesipirini, one of the Algonquin tribes that gathered every
summer to trade with the French on the St. Lawrence River. He
was expected to learn their language, their customs. And of
course, their secrets.

MAIAK ININI. *L'étranger.* A man from another nation;
    a stranger.

MANDAMIN. *Maïs.* Corn.

MAWINEV. *Attaquer.* To attack.

PAKWANDIPEJIKE. *Scalper.* To scalp.

De Vignau spent the winter of 1611–12 with the Kichesipirini,
several days' travel up Kitci sipi, La Grande Rivière, the river that
in time would be known as the Utawa, finally the Ottawa, from the
Algonquin word *atawe,* to trade. It stretched northwest beyond the
main sheet of rapids, or where Kitcikami—"the great wide water,"
the Great River of Canada, the St. Lawrence River—ceased to be
navigable any farther upstream. Kitci sipi drew the traveller out of
the agrarian promise of the St. Lawrence valley and into a primeval
wilderness of pine and spruce, of furious rapids, of ancient igneous
and metamorphic rock smoothed by advancing and retreating gla-
ciers that had been more than half a mile thick. De Vignau had
travelled well beyond where Champlain had ever been, which was
not much past the rapids at the St. Lawrence's height of navigation,
which Champlain in his cartography had labelled *grand sault,* the
Great Rapid. The young man had ventured up Kitci sipi to where
the river's waters plunged into a bowl and boiled like water in a kettle, where the mist rose like steam. He had portaged past the bowl,
and kept going, still days more, the river course rising higher into
the wilderness, through more rapids, until he had reached the village of the Kichesipirini, on an island in the middle of the river.
Below and beside this village, the river was a cascading fury, a natural barricade to unwanted visitors.

In the new year, Nicolas de Vignau had shot one set of rapids
after another in a canoe of his hosts, descending the river course
to rejoin his countrymen. He was now home in France, and he
disembarked with the most remarkable news.

De Vignau informed Champlain that he had seen it himself: the Northern Sea. Seventeen days' journey to its shore from the Great Rapid. There, and back. The Kichesipirini had taken him there, just as their grand chief, Tessöuat, had promised he would.

And de Vignau had seen with his own eyes remnants of a wrecked vessel. *Anglais.* The survivors, he had learned, had came ashore, weak and starving. They tried to steal corn and other necessities from the *sauvages.* A mistake: they were killed. De Vignau had been shown their scalps. But one was taken alive, and not harmed.

KWIWISENS. *Garcon.* Boy
KIWACITO. *Être seul, sans parents.* To be an orphan.
APANINI. *Captif, prisonnier de guerre; esclave.* A captive,
    a prisoner of war; a slave.

This English boy had come to be held by the Nebicerini, who ranged far north through the river systems that led to the Northern Sea, to trade with the Cree. The Nebicerini and the Kichesipirini were not on the best of terms. The Nebicerini were known as the Sorcerers, and the Kichesipirini feared their witch-craft. But the Nebicerini were just a few days' journey to the west of Tessöuat's people, and they wished to make a gift of the boy and the scalps to Champlain. De Vignau was ready and willing to show Champlain the way—to the Nebicerini, to the boy, and on to the Northern Sea.

The things the boy would be able to tell Champlain: about *les Anglais,* and their explorations of the Northern Sea, of what they had learned of the passage west, to the Orient and all its riches. A passage that would circumvent the established trade routes of the Spanish, the Portuguese, the Dutch, and the English. Such a dis-covery would reward spectacularly years of efforts by Champlain to make something of the French presence—of *his* presence—in this new world.

The wealth that lay up Kitci sipi was incalculable to Champlain. He had to reach the Nebicerini. He had to find this English boy.

Twenty

—

NICOLAS DE VIGNAU'S REPORT OF THE ENGLISH shipwreck, the scalps, the boy being held by the Nebicerini for Samuel de Champlain reached his employer in the midst of a stock-taking of the last eight years of his life. Champlain was completing the manuscript for a book, *Les Voyages,* and as he concluded his account of events up to the autumn of 1611, the tale had begun to take on the air of an embittered memoir, rather than of an interim report on his progress in shaping a profitable and populous New France. There was a waning quality to the narrative as it reached Champlain's last days in the New World. He had no obvious way forward.

Champlain had all but taken his place in a long list of failed French colonizers. Their ventures had become misadventures, undermined by a poor grasp of logistics, a lack of appreciation of the obstacles to settlement (not the least of which was the winter), a poverty of funding, a misplaced mania over fabulous riches (jewels and precious metals, cinnamon and nutmeg) awaiting exploitation, and the indifference of commercial partners who were more interested in growing rich in the fur trade than in building a viable settlement. The list went on. Every initiative found a way to repeat the errors of the previous ones while adding new wrinkles of their own.

Les Voyages provided abundant evidence of where and how the vision of a New France continued to go wrong. The book covered considerable geographic and narrative terrain, picking up where Champlain's first published work, *Des Sauvages,* left off. *Des Sauvages* had described his initial summer of explorations along the St. Lawrence in 1603, when he assessed its colonizing potential and weighed the evidence for passage-making opportunities beyond the Great Rapid. *Les Voyages* recounted his four years, from 1604 to 1607, on the Atlantic coast, during which he made three overwinterings, first at Île Ste-Croix, then at Port Royal, and explored from Cape Breton to Martha's Vineyard; then four more years, on the St. Lawrence, where Champlain established a forti-fied habitation at Quebec in 1608 and joined native trading allies in raids on their Iroquois enemies. All the while, Champlain had fought against a rearguard political action by French merchants who were determined to strip him of the trade monopoly that sheltered him.

Champlain had been able to defeat Iroquois warriors, but not the merchants in his own country. No royal monopoly had existed to protect and enrich Champlain since October 1609, and by the time he returned to France in mid-September 1611 from his most recent expedition to the St. Lawrence and the Great Rapid, his ambitions had been all but thwarted. Debarking at La Rochelle, he had proceeded directly to Pons, where his main commercial ally, Pierre du Gua de Monts, was the town's new governor. Champlain wanted to tell him of the progress he had made in forging a military alliance with the Algonquin and the Huron, the "good Iroquois" who lived to the west. It was a pact that was sup-posed to ensure a privileged access to their furs.

Champlain's main news would have been his success in per-suading Algonquin and Huron tribes first to accept young Frenchmen as interpreter-trainees and then to show them the country well beyond the Great Rapid. After meeting with Champlain, a hopeful Sieur de Monts had set out for the royal court at Fontainebleau to plead his case, yet again, for a trade monopoly on the St. Lawrence. Champlain had departed ahead of de Monts, but was delayed when his horse fell on him. Champlain was not a large man—picture a bearded bantamweight of quick movement with a penetrating gaze—and the accident nearly killed him. Or so he complained. However much he was injured, when he was well enough, he carried on to Fontainebleau, where he joined de Monts in lobbying the court. De Monts also met in Paris with his business partners from Rouen, who informed him they had had enough and wanted out. De Monts arranged to buy out their interest in the business at Quebec and to send some men back to Canada to tend to the habitation. But de Monts' hope that a new monopoly would make his fresh investment worthwhile was dashed at court. The Canada trade would remain open, as it had been in 1610 and 1611. Deflated, de Monts returned to governing Pons. He would lease out his Quebec habitation to traders, and in the fall of 1611 he left the remnants of his once grand monopoly for Champlain to do with as he saw fit.

Champlain learned at about the same time how seriously his fortunes had eroded back in New France. One of his teenage interpreters had returned that autumn, rejected, it seems, by his hosts. He informed Champlain that more than two hundred warriors had appeared at the Great Rapid for a rendezvous that Champlain had not kept. Champlain would concede in his new volume that these allies were "greatly displeased" with the fact that he had failed to keep his word and had not joined them in another assault on the Iroquois. A special relationship with the people who lived beyond the Great Rapid was the only advantage Champlain could claim in the fur trade, and he had just undone years of carefully cultivated goodwill. Independent European traders had moved gleefully into the vacuum left by Champlain's return to France, telling natives who came to barter that their erstwhile military ally was in fact dead.

Champlain exacerbated the damage he had already done to his standing with a few native allies by not returning at all to the St. Lawrence in the summer of 1612. The two hundred warriors he had disappointed with his failure to appear in late 1611 had been assured by Champlain's men that he would return the following summer, or never. Champlain wrote that apologies for his absence in 1611 were accepted and that these warriors were asked to promise that they would reappear in 1612 to fight with him. But he had not returned, remaining in France to complete an ambitious map of New France and finish *Les Voyages* while two thousand warriors waited for him in vain to join them.

Nicolas de Vignau was one of the youths left in the care of the Algonquin in the summer of 1611. His host, Tessöuat, did not send him home early. Champlain could only wait for news from the young man, whenever he emerged from the wilderness, provided he emerged at all. There were so many ways the interpreter could come to harm: the privations of the Algonquin life in winter, a fatal wound from an Iroquois arrow or an excruciating death by torture at their hands, or a canoe spill in whitewater. Heaven forbid that de Vignau had learned the hard way the Algonquian word *amonakise:* to capsize a canoe.

But de Vignau had survived, and had returned with greater news than Champlain could have dreamed possible. "This intelligence had greatly pleased me," Champlain would write. Merely listening to de Vignau made Champlain feel as if he had "almost found that for which I had for a long time been searching"—a feasible route to the Orient, above the Great Rapid. De Vignau's words alone made the success veritably come alive.

On its own, Nicolas de Vignau's report would have lifted Champlain from the discouraging air of the final pages of *Les Voyages* and reinvigorated his dormant effort to secure a new monopoly and attract financiers. What made de Vignau's information of the highest priority was the near simultaneous arrival of extraordinary evidence from the Netherlands, which magnified the significance of the interpreter's experiences.

Around midsummer 1612, an unusual volume was published in Amsterdam. Written entirely in Dutch, it was compiled by Hessel Gerritsz, who would succeed Petrus Plancius as official hydrographer of the VOC in 1617. Three distinct works on recent passage-making discoveries were bound within the little volume. The book went through a flurry of editions over the remainder of 1612, with Gerritsz refining its content, and it was released in Latin that same year in order to satisfy the widest possible learned audience.

It took its title, *Description of the Land of the Samoyeds in Tartary,* from the largest item, on the Northeast Passage. Another section addressed the Spanish discovery of Torres Strait, between Papua New Guinea and northeastern Australia. The final item, while consuming the least space, quickly proved to be anything but the least noteworthy. It was a map revealing the latest advances by Henry Hudson in probing the Northwest Passage.

Everything Champlain knew about Hudson's last voyage he knew from Gerritsz's volume. A brief account was printed on the obverse of Gerritsz's map, and additional information on Hudson's last two voyages were included in Gerritsz's introductory essay.

Champlain's own statements on Hudson's final voyage suggest he worked exclusively from a translation of the original Dutch edition. The essay in that edition was thin on details. Gerritsz described how "a certain Mr. Hudson" had been sent out by the VOC's directors "some years ago," and that after failing to find a passage in the northeast, he had sailed west, "whence without having obtained any advantage, he arrived in England." Hudson was then employed by the English on the voyage to the northwest, on which he had "much more prosperity but less good luck." Gerritsz explained how "after much trouble" Hudson arrived at a point three hundred miles west of Terra de Baccaloes, as Gerritsz labelled Newfoundland on the accompanying chart. Hudson "having taken up his winter quarters there and wishing at 52° of latitude to push on further, he was, with all the Commanders, put on shore by the crew, who refused to go further and returned home."

Gerritsz's brief account in Dutch of the *Discovery* voyage on the obverse of the map was better, if not perfect. It must have been added at the last minute, after he had already written and typeset the introductory essay. He now explained how Hudson, after finding his way westward, "would have continued, if the common crew had not shown so much unwillingness; for as they had been out already 10 months, having however been victualled for only 8 months, and had seen only one man on the whole way, who brought them a large animal which they ate, which man however did not return, because he was badly treated." The crew "at last revolted against their masters, who desired to go further, and placed their superiors together in a sloop or boat outside the vessel, and then sailed with the ship to England. For this reason, when they came home, they were all thrown into prison."

The map of Hudson's discoveries in the northwest was a sensation, and as the book was reworked, the Hudson material acquired more prominent billing, until the volume became known as *Detectio Freti Hudson* (Discovery of Hudson Strait). And no wonder: Gerritsz had produced the first map based on the *Discovery* voyage, and nothing like it would ever surface, not even in England. Somehow, Henry Hudson's own cartographic observations had made their way into Gerritsz's enterprising hands.

Already, in January 1612, when six *Discovery* survivors were interrogated by the High Court of the Admiralty, it was well suspected that precious information had crossed the English Channel to the Low Countries. The barber-surgeon, Edward Wilson, was asked "whether he knoweth that the Hollanders have an intent to go forth upon a discovery to the said Northwest passage and whether they have any card [chart] delivered them concerning the said discovery." He replied that "for his part [he] never gave them any card or knowledge of the said discovery but he hath heard say that they intend such a voyage and more he cannot say saving that some gentlemen and merchants of London that are interested in this discovery have shewed diverse cards abroad which happily might come to some of their knowledge." Indeed, by the time the High Court of the Admiralty began questioning the survivors, the materials Gerritsz required to create his chart already may have been in his hands.

And so, in whatever happy manner, and in whatever completed or fragmentary form, Hudson's cartography had been acquired by Gerritsz, who hoped by publishing the map to encourage a Dutch expedition in that direction. The map was the true gem of the little book. A panorama of the Northern Hemisphere swept westward from England, through and beyond the waters explored by Frobisher, Davis, and Waymouth, to a great bay that extended deep into North America. It was as if, in pressing west, well beyond the Furious Overfall, Hudson had unrolled a chart hitherto scrolled tightly closed.

The Gerritsz map might have circulated separately from the main volume, but Champlain seems to have received the Dutch edition of the book in its entirety. It could have found its way to him aboard one of the many Dutch ships that called at his home-town of Brouage on the Bay of Biscay to fill their holds with the region's cultivated salt. Dutch financiers also played leading roles in the French fur trade, and Champlain had a working relationship with two transplanted Low Countries merchants based at Rouen, Corneille (Cornelis) de Bellois and Ludowica Vermeulen. Because Gerritsz's introductory essay referred to a Dutch voyage whose first ship did not return home until July 6, 1612, the book could not have existed before the latter part of that month. It was August, or perhaps September, then, when Champlain first saw the map and the Dutch volume. Nicolas de Vignau was either on his way home with his astonishing report or had just arrived.

Champlain had now heard Henry Hudson's footfalls on the rooftop of his world. They convinced him to plot a new course for his life: a daring expedition beyond the Great Rapid toward Hudson's last known position, with a rescue of his captive son along the way.

Twenty-one

———

NINE YEARS HAD PASSED since Samuel de Champlain had first laid eyes on the Great Rapid and considered what lay beyond it. *Des Sauvages,* the little book he then wrote about his adventures in the summer of 1603, served as his debut in public life. It conveyed almost nothing about who he was, or why he had even come to the river's height of navigation.

Champlain might have been thirty when he saw the rapids that first time. He was a man of modest formal education. His written French was coarse and his delivery direct, unaffected by allusions to classical literature. Latin, the universal language of the educated classes, was most likely a liturgical mumbling at Mass for him. But his world was assuredly much broader than most people would later consider.

Champlain held the rank of naval captain, but the patronage-bloated French navy scarcely had any ships. Champlain was rarely known to hold any command, even a temporary one, and never of a French naval vessel. In the few instances in which he was in charge of some kind of craft, it generally was of a small private vessel being employed for coastal surveying. In keeping with his earlier military service, Champlain would also call himself an *écuyer,* a cavalier. For that matter, he identified himself alternately as the commoner Samuel Champlain and as an implied minor noble, de Champlain. He was in truth a royal spy, an intelligence officer of his king, Henry IV.

The first documentary evidence of Champlain's life would turn up in a military pay record, as he supported Henry of Navarre's right to call himself Henry IV of France over the forceful opposition of the Spanish crown and its allied French Catholic nobles. A payroll notation for Henry's army in Brittany in March 1595 found Champlain being compensated "pour certain voiage secret qu'il a faict important le service du Roy." No one knows what this secret journey, so important to his king, entailed. But later that same year, another Champlain pay entry made discreet reference to "quelque chose important le service du Roy."

The 1590s marked the end of a debilitating period in French history, when a war of succession had become intertwined with protracted and bloody religious disquiet between Catholics and Protestants. Henry IV had helped secure his claim to the French throne by converting to Catholicism in 1593 (allegedly quipping that Paris "was well worth a Mass"). Champlain for his part was most likely born a Protestant, and his conversion to Catholicism might have occurred by the time he entered Henry's service. After the Treaty of Vervins in 1598 brought a fragile peace between France and Spain, Champlain scored spectacularly in the area of espionage when he infiltrated the Spanish Caribbean. He spent more than two years there, from 1599 to 1601, as a set of eyes and ears for Henry IV.

On Champlain's return from the Caribbean, Henry awarded him with a pension, which was probably tied to his naval captaincy. By early 1603, Champlain was ready for a new assignment. He would travel to the St. Lawrence River with nobles from a new monopoly that Henry had just granted for the fur trade.

As he would recall in *Les Voyages,* Henry IV had "commissioned me to make the most exact researches and explorations in my power" on the 1603 expedition. While no personal orders survive, his main assignment was clear. He was to investigate the evidence for a passage upstream of the Great Rapid that could ultimately lead to the Orient.

French colonization efforts in the New World had lost virtually all momentum during the wars of religion and succession in the late sixteenth century. A continuity of knowledge and experience was also broken. Many aspects of sixteenth-century French exploration in the New World were better known in England than they were in France. The voyages of Jacques Cartier in particular were far better documented by Richard Hakluyt than by anyone in Henry's kingdom. The historiographer Gianbattista Ramusio had published the only surviving narratives of the first two voyages, in Italian, in *Navigationi e Viaggi* in 1556. Hakluyt brought out an English translation of Ramusio's Cartier narratives in 1580. No French edition of the first two Cartier voyages would exist until a translation of Ramusio was published at Rouen in 1598. And Cartier's third voyage, of 1541–42, was scarcely known at all in France. The only account in circulation anywhere in the world was a fragmentary report brought out in English by Hakluyt in *Principal Navigations* in 1598, which continues to be the sole surviving version. A published French version of the third voyage still did not exist when Champlain was chosen by Henry IV to determine what might lie beyond the Great Rapid.

The new French trade monopoly's titular leader, a vice-admiral named Aymer de Chaste, did not join the 1603 expedition. Given that he died that May, he may have been too ill. The venture was commanded by François Gravé du Pont ("Pont-Gravé"), a ship captain from St-Malo who had been visiting the Gulf of St. Lawrence since at least the 1570s. Also involved was

Pierre du Gua de Monts, a Huguenot noble who had served in Henry's army. Like Champlain, he was a Saintongeois, and had owned saltworks at Brouage, Champlain's birthplace. Both Pont-Gravé and de Monts had been part of an earlier, failed trade and colonization venture of Pierre Chauvin de Tonnetuit at Tadoussac. Champlain would have no real authority in the enterprise, nor would he have his own ship to command. Instead, he would travel as an observer with Pont-Gravé.

They arrived at Tadoussac, at the mouth of the Saguenay River on the north shore of the lower St. Lawrence, on May 24, 1603. Europeans, especially Basques, had been trading with natives there for several generations. Champlain and Pont-Gravé ventured up the Saguenay, to investigate rumours of where it led. While Champlain proceeded no farther than the rapids at present-day Chicoutimi, he gathered a credible image of the water route north, through Lac St-Jean.

"These *sauvages* from the north say that they live within sight of a sea which is salt," Champlain reported in *Des Sauvages*. "If this is the case, I think that it is a gulf of that sea which flows from the north into the interior, and in fact it cannot be otherwise." Champlain had quickly deduced the existence of Hudson Bay, seven years before Henry Hudson reached it.

Pont-Gravé and Champlain moved on to investigating what lay above the Great Rapid. On June 18, they departed Tadoussac, and for two weeks, Pont-Gravé steered their pinnace up the St. Lawrence as Champlain gathered his first impressions of the land that would become his life's work.

"The farther we advanced," he wrote in *Des Sauvages*, "the finer the country became." The Saguenay had been a granite fjord, high-walled, primeval, devoid of agricultural potential. The St. Lawrence valley stirred in Champlain and his companions visions of tilled fields, seigneuries, a New France proper.

Moving upriver, Champlain employed placenames that had been created by Jacques Cartier, but he was impressively ignorant of Cartier's own explorations. Above the river's narrowing, where Cartier had encountered the village of Stadacona—vanished by Champlain's time—they anchored at "saincte Croix," which was probably Point Platon. Three leagues below Ste-Croix, Champlain explained in *Des Sauvages,* was a tributary of the St. Lawrence, "which was as far as Jacques Cartier went up the river at the beginning of his discoveries, and went no further." He had no idea that Cartier had reached the height of navigation at the Great Rapid and visited there the village of Hochelaga on his second voyage, of 1535–36. And he evidently did not know that Cartier had made a third voyage, in 1541, on which he again visited the rapids.

Champlain must have had little time to prepare himself for the 1603 mission. He plainly had not read Cartier's accounts, and was probably relying on the hearsay of Pont-Gravé—who was, after all, based at Cartier's St-Malo—for knowledge of Cartier's findings. Champlain left the inescapable impression in *Des Sauvages* that he travelled farther up the St. Lawrence than any Frenchmen. Of course, others had already made this journey—not only Cartier but who knows how many other independent traders over the ensuing years.

It was early July when Pont-Gravé and Champlain reached the base of the Great Rapid. Champlain took note of the mountain, "visible at a considerable distance," which Cartier in the Hakluyt translation of Ramusio called Mount Roiall—a Dutch chart spelled it Mont réal, and Champlain would adapt the corruption to his 1612 map of New France with the label montreal, although he located the hill far to the north, in the vicinity of the Laurentians. It was of no concern to him that the palisade village of Hochelaga, visited by Cartier and illustrated in Ramusio, was, like Stadacona, gone, and that the Iroquoian-speaking occupants had vanished.

Nevertheless, Champlain had arrived at his own Furious Overfall, an entrancing gateway to a grand opportunity. It was now up to him to determine if in fact an ocean passage to the Orient could be found beyond it.

Jacques Cartier had called the rapids "the greatest and the swiftest fall of water that anywhere has been seen," after viewing them from the vantage point of Mount Royal in 1536. The cascade similarly stunned Champlain when he arrived on July 2, 1603.

"I saw, to my astonishment," he reported in *Des Sauvages,* "a torrent of water descending with an impetuosity such as I have never before witnessed, although it is not very high, there being in some places only a fathom or two, and at most but three. It descends as if by steps, and at each descent there is a remarkable boiling, owing to the force and swiftness with which the water traverses the fall, which is about a league in length."

One could not look upon this spectacle of whitewater without trying to imagine how it had come to seethe through this river channel. There is nothing anywhere else in the world like the Great Lakes watershed. Twenty percent of the planet's freshwater surface area is represented by the main lakes, fed by a drainage basin of some 290,000 square miles—an area thirty-six percent larger than modern France. Lake Superior drains into Lakes Michigan and Huron—the "middle" lakes, which technically are contiguous, and include the "sixth" Great Lake of Georgian Bay, an arm of Lake Huron. They in turn feed Lake Erie, and Erie— plunging over Niagara Falls—fills Lake Ontario. From Ontario springs the St. Lawrence River. And before the St. Lawrence reaches the Great Rapid (or what we now call the Lachine rapids), it is stoked by the outflow of the Ottawa River system, with its own drainage of some 57,000 square miles, an area about as large as England and Wales. About half of the Ottawa's flow bypasses the Great Rapid by two rivers to the north, after gathering in Lac des Deux-Montagnes (Lake of Two Mountains). The rest chooses the main channel, to the south, after flowing around Île Perrot, through the rapids of either Ste-Anne-de-Bellevue or Perrot, and joining the Lake Ontario outflow in Lac St-Louis. Champlain was watching more than two hundred thousand cubic feet of water per second descend from Lac St-Louis through the Great Rapid in a stampede of spray and standing waves.

Several native guides accompanied Champlain—whether they were Montagnais or Algonquin he did not say. They went ashore, as Cartier had done in 1541, to survey on foot the extent of the rapids. Whatever thought Champlain's party had of attempting to travel above the Great Rapid was abandoned. They had only one canoe: a skiff the French had built specifically for surmounting the rapids had already proved unsuited to the task in fast-moving shallows downstream, in what would become known as the *courant* Ste-Marie, thumping along rocks as the canoe of the guides glided effortlessly forward. Instead, the questioning of the guides began.

Natives had explained to Cartier the passage farther upstream by laying sticks end to end and placing across them branches to indicate the locations of sets of rapids. Perhaps Champlain encountered the same technique, although he also gathered maps they drew for him. A detailed picture of the landscape upstream began to form.

Like Cartier, Champlain heard of a river that branched away to the west, leading into the territory of the Algonquin. It was his first knowledge of Kitci sipi, the Ottawa, which Nicolas de Vignau would ascend eight years hence to live with Tessöuat.

After interviewing his guides at the rapids and, on the way back to Tadoussac, a group of Algonquin at Île d'Orléans and then another young Algonquin farther downriver, Champlain arrived at a description of the Great Lakes system far more developed than anything that preceded his investigation. He learned of Lake Ontario, and Niagara Falls, and Lake Erie—and beyond Lake Erie, some great body of water not even his guides had visited. One interview made this great body of water salty, another did not, and the third interview, conducted with the young Algonquin, made the first great lake upstream initially composed of fresh water but increasingly salty as one travelled west, until "the water is totally salty." A waterfall then led to "a sea so great that they have not seen the end of it, nor heard of anyone who may have seen it." The distance from the Great Rapid "to the salt sea, which is possibly the South Sea, is some four hundred leagues," Champlain wrote. "It is not to be doubted, then, according to their statement, that this is none other than the South Sea, the sun setting where they say."

In returning home to report that the way to the distant sea pointed toward the setting sun, Champlain was bearing the best possible news. He would recount in *Les Voyages* how, in the autumn of 1603, he delivered to his king a report "on the feasibility of discovering the passage to China, without the inconveniences of the ice of the north or the heats of the torrid zone, through which our sailors pass twice in going and twice in returning, with inconceivable hardships and risks." The report has never been seen, but *Des Sauvages* must have substantially reflected its contents.

Champlain's book, a little more than four thousands words, was a product of its age. It was partly a report on serious investigations, partly an adventure travelogue that was not always concerned with veracity. Champlain would be chastised by his contemporary, Marc Lescarbot, for offering up without criticism the native tale of a giant named Gou-Gou, who terrorized the Baie Chaleur and could stuff an entire ship in a pouch on his stomach. Champlain would be noticeably determined to provide sober and careful reportage in *Les Voyages,* but in his fact-finding on the St. Lawrence in 1603, he may already have gilded his results to satisfy prevailing theories about a midcontinental passage.

In late 1602, a book had appeared in London that became an immediate bestseller. *A Briefe and True Relation* was a report on the Bartholomew Gosnold expedition of 1602, which included materials from the trade and colonization promoter Edward Hayes expounding on the possibilities of a midcontinental route to the Orient. Hayes envisioned two great rivers, one draining into the Atlantic, one into the Pacific, with a portage bridging their headwaters. While Hayes argued that, as per Gosnold, the search for this route and an associated colony should focus on the Atlantic coast between latitudes 40 and 44, he also presented evidence that beyond the Great Rapid the river "did lead into a mighty lake, which at the entrance was fresh, but beyond, was bitter or salt; the end whereof was unknown." Hayes argued, as Edward Wright's 1599 world map showed, that the route led north, to the Northern Sea.

Champlain appeared to be as familiar with Hayes's argument and evidence as he was ignorant of Cartier's explorations. Champlain's third anecdote, gathered from an Algonquin youth, which stated the peculiar idea of a lake upstream that was initially freshwater but becomes increasingly salty, appears to have been added as an afterthought to his legitimate results in *Des Sauvages.* The alleged evidence from this youth seemed to be a fabrication meant to satisfy anyone who was aware of and believed in Hayes's recently published evidence for this strange lake. Champlain then bent the route beyond the lake, which Hayes and Wright argued led to the forbidding Arctic, instead to the balmy South Sea, or Pacific Ocean.

Champlain's volume was a landmark work. Once Richard Hakluyt decided to have *Des Sauvages* translated (and turned all of Champlain's references to "wholesome" water into "salty"), its influence on the general perception of North American geography and exploration opportunities was considerable. Echoes of Champlain's analysis could be heard in the public and private writings of the English involved in the Virginia colonization schemes, who also were concerned with finding a midcontinental route along the lines of Hayes's theory. The multinational efforts to find a profitable new route to the Orient had become an echo chamber of evidence and ideas. No one could know if crucial portions of what they were absorbing had been twisted or invented outright to agree with the results of their rivals, the theories of cosmographers, and the schemes of trade and colonization promoters.

And no one was more seriously or secretively affected by Champlain's reportage in *Des Sauvages* than Henry Hudson, as his persistent attempts to find some passage south from James Bay may well have been an effort to connect with Champlain's transcontinental passage to the Pacific, along the water route from the Northern Sea to Lake Tadouac as drawn by Wright. In a way he would never be able to comprehend, Champlain's quest to retrieve John Hudson from the Nebicerini and reach the Northern Sea had begun with his own published report of 1603 on what lay beyond the Great Rapid.

Based in part on the evidence Champlain brought back from the St. Lawrence, the Sieur de Monts—who stepped to the fore when he learned de Chaste had died—was granted a ten-year monopoly on trade between latitudes 46 and 40. The territory included the height of navigation at the Great Rapid and continued unabated into the interior. If Champlain were correct about the nature of the passage, de Monts would also control the transcontinental route to the Pacific. De Monts was also granted exclusive right to the river's longstanding trading site of Tadoussac, which was above latitude 48. On the Atlantic coast, the latitude limits meant the monopoly ran from Cape Breton south, beyond Cape Cod.

Having secured the right to exploit the purported route to the Orient beyond the rapids, the Sieur de Monts had proceeded to do nothing with it, moving his base of operations to the Atlantic coast from 1604 to 1607, more than likely to follow the published advice set down by Edward Hayes for locating a colony and searching for the midcontinental passage.

Champlain had argued in *Des Sauvages,* in purely Hayesean terms, that the headwaters of a river on that coast would come close to the transcontinental passage he argued lay upstream of the Great Rapid. A portage could provide the connection, and the Great Rapid be avoided altogether. "One would accomplish a great good by discovering, on the coast of Florida [i.e., the Atlantic coast] some passage running near the great lake before referred to, where the water is salt: not only on account of the navigation of vessels, which would not then be exposed to so great risks as in going by way of Canada, but also on account of the shortening of the distance by more than three hundred leagues. And it is certain that there are rivers on the coast of Florida, not yet discovered, extending into the interior, where the land is very good and fertile, and containing very good harbours."

Champlain went along with de Monts in 1604, still at the beck and call of his king, and spent four summers charting the Atlantic shore, searching in vain for the river that would lead deep into the continent, toward his passage above the Great Rapid. The English had their own designs on establishing a colony in Norumbega, which would become New England. It was a minor miracle that in four years of exploration, Champlain never actually encountered an English rival on the compact length of coast he was charting between Cape Cod and the Bay of Fundy, although he came within perhaps a half-day's sail of encountering George Waymouth in 1605. Learning from a Pemaquid chief in the vicinity of the Georges River of a recent visit by an English ship, Champlain never appreciated that it was Waymouth he very nearly met.

In 1607, Henry IV abruptly cancelled de Monts' monopoly, bowing to pressure from merchants in St-Malo and the French Basque region. Champlain then shifted his attention back toward the Great Rapid, as de Monts moved his base of operations to the St. Lawrence to take advantage of a one-year monopoly extension from Henry. De Monts made Champlain his lieutenant, granting him his first formal role in a trade venture in New France. If Champlain was going to properly investigate a midcontinental route now, he would have to overcome the Great Rapid. But in the ensuing years, Champlain managed to get no farther beyond the whitewater than a single visit upstream to Lac des Deux-Montagnes.

Nine years after first seeing the Great Rapid, Champlain set himself to producing an ambitious map of New France. Drawn in 1612, the map was not without its problems, but it was still far better than anything then in circulation. He described northeastern North America between about latitudes 38 and 56, from around Cape Cod northward to right about where John Knight had vanished on the Labrador shore, and then westward, well beyond the Great Rapid. The map was most interesting where it was most confused: in Champlain's interpretation of what lay upstream of the Great Rapid. One third of the width of the map was given over to lands and waters he had never seen.

To draw the world that dominated the left-hand third of his map, he relied on anecdotal evidence from natives and their sketches. Champlain showed the Ottawa and the upper St. Lawrence beyond the rapids almost as one waterway, interwoven through a series of islands. There was a best guess as to the shape and length of Lake Ontario, and then beyond it, connected by a narrow, winding strait, a *grand lac,* a great lake, whose full dimensions he could not possibly show.

The lands not yet visited by Champlain were decorated by his engraver, David Pelletier, with a veritable wallpaper of plump deciduous trees, some organized into neat, rectangular forests of military precision on a landscape as flat as a billiard table. There was no sense of the wildness of this place, of the rock and pine and cascading rivers of the Laurentian Shield. The map had nothing to say at all about the geography farther north. Champlain did not permit himself to fantasize about the Septentrional lands depicted by Mercator, or to propose (as other cartographers had) that the Labrador shore was the Estotiland of the Zeno brothers. He understood that somewhere above the St. Lawrence system there was a northern sea, but he refrained from any visual speculation about how far north this shore might be in latitude or leagues. It was geography well beyond Champlain's experience and comprehension, and of no interest to the 1612 map's intended user, a mariner approaching New France from the Atlantic.

But the title description of Hessel Gerritsz's map of 1612, indicating that it showed Henry Hudson's discoveries to the northwest, "suprum Nova Franciam"—above New France—demanded Champlain's personal attention. The Gerritsz map happened to expand the most authoritative portrait of the northeastern part of the continent: the new image of New France that Champlain himself had only just completed. Where Champlain cropped the view at the top of his New France map was where the lower latitudes of Gerritsz's amazing hemispheric sweep began.

Merging the two maps on a single sheet of paper would have challenged a skilled geographer like Hessel Gerritsz, let alone someone like Champlain. Champlain's skills were so elemental that for basic calculations like multiplication and division he turned to printed tables. He knew nothing of spherical trigonometry, the higher mathematics that the leading men of navigation and cartography in England and the Low Countries insisted were necessary not only for mapmakers in transferring the details of a spheroid planet to a two-dimensional surface but also for pilots engaged in exploration who hoped to accurately record where they had been.

However limited his formal education, Champlain had a genuine talent for quickly grasping the sense of a place, and he managed to accomplish a remarkable amount with very basic skills. His noon sun sights produced latitude readings that were consistently accurate to a quarter degree or better, which was very good for his day, and through elementary triangulation and by estimating distances using dead reckoning, he managed to capture credible two-dimensional portraits of harbours and coastlines.

We can well imagine him puzzling through the decisions that would have taxed a far better trained man. Champlain's New France map was oriented to magnetic north, to satisfy old-fashioned navigators, Gerritsz's to true, or geographic, north. They used different schemes for marking out longitude on the earth's surface, and entirely different projections were employed to depict a spherical surface as a two-dimensional plane. But with care, and some fudging, Champlain could meet these challenges. Even crudely pieced together (and in many ways, Champlain's merger was crude), the two maps could create a comprehensive new view of eastern North America, from Cape Cod all the way north, above the Arctic Circle and beyond latitude 69, into Davis Strait. And once this view was in hand, hitherto unimagined opportunities leapt from the paper.

A trail of English placenames on the Gerritsz map, reshaped by a Dutchman's engraving tool, illuminated Henry Hudson's progress into the unknown, beyond the Furious Overfall: Hold with Hoope, Prince Henry, The Kinges Forlant, Quine Anne's Forlandt, C. Charles, C. Worsnam, Salisberis Islandt, Diges Islandt. Champlain took careful note and transferred a few of them faithfully to his new, merged map.

There were no placenames at all on Gerritsz's map beyond Diges Islandt, where Hudson steered into the great bay from which he would not emerge. The naming of landmarks coincidentally ended at the geographic spot where Hudson's journal entries ceased, on August 3, 1610, in the abstract that would finally be published by Samuel Purchas in 1625. The bay itself remained unnamed. Only at the bay's most southern end did the placenames resume, with a single notation: the supplication of "The Bay of gods merces." Nearby was an inscription, referring to an unmarked haven around latitude 52: "The bay wher Hudson did winter." Champlain transferred this last inscription to his new map, preserving the misspelling of *where* in Gerritsz's engraving.

The Gerritsz map could only hint at the narrative of the voyage, but it described an enormous quantity of new geography. The contours indicated that Martin Frobisher had been wrong to call the waters beyond the Furious Overfall the "Mistaken Strait." Far from being a dead end, the strait led not only to the great bay that would also come to bear Hudson's name but to a promise of open water to the north and west of the Digges Islands, labelled Mare Magnum, where a passage through to the Orient might be awaiting discovery.

Gerritsz's map also revealed something that perhaps only Champlain could appreciate. The Bay of God's Mercies, at the southernmost point of Hudson's explorations, was drawn so that it pressed into the lower margin of the chart, at latitude 50. The possibility of a water route south remained in the eye of the beholder. Champlain knew that the Bay of God's Mercies was less than four degrees of latitude north of the Great Rapid. He also knew of several rivers that flowed down to the St. Lawrence from the bay's general direction. One of them was the Ottawa, the very waterway Nicolas de Vignau had just reported to have followed en route to the Northern Sea and the wreckage of an English vessel.

Twenty-two

—

Nicolas de Vignau provided Champlain with a written description of the country he had seen on the way to the Northern Sea, as well as a map. Champlain weighed this evidence carefully, along with what de Vignau had already told him about the wreckage of an English vessel and the other details of the journey, and measured it all against what he had been able to learn from the Hessel Gerritsz book of Henry Hudson's disappearance.

The wreckage, the massacre of survivors, the close proximity of the Northern Sea to the Great Rapid indicated by the merger of Champlain's and Gerritsz's cartography . . . the facts in de Vignau's account were all consistent with what Gerritsz had just produced. Having been informed by de Vignau that the Nebicerini wished to make a gift of an English boy to him, Champlain would have been even more impressed had Gerritsz known and explained that one of the passengers in the shallop cast away by the *Discovery's* mutineers was in fact an English boy: John Hudson.

Champlain realized that there was enough to take to Fontainebleau. Although his new map, which merged the Gerritsz map and his recent one of New France, would not be published until 1613, it was now probably worked up in at least sketch form to illustrate the opportunity at hand. He might, at last, have the basis to be rewarded a new monopoly on the fur trade in New France, which he could use to entice investors to fund an expedition to the Nebicerini and on to the Northern Sea.

Even so, Champlain was too experienced a leader not to appreciate the basic tenet of command: *Never turn your back on your own men.* And he was caught in a strange role reversal with Nicolas de Vignau. In electing to follow the young man into the wilderness beyond the Great Rapid, it would be de Vignau's back that Champlain would be watching, placing absolute trust in his guidance. Not only Champlain's reputation but also his life would depend on this interpreter's competence.

Champlain would relate that he delivered a stern warning to de Vignau as he prepared to visit Fontainebleau around September 1612. If what de Vignau was telling him was true, he could be certain of being well rewarded. But if the youth were lying, he would be placing a noose around his own neck.

De Vignau swore, with stronger oaths than he had yet used, that he was telling Champlain the truth. With that, Champlain made for the royal court bearing his dossier of evidence.

There had been a significant change in power at Fontainebleau since Champlain's career in New France began with the 1603 assignment. Henry IV had been stabbed to death by a deranged priest, François Ravaillac, while riding through Paris in an open carriage in May 1610. Ravaillac's execution rivalled anything in the tortures practised on prisoners of war by Champlain's native allies. The arm that wielded the knife was severed, Ravaillac was doused in boiling oil, and teams of horses attached to the remaining limbs provided the *coup de grâce* by pulling him to pieces. A Paris mob spirited away his remains before authorities could gather and incinerate them.

Henry's patronage had not always been favourable to Champlain; the king had deflected Champlain's overtures for an additional one-year extension to the de Monts monopoly in October 1609. But his assassination brought an end to a long association for Champlain with the most powerful man in France. The crown shifted to his son, the dauphin Louis XIII, who was not yet eleven when Champlain brought de Vignau's news to Fontainebleau. Power resided in the regent, Henry's widow, Marie de Medici.

Most likely Champlain did not meet with either the young Louis or the regent. Rather, he presented his evidence to the court's senior members. He would later drop three prominent names. The first was the grand chancellor, Nicholas Brulart de Sillery, who had negotiated the Treaty of Vervins with Spain in 1598. The second was Charles de Cosse-Brissac, marshal of France, under whom Champlain had served in the 1590s, and who apparently had arranged for the *Saint-Julien,* a ship partly owned by Champlain's uncle, Guillaume Allène, to be chartered for the Spanish evacuation flotilla at Blavet in Brittany after the peace was signed at Vervins. By joining his uncle aboard the *Saint-Julien,* Champlain was able to reach Spain and to then infiltrate the Spanish Caribbean, when the ship was further hired in 1599 for a supply armada to Puerto Rico and Cuba. The third was Pierre Jeannin, a longstanding associate of the late Henry, now president of the *parlement* of Paris and Louis XIII's superintendent of finance.

Champlain considered Jeannin an ally: the statesman and diplomat believed in the cause of France developing an overseas colony, in the manner of England and Spain. It was assuredly Champlain who personally brought the Gerritsz book to the attention of the French court. Jeannin would have been most persuaded by the fresh evidence in Champlain's hands that New France was in danger of being squeezed out of existence in a pincer movement from the north and south.

Gerritsz confirmed that Hudson had explored the Atlantic coast for the Dutch in 1609, which may have been old news to the French, for independent Dutch traders had begun making follow-up voyages to the east coast and the Hudson River in 1610. Word of Hudson's 1609 discoveries and these subsequent voyages would have travelled quickly, for the Dutch already played a leading role in Champlain's world, as financiers and insurers of French merchant ventures.

The Gerritsz book did reveal that, at the time of publication, the Dutch were completing a two-ship expedition under Jan Cornelisz May. It was an epic recreation of Hudson's 1607, 1608, and 1609 voyages, taking in Spitsbergen, Novaya Zemlya, and eastern North America. The first ship, the *Craen,* had returned on July 6, 1612, and Gerritsz noted that the May expedition had done some trading with natives somewhere in "New France," probably on the Norumbega coast, before overwintering in the vicinity of Cape Cod.

Gerritsz's information on Hudson's *Discovery* voyage, above all the map, showed how Hudson's passage search had opened a back door into the lands the French claimed along the St. Lawrence. That alone should have caused sufficient alarm at Fontainebleau, but Gerritsz heightened the anxiety by making it clear that this too was a frontier of exploration in which the Dutch might engage, and by reporting that the English were already sailing in Hudson's wake: "This summer there have again been expedited thither, by authority of the King and the Prince of Wales, vessels to discover the passage further, and to search out Mr. Hudson and his friends." If the passage were found, two of the ships were to sail on into it, while the third was to return home "with the tidings we expect."

Gerritsz's information was excellent. There were two proper ships in the expedition, which had departed London in April 1612:

the *Resolution,* under the command of expedition leader Thomas Button, and Hudson's own refurbished *Discovery.* The third vessel, a knocked-down pinnace, was expected to return with a progress report. In August 1612, probably around the time Champlain was digesting the contents of Gerritsz's book, Button was choosing an overwintering site on the west coast of Hudson Bay, at the mouth of the Nelson River. The English were searching for a passage westward, out of the Northern Sea, while Champlain was planning his own search for a route into it, from below. And if Button truly was seeking "Mr. Hudson and his friends," Champlain could be confident he wasn't going to find any of them. The Nebicerini had their scalps, and the boy.

As Champlain would recount, the seigneurs at Fontainebleau responded to his evidence for a route beyond the Great Rapid to the Northern Sea by proposing that he "ought to visit the place in person." De Vignau's report (no copy of which has ever been seen) would have held out the possibility of a French trade route to the Northern Sea: up the St. Lawrence, inland along the Ottawa, through a lake (as the interpreter explained to Champlain), and on up to the ocean. It was possible that the French could establish a port on the south shore of the bay, and from there dispatch ships to the Northwest Passage. Reaching the Pacific, and the Orient's wealth, might only require a short sail to the west, around latitude 63, through the Mare Magnum of Gerritsz's chart.

But none of it would be possible if Champlain could not first secure the cooperation of Tessöuat. Nine years had passed since he had first encountered the chief of the Algonquin's Kichesipirini people. The meeting was unforgettable, and Tessöuat's stature in Champlain's world had only increased since then.

Champlain had arrived at Tadoussac on his first visit to the St. Lawrence on May 24, 1603. The *sauvages*—Maliséet, Montagnais, and Algonquin—appeared three days later in a fleet of canoes several hundred strong, following a great victory over the Iroquois. They had slain one hundred, and the warriors and their families gathered at the mouth of the Saguenay to celebrate, before trading began.

At first they camped a few miles away, along the St. Lawrence at Pointe aux Vaches, but after a welcoming visit from the French, they broke camp with astonishing speed and built a new sprawl of bark-covered wigwams, each nation keeping to its own compound, at Tadoussac's harbour. Their shelters intrigued Champlain: inside the wigwams he found upwards of ten families sleeping around fires whose smoke escaped through a gap at the peak. "They sleep on skins all together, and their dogs with them," he related in *Des Sauvages*.

"All these people have a very cheerful disposition, laughing often," he reported, "yet at the same time they are somewhat phlegmatic. They talk very deliberately, as if desiring to make themselves well understood, and stopping suddenly, they reflect for a long time, when they resume their discourse. This is their usual manner at their harangues in council, where only the leading men, the elders, are present, the women and children not attending at all."

He appreciated the precariousness of their lives, the threat of freezing and starvation in winter. He supposed that cannibalism could never be far away, but he never suggested they were any more predisposed to it than shipwrecked Frenchmen. Their eating methods he could scarcely tolerate. Meat was retrieved from the boiling water of a cauldron and distributed on serving platters made of bark. They removed grease from their hands, he wrote, by wiping them on their hair, or on their dogs.

Champlain had little to say about the physical appearance of these people. In 1626, Charles Lalement, superior of the new Jesuit mission in Canada, would write from Quebec to his brother, Father Jérôme, explaining how the faces of native men "are usually painted red or grayish brown, and this is done in different styles, according to the fancy of the women, who paint their husbands and children, whose hair they also oil with bear or moose grease." In 1632, Paul le Jeune would arrive at Tadoussac en route to taking command of the Jesuit mission, soon after another successful campaign had been concluded against the Iroquois. A chief and ten or twelve companions came aboard his ship to visit. Le Jeune did not know their particular tribe, but the first impression they delivered was, to say the least, striking. "When I saw them enter our Captain's room, where I happened to be, it seemed to me that I was looking at those maskers who run about France in Carnival time. There were some whose noses were painted blue, the eyes, eyebrows, and cheeks painted black, and the rest of the face red; and these colours are bright and shining like those of our masks; others had black, red, and blue stripes drawn from the ears to the mouth. Still others were entirely black, except the upper part of the brow and around the ears, and the end of the chin; so that it might have been truly said of them that they were masquerading. There were some who had only one black stripe, like a wide ribbon, drawn from one ear to the other, across the eyes, and three little stripes on the cheeks."

Champlain noted that there had been a *tabagie,* a celebratory feast that included a ceremonial smoking of tobacco, among the gathered tribes on June 8, and on the ninth, Tessöuat assembled his people in the public area of the great camp. The chief planted two poles with suspended Iroquois heads, and gathered alongside him his men, with their wives and daughters arranged before them.

The men sang and performed a dance. The wives and daughters then suddenly disrobed. But for necklaces of beads and porcupine quills, they were completely naked. Champlain could not help but take note of their exposed genitals. They too now sang and danced before reclaiming their robes. Then the robes came off again, and the performance resumed. "They do not stir from their position while dancing, and make various gestures and movements of the body, lifting one foot and then the other, at the same time striking upon the ground," Champlain explained.

In the midst of their performance, Tessöuat addressed the Maliséet and Montagnais who had gathered to watch. Someone translated the formal "harangue" for Champlain: "Look! How we rejoice in the victory that we have obtained over our enemies. You must do the same, so that we may be satisfied." And everyone assembled began to chant in agreement: "Ho . . . ho . . . ho . . ."

Tessöuat and the other Algonquin men returned to their stations behind their women, stripping naked as well, but for a small flap of hide over their genitals. It seems that they had symbolically shorn themselves of possessions, and now waited for tribute from their allies.

It came in many forms: the necklaces Champlain called *matachiats,* the meat and fat of elk and seal, and valuable trade goods like iron kettles, hatchets, and swords. The Algonquin helped themselves to what most interested them and carried it off to their camp.

Champlain had probably witnessed one ceremony among several, as the peace treaties between the participating nations enjoyed an annual renewal with exchanges of gifts. But the particular ability of the Algonquin to command such tribute must have been a revelation. A few days earlier, the French had devoted their diplomatic energies to the Montagnais. Champlain, Pont-Gravé, and de Monts had made a great ceremony of returning to them two of their young men who had visited

France, and had joined their chief, Anadabijou, and as many as one hundred of his men for a feast. A few days later, Champlain then watched as those Montagnais, as well as the Maliséet, obligingly surrendered tribute to the Algonquin.

Champlain would come to understand that Tessöuat's power extended beyond his ability to field warriors against the Iroquois. It would be impossible to explore the interior without his cooperation. Champlain did not have the men on the ground, the force of arms, or the desire to bully his way inland, the way Hernando de Soto had carved a swath of pillage across the southeastern United States in the mid-sixteenth century with a Spanish army that consumed whole villages. Even when he was exploring at his greatest strength, on the Atlantic coast between 1604 and 1607, Champlain never had more than a few dozen men in support. Once Champlain had moved his theatre of operations back the St. Lawrence in 1608, he was entirely dependent on the goodwill of the native traders to permit him any glimpse of the territories beyond the Great Rapid.

As he prepared for a 1613 return to New France with de Vignau, Champlain had still not been more than a few miles beyond the Great Rapid. The Algonquin and Huron emerged as if from behind a primeval curtain, shooting the whitewater in their ingenious little boats. They made personal gifts of pelts to Champlain, fought alongside him, pledged their friendship, then took up their paddles, their prisoners of war, and any trade goods they had gathered from the clamouring merchant vessels and melted back into the wallpaper-pattern forests of Champlain's cartography.

The Algonquin protected their middlemen role in the fur trade of the Great Lakes basin (and beyond) as jealously as did the Montagnais on the routes north from the St. Lawrence. It was not in their best interest to allow the French to bypass them and establish direct relations with the nations deeper inland.

Some relationship between the French and the more distant and powerful Huron was inevitable: the Algonquin needed them as military allies against the Iroquois. But Tessöuat still controlled the traffic on the river at the strategic position of his summer village. The chokepoint defined his tribe: their name, Kichesipirini, meant "people of the island," and the French accordingly would call them the *Nation d'Isle*. Tessöuat could allow war parties of allies to come and go, but demand steep tribute from the trading canoes of those allies.

How he would react to a reappearance of Champlain was difficult to predict. Champlain must have been assured by de Vignau that Tessöuat would receive him warmly, even though he had not lived up to his promise to go to war with the Algonquin in 1611 and 1612. If there was in fact lingering displeasure with Champlain's failure to keep his word, Tessöuat might now be cool to help him in any way. Even if all were well, Tessöuat could decide that allowing Champlain to travel beyond his river chokepoint, to make direct contact with other peoples, particularly the Nebicerini, was not, at this time, in his people's best interest. And Champlain first had to reach him. Several other Algonquin tribes, who lived farther downriver, were in the way. Their disenchantment over Champlain's failure to go to war with them, already expressed in the abrupt return of interpreter-trainees in 1611, could deny him the assistance he needed just to reach Tessöuat's village.

And if Champlain did manage to get to the village, what did he expect to tell Tessöuat about his failures to go to war, and how did he intend to explain his current ambitions? He clearly understood from de Vignau that the less he said to Tessöuat about his desire to collect the gift of an English boy from the Nebicerini and visit the Northern Sea with them, the better. Champlain's only recourse would be to lie about his earlier absences, and about where he was now going, and why. Who could say what might happen to Champlain's party if he were caught in such lies, far in the interior, far from the aid of any other Frenchmen.

The essential hazards of the journey encouraged a persistent doubt in Champlain as to why de Vignau was so willing to take the associated risks. He had questioned the young interpreter enough, and decided to place de Vignau aboard a ship of a trusted associate, the merchant Samuel Georges of La Rochelle, who had participated in de Monts' earlier monopolies. Georges could transport de Vignau to La Rochelle and chat him up along the way.

There was more to this arranged voyage than Champlain admitted. Samuel Georges and his brother-in-law, Jean Macain, were critical participants in the fur trade. They had held a forty percent interest in the Sieur de Monts' company during the monopoly years, and after de Monts' Rouen partners decided they wanted out in 1611, the pair began leasing the Quebec habitation from him. They were also important financiers for the Sieur de Poutrincourt's revival of the Port Royal settlement in the Annapolis Basin on the Bay of Fundy, abandoned by de Monts in 1607, securing from him exclusive rights to the furs of Acadia. If Champlain were planning to secure a new trade monopoly on the St. Lawrence, he would inevitably invite the participation of the Georges-Macain alliance. And that alliance would wish to satisfy themselves that de Vignau was trustworthy before agreeing to back a journey by Champlain to the Northern Sea as part of the bargain.

According to Champlain, de Vignau told Georges that he didn't expect any reward from anyone except the king, and presumably only if the journey were a success. He told the merchant that he wished to make the voyage so that Champlain could see the Northern Sea, as he had. De Vignau swore out an affidavit to this fact at La Rochelle for Georges, in the presence of two notaries.

The young man had been pestered enough. It was time to build a new monopoly from his report and mount the expedition beyond the rapids. But regardless how sweeping a privilege Champlain might secure from Fontainebleau, and how many merchants he could attract with it, the success or failure of Champlain, de Vignau, and their companions would depend almost entirely on Tessöuat and the Algonquin peoples. And Champlain's faith in them was less than absolute.

"I believe that if one were to teach them how to live, and instruct them in the cultivation of the soil and in other respects," Champlain had proposed in *Des Sauvages* of the tribes he had first met at Tadoussac, "they would learn very easily, for I can testify that many of them have good judgment and respond very appropriately to whatever question may be put to them. They have the vices of taking revenge and of lying badly, and are people in whom it is not well to put much confidence, except with caution and with force at hand. They promise well, but keep their word badly."

Twenty-three

—

IN THE AUTUMN OF 1612, Samuel de Champlain turned Nicolas de Vignau's report into a new shelter from the vicissitudes of the free-market system by arranging another trade monopoly under a powerful protector. He had been a military and political ally, as well as a first cousin, of the late Henry IV: the governor of Normandy, Charles de Bourbon, Comte de Soissons. Approached by Champlain through one of the king's councillors to front the venture, the count agreed to serve as Champlain's protector. Champlain prepared the necessary paperwork on the count's behalf, including the petition to be presented at Fontainebleau. Named lieutenant-general of the territory in late September, the count in turn made Champlain his lieutenant.

Champlain was preparing to have notices of the monopoly posted in French ports when he suffered an abrupt setback. An unspecified illness—it was probably smallpox—was sweeping the country and claimed the count. Champlain quickly had a replacement benefactor lined up: the dead count's twenty-four-year-old nephew, Henri de Bourbon II, Prince de Condé, who was a second cousin of the dauphin, Louis XIII.

The letters patent spelling out the monopoly issued to the prince on November 13 granted him exclusive trade and mining rights on the St. Lawrence and its tributaries for twelve long years, making special mention of the trading posts at Tadoussac and Quebec. It called upon him to spread the Roman Catholic faith among the local people, proceed with colonization, and discover the "easiest route for reaching China" by the rivers and lands of his new domain, "with the assistance of the inhabitants of these lands." On the same day, a notice was prepared for the admiralty officers in the coastal provinces of Normandy, Brittany, Picardy, and Guyenne (of which the prince was governor), warning off any independent traders who thought they might infringe on the prince's new rights.

In late 1612 or early 1613, the merchants of St-Malo issued a vituperative response, which might have been expected from a group of people who had just seen their livelihoods cut off at the knees. They were also still embroiled in legal action with the Sieur de Monts. Henry IV had decreed that de Monts be compensated 6,000 livres by merchants who benefited from the earlier termination of his monopoly, but left it entirely up to him to figure out how to get the money out of them. Although it was unsigned, the published factum from St-Malo must have represented opinions of de Monts' former partners. They took direct aim at Champlain in a scathing objection to his newly won privileges, considering the prince a mere front for a favour bestowed upon the former lieutenant of de Monts. The Malouins all but branded Champlain a liar and a parasite.

The factum began with a withering critique of the previous monopoly of de Monts, alleging he had lost close to 50,000 écus through various misadventures and disadvantages, and that the late king had then properly opened trade. Unrestricted trade was pursued (and, it went without saying, cultivated) by the merchants of St-Malo and other parts of France until Champlain secured the latest monopoly. To this trade, the Malouins charged,

Champlain and his "so-called partners have not contributed a single denier." They compared Champlain to a stowaway, literally someone taking a free ride on their endeavours, and dismissed him as a mere "painter"—*peintre* being a profession that encompassed mapmaking. Champlain, they fumed, had been tempted by the "lucre" of seeing the said lands, "always with the help of the companies he led there, from which he on every occasion drew a grand salary, which he cannot deny."

The Malouins scorned any idea that Champlain could claim credit for having discovered the lands for which he now enjoyed the exclusive right to exploit. The Normans and Bretons had discovered and fished these waters since 1505, they argued. And already, Sebastian Cabot had discovered part of it for the king of England in 1507, and Gaspar Cortereál had found the rest for Portugal, in resolving to prove a passage to China or the Moluccas. But as an atlas, or supplement, to Ptolemy, published at Douai in 1603 indicated to the Malouins, such a passage search was in vain.

The Malouins were especially galled by Champlain's assertions of trailblazing discovery made in *Des Sauvages*. They heralded the achievements of their local hero, Jacques Cartier, who at his own expense and risk to his life, they asserted, and under the authority of the king of France, penetrated the St. Lawrence beyond Quebec and Lac St-Pierre. And after him, for thirty-five years or so, they argued, many Normans, Basques, and Bretons, along with the Sieurs de Pont-Gravé and Prévert, as well as the Basque captain Fabien de Meriscoiena (who records show was hired by de Monts to fish and hunt whales and trade in Canada in 1605), had been trading at Lac St-Pierre and beyond with the *sauvages*. And when, "ten or twelve years ago," Champlain was taken to the main rapids by a Malouin, Pont-Gravé, he found himself among "an infinity of people from all regions of France, as many as nine or ten barks, all gathered and bargaining in this place." One could find ample testimony, the Malouins argued, that this place at the time of Champlain's 1603 visit was already discovered and being frequented by others: evidence enough to revoke his present commission.

And how had Champlain managed to secure the precious Canada trade with this new monopoly? By making his ridiculous claims about a route to the Orient awaiting discovery beyond the Great Rapid.

They belittled his evidence for such a passage. Referring to alleged claims by Champlain that he had discovered "four or five hundred leagues" into the country, "the truth," they stated, was that in 1610, Champlain had sent a "boy" away with the *sauvages*. This was the interpreter-scout Étienne Brûlé, the first youth Champlain had sent to live among native allies. And this boy, the Malouins argued, did not report to Champlain anything "worthy of recollection or of enterprise."

Furthermore, Champlain was not the only person who had arranged for young men to live with the natives. Rouen interests, they noted, had also sent in a servant who had returned to France in 1612. He was a youth remembered through Champlain's writings only as Thomas, who was employed by the Rouen merchant and Champlain associate Daniel Boyer. When Thomas returned, the Malouins stated, he reported only on the "misery of the said country," the rapids and falls on the entire river he travelled. This river, the Malouins had gathered, was navigable "only by small bark canoes capable of carrying only three or four people." Lest anyone think that ships could reach the Orient by this route, the Malouins described how at the rapids one must, on foot, "carry on the shoulders the said canoes a long way in the woods." In this way, one was supposed to "traverse about three or four hundred leagues of route, with labour intenable for the French, without having seen other discoveries of merit."

As for the factual promises that Champlain said had been made to him by the *sauvages,* that in four days they could reach the Southern Ocean, about four hundred leagues distant, in order to then reach China, the Malouins argued "one could legitimately demand assurance from the said Champlain of the validity of such promises made by miscreants and infidels."

There were more words to this effect, all of them contemptuous, all of them resentful of Champlain's having made off with an exclusive right to the Canada trade for a dozen years. "For the execution of the plan proposed and researched for ten years," Champlain would "engage and exhaust the treasury of a monarch," depending on royal altruism "to acquire some vainglory" by "penetrating a desert eight hundred leagues," while taking care not to risk "a single denier" of his own.

The Malouins, in their attack on Champlain's passage-making ambitions, relied overwhelmingly on the evidence and arguments he had presented in *Des Sauvages.* And while they also knew about the hinterland travels of Brûlé and of the youth named Thomas, they were completely in the dark about de Vignau, and where the evidence he had returned with was actually leading Champlain in 1613.

Champlain had an ideal platform for rebutting the Malouin allegations: his manuscript for *Les Voyages.* On January 9, 1613, the Paris printer and bookseller Jean Berjon (doing business out of his shop, the Cheval volant, or Flying Horse) received the licence from Fontainebleau to publish it. Champlain may have included the diatribe against the merchants of St-Malo that appeared in its final pages as a last-minute rebuttal to the factum. But the main manuscript was probably completed by late summer 1612, as he had made no mention of the news from de Vignau or the new monopoly secured through the Prince de Condé. Even without an addition directly addressing the factum, the narrative, while undeniably self-serving, painted a harsh portrait of independent merchants like the Malouins who had been operating on the St. Lawrence without restraint since the de Monts monopoly expired for good in 1609.

Of the Malouins, Champlain complained in the concluding words of *Les Voyages* that "all they want is that men should expose themselves to a thousand dangers, to discover peoples and territories, that they themselves may have the profit and others the hardship. It is not reasonable that one should capture the lamb and another go off with the fleece. If they had been willing to participate in our discoveries, use their means, and risk their persons, they would have given evidence of their honor and nobleness, but on the contrary they show clearly that they are impelled by pure malice that they may enjoy the fruit of our labors equally with ourselves." And on his last visit to the rapids, in 1611, Champlain wrote that he found the Huron fearful of the traders who had massed there. The natives complained to him of maltreatment, including beatings, and Champlain had to explain to them that these brutal men had nothing to do with him.

Champlain's countercharges about abusive behaviour were probably true, as he took care in the agreement he would shortly draw up with his commercial partners to insist that the traders behave in a Christian manner in their dealings with the native peoples. Still, the factum was more than a little true where it charged that Champlain persisted in denying Jacques Cartier proper credit for his discoveries, which was key to their claim that Champlain had no right to monopolize the river's trade. He stubbornly insisted in *Les Voyages* that Cartier had never been beyond Trois-Rivières, downstream from Lac St-Pierre, which was some ninety miles shy of the Great Rapid.

While Malouin agitation threatened his monopoly, Champlain rushed to round up the necessary participating merchants and their capital in order to exploit its privileges. To lose the monopoly now would mean the loss of Champlain's main chance in life. Lost as well would be any hope of a Frenchman being bold enough to attempt to reach the Northern Sea by travelling up the Ottawa River, and of collecting an English boy from the Nebicerini.

On January 16, Champlain met with the La Rochelle merchant Mathieu Georges—Samuel's nephew—in the presence of two Paris notaries, Germain Tronson and his stepson, Claude Dauvergne. They might have gathered at Champlain's residence on rue Terravoche, a few blocks from the Seine and Île-de-la-Cité in the first arrondissement, the oldest part of Paris. They worked out an initial accord for a partnership to consist of merchants from La Rochelle and Rouen. A more elaborate agreement followed on February 5. Again Tronson and Dauvergne managed the paperwork, while Daniel Boyer now joined Champlain and Georges as a signatory, on behalf of the Rouen participants. The Malouins, not surprisingly, were nowhere to be seen—and Pont-Gravé by now had moved his base of operations to Normandy, commanding ships out of Dieppe and Honfleur.

The initial accord had imagined an enterprise with two ships, one from La Rochelle, the other from Rouen, each of 120 tons. The second agreement spelled out a four-ship operation—three from Rouen, one from La Rochelle. Champlain handed over passports for each ship from the Prince de Condé, authorizing trade in the monopoly territory. Two thirds of the company's profits would go to the Rouen participants, one third to the Rochelais, and the prince would cream off five percent of the net proceeds. Other traders could be accommodated with additional passports signed by the prince and issued by the partners.

The Rouennaise members were well established in Champlain's world, and drew on the ranks of expatriate merchants and financiers of the Low Countries. The largest Rouen ship, of one hundred tons, would be provided by the Sieur de Monts in association with the Rouen-based Fleming merchant Ludowica Vermeulen, who had already done business with Pont-Gravé in a 1611 fur-trading voyage that had been Dutch in all but name. Boyer agreed to provide a vessel of eighty-five tons, in association with his niece's husband, the transplanted Dutch merchant Corneille de Bellois. And the third Rouen ship, of forty-five tons, would come from Lucas Legendre, who had been involved with the earlier de Monts monopoly as well as in leasing the Quebec habitation. An unnamed group of Rochelais merchants would provide the single largest ship, of 120 tons.

Champlain's money men assuredly were less enamoured with finding a passage to China or a missing English boy than he was. Control of the fur supply was what they desired; a search for a route to the Orient was to them probably window dressing to justify the cartel's existence. Champlain settled for terms less favourable than in the initial agreement, which had called for up to thirty men to be placed at his disposal, presumably for exploration and waging war alongside native allies. The merchants in the February 5 partnership agreed to provide Champlain with only four men from each ship, for a possible total of sixteen, to explore beyond the Great Rapid, and only after trading was concluded with the Algonquin. And he was to strive to be back with them at Tadoussac by August 20 so that pelts could be shipped to France without undue delay.

Champlain's most important companions would be his own servant, Nicolas de Vignau, and the youth named Thomas. Champlain also fully expected to go to war alongside the Algonquin and Huron, to make amends for his absences in 1611 and 1612. To that end he invited along a nobleman adventurer, the Sieur de L'Ange, who was denied any financial interest under the February 5 agreement.

If the Malouins required further evidence of Champlain's

propensity for mounting expeditions "always at the expense of the companies which he led, from which he on every occasion drew a grand salary," they would have found it in the terms of the new agreement. Champlain was promised, on his return to Honfleur at the end of the expedition, eight hundred livres. The fee was meant to "give courage" to him, and to ensure that he would "behave virtuously" and have the "means as well to maintain himself during said voyage." By way of comparison, in 1604 de Monts hired a pilot to serve him in Acadia for sixty livres, and a surgeon and two sailors for twenty-four livres each.

There was an aggravating last-minute legal distraction: on February 9, the *parlement,* or parliamentary court, at Rouen recognized a petition by Malouin merchants and citizens opposing the Prince de Condé's monopoly. The power of this court (also known as the *parlement* of Normandy), was exceeded only by that of the *parlement* of Paris and of the crown. The Malouin action meant that Champlain could not get his commission published in the ports of Normandy, or in St-Malo. "This greatly embarrassed me," Champlain would write, "and obliged me to make three journeys to Rouen, with orders of his Majesty, in consideration of which the Court desisted from their inhibition, and the assumptions of the opponents were overruled."

Only on March 4 did the Rouen *parlement* order the monopoly's letters patent registered. According to Champlain, the Malouins simply were told that they were free to join the trade company he had formed under the monopoly. Champlain scarcely had time to publish his commission in the outstanding French ports, including St-Malo, before departing Honfleur on March 6 with Pont-Gravé, who was probably commanding the Rouen ship of de Monts and Vermeulen.

Champlain was moving at breakneck speed. The February 5 agreement had promised to produce the names of the La Rochelle participants in nine or ten days, but no list would survive. Since Champlain would write that signatory Mathieu Georges' uncle, Samuel, had de Vignau swear out an affidavit at La Rochelle, Samuel Georges more than likely planned to be involved that season with his regular partner, Jean Macain. Nevertheless, the four-ship venture was described as "hors ceste année presente"—"except for" or "beyond" the present year. The plan was the ideal configuration, but the principals telling Tronson and Dauvergne what to write down were unsure whether Rochelais interests would be able to sail that spring. A paragraph was needed to address the thorny problem of how to divvy the proceeds should a large Rochelais vessel not materialize for 1613.

Champlain, who would be travelling with Pont-Gravé, had to get to Tadoussac without delay, even if it meant risking a 1613 season without the participation of the Georges-Macain partnership. It was critical that Champlain post the prince's commission there and avoid a repeat of the traumatic beginning to the one-year extension de Monts had secured for his trade monopoly in October 1607.

Pont-Gravé had arrived aboard the *Lièvre* (the *Hare*) at Tadoussac just ahead of Champlain in May 1608, and found a French Basque ship under the command of a man named Darache already trading with the natives. Darache responded to Pont-Gravé's effort to enforce the monopoly extension by opening fire on the *Lièvre* with cannon and musket, striking Pont-Gravé and three of his men, killing one.

The Basques then matter-of-factly boarded the *Lièvre,* confiscated all of her cannon and other arms, and informed the seriously wounded Pont-Gravé that they would continue their trade with the gathered natives. When their trading was done and they were ready to return to France, and Pont-Gravé was no longer a nuisance, they would be pleased to return Pont-Gravé's weapons and ammunition to him.

Champlain, arriving soon after, had no real chance of liberating Pont-Gravé by force, or of evicting Darache. Champlain was rowed to the Basque ship for a lengthy negotiation. When he was done, Darache was free to continue trading, and Pont-Gravé and the *Lièvre* were allowed to retreat from the harbour, licking wounds.

It had been a feeble beginning to Champlain's operations as de Monts' lieutenant on the St. Lawrence. In the spring of 1613, neither Champlain nor Pont-Gravé wished to relive the experience.

On April 29, 1613, having endured a lengthy crossing and survived a violent gale in the Gulf of St. Lawrence, Champlain and Pont-Gravé arrived at Tadoussac. Once again, there was already another ship in the harbour.

Twenty-four

—

C HAMPLAIN WAS SHOCKED by the emaciated state of the Montagnais who paddled out to greet him at Pointe aux Vaches, off Tadoussac, in the spring of 1613. The winter he concluded had been hard, by which he meant mild—there had not been enough snow to slow down large game for hunters. He held back from revealing himself to these famished people, who cried out for bread as they clambered aboard Pont-Gravé's vessel.

The Montagnais examined the faces of all the Frenchmen on board, only then asking where Champlain was. He had the crew tell them that he was back in France. "But this they would not think of believing, and an old man among them came to me in a corner where I was walking, not wanting to be recognized as yet, and taking me by the ear, for he suspected who it was, saw the scar of the arrow wound, which I received at the defeat of the Iroquois. At this he cried out, and all the others after him, with great demonstrations of joy, saying, 'Your people are waiting for you at the harbour of Tadoussac.'"

The ship that had beaten Champlain and Pont-Gravé to Tadoussac was one of their own.

—

Champlain had witnessed starvation among the Montagnais before. They were nomadic hunters, not agriculturalists like the Huron or, to a lesser degree, some of the Algonquin tribes on the Ottawa River. Any failure of the hunt was catastrophic. What is more, the fur trade was transforming the Montagnais culture, making them utterly dependent on the French.

When the members of Champlain's company who reached Tadoussac before him rowed out to greet him, they brought with them three geese and two rabbits. They gutted them and threw the entrails overboard, which the Montagnais lunged for and devoured. "They also scraped off with their nails the fat with which our vessel had been coated, eating it gluttonously as if they had found some great delicacy," Champlain reported with undisguised repugnance.

Champlain offered no evidence of French attempts to relieve this starvation among the Montagnais. His own frustration with these people was longstanding. After the privations he experienced at the Quebec habitation in the winter of 1608–09, he complained about their failure to set aside food to prevent famine, and wished that they would grow corn like their neighbours. During his time in the Caribbean, Champlain may have absorbed inspiring details about the Spanish colony in Florida, specifically about the relationship between the natives, the Catholic Church, and the settlements. The Spaniards baptized the natives and settled them next to their own posts. Through a corn tax, the Christianized *india* helped to feed the Spanish residents. The Montagnais were failing to meet Champlain's expectations. They were a people his vision was passing by, their suffering mere background to his quest to now reach the Northern Sea and the English boy.

The next day, two ships from St-Malo appeared at Tadoussac. They had left port before Champlain had been able to have his commission posted in all the French ports. He now headed over to the Malouins to inform them of their intrusion.

Champlain took the Sieur de L'Ange with him. Several armed men would have accompanied them. Champlain would have done everything possible to avoid repeating the disaster of the Darache episode of 1608.

Champlain read aloud to nobles aboard the Malouin ships the royal commission. Infringement of the Prince de Condé's rights invited a 10,000-livre fine and the seizure of vessels and merchandise. As well, anyone attempting to provide arms to the natives would pay an equal penalty and face corporal punishment.

It was vital to Champlain that powder weapons were kept out of the hands of the *sauvages*. His ability to provide unsurpassed military support had been the foundation of his role as a privileged customer for native furs during the free-trade years. No one else apparently dared trade powder weapons to the natives during that time. If weapons did not continue to be reserved exclusively for French hands, the natives would have no reason to recognize his monopoly role. They could seek out smugglers—as some native traders had already been wont to do, farther downriver in the Matane region—to bargain for the best possible prices, and receive the guns and ammunition they must have desired. The Huron and Algonquin could turn the guns on the Iroquois without any aid from Champlain. And if Champlain objected, he would risk having the weapons turned on him.

Had the Malouins begun trading, they would have faced the seizure of their ships and goods as well as the fines, with half the take going to the Prince de Condé "or his lieutenant," Champlain, the other half to the merchant partners. But a forceful subjugation was in no one's best interest, and quite possibly beyond the capabilities of Champlain and de L'Ange. Fortunately, the Malouins "replied that they were subjects and faithful servants of his majesty, and that they would obey his commands," according to Champlain. A Malouin noble, the Sieur de Maisonneuve, was issued one of the Prince de Condé's trading passports. Tadoussac, a port that had hosted exchanges between Europeans and natives for the better part of a century, was now Champlain's exclusive trade zone. After enduring the vitriol of the Malouin factum and the petition filed at the Rouen *parlement,* Champlain had turned a corner with at least some of the Breton merchants.

On May 2, Champlain was ready to proceed to the habitation at Quebec. Two shallops had been assembled by his company. They would carry Champlain, de L'Ange, the interpreters de Vignau and Thomas, traders and their goods, and an unknown number of men from the merchant vessels who were to accompany Champlain on his journey up the Ottawa, as Champlain never did reveal how many ships the partnership sent out in 1613. Champlain travelled in de L'Ange's company, most certainly with the two interpreters as well. Their shallop soon lost its mast in violent weather, which sank a Malouin shallop on its way upriver, but all the Malouins were saved, and Champlain's party was able to reach Quebec in five days.

The taste of salt was all but gone from the river here. The trees were coming out into leaf, and the first wildflowers were beginning to blossom. Champlain did not know what he would find, after two years away from this modest post at the great river's narrowing above Île d'Orléans. Hopefully the men sent out by the La Rochelle merchants who leased the property from the Sieur de Monts would be in better health than the starving Montagnais at Tadoussac. When he made this same passage upriver to build the habitation in 1608, after brokering Pont-Gravé's escape from a defiant Basque trader, Champlain had no idea that his own men were preparing to murder him.

It was not Champlain's wits that saved him that summer, but pure chance, and a guilty man's conscience. He learned of the plot against him only a few days after arriving at Quebec on July 3, 1608, to begin construction of the habitation. By all rights, Champlain should have been dead by then. All of his close associates, the ones he could confide in, had sailed back to Tadoussac for supplies, and the conspirators were debating the best way to kill him without drawing attention to themselves: whether he should be surprised alone and strangled, or (better yet) lured by a false alarm of some threat in the night and shot.

They planned to act before the vessels returned from Tadoussac, but a shallop arrived early, on the very day the deed was to be done. One of the men who had reluctantly agreed to join the conspiracy had changed his mind, and the plot was revealed. Champlain promised to pardon four of the conspirators in return for their testimony. Six main conspirators—two of whom soon proved to be wrongly accused and were duly released—were seized.

The ringleader was Jean Duval, a locksmith first hired by de Monts to serve at Port Royal in 1606. Champlain would state that Duval had been recruiting collaborators since the expedition left Honfleur, but the recent events at Tadoussac may have been the true inspiration. Duval could have concocted the plan in concert with the Basque trader Darache. According to Champlain, it was Duval's idea to kill Champlain and then hand over the new post at Quebec to "Spaniards and Basques" at Tadoussac for a handsome reward.

Champlain attested that the conspirators, confronted by their accusers, confessed to their crimes. "Duval knew not what to say," he would write, "except that he deserved death, that all stated in the depositions was true, and that he begged for mercy upon himself and the others, who had given in their adherence to his pernicious purposes."

Deciding to take justice into his own hands as the lieutenant of de Monts, Champlain had assembled a distinctly partial jury, which included himself and Pont-Gravé, to hear the charges. Three of Duval's co-conspirators, condemned to hang, were sent back to France, where de Monts could arrange the punishment deemed most appropriate. Duval too was condemned to death, but was to "serve as an example to those who remained, leading them to deport themselves correctly in future, in the discharge of their duty; and that the Spaniards and Basques, of whom there were large numbers in the country, might not glory in the event."

And so Duval was strangled, and hanged, and then decapitated, his severed head set on a pike and placed "in the most conspicuous place on our fort." As the habitation rose from the ground, Duval's lifeless expression greeted any traveller on the river, European and native alike: a reminder of how forthrightly Champlain was prepared to deal with anyone who dared to cross him.

Arriving at the habitation on May 7, 1613, Champlain saw before him a two-storey wooden redoubt with an upper gallery from which muskets could be fired in any direction. Cannons set on platforms overlooked the St. Lawrence. But even at this considerable narrowing, the river was about three quarters of a mile wide. While no one could pass upstream unnoticed during daylight, this modest base could do little to prevent a well-armed and determined force from proceeding upriver. Access to a territory larger than Europe was controlled by a structure that no self-respecting harbour in France would rely on for its defences.

Champlain remained six days at the habitation. He was relieved to find "in good condition those who had wintered there, they not having been sick. They told us that the winter had not been severe, and that the river had not frozen." Conditions that had ravaged the Montagnais had proved kind to the French at Quebec.

Champlain's first overwintering at Quebec in 1608–09 had been his worst in New France. More than fifty men had perished during his three consecutive overwinterings in Acadia, but the losses had been progressively less traumatic. When Pont-Gravé, who had sailed for France after the Darache assault, returned to relieve Champlain at the Quebec habitation in the spring of 1609, he found de Monts' lieutenant knee-deep in death, suffering, and starvation among his own men and the Montagnais.

Twenty of twenty-eight Frenchmen had died during Champlain's first command, some of dysentery, most of scurvy, the cause or treatment of which Champlain was unable to comprehend. He thought the illness was caused by unhealthy vapours emanating from the ground, and by blood becoming overheated. He believed fresh meat was the answer, but there was none to be had that winter, as hunting was especially poor.

Of the eight Frenchmen still alive when Pont-Gravé appeared, half of them were ill. The de Monts monopoly extension had expired, and there scarcely seemed to be a point to the misery and loss Champlain had just overseen. If he returned to France at that point, Champlain would be able to report only abject failure. He decided instead to cement his commercial relations with the native peoples in one bold stroke, by becoming a brother in arms. He gathered eleven men with him in a shallop and proceeded upriver with a Montagnais war party.

Promises of military assistance had been made before, during the brief Chauvin monopoly, but never fulfilled. In *Des Sauvages*, Champlain had expressed hope that the Iroquois could be made allies of the French. The dream of French neutrality in the endless cycle of native conflict now went firmly by the board. From a pit of despair as his men died and the Montagnais were reduced to eating putrid carrion, Champlain rapidly and decisively moved forward. If he could survive the coming raid on the Iroquois, he would bind his future to the Montagnais and their Algonquin and Huron allies.

Twenty-five

—

O N MAY 13, 1613, Champlain's two shallops departed Quebec. They had about eighty-five miles to cover to reach Lac St-Pierre.

Champlain's party would have found the great river eerily empty of human activity, especially now that a fresh monopoly was barring unauthorized traders from the river. The persistent threat of Iroquois raids having long ago cleansed the landscape of any permanent villages, Champlain sailed past mile upon mile of prime farmland begging cultivation. Thanks to de Vignau's report, he had been able to secure a monopoly that gave him at least twelve years in which to make something of the promise that this landscape had first suggested to him in 1603. From his vantage point in the small open boat, he could not have helped but imagine the seigneuries and villages that could spring from this fertile ground, if the merchants backing him could be convinced that there was more to this country than the fur trade.

He would report almost nothing about the journey upriver, but it would only have taken a few days to reach Lac St-Pierre. Another day would make easy work of the length of the riverine lake. The St. Lawrence then constricted into a sieve of islands and channels. Here, on its south side, the River of the Iroquois emptied into it. It was the entrance to a major transportation corridor, and the locus of some of the most critical episodes in Champlain's history in this country.

Champlain had first encountered the River of the Iroquois on his 1603 mission. It flowed from the south, into the St. Lawrence, fifty miles downstream from the Great Rapid. Cartier had named it: the river was a main route into and out of the territory of the enemy of the tribes with whom the French traded. A war party of several of these allied tribes had assembled at the river mouth for an assault on the Iroquois when Champlain and Pont-Gravé paused there, en route to the Great Rapid, in 1603.

The river, which we know as the Richelieu, greatly intrigued Champlain and Pont-Gravé. So determined were they to press on that they tried to drag the pinnace over land, past the rapids, but could not force the little bark through the trees. Instead, they took their skiff farther upstream to test the river, but the current was too much for them, and they abandoned the effort. (By then, Champlain was fully persuaded of the ingenious utility of the birchbark canoe.) Thwarted by his clumsy boats, Champlain could only listen to his guides describe what he was unable to reach.

In being told about this river in 1536, Cartier was assured that it provided a passage from the St. Lawrence to "Florida," a term that applied to much of the Atlantic seaboard. It was Cartier's evidence that encouraged Edward Wright to draw the selfsame waterway on his 1599 chart. Champlain could not have been unaware of so famous a map, but in 1603 he was footloose in Canada with precious little knowledge of what Cartier had already learned. Which may have been for the best, as he listened carefully, and without prejudice, to what was described for him.

At the head of the river of the Iroquois, the natives told him, was a large lake, "some forty or fifty leagues long and some twenty-five wide, into which as many as ten rivers flow, up which canoes can go for a considerable distance." Beyond this large lake, there was a portage to another lake, at the end of which was an Iroquois encampment. And nearby was a river "extending to the coast of Florida, a distance of perhaps some one hundred or one hundred and forty leagues from the latter lake."

The river to the coast ran about two hundred miles from the portage to the sea. Champlain was absolutely correct about there being two lakes and the general configuration of the route. In writing up his findings in *Des Sauvages,* he described with unprecedented precision the components of the vital corridor linking the St. Lawrence with the Atlantic seaboard, a place where multinational ambitions would soon converge from opposite directions.

Six years later, Champlain at last seized the chance to explore the River of the Iroquois as he joined the war party of Montagnais, Algonquin, and Huron after the near disaster of his 1608–09 overwintering at Quebec. And nothing was going to prevent him from overcoming the river's obstacles this time. When the Chambly rapids rebuffed his shallop, as it had his pinnace in 1603, he walked away from it, telling most of his men to take the vessel back to Quebec. He chose two Frenchmen to carry on with him in a canoe.

It took Champlain the better part of July 1609 to negotiate the length of the lake he found beyond the Chambly rapids, which he named for himself. As the Montagnais, Algonquin, and Huron warriors approached within a few days of the southern end of the lake, they began to travel only at night.

Champlain was asked routinely to tell them of his dreams, whether he saw their enemies. Dreams were elemental to the lives of his allies. They were believed to be a revelation from the spirit world, working through the subconscious, or an expression of the desire of the soul of the dreamer. They also foretold the future, and no one would act in a way that defied a dream's prediction. "If during the night they dream they must kill a Frenchman," Jesuit superior Charles Lalement would allege in 1626, "woe to the first one whom they meet alone. They attach great faith to their dreams. Some of them will tell you two days before the coming of a ship the hour of its arrival, and will give no other explanation except that they have seen it while asleep."

Loathing what he called their superstitions, Champlain continually turned aside the enquiries of his travelling companions, until one night he had the dream they were seeking.

He saw the Iroquois drowning in the lake, near a mountain. Champlain wanted to help them, but his native allies told him they must let them all die, because they were of no importance. When he awoke, Champlain decided to share this dream, and he saw that it "gave them so much confidence that they did not doubt any longer that good was to happen to them."

Champlain came within a few miles of the end of his eponymous lake at Crown Point, where Lake George drains into Lake Champlain. It was as he had been told in 1603: a large lake led to a smaller one, and from there, a portage led to a river that flowed to the Atlantic coast. He was now told the portage to this river was a two-day journey overland. Standing in his way was an Iroquois war party. And at ten o'clock on the evening of July 29, the two sides made contact.

Warfare between these nations at this time was a matter of ritual, of blood vengeance, of personal prestige. The opposing forces conferred with each other through emissaries, and agreed they should wait until daylight "so as to be able to recognize each other," Champlain wrote.

The enemy warriors were known by many names. To the four other tribes in the Iroquois confederacy, they were the "keepers of the eastern door." They called themselves Kahniankehaka, "the people of the flint." The Huron, who shared their language, called them the Agniehronnon. In English, they would become best known as the Mohawk, a variant on a pejorative of the Narragansett tribe, Mohowaanuk, meaning "man eaters." They promised to offer battle at daybreak.

There was a new moon; the night was pitch dark. Champlain noted it was spent "in dancing and singing, on both sides, with endless insults and other talk; as, how little courage we had, how feeble a resistance we would make against their arms, and that, when day came, we should realize it to our ruin. Ours also were not slow in retorting, telling them they would see such execution of arms as never before, together with an abundance of such talk as is not unusual in the siege of a town."

The sun, concealed behind the Green Mountains, rose about 5:45. As the two forces prepared to meet, Champlain and his French companions concealed themselves from the Iroquois, to maximize surprise. They donned light armour, selected a harquebus each, then watched as two hundred Iroquois emerged from behind a barricade they had built overnight. The closest any of them had come to a European, it seemed, was the trade goods they had gained in raids on Champlain's native allies, as he remarked on the few cheap iron axes they had used alongside traditional stone ones to throw together their defensive works.

The Iroquois were "stout and rugged in appearance. They came at a slow pace towards us, with a dignity and assurance which greatly amused me, having three chiefs at their head." Champlain had every intention of killing as many of these imposing warriors as possible.

"Our men also advanced in the same order, telling me that those who had three large plumes were the chiefs, and that they had only these three, and that they could be distinguished by these plumes, which were much larger than those of their companions, and that I should do what I could to kill them." Champlain was sorry that he did not speak the languages of his allies and could not do more to arrange a proper military assault. But he was determined to show them his courage, and his goodwill, in joining them in this engagement.

As Champlain's allies approached the enemy, they shouted back to him, then parted to allow him to emerge into view. He marched out, alone, twenty paces ahead of his own force, thirty paces from the Iroquois.

They paused, and stared at him. They had seen nothing like him before: a compact, bearded stranger, in a skin of steel, brandishing strange tools.

A drawing of the confrontation published by Champlain in *Les Voyages* showed him sporting the armour of a cavalier, including a breastplate and a helmet festooned with what appeared to be an ostrich-feather plume. His feet were widely planted, bracing himself against the kick of the heavy gun.

The harquebus was a powerful weapon, but not particularly accurate, and required time and care to reload. It was most effective in a massed volley of shooters. Champlain was counting on absolute surprise and a devastating impact from that first shot to turn the entire battle in his favour. He had stuffed four musket balls down the barrel. If the gun didn't explode in his face, it would kill more men more quickly than the natives on either side of the battle line had ever witnessed.

When the Iroquois recovered from the shock of the sight of him, and moved to loose their arrows, Champlain vanished with a thunderclap, in a wreath of smoke that spouted fire.

A single harquebus ball could pierce a thick oak plank. His four-ball charge ripped effortlessly through the woven body armour and wooden shields of the enemy, and on through flesh and bone. Two chiefs dropped dead, and a warrior with them was mortally wounded. As arrows flew from both sides, Champlain's French companions fired from concealed positions in the woods, and the third Iroquois chief was slain.

The Iroquois quickly broke ranks and fled the field. "I pursued them, killing still more of them," Champlain recalled. "Our savages also killed several of them, and took ten or twelve prisoners. The remainder escaped with the wounded. Fifteen or sixteen were wounded on our side with arrow-shots, but they were soon healed."

Champlain had made himself a firm ally of his trading partners, and embroiled the French in bloody battles with the Iroquois that would persist for most of the next century.

On the journey back up Lake Champlain after the battle, Champlain's native allies paused as evening approached, to enact their vengeance on one of their Iroquois prisoners. They made a harangue, "enumerating the cruelties which he and his men had already practised towards them without any mercy, and that, in like manner, he ought to make up his mind to receive as much. They commanded him to sing, if he had courage, which he did, but it was a very sad song."

A fire was lit; branches were heated into white-hot brands. They "burned this poor creature gradually, so as to make him suffer greater torment. Sometimes they stopped, and threw water on his back." The prisoner's nails were torn out, and fire then applied to the ends of his fingers and his genitals. He was scalped, and heated sap poured onto his skull. Next, "they pierced his arms near the wrists, and, drawing up the sinews with sticks, they tore them out by force; but, seeing that they could not get them, they cut them. This poor wretch uttered terrible cries, and it excited my pity to see him treated in this manner, and yet showing such firmness that one would have said, at times, that he suffered hardly any pain at all."

Champlain was urged to join in the torture, to burn the man, but he was appalled and angered by the treatment of this prisoner of war. "I remonstrated with them, saying that we practised no such cruelties, but killed them at once." If they wanted Champlain to shoot him with a musket, he would be glad to do so, he explained. "They refused, saying that he would not in that case suffer any pain. I went away from them, pained to see such cruelties as they practiced upon his body. When they saw that I was displeased, they called me, and told me to fire a musket-shot at him. This I did without his feeling it, and thus put an end, by a single shot, to all the torments he would have suffered, rather than see him tyrannized over."

But Champlain's allies were not finished with their prisoner. They cut open his body and threw his entrails into the lake. His head, arms, and legs were also removed and "scattered in different directions." Only his scalp was kept, as a trophy of war, along with the others taken from Iroquois dead after the battle. His heart was removed and cut into several pieces, which were given to the other prisoners, among which were his brother. They were ordered to eat the pieces, but while they took them in their mouths, they refused to swallow. Some Algonquin who were guarding them made them spit the pieces out, and the chunks of heart were thrown in the lake.

"This is the manner in which these people behave towards those whom they capture in war," Champlain would write, "for whom it would be better to die fighting, or to kill themselves on the spur of the moment, as many do, rather than fall into the hands of their enemies. After this execution, we set out on our return with the rest of the prisoners, who kept singing as they went along, with no better hopes for the future than he had had who was so wretchedly treated."

On September 22, 1609, Henry Hudson and the *Half Moon* reached the height of navigation on the river that would be named for him. Hudson came within perhaps eighty miles of where Champlain had fought the Iroquois seven weeks earlier. He could have known of Champlain's 1603 report of the configuration of this transportation corridor, from an unpublished translation of *Des Sauvages* provided to him by Richard Hakluyt, and so would not have been entirely surprised when the river failed to pass through to the St. Lawrence, as the Wright map suggested. Champlain for his part had known the portage route south to the Atlantic was there to be discovered in 1609, but he had no chance of forging forward, into Lake George and then overland to the uppermost reaches of the Hudson River. When Robert Juet was blasting angry natives on the lower Hudson with the *Half Moon*'s falconer, Champlain was east of the Grand Banks, on the way back to France with Iroquois scalps to show his king, but without any real hope of having de Monts' monopoly extended. On order of the *conseil d'état* on October 6, 1609, the Canada trade had already officially been thrown wide open.

Champlain never commented on the fact that Hudson had discovered his river in the same year that Champlain had discovered his lake, between them inspecting all but a few bridging miles of that vital corridor. Nor did Champlain ever indicate he knew that, while he was almost being swallowed whole by the Canadian winter at the Quebec habitation in 1608–09, Hudson had almost been hired by Henry IV to sail for France.

Pierre Jeannin, who was at The Hague helping broker the truce between Spain and the Dutch Republic, had been fomenting a plan for about a year to set up a French rival to the VOC with the help of a prominent disgruntled VOC investor, a transplanted Fleming based at Amsterdam named Isaac Lemaire. In January 1609, Lemaire suddenly had another plan for Jeannin's consideration: Henry IV should hire through Lemaire an English pilot footloose in Amsterdam, to make a northeast passage attempt. Henry Hudson was supposed to be making such a voyage for the VOC, but Lemaire understood that a snag had developed in the contract negotiations.

Jeannin was intrigued, and sought out Petrus Plancius for his advice on the feasibility of the route, without (he hoped) giving away a French interest in hiring Hudson. Henry IV was persuaded to provide the 4,000 crowns that Lemaire requested to mount the expedition, but he sent it on February 28—far too late to engage Hudson, who had signed his VOC contract on January 8. In settling for a modest fee from the VOC for the *Half Moon* voyage, Hudson assuredly never knew how much his services were in play.

The worlds of Henry Hudson and Samuel de Champlain had been converging for longer than Champlain knew, in a mounting series of near misses. By rescuing John Hudson, Champlain could at last close the gap between them, completing a union of vision and ambition he had begun by merging his map of New France with that of Hessel Gerritsz's rendering of the *Discovery* voyage's geographic revelations.

—

Twenty-six

CHAMPLAIN WAS APPROACHING THE GREAT RAPID
when a new moon, a disc invisible to the world, rose in
close company with the sun on May 19, 1613. Only an
eclipse could indirectly reveal the moon's presence—an event that
Englishmen on the western shore of Hudson Bay were awaiting at
that very moment.

Thomas Button's expedition followed instructions drawn up
by the esteemed navigation authority and mathematician Edward
Wright. Charged with continuing the search for the Northwest
Passage last pursued by Henry Hudson, Button had been told to
proceed westward once beyond Hudson Strait, and to measure the
tides around latitude 58 for some clue of where the passage might
lie. But this only brought him to the impassable barrier of the
western shore of Hudson Bay. His two ships, the *Resolution* and
the *Discovery*, had then braced against the enclosing winter in the
mouth of a river at latitude 57.

The *Resolution* was destroyed, and many of the expedition's
men, including Button's master aboard the *Resolution*, Robert
Nelson—in whose memory Button named the river—were lost to
scurvy over the winter of 1612–13. As the survivors waited for the
ice to release the *Discovery*, Button turned to another item in

Wright's instructions: he was to observe the local time of an eclipse of the sun on May 19. Once Button was home, his results could be compared with observations of the same eclipse back in London. The time differences could be translated into the separation of the two points of observation in degrees of longitude. In this way, Button's position at the place of observation could be determined precisely, helping enormously in mapping the passage.

Alas, Button was too far south to observe an eclipse. He would have had to be at least as far north as latitude 80 even to see the rims of the two bodies touch. The sun and moon closed within about half the moon's diameter at Button's latitude around noon, and then went their separate ways again. Some twelve degrees of latitude farther south, where Champlain approached the rapids, they came within about one moon's diameter.

If he attempted a noon sight of the sun that day, Champlain might have been aware of the celestial near miss. It was an apt portent of his arrival at the *saults*. When he reached the foot of the Great Rapid on May 21, he learned from the other shallop, which had arrived ahead of him, that a party of Algonquin had just come and gone. Returning from a raid on the Iroquois, they were told of Champlain's imminent appearance, that he was on the way with men to assist them in their wars, as he had promised in 1611, and that he wished to travel into their country "and enter into an alliance with all their friends."

This news, Champlain would write, "greatly pleased" the Algonquin, but evidently not enough to persuade them to wait for him. They had two Iroquois captives, and were eager to return home "to assure their friends of their victory, see their wives, and put to death their prisoners in a festive *tabagie*." They promised they would return for Champlain before the middle of the first moon.

"I regretted very much that I was not prepared to go with them to their country," wrote Champlain. As with his reluctance to reveal himself on his arrival at Tadoussac, Champlain seemed to have been deliberately holding back from making contact with natives at the *saults,* allowing the other shallop to arrive first. It was as if he wanted to be sure that he would be welcomed on his reappearance. But now he would have to wait for the Algonquin to make good on a promise of their own, to return within a few days. It must have caused Champlain considerable anxiety to know that he was now depending on people whose trustworthiness he had so maligned in *Des Sauvages* to be more reliable than he was.

Downstream of the Great Rapid, Champlain's two-shallop expedition waited, counting the days. There was no question of attempting to travel deeper into the country without the assistance or approval of the Algonquin.

In the difficult years that had followed the irreversible loss of de Monts' monopoly in October 1609, the anchorage downstream of the *saults* became the most important base of operations for Champlain. Without an exclusive right to the St. Lawrence trade, he could not wait for the Algonquin and Huron to travel all the way to Tadoussac or Quebec to do business with them. He had to meet them where they first emerged from the wilds beyond the Great Rapid. It was here, in the summer of 1611, that Champlain had struck the bargains he was unable to keep.

In the first decade of the seventeenth century, the French relied on the natives to bridge the cultural gap. Champlain was fortunate to inherit, particularly with the Montagnais on the lower St. Lawrence and the Mi'kmaq in Acadia, native groups already acclimatized to the French through decades of trading. A few of their number, in the time-honoured tradition, were taken back to France for education and indoctrination. And by the time Champlain came along, there was probably already a well-established language of trade, a creole that would have drawn heavily on Basque, a tongue so ancient and so utterly different from neighbouring Indo-European languages like French and Spanish that it may have been in use in the historic Basque region during the paleolithic era.

The first time Champlain went to war with his native allies, in 1609, he was frustrated by his lack of native language skills. The trade creole evidently was incomprehensible to him, and he would never demonstrate any facility with the challenging Algonquian and Iroquoian languages. (Nevertheless, the Basques had apparently given the natives with whom they traded a word for the sun that a Frenchman could understand: Jesus.)

For their part, the Algonquin and Huron peoples seem to have found French all but impossible to comprehend. According to the Jesuit missionary Francesco Giuseppe Bressani, a gifted Italian astronomer and professor of mathematics who visited Huronia in the 1640s, they could not master the pronunciation of the consonants *b, f, l, m, p, x, z,* or the vowels *i* and *u,* nor could they manage "the accents, the aspirations, the changes in tone" necessary to be understood. Not having an indigenous writing system didn't help their learning process.

Champlain's singular willingness among the commercial traders to participate in native wars made possible the appropriate strategic move: having Frenchmen live among the tribes above the Great Rapid. His interpreters-in-training could infiltrate the world beyond the rapids, one intrepid teenager at a time.

According to Champlain, Étienne Brûlé had already spent two winters at the Quebec habitation—making him a survivor of the horrific privations of 1608–09—when he made known his desire to live among natives and learn their language. They were at the mouth of the River of the Iroquois in 1610, and Champlain turned to Pont-Gravé to discuss the youth's request.

Brûlé could not have asked for his assignment at a more trau-
matizing moment. Champlain's second battle against the Iroquois
with native allies had just been won, but he was bandaged and
bleeding; a stone-tipped Iroquois arrow had split his ear and
pierced his neck, and he had torn it out with his own hands. The
harvesting of scalps and the agonizing torture of Iroquois prisoners was bloodstain fresh, an episode made even more shocking to
Champlain by the participation of women among his allies in
ingeniously inflicting excruciating pain.

Brûlé had no qualms about immersing himself in the
Algonquin world. When queried on his willingness, "he answered
the question at once," Champlain related, "by consenting to the
journey with great pleasure."

Champlain found Brûlé a host when Yroquet, an Algonquin
chief he had met in 1609, arrived with eighty men, too late to
have joined in the battle. Champlain persuaded Yroquet to have
Brûlé stay with him and his people, who were one of perhaps
eight Algonquin tribes at the time of contact in the Ottawa River
watershed, which numbered in total about six thousand people.

Yroquet's people (whom Champlain also called the Yroquet)
were the Onontchataronon. They lived on the south side of the
Ottawa River, in the triangle of terrain formed roughly by
present-day Ottawa, Lac des Deux-Montagnes, and what is now
Kingston, on eastern Lake Ontario. There was a pronounced
bond between the Arendarhonon (the Rock People) of the Huron
confederacy and Yroquet's people. (Onontchataronon was an
Iroquoian name given to them by the Arendarhonon. It meant
People of the Mountain, which supported a tradition that they
had once lived on the island of Montréal.) The Huron, who
might have numbered twenty thousand, were more sedentary
than their Algonquin allies, practising slash-and-burn agricul-
ture to grow corn, beans, and squash and living in longhouses

in palisaded villages that were home to anywhere from perhaps three hundred to eighteen hundred individuals. Yroquet's people travelled to Huron country every winter to live with the Arendarhonon, and it was through Yroquet that Champlain first met any member of the Huron confederacy.

Yroquet's son had observed Champlain and Pont-Gravé in 1608, and was sufficiently impressed to encourage his father to travel down the St. Lawrence in 1609 to meet these Frenchmen. Yroquet brought with him an Arendarhonon chief, Ochateguin. Champlain struck an alliance on that first encounter with both tribes, before fighting the Iroquois alongside them.

As he prepared to go to war against the Iroquois that first time in 1609, Champlain had secured grand promises from his native allies. The Montagnais said they would take him in 1610 "to a sea so large that the end of it cannot be seen, whence we should return by way of the Saguenay to Tadoussac." And his new allies, the chiefs Yroquet and Ochateguin, vowed "to show me their country, the great lake, some copper mines, and other things, which they had indicated to me. I accordingly had two strings to my bow, so that, in case one should break, the other might hold."

When Champlain returned to Canada from France in 1610, he had reminded the Montagnais of their promise to take him to that distant sea. They said they would, but not this year, a response that Champlain said "pleased him," although it was the beginning of a pattern of promises by native allies being deferred rather than made good when it came to revealing the world beyond the St. Lawrence and the Great Rapid. Champlain in the meantime had come to pin his greatest hopes for establishing a new trade monopoly on the second string: the peoples of Yroquet and Ochateguin. Even though Henry IV had rebuffed, in the autumn of 1609, overtures for another monopoly extension, solidifying a special relationship with these peoples, and learning everything possible about their territories, continued to be Champlain's priority.

When Yroquet accepted responsibility for Brûlé in 1610, he asked Champlain to take to France on behalf of the Arendarhonon one of their youths, Savignon, the brother of a chief named Tregouaroti. Champlain returned to the Great Rapid in 1611 with Savignon, accompanied by a youth named Louis, an employee of the Sieur de Monts. In a few days, Brûlé would be returned to Champlain, and Savignon would rejoin his people. While they awaited the rendezvous, Louis persuaded Savignon to paddle him to an island in the rapid so that he could hunt herons. A Montagnais chief, Outetoucos, went along with them, then insisted on their shooting the rapid after the hunt was finished. The canoe capsized, and although Savignon survived, both Louis (who could not swim) and Outetoucos drowned.

Champlain was paddled to the site of the tragedy in the heart of the Great Rapid the next day, in vain hope of recovering the bodies. "I was horrified at beholding such a terrible place, and astonished that the deceased should have been so lacking in judgment as to pass through such a fearful place, when they could have gone another way. For it is impossible to go along there, as there are seven or eight descents of water one after the other, the lowest three feet high, the seething and boiling of the water being fearful. A part of the fall was all white with foam, indicating the worst spot, the noise of which was like thunder, the air resounding with the echo of the cataracts."

Champlain named the killing rapid and the riverine lake upstream St-Louis, ostensibly for a canonized thirteenth-century French king but plainly in honour of a youth who had been lost in "a sad death." It had been an utterly needless and costly one. Louis would have been a prime candidate for an interpreter trainee. And had Savignon perished, Champlain's interpreter-training plan might have crumbled, and with it his ambitions to cement his special relationship with the natives beyond the Great Rapid.

The only person Champlain could think of to blame for the tragedy was Outetoucos, a man he had considered "very respectable." But Outetoucos had ended up in this treacherous section of river only because Louis had insisted that Savignon take him hunting birds on an island in the heart of the Great Rapid. It was impossible ever to know how this reckless country could affect a young Frenchman's judgment.

After the loss of Louis and Outetoucos, Champlain travelled above the Great Rapid with Savignon, reaching Lac des Deux-Montagnes, the swelling of the lower reaches of the Ottawa River. There, on June 13, 1611, they met a party of two hundred warriors, who were probably a mix of Algonquin and Huron. In command were three chiefs: the Onontchataronon's Yroquet; Savignon's brother, Tregouaroti; and Ochateguin of the Arendarhonon. With them was Brûlé, who was dressed entirely in native clothing.

Brûlé reported that he was well treated by his hosts, and Savignon in turn "commended the treatment I had shown him in France, and the remarkable objects he had seen, at which all wondered." It would later turn out that Savignon was appalled by many aspects of French society, among them the way children were beaten, and would later discourage his people from sending their offspring away with the French.

Over the course of July and August 1611, there was much manoeuvring among the Algonquin and Huron tribes to curry favour with Champlain, and by Champlain to curry favour with them. The explorer had not mastered the precise identities of tribes or the complexities of the relationships between them, but he did his best to secure an advantage. In his meetings with the Arendarhonon of the Huron, assuredly brokered by Yroquet,

Champlain pressed them for geographic intelligence. "Four of them assured me that they had seen a sea at a great distance from their country, but that it was difficult to go there, not only on account of the wars, but of the intervening wilderness."

The Arendarhonon sought a stronger alliance with Champlain, telling him he could take as many of their people as he wished to France. While they had been predictably discouraging about the hazards of travelling beyond Huronia toward the distant sea, the Arendarhonon promised to assist Champlain and any Frenchmen he wished to name in travelling at least to their own country. Champlain assured them he would ask his king to provide forty or fifty men for a summer's reconnoitre of their country, if the Arendarhonon would provide the necessary provisions. He also would "take presents for the chiefs of the country through which we should pass"—a tacit admission that it was up to him to deal with the difficulty of moving through the chokepoint on the Ottawa held by Tessöuat. Champlain went so far as to promise, should he find their country "favorable and fertile," to establish French settlements in Huronia.

For now, a single French youth was provided to travel to Huronia in the company of Tregouaroti. It most certainly was Brûlé, who had probably already overwintered there when he was in the care of Yroquet, in 1610–11. And before Champlain sailed back downriver from the Great Rapid, at least two more French youths were placed with native hosts.

One was the youth remembered only as Thomas, the servant of the Rouen merchant Daniel Boyer. Boyer was also a surgeon, and had tended to the arrow wound in Champlain's neck in 1610. Boyer again had ventured up the St. Lawrence to trade in 1611, and approached Yroquet directly about taking the youth with him. Champlain took great pains to explain in *Les Voyages* that Yroquet agreed to do so only on Champlain's approval.

A formal overture to Champlain was then made by Tessöuat's people, the Kichesipirini, who arrived in fourteen canoes at the site of present-day Montréal, below the Great Rapid, on August 14. "They begged me to continue my good will to them, which I promised to do," Champlain wrote in *Les Voyages*. "They spoke with me very especially respecting certain explorations towards the north, which might prove advantageous; and said, in reference to them, that if any one of my company would like to go with them, they would show him what would please me, and would treat him as one of their own children."

The Kichesipirini must have become alarmed by the special relationship Yroquet was shaping between Champlain and his Algonquin tribe, the Onontchataronon, and through them the Arendarhonon of the Huron confederacy. If the Iroquois could be beaten back with the help of the French and their marvellous powder weapons, an alternative route between Huronia and the Great Rapid, employing the upper St. Lawrence, could be safely revived. There would no longer be a trading chokepoint on the Ottawa held by Tessöuat. The Onontchataronon and Arendarhonon could serve as the new trade middlemen for other distant tribes. They could already boast of good relations with the Nebicerini, the Algonquian-speaking people who lived around Lake Nipissing on the route between northern Georgian Bay and the Ottawa River, and who made annual trading journeys north to the Cree who lived along the shore of James Bay. And like the Onontchataronon, the Nebicerini travelled to Huronia every winter to live with the Arendarhonon.

Tessöuat made a countermove: a magnanimous offer to show one of Champlain's men the territories to the north. He probably hoped to make the connection for the French with the Nebicerini, however much his people feared them as sorcerers, before the Arendarhonon and Onontchataronon exploited their good standing with them first.

"I promised to give them a young man," Champlain wrote, "at which they were much pleased." He presented Nicolas de Vignau. "When he took leave of me to go with them," Champlain continued, "I gave him a detailed memorandum of what he was to observe while with them."

Anchored at the base of the Great Rapid in May 1613, waiting for the Algonquin to return as promised, Champlain's hopes for anything more than abject failure on this expedition would have become vanishingly small. The merchants were sitting on goods they had probably financed at the usually rates of twenty-five to thirty percent interest, and there was no one to trade with. The Great Rapid was a shimmering, shuddering, thundering impediment to the two French shallops. But the greater impediment was the native peoples, and the state of their relationship with Champlain.

If the Algonquin did not return to the Great Rapid, and extend to Champlain their full cooperation, Champlain would be reduced to the most base categorizations of his Malouin detractors: an interloper who worked with other people's money, making ridiculous claims about the existence of a passage beyond the Great Rapid to the Orient that were based on the testimony of miscreants and infidels, who now had decided they wanted nothing to do with him.

—

Twenty-seven

THE FIRST SILVERING OF THE MOON'S CRESCENT appeared on the night of May 23, 1613, and the next day, just as they had promised, the Algonquin reappeared from beyond the Great Rapid.

It was a relief to the French, but hardly a rousing reception. There were only three canoes, carrying perhaps nine men. Furs were produced to barter. Champlain's trading partners would have proffered some of the standard European goods: "cloaks, blankets, nightcaps, hats, shirts, sheets, hatchets, iron arrowhead, bodkins, swords, picks to break the ice in winter, knives, kettles, prunes, raisins, Indian corn, peas, crackers or sea biscuits, and tobacco," as the Jesuit superior Charles Lalement would itemize in 1626. In return, the traders would receive "hides of moose, lynx, fox, otter, black ones being encountered occasionally, martens, badgers, and muskrats; but they deal principally in beavers, in which they find the greatest profit."

Champlain would write that the natives had been treated so badly by traders at the rapids in 1612 that they had decided not to come any more. They had also concluded that they would never see Champlain again, "on account of the wrong impressions which those jealous of me had given them respecting me." Having given up hope of further military support from the French, twelve hundred men, who must have been a combined force of Algonquin, Huron, and Montagnais, had already gone to war in the summer of 1613 against the Iroquois.

The news, Champlain admitted, was "disheartening" for the traders who had come with him to the *saults*. As for Champlain himself, his reception by the visiting Algonquin was at best cordial, but very close to indifferent. In *Des Sauvages* and *Les Voyages* and at Fontainebleau, he had touted himself as a fearless adventurer with a special relationship with the indigenous people, respected above all other Frenchmen, deserving the protection of a sweeping, long-term monopoly. Here at the Great Rapid, his reputation had all but collapsed, in full view of his trading partners.

The new monopoly could function only if the natives agreed to participate, and the apparent ease with which the nations above the Great Rapid had given up the trade with any Europeans suggested that Champlain's assistance in war had been more important to them than the goods his merchant partners were now proffering. However much Champlain claimed that the trade had collapsed because of poor treatment of the natives in his absence, the people to whom Champlain had made great promises had resigned themselves to his disappearance, written off the trade, and carried on waging war without him. His reappearance did little to overcome his irrelevance.

Champlain knew that in addition to reaching the English boy and the Northern Sea, he would have to persuade the people he met along the way to travel to the Great Rapid and trade with his merchant associates. No less was required to salvage their investment, not to mention his reputation among them. But Champlain was in danger of not even being able to travel inland. He needed Algonquin canoes and guides to take him and his party up the Ottawa, and these particular Algonquin were decidedly lukewarm about extending him any favours.

When Champlain asked for all three of their canoes, along with three natives to guide him, they balked. It was only after "much difficulty" and "by means of some presents" that Champlain received two canoes and a single Algonquin. Having been prepared to take up to sixteen men from the trading vessels with him, he had room for only four. One of the canoes would have to be handled exclusively by Frenchmen. Two of Champlain's French companions were anonymous men from the merchant investors. The other two were the interpreters, de Vignau and Thomas.

This is what life had come to for the Prince de Condé's lieutenant in New France, after a decade of hardship and relentless politicking: five men preparing to set out for the Northern Sea in two birchbark canoes with a single, reluctant native guide.

Champlain turned to de Vignau in the presence of the entire company and asked him, one last time, "that if what he had previously said was not true he must not give me the trouble to undertake the journey, which involved many dangers. Again he affirmed all that he had said, on peril of his life."

The canoes were loaded with weapons, some gifts for the people they would meet, a minimum of personal items, and enough provisions to send them on their way. A fishing net would help them feed themselves. Sieur de L'Ange and the rest of the expedition's members were to wait below the Great Rapid for Champlain's return. The men remaining behind in the shallops fired a salute, and Champlain was off, paddling toward the whitewater.

It was May 27, Whitsunday. De Vignau's report had promised a return trip to the Northern Sea in seventeen days. It took Champlain until the twenty-ninth just to overcome the Great Rapid.

Poor weather did not help, but Champlain was slowed by the sheer difficulty of the journey for inexperienced Frenchmen, who were forced to manage the unfamiliar canoes rather than be paddled around by native guides. Champlain had admired the birchbark craft since first seeing them in 1603 (although he warned in *Des Sauvages,* "They are very liable to turn over, if one does not understand how to manage them"). He was taken with their speed and lightness, the way they could be carried overland by a single man on portages yet still bear a heavy load in the water. But the labour required just to gain the Ottawa was almost too much for these Frenchmen.

Champlain had been to Lac des Deux-Montagnes before, but never beyond it. The two sets of rapids he had to surmount to reach it, the Great Rapid and Ste-Anne-de-Bellevue, were effort enough, but then came the extended set above the lake, the Long Sault.

Many of the daunting sections of the river's whitewater, like the Long Sault, would eventually be obliterated or severely curtailed by flooding behind hydroelectric dams. Champlain offered terse descriptions of this original, lost watercourse. More elaborate recollections of specific features would await later travellers, such as the explorer and trader Alexander Mackenzie, who described the route in a book published about 1801, and Nicholas Garry, deputy governor of the Hudson's Bay Company, who made the same journey in 1821.

Father Bressani would also venture up the Ottawa in travelling to the Jesuit mission in Huronia in 1642, and attest to the difficulties of the journey: "The cascades are dangerous, if travelers go into the strongest part of the current; the savages themselves often founder." The techniques that Bressani, Mackenzie, and Garry employed in overcoming these obstacles were no different than the ones introduced to Champlain by the Algonquin. Some of the smaller drops could be paddled, but the canoes and their contents often had to be carried, or portaged, around the most difficult rapids. Sometimes the contents alone were offloaded and carried at what would become known as a *décharge,* while the canoes were "tracked," floated through the rapids on the end of a tether. Occasionally, the loads were left in the canoes as they were tracked. "But this is not without danger, nor without great difficulties," Bressani wrote of the natives' ordeals in tracking. "Often they are obliged to place themselves up to the waist in icy water. They are also sometimes up to the neck, then need to save themselves by swimming. More than once the boats perished, because their handlers could no longer resist the violence of the current."

The Long Sault rapids, along which the Ottawa dropped more than sixty feet, presented a difficult sequence of portages and *décharges.* Champlain was very nearly lost when the current seized the laden canoe he was tracking, yanking him into the water. He could not swim a stroke, and if the current took hold of him, he was a dead man. Champlain tumbled between two rocks, which saved him, but the lanyard dug so deeply into his wrist that he thought he might lose his hand.

Champlain "cried out to God," and an eddy returned the canoe to him. "Having thus escaped, I thanked God, begging Him to preserve us." His companions had several near-fatal mishaps of their own, and all were so exhausted that, after clearing two sets of rapids in this section, they spent the remainder of the day recovering their strength. It was Saturday, June 1, and the journey had scarcely begun.

The next day, with the ordeal of the Long Sault behind him, Champlain began making steady progress upriver. After passing a "small lake," the widening at present-day L'Orignal, he encountered a party of downbound Algonquin in fifteen canoes. The two groups saluted each other; these Algonquin had been told of Champlain's arrival by the returning war party that had just missed him as he approached the Great Rapid. Champlain signalled to them, indicating that he wished to stop and speak. The Algonquin agreed. They chose an island, and camped there through the following day.

They were Kinounchepirini, the Pike People, who lived immediately south of Tessöuat's Kichesipirini. The next day, Champlain served up what was becoming his standard explanation for why he was on the river. Nothing was said of retrieving an English boy from the Nebicerini or of reaching the Northern Sea. Champlain told them, "I had gone into their country to see them and to keep the promise I had previously made to them." If they were prepared to go to war, he would be most pleased, as he had brought men for the purpose, "at which they expressed much satisfaction."

But the Kinounchepirini were less satisfied with his plan "to go on farther to alert other tribes" that he was ready to fight the Iroquois with them: "they tried to dissuade me, declaring that the way was bad and that we had seen nothing like it yet." He turned their discouraging words to his advantage. If this were the case, then they should assist him. "I begged them to give me one of their men to steer our second canoe, and also to act as guide," because, he said, his own guides no longer knew the country. It might have been true that his lone Algonquin guide was unfamiliar with the entirety of the passage to Tessöuat's village, and the Kinounchepirini agreed to help, a decision encouraged by a gift from Champlain.

For an additional Algonquin guide Champlain exchanged his least useful Frenchman, whom the downbound Algonquin party would take back to the shallops below the Great Rapid. Champlain tore a page out of his notebook, scribbled a message on his progress and plans, and handed it to the discarded expedition member to present to the rest of the company.

Under the accord for the venture signed by Champlain on February 5, half of the value of any gifts of pelts the natives made to the expedition beyond the Great Rapid, and of any gold, silver, copper, and precious stones they found, would go to Champlain and the men he commanded, and the other half to the merchant partners. Ridding himself of one Frenchmen thus granted Champlain and his remaining three French companions a larger share of whatever bounty awaited them. But at this point, enhancing personal profit would have been the furthest thing from anyone's mind. Champlain now had the additional native expertise he desperately required just to keep moving forward, and a struggling crewmember from one of the merchant ships had lucked into an escape from this hazardous mission.

The river was on its best behaviour now, and in a day Champlain reached the site of the present city of Ottawa, where the Rideau River splashed over a limestone shelf into the Ottawa River. Champlain would publish a ridiculously oversized description of the falls, turning it into a veritable Niagara: "from a height of twenty or twenty-five fathoms, it falls with such impetuosity that it forms an archway nearly four hundred yards in width." The natives, he noted, enjoyed walking behind the *rideau,* or curtain, of falling water for amusement, and there was good hunting above the falls.

But it was also a dangerous place. The Rideau River provided a corridor for Iroquois raiding parties moving up from Lake Ontario to ambush travellers on the river there. Just ahead in the main river was a series of steep, wide rapids, which Champlain was assured the Iroquois never ventured past. Akikodjiwan, the Algonquin called the set farthest downstream, the rapids where the river plunged into a rock basin and boiled like water in a kettle, which the French accordingly would call La Chaudière. "This waterfall makes such a noise in this basin that it can be heard for more than two leagues away," Champlain declared.

Alexander Mackenzie would write that the river here "falls twenty-five feet, over cragged, excavated rocks, in a most wild, romantic manner." Nicholas Garry would create a more detailed word portrait of a stretch of whitewater that would be greatly altered by damming: "The Utawa dividing itself into two streams forms an extensive island covered with the finest trees (principally oak), in a bed of long grass and beautiful verdure. The river then uniting becomes an immense body and as if angry at the interruption to its course is rough and agitated, and in this state runs over a bed of rugged, uneven, excavated rocks for several hundred yards in a breadth of nearly a mile. One of the rocks in the middle of the fall more excavated than the others has the appearance of a kettle of boiling water from which the fall takes its name, and into this vast abyss, *gurgite vasto,* the waters fall. The surrounding country is rocky and mountainous and covered with black pine. The rock is a sort of slate in strata which time has mouldered into the oddest shapes which have the appearance of ruins."

It was a hard paddle against the current to reach the foot of these rapids, with the threat of an Iroquois ambush at their backs. There the Algonquin paused to perform a ceremony at the thundering basin. As Champlain would explain, "They assemble in one spot, where one of them takes up a collection with a wooden plate, into which each one puts a bit of tobacco. The collection having been made, the plate is placed in the midst of the troupe, and all dance about it, singing after their style. Then one of the captains makes a harangue, setting forth that for a long time they have been accustomed to make this offering, by which means they are insured protection against their enemies, that otherwise misfortune would befall them, as they are convinced by the evil spirit. And they live on in this superstition, as in many others . . . This done, the maker of the harangue takes the plate, and throws the tobacco into the midst of the cauldron, whereupon they all together raise a loud cry."

Champlain had no time for native beliefs, and would have been impatient to move on, beyond the reach of Iroquois raiders. For them, capturing Champlain, after an untold numbers of Iroquois had fallen to his harquebus and sword, would have been an unimaginable triumph. For Champlain, his fate would have been equally unimaginable. "These poor people are so superstitious," Champlain declared, "that they would not believe it possible for them to make a prosperous journey without observing this ceremony at this place, since their enemies await them at this portage." Only when the gift of tobacco had been made to the booming cauldron would the Algonquin proceed any farther.

Two more sets of rapids, the Petite Chaudière and the Remic, lay immediately upstream. They were wide and ragged, and the water's edge was lined with broken rock. Champlain and his companions carried the canoes, paddled for a short stretch, disembarked again and forged through several hundred yards of underbrush, and finally waded into the river to drag the boats over sharp stones. Champlain had time to take a noon sun sight, and arrived at a latitude of 45 degrees, 38 minutes. It was a good result, off by less than 13 minutes.

After forging through nearly five miles of river they came to a final sheet of rapids, the Deschênes. Before them was a welcomed calming and broadening of the Ottawa as it began a northwesterly jaunt: Lac Deschênes (more properly *des chênes,* the lake of oaks) some twenty miles long. They paddled to an island and spent the remainder of the day at rest.

It had been eight days since they left the shallops. According to Nicolas de Vignau's report, they should have been at the Northern

Sea by now, if they were to make it there and back to the Great Rapid, as he did, in seventeen days. But they were a little more than halfway to Tessöuat's village.

Twenty-eight

—

LAC DESCHÊNES DELIVERED THEM to the awesome impediment of Rapides des Chats. Like Rideau Falls, "Cats' Rapids" was not quite as spectacular as Champlain attested—"a large rapid, which is nearly three leagues wide where the water descends a slope some ten or twelve fathoms high and makes a wonderful noise." The actual drop of some thirty-five feet nevertheless was studded with islands that broke the falls into a series of explosive chutes. A hydroelectric dam in 1931 would submerge these rapids, but not before Nicholas Garry had more precisely described how "the whole body of the river being fully two miles in breadth runs over rocky islands and pinnacles and covered with wood, and forms an innumerable number of falls (you see at once fifteen) . . . a battle between rock and water over a mile of rocks ragged and uneven. The portage is here very difficult and dangerous but only 270 paces."

Writing of this natural spectacle in the late nineteenth century, George Grant would remark that the number of chutes "are generally counted as sixteen; in reality, we observe many more, and as we get nearer, realize the fact that the entire strength and stress of the Ottawa is bent on forcing its way over this barrier of limestone precipice . . . Between the cascades, the rocks appear like separate islands, where the thirsty cedars and willows cling with serpent-like roots in the water-hollowed stone; maple and birch brightening the sombre pines and veteran firs, gaunt with years, keeping guard." Grant took particular note of the main chute, whose spray formed "a pillar of mist, which but for its purer whiteness, might be mistaken for one of the columns of bush-fire smoke in the country around."

In early June, when Champlain reached it, the spring flood from snowmelt still would have been strong. Even in average conditions, more than three times as much water spilled over Rapides des Chats as flowed through the Seine south of Paris. And waiting above the main plunge was what Alexander Mackenzie called a "serpentine channel," with Nicholas Garry recounting that this passage "consists entirely in the most frightful rapids, running at least ten miles an hour over beds of rock."

Rapides des Chats may have been the most difficult portage yet. The Algonquin tribes of the upper Ottawa and the Huron were accustomed to hauling French goods over this impediment on their return from trading, but the guides leading Champlain had no enthusiasm for carrying more than was absolutely necessary; doing otherwise would require repeated ascents of the mist-slickened rocks of the treacherous drop. They insisted that Champlain's party strip its possessions to bare essentials. Champlain observed that "we were obliged to give up our maïze or Indian corn, and some few other provisions we had, together with our least necessary clothes, retaining only our arms and lines, to afford us means of support from hunting and fishing as place and luck might permit." Considerably lightened, they then alternately carried, paddled, and poled the canoes along the sandstone bed of the swift, undulating channel above the main drop: "our *sauvages,* who are indefatigable in this work and accustomed to endure such hardships, aided us greatly."

The way had jogged southwest, opening into another riverine lake, Lac des Chats. The Madawaska flowed into the Ottawa here from the south, tumbling through a parade of falls and rapids as it carved down through more than 750 feet of elevation on its way out of the country of another Algonquin tribe, the Mataouchkairini. Much of the pine forest around Lac des Chats was burned away, and Champlain assumed that Algonquin had cleared the land for crops.

They sought rest and shelter on one of Lac des Chats' islands. Champlain named it Ste-Croix, and erected a cross he fashioned from red cedar, emblazoned with the French coat of arms. Champlain had erected these crosses wherever he stopped along the river, pressing Louis XIII's realm deeper into the hinterland.

Ahead, the prow of Bonnechere Ridge, a plateau of dense pine forest, rose some four hundred feet from the river. The watercourse approaching the ridge was constricted by the rapids of the Chéneaux, literally "gutters" running through a clutch of islands. The way upstream turned from west to north at the promontory of the ridge, and presented the most imposing obstacles yet.

Dark Precambrian rock emerged from beneath the sedimentary deposits of what, 500 million years earlier, had been the bottom of a tropical sea. Here was the first forceful impression of the Laurentian Shield, the landscape of metamorphic and igneous stone scraped bare by ice ages, of forests dominated by pine and spruce, of rivers that found courses in rock seams shattered by glacial passage. The French knew they were in another country now.

For about a mile, the water surged through the rapid that would be known as Portage du Fort, another tumultuous drop that hydroelectric damming would eliminate. Garry would camp here in 1821, describing a night spent before "a violent rapid, with the foam, spray and loud noise." Above the Portage du Fort rapid, the Ottawa divided around Grand Calumet Island. The western course, Rocher Fendu (split rock), remains today a tortuous series of seven punishing rapids, with multiple channels coursing through dozens of islands. The eastern course was less imposing, but still presented several falls and rapids, whose mist may have inspired the coming French traders to name the main island Grand Calumet, or great pipe. When the river rejoined above Grand Calumet, it made a loop through more rapids, the way upstream bending south before leading northwest. The river's main channel completed the loop by wending around the south side of an island that would be called Allumette: the match that lights the great pipe.

In the middle of this channel, between the mainland and Île d'Allumette, was a natural defensive position, now called Morrison Island. This was where Tessöuat and the Kichesipirini made their summer camp, secure above the fifty-odd miles of convoluted river passage upstream of the Chéneaux, which were punctuated by the most forbidding whitewater barricades on the entire course of the Ottawa.

The Grand Calumet section of the river could be overcome most readily by staying to the eastern channel and avoiding Rocher Fendu. It was how Bressani, Mackenzie, and Garry would make their way upriver. But as at Rapides des Chats, the river was still in spring flood when Champlain arrived, as it was only June 6 when he reached the Chéneaux. As his party confronted the lengthy rapid of Portage du Fort, the first of a series of major tests before them, Nicolas de Vignau and the Algonquin guides fell into deep disagreement over where next to proceed.

De Vignau fully expected to carry on up the Ottawa, through Portage du Fort and then around Grand Calumet, one portage and *décharge* at a time. Champlain's guides would not hear of it. *You are tired of living,* they told de Vignau. To Champlain, speaking through Thomas, they declared that the youth was not telling the truth.

The route was certainly feasible, but de Vignau had made the series of portages around Grand Calumet in late August of 1611, when the river's flow might have been less than half that of the spring flood. The Algonquin insisted that at the foot of the Portage du Fort rapid, they would ascend to the high ground of Bonnechere Ridge, and then strike out overland, on a fairly direct path to Tessöuat's summer camp, following a chain of ponds and small lakes. It was about half the distance of the route around Grand Calumet that de Vignau advocated, and without any of the fast-flowing hazards.

But Champlain's Algonquin guides expected their party to leave behind the canoes and cover the entire portage on foot, unless assistance could be gained from the Kinounchepirini, who lived along the route. One of his guides was a Kinounchepirini, and the overland march would allow him to deliver Champlain directly to his chief, Nibachis.

The dispute between the Algonquin guides and de Vignau tested Champlain's faith in the young man. He began to suspect that de Vignau, for reasons unknown, was determined to lead him into impassable rapids, "in order to ruin me or to disgust me with the undertaking." Champlain would not allow de Vignau the perplexing pleasure of sabotaging the expedition. He chose to heed the word of the guides, and at this point may have begun turning exclusively to Thomas as an interpreter.

The canoes were abandoned. Champlain took up three harquebus, three paddles, his cloak, and a few small articles and struck out on foot for the high ground of Bonnechere Ridge.

Depending on the style of harquebus Champlain was using, the three guns he was carrying weighed alone somewhere between forty-five and seventy-five pounds. But the burden of their gear was not the worst aspect of the journey, according to Champlain.

The mosquitoes were almost intolerable as the men followed a crude trail through the enclosing pine forest, and they were famished, having left all their food behind at Rapides des Chats. In the last twenty-four hours, Champlain would note they had eaten only fish they had caught—broiled and unseasoned. After about eight miles of bushwhacking, they were forced to stop. The party had passed along several small ponds, and retired for the day on the shore of what would be named Jeffreys Lake by nineteenth-century homesteaders when the vast stands of ramrod-straight pine were cleared for timber and farming began.

Much as Bressani would note of his Huron travelling companions, Champlain's guides probably carried with them a makeshift shelter—"a piece of bark that serves to keep off the rain during the night." A fire was lit to drive off the mosquitoes, and the men cast lines for fish in the lake, which Champlain found quite pleasant.

After a night's rest, they were on their way again, walking the length of Jeffreys and the adjoining Olmstead Lake before continuing over land for three leagues, "through a country worse than we had yet seen," wrote Champlain, "since the winds had blown down the pines on top of each other. This was no slight inconvenience, as it was necessary to go now over, now under, these trees." Champlain had come upon a *chablis,* a flattening of trees caused by a fierce thundersquall or weak tornado. He also may have been following the course of the Muskrat River, with trees whose roots had lost their grip in the sandy soil of the banks having collapsed in their way. The river would have delivered them directly to the shore of Muskrat Lake, the largest in the chain along this portage, and into the village of Nibachis.

They made camp outside the Kinounchepirini settlement, and Nibachis "came to visit us with his followers." The Algonquin guides were questioned about Champlain. Satisfied with the answers, Nibachis offered Champlain's party tobacco to smoke, and then addressed his own people. Their chief declared "we must have fallen from the clouds, for he knew not how we could have made the journey, and that they who lived in the country had much trouble in traversing these bad ways: and he made understand that I accomplished all that I set my mind upon; in short, that he believed everything the other *sauvages* had told him about me."

The village was bordered by tilled fields of maïze, and Champlain could see people fishing in the lake, which stretched eight miles to the northwest before narrowing into the Muskrat River and finally draining into the Ottawa, just upstream of Tessöuat's village. Seeing their hunger, the Kinounchepirini gave them some fish. When the meal was done, Champlain turned to Thomas to convey to Nibachis the pleasure he had in meeting him, and to explain his purpose for coming. He wished to assist them in their wars, he said, and had to travel still farther to the chiefs beyond him, to deliver the same message. Nibachis was pleased to help, promising them canoes for the journey they would resume the next day.

They followed the narrow lake and the river issuing from it, until they were within about three miles of the Ottawa. Trails that were easy walking led them through "very beautiful" country. And then Lac des Allumettes, the widening of the Ottawa above Île d'Allumette, was before them. It was June 8. Across a short stretch of water was the Kichesipirini summer camp, on Morrison Island.

Tessöuat maintained his own wigwam on the shore opposite the island redoubt. He was conferring with the chief of a neighbouring tribe when Champlain appeared without warning.

"I thought you were a ghost," the aging chief confessed. An apparition was almost more credible than the truth: that Champlain, through sheer force of will and at tremendous personal risk, had overcome about 125 miles of rapids-riven river and wilderness and the hovering threat of Iroquois raiders over the course of thirteen days, to travel from the Great Rapid to Tessöuat's village.

Champlain, de Vignau, and their companions were welcomed, and taken to the island camp.

Twenty-nine

—

CHAMPLAIN ADMIRED WHAT TESSÖUAT HAD ACHIEVED on Morrison Island. Although the wigwams were roughly built, the summer camp was "strongly situated." The island was a slab of limestone, free of flooding in the spring melt. Rapids discouraged a downstream approach, and also churned the water separating it from Île d'Allumette. Attackers would have to make their way up the same arduous portage Champlain had just completed, or struggle through the chain of portages and *décharges* around Grand Calumet. A surprise assault seemed virtually impossible, as an Iroquois force bold enough to attempt one would be easily scouted and ambushed at any number of points where they were exposed and moving awkwardly in single file, all the way downstream to the Akikodjiwan rapids.

And as he strolled about the island, Champlain realized that this natural redoubt was also a cemetery.

The dead were placed on wooden platforms, with their faces carved simply on one end. The largest platform was six or seven feet long and four feet wide, and all were "painted yellow and red, with various decorations as fine as the carving"—by which Champlain meant rather crude.

"If it is a man, they put a shield, a sword with a handle such as they use, a club, a bow and arrows," Champlain explained. A chief would have a *panache,* a bunch of feathers, placed on his head, "and some other ornament or embellishment." A child received a bow and arrow, a woman or girl "a kettle, an earthen pot, a wooden spoon, and a paddle."

A dead man was provided with "his beaver or other skin, which he made use of in his life, and they place beside him all his valuables such as axes, knives, kettles and awls, so that these things may be of use to him in the land to which he goes: for they believe in the immortality of the soul." Only warriors, Champlain stressed, merited the carved burial platforms. Other men received no more special regard than a woman, being "useless people." He found few warrior burials in this cemetery. It must have occurred to him that not many Kichesipirini who went to war managed a peaceful death and interment at home.

For his initial meeting with Tessöuat and a few other Kichesipirini, Champlain decided that explaining the purpose of his visit could wait. Instead, he questioned the natives about their location. As much as he admired the island's defensibility, he had taken note of the poor soil on the mainland, and while fish were plentiful, the hunting was not the best. "I asked them how they could waste their time in cultivating such a poor region, seeing there was much better land which they left untilled and abandoned." Such land, he argued, could be found along the shore below the Great Rapid.

Champlain surely anticipated their answer. The Kichesipirini told him they were forced to live here "to be safe from their enemies," but that if Champlain would establish a French settlement below the Great Rapid, as he promised, they would "come and live near us, feeling assured that their enemies would do them no harm while we were with them."

Champlain had already begun making plans for a settlement below the Great Rapid. On his arrival in June 1611 he had ordered a spot cleared at the river's edge, where the city of Montréal would rise. He called it Place Royale, and planted some seeds, which germinated quickly and gave him hope for the location. Employing local clay for what must have been mud bricks, he had a test wall built four feet high, three or four feet thick, and about seventy feet long, to see if flooding would reach the site the following spring. Two nearby islands also struck him as promising locations for a more easily defended habitation.

Having at last returned to the foot of the Great Rapid in 1613, Champlain had concluded that a fortified settlement should be established there. He now told the Kichesipirini "that this year we should prepare wood and stone in order next year to build a fort and plow the land. When they heard this they gave a great shout in sign of approval."

Champlain then invited all the chiefs and leading men to meet him the next day over on the mainland, at the wigwam of Tessöuat, who was going to give a *tabagie* in Champlain's honour. There, he announced, he would reveal his plans. The Kichesipirini he addressed promised to be there, and immediately sent out invitations to their neighbours.

Nicolas de Vignau had stayed with Tessöuat and his family when the youth overwintered with the Kichesipirini, and a visitor as important as Champlain would have been given no less a place of honour. Tessöuat's wigwam must have been substantial if it was expected to host a *tabagie,* and could have been as large as the ones Champlain had encountered at Point aux Vaches in 1603, which held up to ten families. Champlain, and likely de Vignau, Thomas, and their anonymous French companion, would have spent the night of June 8 in a bark-covered structure with a framework of bent saplings, bedding down on spruce boughs and furs with Tessöuat's extended family and their dogs. This grand wigwam would have been more rectangular than circular, with more than one hole in the roof carrying away the smoke from fires left burning to ward off mosquitoes.

Although Champlain had travelled with native allies, until this night he had not truly lived among them. As austere as life was in a habitation like Quebec, it was still far removed from that of Tessöuat's people. There was no surgeon, no plank-on-frame shelter, no defensive cannon, no singing of "Te Deum." Most Europeans, including Champlain, found the food disgusting: filthy by their standards, sometimes putrid.

To create civilization from wilderness, to bring to heel the landscape and its peoples, Champlain needed young Frenchmen to forge into it ahead of him, to live with the *sauvages* and begin the long process of making them good sedentary Christians. Even so, when Étienne Brûlé volunteered to live among the Algonquin in 1610, Champlain and Pont-Gravé had been sufficiently surprised to want to be assured that this was his true desire. Others, like Thomas and de Vignau, had followed enthusiastically in his wake. What made these French youths so ready to leave behind the relative comforts of civilization, the touchstones of their own culture, the bonds of friends and family, and embrace the life of the *sauvages* that was so (Champlain had no other word for it) barbaric, so devoid of the Lord's presence, of a Christian moral order?

For some of these youths, and those who would follow as woodsmen of any and all description, a bracing liberation was to be found in a land almost inconceivably vast and unbroken in its spirit. Newcomers were often captivated by its untamed and seemingly untamable nature: its ragged dangers, its "wild, romantic manner," as Alexander Mackenzie would say of the Chaudière rapids. The Great Rapid might have entombed the youth Louis, but others had stepped forward, and to a large measure their daring had brought Champlain to this place in the wilderness, to this point in his life and career.

The country, and its people, were raw material for Champlain, waiting to be reshaped as a true New France. In the meantime, the landscape was virtually Godless. There were no priests at either the habitation at Quebec or among the natives, spreading the message of Christ to the heathen and supervising the lives of the young Frenchmen abroad. And there, rather disquietingly, the answer to the question of the country's appeal may have been found by someone like Champlain. Perhaps these youths revelled in a life scandalously liberated from the strictures of any sort of Christian church, without the dense and suffocating social hierarchies of a still-feudal France.

Champlain was hardly unaware of the narcotic allure of young native women, the teenage girls who were free in their culture to have sex with whatever young man they so chose, whenever they so chose, until the day that they selected a mate. He had delicately taken note of native sexual mores in *Des Sauvages*. "When a girl attains the age of fourteen or fifteen years, she may have several suitors and friends, and keep company with such as she pleases. At the end of some five or six years she may choose that one she fancies as her husband." He would later profess his alarm at the overtures Huron girls made toward him. Casual liaisons between the French and these curious and willing and entirely self-assured young women would have been unavoidable. How spectacularly foreign this freedom of behaviour and choice was to a minor noble like Champlain, who advertised his devout Catholicism regularly in his writings, and whose own largely inscrutable private life nevertheless was highlighted by an arranged marriage in December 1610 to a twelve-year-old girl.

Champlain's union with Hélène Boullé was assuredly entirely loveless. While Huron marriages required the approval of parents, who sought alliances through their children, Champlain's marriage contract forbade him to consummate the relationship for two years, unless her father gave specific permission. That consummation probably waited several years more: the balance of her 6,000-livre dowry, on which Champlain had collected an initial 4,500 on their wedding, was not paid out until 1619. It was a union about power, and strategic relationships, and in no small part the enormous dowry. Hélène was the daughter of a prominent Huguenot, Nicolas Boullé, secretary of the royal chamber. Champlain probably named Île Ste-Hélène, below the Great Rapid, in his bride's honour, yet they lived together intermittently and would never have children.

The women of the country were a profound mystery to Champlain. Their sexual mores were scandalous in Christian eyes, and this strange empowerment seemed also to express itself in their willing and inventive participation in the torture of prisoners. Sometimes, they became victims of torture as well: Champlain once liberated an Iroquois woman while his allies were removing her fingers. There was no weaker sex; in many tribes, hereditary rights of chiefs were matrilineal. While Champlain's dealings in the New World were with the warriors and the chiefs, the women for him were an unacknowledged force, hardly as "useless" as he claimed after touring the island cemetery.

After witnessing the nude dancers at Tessöuat's *tabagie* at Tadoussac in 1603, Champlain all but averted his gaze from the country's women. He became something of a warrior-priest who moved through a landscape that mocked the neat rectilinear woodlots of David Pelletier's engraving on his maps, acknowledging his own suffering and hardship but no pleasure. That first night in Tessöuat's village on the shore of the Ottawa, de Vignau and Thomas might have slipped away, into welcoming arms, but Champlain lay alone. Exhausted and bruised by the ordeal of the river, he was determined to keep moving forward: higher up the watershed, deeper into the wilderness, and among peoples stranger still. The Sorcerers had been waiting for him for almost two years, and so had the English boy.

Thirty

—

THE GUESTS ASSEMBLED AT TESSÖUAT'S WIGWAM for the *tabagie* in Champlain's honour on June 9, each carrying his own wooden bowl and spoon, and seating themselves on the ground without ceremony or any apparent regard to rank. By strange coincidence, it was ten years to the day that Champlain had first met Tessöuat at Tadoussac, when the chief had planted the poles adorned with Iroquois heads and presided over the singing and dancing of the warriors and their wives and daughters, before demanding tribute from the Montagnais and Maliséet.

Tessöuat served to his guests chowder "made of maïze crushed between two stones, mixed with meat and fish, cut into little pieces, the whole being boiled together without salt. They also had meat roasted on coals, and fish boiled apart, which he also distributed."

Champlain was not having any of it. They prepared their food, he wrote, "in a very dirty manner." He asked for some fish and meat to prepare in his own way, which the Algonquin obliged him. For drink, they had "fine, clear water." Following the custom of the *tabagie,* Tessöuat ate nothing as his guests dined.

When the feast was over, the young men withdrew from the great wigwam. There were no windows to provide illumination or ventilation. Shafts of light, reaching down from the smoke holes in the bark roof, in a spectrum running from cream to grey, would have been diffused by the fine airborne ash and the powdery dust of the hardpacked ground. Much of the interior would have been left in deep shadow, as a late-spring sun warmed the structure and brought its many aromas alive. The wigwam was a place where the Algonquin not only lived, slept, and prepared and ate their meals but stored their food, including maïze and smoke-cured game.

Tessöuat's wigwam would have brimmed with the spoils of contact. As dogs moved among the *tabagie*'s participants, seeking handouts from the meal, Champlain and his companions could have caught glimpses of the treasured red blankets, the iron kettles and trivets and knives—goods that Tessöuat had gathered from the merchants who came to trade below the Great Rapid, as well as from Huron and Onontchataronon who surrendered the items as tolls in passing through his territory. The many Iroquois scalps Tessöuat had personally harvested, from enemies killed in battle and prisoners brought back to this redoubt for torture and execution, also must have been on prominent display.

The elders lit pipes and passed them around. For half an hour, the tobacco was ceremonially shared, without a word being spoken, while a sweet fog settled over the gathering.

It did not matter that these people lived in conditions that would offend the poorest denizens of Paris, that Champlain found wretched the best meal they could offer him, or that their faces routinely were decorated by vivid paints. Champlain did not doubt their intelligence, their sagacity, their present advantage over him. They were sitting in judgment of what he had done for them to date, and of what he hoped to do next. Years of ambition had become focused on this meeting and the speech he had to deliver, whatever aches and exhaustion lingered from the gruelling journey up the river.

Champlain turned to Thomas in order to make his address. He could not have had a more expectant audience.

Champlain explained that he had made the journey only to assure them of his friendship, and of his desire to help them in their wars, as he had done before. He explained that he had been prevented from coming to them in 1612, as he had promised, because his king had employed him in other wars. It was a lie they were in no position to challenge. He assured them that his king had ordered him to visit them and fulfill his promises. To that end, he had men waiting at the Great Rapid, prepared to join them in a raid on the Iroquois.

Champlain also noted that he had come to their country to observe the fertility of their soil, to see their lakes and rivers—and to visit the sea that they had said was in their country. And he wished to visit a tribe that was six days' journey from them, the Nebicerini, so that he could invite them to war as well. In order to reach the sea and extend the invitation to the Nebicerini, he would require four canoes and eight Algonquin to guide him.

As the word *Nebicerini* left the lips of Thomas, Champlain could see his audience become more attentive.

"After I had finished my discourse," Champlain would write, "they began again to smoke, and to confer among themselves in a very low voice respecting my propositions." Then Tessöuat replied, on behalf of everyone assembled.

He had always regarded Champlain as more friendly toward the Algonquin than any other Frenchman, Tessöuat began. The past proofs they had of this made them more at ease about the prospects for the future. And Champlain had shown himself to be a true friend, by taking so many risks to visit them and invite them to war. All of these things made them feel as kindly toward him as they did to their own children.

Nevertheless.

Last year, Tessöuat told Champlain, you broke your promise. Two thousand warriors had gone to the rapid, expecting to join him there for an assault on the Iroquois and to make presents to him. But he was not there. They were "greatly saddened" by this. They concluded, as some French traders told them, that he was dead. And the Frenchmen they did meet at the rapid did not want to go to war with them, and they treated some of their number badly. Never expecting to see Champlain again, the Kichesipirini and their allies had already gone to war this year without him, twelve hundred men in all.

It was all well for Champlain to say that he had men waiting at the Great Rapid, but Tessöuat told him they were not prepared to go to war yet again this year. And they were most displeased with his desire to visit the Nebicerini. Tessöuat spoke of the hardships of such a journey, and of the Nebicerini themselves. These people were sorcerers, *mitek,* who had caused the deaths of many of his own tribe by charms and poisoning, and so were not friends of the Kichesipirini. And as for war, Champlain was not to think of them. They had little courage.

But Champlain was not to be deterred from visiting the Nebicerini, collecting the English boy, and gaining the Northern Sea.

It was not far to the Nebicerini, he replied, and the way could not be worse than what he had already travelled. And their witchcraft could not harm him, because his god would preserve him. Champlain further claimed to know the herbs they used for their potions and so could avoid eating them. It was also his desire, he explained, to make friends of the Nebicerini and the Kichesipirini. To that end, he would make presents to the Nebicerini, as he was confident they would do "something" for him.

That was as close as Champlain was willing to come to mentioning the gift of the English boy.

The Kichesipirini considered his proposal. The offer to serve as an ambassador, to broker a firm alliance between them and the Nebicerini, must have had an effect. Champlain was told he could have his four canoes and paddlers.

Champlain was delighted. The decision, he would write, made him forget all of the troubles he had gone through so far to reach the "much-desired sea."

After leaving the *tabagie* triumphant, Champlain wandered in the village's gardens, inspecting the pumpkins, beans, and peas. Then Thomas came to him. The interpreter, "who understands their language very well," reported that after Champlain left the meeting, the Algonquin continued to discuss his plans and had made different ones of their own.

The Kichesipirini had decided that if Champlain were to travel to the Nebicerini, he would die at the hands of these sorcerers, as would the Kichesipirini who went along with him. They could not give him the canoes they promised, because no one was willing to guide him. They now thought Champlain should wait another year to make the journey. They would tell Champlain he could travel then with a good escort of Kichesipirini, who would protect him against these evil people.

Infuriated, Champlain stormed back to Tessöuat and his elders. Champlain had Thomas tell them that "he held them to be men, and true to their word, but now they were showing themselves children and liars." If they did not wish to keep their promises, Champlain charged, then they should not pretend to be his friends. But if it was instead the case that they felt inconvenienced by his request, he could make do with two canoes and four guides.

The Kichesipirini reiterated their objections: the difficulties of the portages, the number of rapids, the wickedness of the Nebicerini and other tribes he would encounter. It was only on account of their fear for his safety, they stressed, that they were now refusing his request.

"Tell them I am sorry they have showed themselves so little my friends," Champlain instructed Thomas. "That I should never have believed what they said." And, pointing to de Vignau, he had Thomas announce that he had a youth "who had been in that country and had not noticed all the difficulties they presented, nor found those tribes as bad as they were saying."

The Kichesipirini looked to de Vignau, none of them more carefully than Tessöuat.

"Nicolas, is it true that you have said you had been in Nebicerini country?" the old chief asked.

There was a lengthy silence, until at last de Vignau said to them in Algonquin: *Enh.* Yes. Yes, I have been there.

The Kichesipirini erupted. "Immediately they regarded him with anger, and rushed upon him, as if they would have eaten him or torn him apart, shouting very loudly," recalled Champlain.

They were hurling words at de Vignau that Champlain could not understand. "You are a brazen liar," Champlain heard Tessöuat say to de Vignau, through the translation by Thomas. "You know well that every night you slept beside me and my children, and rose every morning at that place. If you visited those tribes, it was in your sleep. Why have you been so shame-faced as to tell lies to your chief, and so wicked as to wish to jeopardize his life amid so many dangers? You are a miserable wretch who ought to be put to death more cruelly than we do our enemies. I am not surprised Champlain scolded us so much, having confidence in what you told him."

Champlain turned at once to the set-upon de Vignau. "I must reply to these people," he told the youth. "And since you have been in those parts, you must give evidence of that to convince me, to get me out of the difficulty you've placed me in."

De Vignau "remained silent and quite abashed." And so Champlain drew him aside, away from the angry Algonquin.

Champlain "begged him earnestly to tell me the truth, and said that if he had seen this sea, I would have the promised reward given to him." And "if he had not seen it, he must tell me so, without giving me any more worry."

Champlain needed the truth of what de Vignau knew, and how he knew it. But whichever way de Vignau answered, someone would see him dead. If he insisted he had told the truth, the Algonquin would continue to call him a brazen liar and insist on his death—which Champlain might not be able to prevent if he wished to escape with his own life. And if de Vignau said he was lying, the Algonquin would probably still wish him dead, and Champlain himself could see to it that he was executed as brutally as he had the traitorous locksmith Duval, for all the trouble he had caused.

"Once more with oaths he affirmed all that he had before asserted," wrote Champlain, "and said that he would show me this if these *sauvages* would give us the canoes."

Thomas then came to Champlain and de Vignau. He said he had discovered that the Kichesipirini were secretly sending a canoe to the Nebicerini, to warn them of Champlain's arrival. It was a bewildering development. Were the Kichesipirini fearful of the Nebicerini or not? Why did the Nebicerini need to know about Champlain's intentions? Was Tessöuat in fact aware of the English boy, and wished the Nebicerini to remove him, for now, from Champlain's reach?

Champlain decided to turn the intelligence to his advantage. He went back to Tessöuat and his people and told them: *Last night, I had a dream.* In this dream, Champlain explained, he had seen that they were going to send a canoe to the Nebicerini, without telling Champlain, which astonished him, he confessed, since the Kichesipirini knew he wanted to visit them.

Dreams were not to be trifled with. If Champlain saw Kichesipirini preparing to send a canoe to the Nebicerini, then that was what must happen, and Tessöuat could not now be convinced to do otherwise. But if Champlain was inventing the vision, then he was committing a great offence against their beliefs.

The Algonquin plainly believed Champlain had fabricated the dream, telling him he had done the Kichesipirini "a great wrong." He had more confidence in a liar who wanted to kill him than in so many honest chiefs who were his friends and held his life dear.

But Champlain would not retreat, and he laid down the card he had never intended to play. He declared that de Vignau had been to that region with one of Tessöuat's own relatives, that he had seen the sea, and the broken fragments of an English ship, along with English scalps in the possession of the Nebicerini. And that the Nebicerini were holding prisoner an English youth, and wished to make to him a gift of the youth and the scalps.

At this, the Kichesipirini "exclaimed more loudly than before that he was a liar," and hurled other words at de Vignau that made "the greatest insult they could offer to him. With one voice, they declared that he should be put to death, or that he should name the person with whom he had gone there, and should state the lakes, rivers, and trails by which he had passed."

A terrified de Vignau replied that he had forgotten the name of the person—"although he had mentioned his name to me more than twenty times, and even on the previous day," wrote Champlain. There was no way for Champlain himself to identify the man, who must have been present, without de Vignau's corroboration. Champlain would be accusing a relative of Tessöuat of lying in concealing his role in de Vignau's journey, without any evidence to support the grave insult. As for the details of that journey, there was the map de Vignau had drawn, which Champlain was carrying. Champlain now showed it to the furious Algonquin, who began grilling de Vignau on its details. The youth would not reply.

His doubt growing, Champlain withdrew from the quarrel to review in his own mind what he knew of the Hudson voyage, and confirmed de Vignau's statements to be consistent with everything he had learned from the Hessel Gerritsz book and map. It was so unlikely, Champlain decided, that de Vignau could have invented all of what he had revealed and not have made the journey. "It was more than likely that he had seen these things," Champlain concluded. He was sure it was de Vignau's ignorance of details of the landscape that left him unable to answer the particular questions of the Algonquin who were so aggressively critiquing his map.

Champlain's isolation and vulnerability were now profound. He had deeply angered Tessöuat and his people, and was many days' travel from the Great Rapid, far beyond the reach or knowledge of any Frenchman. A canoe was being prepared to speed a messenger to the Nebicerini for reasons unknown, while Champlain himself could go nowhere, neither upriver nor down, without the great chief's assistance or goodwill. And de Vignau was on the verge of being torn to pieces.

Champlain sent for de Vignau to come before him, Thomas, and the hapless, anonymous Frenchmen they had dragged along from the Great Rapid.

Champlain told de Vignau that "the time for dissimilation was past, that he must tell me whether or not he had seen the things he had related. I said that I wished to seize the opportunity that presented itself, that I had forgotten all that had happened, but that if I had to proceed farther, I should have him hanged and strangled without any mercy."

The arguments had attracted the village's attention. Children were gathering, as eager as the elders to have the interpreter who had lived among them put to an excruciating death. Spring flood-waters were moving out of the stillness of the riverine lake upstream, tumbling past the island into an irresistible, eruptive descent. They were all on the brink of something wild and terrible.

Nicolas de Vignau collapsed to his knees before Champlain.

PART III

—

The Returning

Thirty-one

—

IN THE DAYS THAT FOLLOWED THE MUTINY OF JUNE 22,
1611, the *Discovery* moved closer to anarchy than to England.
The Trinity House transaction record of October 24, 1611,
which gave a basic accounting of the fate of the entire *Discovery*
crew, would state: "After Hudson was put out, the company elected
Bylot as master." But Habakkuk Prickett would not attribute any
formal authority to Bylot, proposing instead that the crew "had
many devices in their heads, but Henry Greene in the end was their
captain, and so called of them."

Robert Bylot was a complete unknown to the historical record
when he appeared in the general crew ranks of the *Discovery,* but he
had skills that Hudson respected. When Hudson sent the shore
party to East Digges Island in August 1610, he must have been relying on Bylot to observe the tide for clues to the direction a passage
might lie. But in the summer of 1611, Bylot, with the *Discovery*
mutiny so close astern and his own culpability in question, struggled to maintain control of the *Discovery's* course, as if cursed by
some of Hudson's last purported words: that "they were all dead
men" because "there was no man left able to carry the ship home."

Within a few days of the mutiny, the *Discovery* came to some
islands—James Bay is littered with them—where some of the crew

went ashore, gathering what Prickett called "cockle grass" in hope of alleviating the scurvy cases. Two birds were also shot. They remained at anchor for a night and "the best part of the next day, in all which time we saw not the shallop, or ever after," wrote Prickett. The time had come to sort out who was in control.

After the mutiny's events were related by the chaotic chorus of survivors in depositions before the High Court of the Admiralty, the narrative for the remainder of the *Discovery* voyage returned to the care of Prickett. The haberdasher wrote that he was approached by Greene, who informed him that the crew wished Prickett to take charge of Hudson's cabin and possessions, presumably because he was the owner's representative. Prickett disagreed, saying the responsibility lay with Juet. At this point, Prickett evidently understood that Juet was going to take command of the vessel.

Greene replied that Juet wanted nothing to do with Hudson's things: "he said he should not come into [the cabin], nor meddle with the master's card or journals."

At that, Prickett agreed to take responsibility for Hudson's effects. Greene gave him the key to Hudson's chest, but revealed that he had already been through it and "had laid out the master's best things together, which he would use himself when time did serve." The quantity of biscuit that Prickett said was found in the cabin was turned over to Prickett's care.

Both Juet and Greene seemed determined to exercise their own particular authority. Juet was interested in seizing nautical command, the day-to-day working of the ship, while Greene desired control over their ultimate destination and the pecking order of men. But neither Greene nor Juet wanted to be seen to have replaced Hudson. Juet's aversion to touching Hudson's effects was most likely a ruse to avoid assuming control of the charts, log, and journal, which would be a sure sign of guilt in the mutiny. And so

Greene and Juet had settled on persuading Prickett (at the alleged wishes of the crew) to be responsible for the cabin and Hudson's effects. If Prickett took possession of the ship's papers and Hudson's cabin, then Prickett would also serve as acting master.

The problem with the scheme was that the majority of the crew was unwilling to go along with it. While Greene fancied himself the commander, he was no sailor, and the weight of his authority rested largely in the persuasiveness of his thuggish accomplices, William Wilson and John Thomas foremost among them. Despite Juet's navigation skills, support for his fiery leadership must have been thin as well. And no mariner could have imagined granting Prickett command of the vessel.

So the crew held their vote and chose Bylot to serve as master. But Juet immediately challenged Bylot on the best course to steer. While Bylot in Prickett's telling enjoyed the last word (a sign that he was in fact the master, as the Trinity House record stated), the arguments with Juet would persist. They were trapped in a dense ice field for two full weeks, then could not even agree between themselves (with Prickett providing his own opinions) whether they had reached Cape Wolstenholme or had sailed past it. Neither Bylot nor Juet were such poor navigators that incompetence could explain the problems. Hudson's chart for Hudson Bay was probably rudimentary, and their course south in 1610 had most likely been farther west. This must have been the first time the Discovery crew had seen the east shore of the bay. And the sky would have been persistently overcast, frustrating efforts to secure a latitude fix.

Meanwhile, Greene (as always, in Prickett's telling) represented a perpetual threat to shipboard order. Prickett claimed that Greene began stealing things, and then contriving to conceal his guilt by sending Prickett looking for them, as if they were misplaced. Prickett also alleged that Greene accused him of nicking thirty biscuits from the supply found in Hudson's cabin, which had been entrusted to the haberdasher.

While Juet and Bylot bickered over the course steered and their very location on the surface of the earth, Greene made known that he was determined the *Discovery* would not "come into any place (but keep the sea still) till he had the king's majesty's hand and seal to show for his safety." Prickett would also testify to the High Court of the Admiralty that about this time "Greene, [William] Wilson and Thomas had consult him together to turn pirates," and that they would have done so were it not for what happened upon the *Discovery*'s return to the murre colony.

Food was running perilously low by the time the *Discovery* reached Cape Wolstenholme on July 26, more than a month after the mutiny. They had failed to reconnoitre the Belcher Islands, which teemed with walruses, or to avail themselves of Hudson Bay's seals and beluga whales. But none of that mattered now that the murre colony was within sight. They ran the *Discovery* hard aground on a shoal in Digges Sound in their ecstatic approach, and hung there for a good eight hours, waiting for the flood tide to free them. The crew killed about thirty Icelandic gulls nesting in the cliff face with their muskets, but the bird harvest was difficult and the anchorage uncertain. And so, on the twenty-seventh, they sailed over to Cape Digges, on East Digges Island, to restock on its murres.

As Prickett would tell it, a shore party that included (and was most certainly led by) Henry Greene encountered seven boats manned by "savages," who were camped in tents to the west of the murre colony. They were Inuit, and like the *Discovery*'s men were drawn to the island by the hundreds of thousands of seabirds on the cliffs.

These Inuit could have watched the *Discovery*'s progress as Hudson brought her through these waters in 1610. The Inuit maintained rich oral histories, and through contact with other groups, this band may have had some knowledge of the Frobisher and Davis expeditions, and of Waymouth as well. There would have been a broad appreciation of the sorts of marvellous goods to be gained from people who came in great wooden boats.

The *Discovery*'s men agreed to follow the Inuit to their summer camp. They exchanged hostages, with a *Discovery* crewman remaining in a tent while an Inuit accompanied the Englishmen to the bird colony. The sheer granite cliffs rose five hundred feet from the sea. Their guide showed them how the birds were caught, by knocking them down with a long pole. The *Discovery*'s men in turn demonstrated the power of a musket, which could knock "seven or eight" birds out of the air with a single shot.

On the boat's return to the summer camp, the Inuit "made great joy, with dancing, and leaping, and stroking of their breasts," according to Prickett. "Diverse things" were offered to the *Discovery*'s men, but the English were interested only in walrus ivory, which was secured for "a knife and two glass buttons." Greene came away with the impression, gained through signs, that he could return to trade for fresh meat. The next day, July 29, he did just that, taking with him William Wilson, John Thomas, Michael Perce, Adrian Moter, and Prickett, who claimed still to be lame but was expected to serve as the ship's cape merchant, bringing "such things as I had in the cabin, of everything somewhat" as trade goods.

"And so, with more haste than good speed (and not without swearing) away we went," Prickett recalled of the madcap departure from the *Discovery* in the ship's boat.

As they approached the cove where the Inuit were camped, Prickett could see people on the hills "dancing and leaping." The ship's boat was brought into the beach and fastened to a rock. The Inuit surged forward, everyone holding something for barter.

Greene was firm: there was to be no trading for anything until he had venison.

Greene and Wilson showed off some bells and mirrors and a jaw harp; Perce and Moter went ashore to gather the antiscorbutic "sorrel." One of the Inuit men clambered into the bow of the boat, where Prickett was seated. He had "a bottle" to show Prickett—an interesting artifact of some trade, perhaps second- or third-hand, with Europeans.

The man's presence made him nervous, and Prickett made signs for the Inuit to go ashore. When he seemed—or pretended, in Prickett's judgment—not to understand, Prickett stood up and pointed the way, and the man obediently disembarked.

Prickett sat down again, but was surprised then to see a leg and foot next to him. Someone was standing over him. He craned his neck to take in another Inuit, and glimpsed the knife coming down.

Unless indigenous people saw an immediate danger in the newcomers they encountered, they usually attempted to establish some exchange with them. Europeans had wonderful things to offer, above all metals. While North American natives often possessed decorative items, and occasionally weapons, made from annealed copper, there was no locally produced iron. Europeans were wide-eyed at the masses of copper worn by some tribes, but it was the mines that produced the copper they were most interested in reaching. For the native groups, the iron goods that Europeans offered, such as hatchets, knives, and kettles, offered immediate, practical gratification.

Of all the native groups encountered during the contact period of the sixteenth and seventeenth centuries, in their reaction to Europeans none was more complex, more unpredictable, than the Inuit. The Europeans themselves were unpredictable enough, and sometimes devastatingly so. But even a man like John Davis, who was unusually determined to treat the Inuit kindly—leaving aside his one unfortunate if predictable incident of kidnapping a man—was pressed beyond exasperation by how quickly cordial relations along Davis Strait broke down as the Inuit turned to unrestrained pilfering. Once they attempted to steal a ship's anchor from Davis in broad daylight. And when Davis began assembling a pinnace on shore, the Inuit dismantled it as fast as he could put it together, in order to have the nails.

The best-known cases of Inuit attack at the time the *Discovery* called at East Digges Island in July 1611 had come on the Labrador coast, with John Davis's loss of four men to an ambush in 1586, and with the disappearance of John Knight and the subsequent massed assault on the grounded *Hopewell* in 1606. Regardless of who initiated them, bloody confrontations were routine occurrences between Europeans and native peoples all along the coast of eastern North America. Hudson had experienced a few himself on the 1609 voyage, and had been wary enough on the *Discovery* expedition to establish the policy during the James Bay overwintering that anyone who went ashore was to carry a musket and be accompanied by someone with a pike.

Henry Greene had rushed to his trading appointment with the Inuit, armed only, according to Prickett, with a pike, which he held as he stood on shore, displaying his gewgaw wares and insisting on fresh meat in exchange. And rather than keeping the boat safely away from shore, as East India sailors did when trading with local people, Greene had the *Discovery*'s boat tied to a rock, where it could easily be gained by the Inuit, with only the ailing Prickett aboard it.

Prickett wrote that he was able to bring an arm across his chest in time to deflect the thrust of the Inuit who had stolen up on him from behind in the shallop, although the knife still wounded his arm and pierced his chest below his right nipple.

Prickett raised his left hand to prevent the next thrust, and nearly lost his little finger; a third stab found his right thigh. At that, Prickett was able to grab the tether on the knife's handle, and the Inuit's sleeve with the other hand, and pull the man over. Grasping his own knife, he quickly stabbed the fallen assailant in the chest and throat.

Around him, his shipmates were being butchered.

John Thomas and William Wilson were disembowelled, and both Greene and Perce were seriously wounded. They all fell into the boat; Moter raced down from the rocks where he had been gathering sorrel and dove into the sea, swimming after the boat as its bleeding and gutted occupants tried to clear the shore. Perce fended off Inuit who were pressing the attack at the bow, knocking one into the sea with a hatchet blow, as Greene shouted "Coragio" and flailed at their attackers with a truncheon. Moter, crying out at the stern to be pulled aboard, was retrieved by Perce.

The Inuit took up their bows, and the arrows sang home. Greene fell dead. Others took many hits. Prickett was struck in the back as they fought to turn the boat around and make for the *Discovery*. Perce and Moter took to the oars and rowed them clear. Prickett watched with dismay as the Inuit ran for their own boats, but was relieved when they decided not to launch them.

Once the survivors had rowed a good distance from shore, Perce fainted at his oar. Moter stood in the bow and waved frantically at the *Discovery*, whose men finally awoke to their shipmates' desperation, weighed anchor, and closed with the boat.

Greene's body was dumped from the boat into the ocean. The rest, including the Inuit man who had attacked Prickett and who was still alive "yet without sense," were brought aboard.

There was little the barber-surgeon could do for them. The Inuit, Thomas, and Wilson all died that day, with Wilson, stomach sliced open, "swearing and cursing in a most fearful manner." Perce lingered for two more days. Only Moter and Prickett lived.

Nevertheless, there was something not quite right about Prickett's account. It was doubtful that the Inuit would have planned an attack in advance. Even if the shore party seemed vulnerable to them, they had been shown the devastating effect of musket shot on their first meeting, and the *Discovery* was anchored offshore. The prospect of a counterattack must have been high, and this was a family camp. The Inuit may have been on their guard, but not prepared to launch an actual assault. More likely is that the trading session had rapidly spun out of control.

Prickett of course blamed Greene for what happened. He charged that "Henry Greene (more than the rest) was so confident, that (by no means) we should take care to stand on our guard: God blinding him so, that where he made reckoning to receive great matters from these people, he received more than he looked for, and that suddenly . . ." Greene had been made "a good example for all men . . . that mean no conscience of doing evil, and that we take heed of the savage people, how simple soever they seem to be."

However the attack had come about, now there were nine left aboard the *Discovery* from the original complement of twenty-three. And they still did not have enough food to get home.

They remained in the vicinity of the attack for several days, the *Discovery* sailing back and forth, unable to anchor safely, as men were dispatched to harvest birds in difficult, dangerous conditions. "For if the wind blew there was a high sea, and the eddies of the tide would carry the ship so near the rocks as it feared our master, as I will now call him." Only with the death of Greene was

Prickett willing to grant Bylot the master's role, but he did so without ever using Bylot's name.

They killed three hundred birds, and then moved on, back east along Hudson Strait. They nearly ran aground on the islands at the tip of Chidley Cape, which marked the southern extreme of the Furious Overfall. The fog was so thick that they "were ready to run [their] bowsprit against the rocks" when they saw their way clear. The small band of survivors shaped a course for John Davis's Desolation, at the southern end of Greenland.

From there, they planned to make for Ireland. The crew went on a "hard allowance" of half a bird a day with their porridge. They had been skinning the murres because they could not be plucked, but Juet began preparing their skins as well to eat, by burning away the tiny feathers. There was little they did not eat: the skins became "a great dish of meat, and as for the garbage, it was not thrown away."

Their effort to steer for southern Greenland was thwarted by the wind, which forced them away. Juet persuaded the ship's company that they should now make for Newfoundland, where they could find "great relief" from the English fishermen there. Even if the fishermen were gone, Juet argued, they could find a "great store of bread and fish left ashore by them."

The wind pressed them west-southwest, away from Greenland, until they had almost reached latitude 57. If the wind remained against them, they were in danger of being forced to seek refuge along precisely the same part of the Labrador coast where John Knight had vanished.

The wind shifted, to the west-southwest. Their options at once widened. They could sail for Newfoundland, as Juet argued, or for Ireland. Bylot, wrote Prickett, came to him and asked what course they should choose. They might have been less than four hundred miles from Newfoundland, some eighteen hundred from Ireland.

"I said it was best to go where we knew corn grew, and not to seek it where it was cast away and not be found," Prickett advised. Bylot agreed with him. "Toward Ireland we now stood," wrote Prickett, "with prosperous winds for many days together."

But the wind was fickle, and the food was running out.

Bennet Mathew cracked the bones of the last of the *Discovery*'s bludgeoned birds and fried the marrow in candle grease till crisp, then dressed the offering in vinegar. The men took their despairing turns at the whipstaff, so famished that they had to sit rather than stand, with the *Discovery* wandering in response to the desultory guidance of their weakening hands. The sails flapped through inattention; the horizon provided nothing to steer for. Robert Bylot strove to bring the ship to Galway Bay while overseeing the feeble efforts of those around him.

Somewhere at that same time, on that some ocean, Samuel de Champlain was sailing from Tadoussac to La Rochelle, remarking on the "fair" weather that blessed his crossing after a few days of fog in the Gulf of St. Lawrence. Nicolas de Vignau was now in Tessöuat's care, and on the verge of reaching the Kichesipirini summer camp, secure above the whitewater barricades of the Ottawa River.

Juet struggled with the chart and their undisciplined helmsmanship to reach a dead-reckoning estimate of when Ireland might at last be sighted. When he estimated that they were within sixty or seventy leagues of landfall, those leagues passed without any interruption to the smooth rim of the bowl of the eastern horizon, and then more leagues still. The world made no sense to him. And Juet, "for mere want," Prickett attested, then died.

The remaining men would have heaved the aging navigator's body overboard. They began to fear that they might have missed

Ireland altogether, that the *Discovery* had wandered too far south. But on September 6, some 130 leagues beyond where Juet had asserted Ireland would appear for them, the rim of the bowl acquired a blessed imperfection: Dursey.

—

Thirty-two

WITH THE ASSISTANCE OF THE FISHERMEN hired off Dursey, the *Discovery* was able to reach England. Having survived starvation and cold, uncharted Arctic waters, the cruel division of the crew, and an Inuit attack, the eight remaining members of Henry Hudson's last voyage now had to plot a course through the legal hazards awaiting them in London.

The ship anchored off Plymouth Castle, but did not "stop or stay," according to Habakkuk Prickett. He and Bylot could not allow the crewmembers to disperse. They had to keep their story safely aboard. Taking advantage of fair winds, they pressed down the English Channel, making for the capital with all speed. As to what terrible events might have occurred aboard the *Discovery,* watchers of the coast would have gathered scuttlebutt from English fishermen returning from Dursey, and from the extra hands who had been hired to bring the ship home. The survivors had to race such rumours to London, and not allow an advantage to slip to anyone who might hear the tale before they could deliver it in person.

At Gravesend, Prickett recalled, "most of our men went ashore." Among them was Bylot, who left it to Prickett and an unknown complement to get the *Discovery* up the Thames. Bylot would have gone ahead to judge the nature of their reception, to ensure that they would not be immediately tossed into Marshalsea Prison in Southwark by the Lord High Admiral, who was also one of the voyage's sponsors. When the *Discovery* halted at Erith, just down-river from the capital, Bylot "came aboard, and so had me up to London with him," Prickett wrote. Together they made for the home of Sir Thomas Smythe on Philpot Lane, to hand over the ship's papers and do whatever they could to ensure their freedom.

The less brave and ambitious among the survivors could opt for flight, but the rest would hope to preserve their good names. Without Smythe's protection, their situation was hopeless. They needed to harness his peerless influence within London's trade companies, political offices, and the royal household.

Presenting a plausible alibi was critical, but it would not be nearly enough. They had to dangle some uncollected prize before men of influence, something only the survivors could deliver up. Certain formalities of justice would still have to be respected, and miserable days might be spent in prison waiting for their deliverance, but those who had the stomach for the risks and the confidence in their patrons would ultimately be rewarded.

Trinity House at Deptford Strand had the first crack at passing judgment on the *Discovery*'s survivors. Essentially a guild for ship pilots and masters like Henry Hudson, the corporation had gained the power to punish seamen under its extended charter of 1604. But that power did not amount to much when it came to an event like the *Discovery* mutiny. In a 1611 case, its master and elder brethren conceded that the greatest punishment they could inflict on men guilty of mutiny was a denial of wages. What if any action Trinity House took against the *Discovery*'s survivors is unknown, but docking their pay for the loss of Henry Hudson and the others would hardly have seemed a satisfactory resolution. On October 24, Trinity House's transaction records gave a basic summary of who had lived and who had died, and not much more. The survivors' first legal hurdle had been cleared.

The impression Prickett and Bylot made on Smythe and other investors was sufficient to encourage a continuation of the passage search. On December 4, John Chamberlain wrote to Sir Dudley Carleton, King James's ambassador to Venice, with London gossip, noting that Sir Dudley Digges is "busy with the discovery of the north-west passage." And before 1611 was out, Smythe's East India Company decided to commit 300 pounds annually for the next three years to supporting the quest.

Prickett may have further stoked the enthusiasm for an imminent passage success at this time by conveniently recalling that the knife the Inuit man had used to stab him looked rather East Indian in origin. It was a fact he failed to note in his written narrative, but it was recalled by Samuel Purchas in *Purchas His Pilgrimes* in 1625: "The weapons and arts which they saw, beyond those of other savages, are arguments hereof [for a passage to the Pacific]. He which assaulted Prickett in the boat, had a weapon broad and sharp indented, of bright steel (such as they use in Java), riveted into a handle of morse tooth." It followed that either these savages had come from the Pacific, or trade through a passage to the west had placed the knife into the hand of Prickett's attacker.

The search would resume in the spring, and it inevitably invited the participation of some of the survivors, who could help guide the expedition. Whether or not they would be allowed to join, or even be allowed to live, was up to the High Court of the Admiralty.

The High Court of the Admiralty was rather more empowered than Trinity House, its considerable authority extending beyond the Royal Navy to indictable actions on British merchant ships, on navigable waters within the kingdom and on the high seas. On January 25, 1612, England's Lord High Admiral—Charles Howard, Earl of Nottingham and soon to be Baron of Effingham—formally took an interest in the disappearance of Henry and John Hudson and their seven companions.

Lord Howard's position bore the usual complications of the times. As Lord High Admiral, he upheld the kingdom's laws through his court. But through his 1585 patent from Elizabeth I (a cousin of his), the admiralty was very much his personal property. And as an investor in Hudson's voyage who was prepared to continue funding the passage search, he had his own interests to consider, as well as those of friends and relatives. Two powerful members of the Howard family had also backed the Hudson voyage: the Lord High Admiral's uncle, the Earl of Northampton, who was Keeper of the Privy Seal and would be named Lord High Treasurer in 1612, and the Lord High Admiral's cousin, the Earl of Suffolk, who as Lord Chamberlain was head of the king's household.

On criminal matters within its purview, the High Court of the Admiralty operated as a Commission of Oyer and Terminer—"to hear and determine." Cases originated with the Lord High Admiral himself, or on direction from the Privy Council (of which he was a member); a citizen could also launch a case through a petition to the Lord High Admiral. A commission panel, led in strict legal terms by the Lord High Admiral's chief justice, Dr. Julius Caesar, but more practically by a deputized judge drawn from Doctors' Commons, questioned suspects and witnesses. The sworn testimony, set down in signed depositions, was then submitted to a grand jury, which would decide whether to indict any of the accused on particular charges. Those indicted would then go to trial.

Six of the eight *Discovery* survivors—the supercargo/haber-dasher, Habakkuk Prickett; the barber-surgeon, Edward Wilson; the acting master, Robert Bylot; the boatswain's mate, Adrian Moter; the common hand, Francis Clement; and the cook, Bennet Mathew—were called before the court's commission on that late-January day. Neither the ship's boy, Nicholas Sims, nor the cooper, Silvanus Bond, were ever formally interviewed, and could well have fled at Gravesend, catching a ride on the first downbound ship headed out of the kingdom.

The interrogated survivors may already have spent some unpleasant time in prison, as Hessel Gerritsz would avow, but Gerritsz's account left the erroneous impression that justice was about to be served.

Britain's naval affairs seethed with corruption, and the admiralty court inquiry was deeply compromised. The deputy judge presiding over the 1612 depositions was Dr. Richard Trevor, the uncle of four influential brothers in naval affairs who enjoyed the patronage of either the Lord High Admiral or other members of the Howard family. The nephew of the judge who was most critical to the *Discovery* affair was Sir John Trevor. A career parliamentarian who represented Welsh boroughs controlled by the Lord High Admiral, he was made surveyor of the navy in 1598 and a gentleman of the privy chamber in 1608. Sir John was close to Henry, the Prince of Wales, advising the youth on his pet enthusiasm for discovering the Northwest Passage. Sir John thus bore some responsibility for the prince's having served as the 1610–11 *Discovery* voyage's patron. Sir John had also been involved in the Virginia initiative since joining the London wing of the 1606 company, and so would have known Sir Thomas Smythe and many other principals in the *Discovery* venture whose commercial interests included the Jamestown colony.

Among the likeminded men in the Lord High Admiral's and the Trevors' circle involved in promoting the ongoing passage search was Sir Robert Mansell, a relative and favourite of the Lord High Admiral. He distinguished himself in action at sea and was involved in privateering ventures with both the Lord High Admiral and Sir John Trevor. Mansell called on the support of Trevor to secure the post of treasurer of the navy in April 1604. While in Parliament, serving in a Welsh riding controlled by the Lord High Admiral, he acted as spokesman for the navy. He became part of the clique advising the Prince of Wales on the Northwest Passage search, and backed Hudson's *Discovery* voyage.

Mansell was also a thief, and his corrupt practices in navy victualling had been exposed by the naval commission investigation launched in 1608 to sort out the mess that the kingdom's first line of defence had become under the Lord High Admiral, Sir John Trevor, and Mansell. In 1609 the chief commissioner, Sir John Coke, declared that "the whole body is corrupted, as there is no sound part almost from the head to the foot." Despite the evidence, Mansell and his regular accomplice, Sir John Trevor, managed to avoid punishment, when an ineffectual king asked offending parties to henceforth be on their best behaviour. Mansell invested in the Muscovy Company during Sir Thomas Smythe's governorship, an ideal place to park the proceeds of his embezzling. The company was a major supplier of goods to the navy, such as timber, cable and cordage, and train oil for grease, and so Mansell was positioned to earn even legitimate profits from his own naval office.

The general tone of Dr. Richard Trevor's deposition-taking in January 1612 was set by the questioning of Edward Wilson. In addition to asking the barber-surgeon what he knew of any charts from Hudson's voyage having fallen into Dutch hands, and whether he was aware of any plans by the Dutch to follow Hudson into the northwest, the commission invited his opinion on the feasibility of the route. Wilson thought it could be found—provided, of course, that survivors of the *Discovery* voyage were involved. "Being asked further whither there be a passage through there he sayeth that by all likelihood there is by reason of the tide of flood came out of the western parts and the tide of ebb out of the eastern which may be easily discovered if such may be employed as have been acquainted with the voyage and knoweth the manner of the ice." The forces of commerce and politics were far more concerned with securing an advantage over the Dutch than they were with finding guilt in the disappearances of Henry and John Hudson and their companions in the shallop. It was imperative to the men who had sent out Hudson, who were among the most influential political and commercial figures in the realm, that they press on with the passage search at the earliest opportunity. And as Edward Wilson pointed out, they needed the survivors to carry forward.

No further action seems to have been taken against the survivors after they made their January 12 depositions. No dated indictment survives from the time, nor any record of a trial. Instead, Prickett, Bylot, and Wilson joined the follow-up expedition in the spring of 1612. The *Discovery*, with a captain named John Ingram, was sent out in support of the larger *Resolution*, under the charter of the Company of Merchant Discoverers of the North-West Passage—better known as the North-West Company, with the Prince of Wales serving as their patron. The letters patent (which wasn't issued until July 26, several months after the expedition sailed) said that its principals were the same ones to have backed Hudson. They included the various Howards and the Lord High Admiral's favourite, Sir Robert Mansell, but of the twenty-four directors, twenty-one were London merchants. And among the 288 subscribers for the 1612 voyage were the names of Prickett, Bylot, and Wilson.

The expedition leader, Thomas Button, was an accomplished mariner who would rise to the rank of admiral. Nevertheless, the era's predictable nepotism had moved forward his candidacy for command. Button was part of the circle of Welsh landowners and mariners who had the Lord High Admiral at their epicentre. He had commanded a privateer, the *Wylloby*, in 1602 that was owned by his uncle, Sir Robert Mansell, and Sir John Trevor.

The idea circulated (and was no doubt encouraged by the backers) that the Button expedition was to search for Henry Hudson and the other missing crew. But there was no mention of any such duty in the sailing instructions drawn up by Edward Wright in the name of the prince, and the two ships went nowhere near Hudson's last known position.

The instructions did, however, indirectly acknowledge the more desperate events of the Hudson voyage. Item 10 prescribed: "You must be careful to prevent all mutiny amongst your people, and to preserve them as much as may be from the treachery and villainy of the Salvages, and other Eastern people; wherever you arrive have as little to do with them as may be."

Button did well to behave in pronounced antithesis to Hudson's secretive manner with respect to where his ship was and where it was going. He encouraged the men to take an interest in their course and position, and to compare their notes with each other, and he consulted them on his actions. As for avoiding the "Salvages," Button failed utterly to give them the prescribed wide berth. When the expedition paused at the Digges islands to assemble its pinnace, it encountered Inuit. Neither side would have forgotten the clash of 1611 that claimed four members of the *Discovery* crew and several Inuit. Button's men attempted to steal two umiaks from the Inuit, presumably to prevent them from mounting an assault on the pinnace construction site. Five Englishmen were slain in the process.

Wright's instructions to Button strongly suggested that Hudson, after passing the Digges islands on his inbound course, did reach or

approach the western shore of Hudson Bay on the way to James
Bay. After passing "Salisbury His Island" at the western end of
Hudson Strait—the instructions were the first time Hudson's name
was attached to what had been Frobisher's Mistaken Strait—Button
was to "stand over to the opposite Maine in the Latitude of some
58 degrees" and take note of the direction of the tide for clues as to
whether the passage lay to the southwest, north, or northwest. The
directive brought the Button expedition to the mouth of the Nelson
River near latitude 57, where an untold number of men died
during the overwintering and the *Resolution* was destroyed in the
ice. Button would subsequently remark to explorer and chronicler
Luke Foxe that he could not send a boat ashore on the return
voyage to measure the tide at Nottingham Island (named by Button
for the Lord High Admiral) "for I had not above eight sound men."
Button's staggering losses further underscored Henry Hudson's
superb record in keeping his men alive. And Prickett, Bylot, and
Wilson managed again to be among the *Discovery*'s survivors.

On his return in 1613, Thomas Button was knighted by King
James and given an admiralty for the Irish coast by the Lord High
Admiral. A less ambitious single-ship voyage was planned for 1614,
and Button recommended that command of the *Discovery* be
given to William Gibbons, a cousin and friend who had been a
volunteer on the 1612–13 expedition. Button declared that
Gibbons was "not short of any man than ever yet [I] carried to
sea." Gibbons got the assignment, assuredly with some assistance
at court from Button's uncle, Sir Robert Mansell, for whom
Button had named Mansel Island, next to Nottingham Island at
the north end of Hudson Bay.

For the Gibbons voyage, at least one of the mutiny survivors,
Robert Bylot, was aboard the *Discovery* for the third time since
1610; any further involvement by Prickett and Wilson in the

passage search cannot be confirmed. Little is known about the Gibbons venture, which appears to have been largely stymied by the sort of pack ice in the Labrador Sea that led to the loss of John Knight in 1606. According to Foxe, the *Discovery* was trapped by ice for twenty awful weeks—the entire summer—around latitude 57, in the very area of Knight's loss, before returning to England.

Control of the passage search then fell firmly to Sir Thomas Smythe, who ran the North-West Company as governor, with Sir Dudley Digges and Sir John Wolstenholme (a London merchant who, like Smythe, was a customs official) serving as fellow directors. Key financing was provided by Sir Francis Jones, a London alderman who would be the city's lord mayor in 1620. Bylot was promoted to master of the *Discovery* and commander of the passage search, with William Baffin assigned as his pilot. Baffin had explored Greenland with James Hall in 1612, on a voyage backed by the London alderman William Cokayne. It went rather badly: Hall was murdered by the Inuit in retribution for earlier atrocities committed while he was exploring for the Danes. Baffin was then employed as chief pilot for the Spitsbergen whale fishery by Smythe's Muscovy Company. In his 1615 voyage journal, Baffin complimented Bylot as "a man well experienced" in the passage search, and dismissed the Gibbons voyage as one "in which by some sinister accident, was little or nothing performed."

Bylot and Baffin made a careful survey of the north shore of Hudson Strait and probed the open waters beyond it that led to the west side of Baffin Island, which would be known as Foxe Strait and Foxe Inlet. Baffin's navigational skills were above and beyond anything exhibited by Hudson or even Juet. He carried a massive quadrant with a four-foot semidiameter, which he used for observations of the sun, moon, and stars to calculate latitude, compass variation, and longitude. He was also the first navigator to record headings in degrees rather than points of the compass, and set a new standard in ship journals. Two centuries later, the Arctic explorer Captain Edward William Parry would salute Baffin as an "able and indefatigable navigator," after experiencing first-hand the accuracy of his work. Indeed, the quality and meticulousness of Baffin's results were exceptional for the early seventeenth century.

Baffin rightly concluded that Hudson Strait would not produce a navigable passage, and the search threatened to enter another period of stasis. On January 24, 1616, George Carew, Earl of Totness, wrote to Sir Thomas Roe, ambassador to the court of the Great Mogul, providing a summary of the past year's events. For January 1616, he noted that there is "nothing done" with respect to the "north-western or northeastern passage." But the search did not die. In 1616, Smythe's North-West Company again dispatched Bylot and Baffin in the *Discovery*, this time to press north, up Davis Strait, in search of a high-latitude passage west. They found the expansive Baffin Bay, and reached the latitude of 78 degrees, 45 minutes, an extraordinary effort in these waters that would not be bettered until 1856.

The letters patent of the North-West Company in 1612 had promised Thomas Button all of the customs revenues that would accrue from the traffic a proven Northwest Passage would generate in the fifth year after the patent's issue, with the same revenues going to the company's investors in the seventh year. But by 1617, when Button should have been reaping his considerable rewards, the search had come up dry. When Bylot and Baffin left Gravesend on March 26, 1616, they were expected to sail up Davis Strait to latitude 80, turn west, and eventually fetch up in Japan. Failure was announced by their reappearance, at Dover Roads, on August 30. "There is no passage, nor hope of passage, in the north of Davis Strait, we having coasted all or nearly all the circumference thereof, and find it to be no other than a great bay," a defeated Baffin wrote Wolstenholme on his return. The following January, when George Lord Carew sent Sir Thomas Roe his next annual list of noteworthy events, his concluding item for October 1616 was: "The North-west Passage discoveries have failed."

"I cannot but much admire the work of the Almighty," Baffin also observed to Wolstenholme, "when I consider how vain the best and chiefest hopes of man are in things uncertain. And to speak of no other matter, than of the hopeful passage to the North-West. How many of the best sort of men have set their whole endeavours to prove a passage that way? . . . Yea what great sums of money have been spent about that action, as your worship hath costly experience of."

Ironically, Baffin had declared the search hopeless when he had unwittingly found the entrance to the Northwest Passage. The bay he had named for himself was not enclosed, as he thought. On July 12, 1616, he and Bylot entered a broad indentation more than forty miles wide above Baffin Island at latitude 74. They called it Sir James Lancaster's Sound, in honour of one of the company's investors. It was Lancaster, in returning from the first East India Company expedition to the Far East, who had borne the intelligence that the Northwest Passage lay along latitude 62½, which roughly coincided with the location of Lumley's Inlet and the Furious Overfall. Neither Baffin nor Bylot realized that the seeming dead end they named for Lancaster, some twelve degrees of latitude higher, in fact was the eastern entrance to the passage. Lancaster, who died in June 1618, would never know it. The "sound" would not be recognized as the passage entrance until 1819.

The apparent failure of the search was of far greater consequence for Bylot than for Baffin. For so long as Bylot remained employed by Smythe's North-West Company, the ugly matter of justice being served for the *Discovery* mutiny of 1611 was kept at bay. The protection from prosecution all of the survivors enjoyed through the continuing passage search, however, evaporated soon after the *Discovery* returned to London in September 1616. Now that Baffin had pronounced the search futile, there was no longer any need to shield Bylot and others in hope of exploiting their knowledge.

On February 7, 1617, Habakkuk Prickett and Robert Bylot again stood before a commission of the High Court of the Admiralty, this time to answer far more probing, even alarming questions.

Thirty-three

—

THE IMPETUS FOR THE REVIVAL of the *Discovery* case is unknown. Henry Hudson's chief supporters at court, who might have demanded it, were gone. Sir Walter Cope had seen his influence diminish considerably with the death of Sir Robert Cecil in 1612, and had himself died in 1614, taking the influence of Sir Thomas Challener with him. Henry, Prince of Wales, had died in 1614, and no one else in the royal family exhibited anything close to his enthusiasm for the search, let alone for getting to the bottom of Hudson's loss. Nor was there a discernible motivation for Sir Thomas Smythe or his fellow directors of the North-West Company, Digges and Wolstenholme, to stir up old issues. On the contrary, Bylot obviously had enjoyed the full confidence of these investors.

Smythe was not without his enemies, however, and reviving the mutiny case would have been an opportune way to cause him embarrassment and undercut his power and influence. His stature in overseas ventures (which included the new Somers Islands Company for Bermuda, a spinoff of the Virginia Company of which he was elected its first governor in 1615) was resented by investors elsewhere in the kingdom. Smythe was acquiring a for-midable foe in Sir Edwin Sandys, a non-merchant investor from

Kent in the 1610–11 *Discovery* voyage and the succeeding North-West Company's Button expedition. A Puritan sympathizer who led the House of Commons in the brief and entirely unproductive "Addled Parliament" of 1614, Sandys opposed unchecked royal power, which put him at odds politically with Smythe, who was James's loyal servant in the House. Sandys was also an investor in the East India, Virginia, and Somers Islands companies, and he was en route to taking on Smythe in a vicious struggle for control of all three of them.

Sandys' main ally in his investment agitations was Henry Wriothesley, Earl of Southampton, a likeminded parliamentarian who was a fellow investor in Hudson's final voyage, as well as in the North-West Company. He was honoured by the Button expedition with Southampton Island in northern Hudson Bay, and he also invested alongside Sandys in the Virginia, Somers Islands, and East India companies. As a Bermuda plantation owner, Southampton backed Sandys' agitations in the governing company. Southampton also supported Sandys as he pressed for an audit of the Virginia Company books, the insinuation being that Smythe had abused his power as treasurer.

Although Sandys would not aggressively and openly challenge Smythe for outright control of the Virginia and Somers Islands companies until 1618 (and waited until 1619 to mount an apparent bid for the governorship of the East India Company), he had been prominent in the two related companies since their creation, and had already secured a base for his multipronged assault on Smythe in being elected an assistant, or director, of the Virginia Company, in 1616. Dissatisfaction with the state of the Virginia and Bermuda colonies was widespread. In George Lord Carew's summary of events for Sir Thomas Roe of January 24, 1616, his list for the past month disparagingly reported, "The Virginia and Bermuda plantation sleeps."

As leading investors in the 1610–11 voyage, Sandys and Southampton could have petitioned the Lord High Admiral's court to seek fresh depositions from the survivors. They may have genuinely believed that guilty parties had for too long gone unpunished. But they also would have expected the evidence to reflect poorly on Smythe, whom they were determined to unseat at the Virginia, Somers Islands, and East India companies.

Smythe would not be questioned, but he was vulnerable to accusations of having shielded the survivors in 1612, registering his support by having employed them in further passage ventures. In the renewed investigation of 1617, Smythe's was the only name among hundreds of investors to be invoked by the interrogators.

Habakkuk Prickett and Robert Bylot were the first survivors to be rounded up by the High Court of the Admiralty for fresh interrogation. After Prickett and Bylot were questioned in February, Bennet Mathew was deposed on March 8, Francis Clement on May 13, and Edward Wilson on August 2.

The presiding judge from the 1612 depositions, Richard Trevor, had died in 1614. In his place was another deputy justice, one Dr. Amy, assuredly the same one who sat in the House of Lords with the Lord High Admiral in the Parliaments of 1610 and 1614. Dr. Amy marshalled a far more probing and insinuating investigation. Notwithstanding that some of the surviving depositions are fragmentary, all of the men appear to have been interrogated by the court commission using much the same series of twenty-three questions or "articles."

The deliberate casting away of sick men in the mutiny was indefensible. Ever since Sebastian Cabot laid down his ordinances of 1553 for the forerunner of the Muscovy Company, care of the sick had been a primary directive of shipboard discipline. Prickett's written account, however much he had intended it to clear his name, was a self-incriminating record of the widespread failure among the survivors to oppose the cruel and selfish plan to dispose of the weakest crewmembers, along with the Hudson father and son, and their acolytes.

None of the actual questions the admiralty court posed to survivors are preserved, but the answers from the inquiry of 1617 indicate that the court's commission had pulled together a body of knowledge or rumour from unknown sources. There may have been loose lips among the survivors, indiscreet confessions in taverns and alehouses. Troubling information also could have been passed along from Sandys or Southampton.

Prickett was forced to state that "he for his part told the masters of the Trinity House the truth of the business aforesaid, but he never knew or heard that the masters said they deserved to be hanged for the same." And he alone faced a twenty-fourth question in 1617, stating that "for his part [he] made no means to hinder any proceedings that might have been taken against them. Neither knows who."

Dr. Amy's commission wanted to know what had been told specifically to Smythe, and what Smythe might have told others. To the seventeenth question posed to Prickett in 1617, his deposition noted, "He says they told Sir Thomas Smith the truth how the said Hudson & the rest were turned out of the ship. And more to this article he knows not."

Prickett's answer suggested that the court was trying to take the haberdasher to task for having lied to Smythe, but Bylot's response to the same article indicated a more complex interest. Bylot was compelled to state: "He told Sir Thomas Smith the manner how Hudson and the rest went from them, but what Sir Thomas said to their wives he knows not." Bylot's answer showed that the court sought to establish disagreement between what the key survivors claimed to have told Smythe about the mutiny and what the court understood (or alleged) Smythe had told the widows of those cast away. A pathway of information apparently had been opened between the admiralty court and the widows. No widow would have been more vociferous in her questioning of the integrity of the survivors than Katherine Hudson, who had lost a husband and a son. In 1614, she applied to the directors of the East India Company, asking for some consideration for her youngest son, Richard. The directors, led by Smythe, found Richard Hudson a position aboard a ship called the *Samaritan,* provided five pounds for his "apparels and necessaries," and sent him to Bantam. So began a career in which Richard Hudson rose to become the East India Company's chief representative in the Bay of Bengal, while his mother made her own remarkable way to India and entered the import-export business through the company.

The admiralty court confronted the survivors with disturbing new allegations. All denied that shots were fired at the men in the shallop. They also refuted the idea that the ship was in fact well stocked with hare and partridge at the time of the mutiny. And Bylot was forced to deny that he "took any ring out of Hudson's pocket, neither ever saw it except on his finger, nor knows what became of it." It was an astonishing accusation, having been put to a man whom Smythe had employed as his master and commander in the North-West Company voyages of 1615 and 1616.

The questioning extended to misdeeds beyond the mutiny itself, to shipboard murder. It was alleged that the blood found on the preserved clothing and in the ship was not produced by victims of an Inuit attack, but rather that the men whom the survivors blamed exclusively for the mutiny (and perhaps even Hudson and his fellow castaways) actually had been killed in their berths while they slept. For as Prickett's narrative confidently stated after recounting the Inuit attack, "Thus you have heard the tragical end of Henry Greene and his mates, whom they called captain, these four being the only lusty men in all the ship." In response to his latest interrogation, Bylot insisted, "from their wounds [inflicted by the Inuit] the cabins, beds and clothes were made bloody."

Of all the statements made by survivors in response to the admiralty court's more heated questioning of 1617, none suggested a stranger suspicion than the ones dealing with the fate of the carpenter, Philip Staffe.

Robert Bylot avowed that Staffe went into the shallop "of his own accord, without any compulsion; whether he be dead or alive, or what has become of him, he knows not." Prickett too was asked to address Staffe's fate that day, saying "he does not know whether the ship's carpenter be dead or alive, for as he says he never saw him since he was put out of the ship into the shallop." The court nevertheless persisted. On May 13, Francis Clement stated that Staffe "was one of them who were put into the shallop with the master and the rest; whether he is dead or not, he knows not."

Dr. Amy's commission seemed to be pressing the survivors for evidence that Staffe was alive—as if the carpenter, against all odds, had been spotted strolling the streets of his native Ipswich. The court may have been suspicious of the fact that Staffe's chest, which survivors avowed was placed with him in the shallop, was the only one belonging to a castaway that didn't return with the *Discovery.*

The 1617 interrogations also took aim at what the survivors could tell the court about Thomas Woodhouse. The Trinity House transaction record had already noted that Woodhouse had not gone quietly into the shallop, and the admiralty court now belatedly wanted to know what some of the key survivors could reveal of his alleged attempt to bribe his way back aboard by providing the keys to his chest. Nothing, as it turned out. Woodhouse's writing had also surfaced. His sole surviving note regarding Juet's September 1610 hearing, at which he lost his mate's position to Bylot, revealed that the full story of the mutiny had not been told by Prickett, who had pinned virtually all responsibility on Henry Greene perhaps to shield from embarrassment a patron of Robert Juet's and to protect Robert Bylot. (Purchas would state that the Woodhouse note was in the papers of Richard Hakluyt, along with Hudson's journal abstract and Prickett's narrative.) The survivors were now asked whether they could recognize Woodhouse's handwriting and if they knew what it was he had been committing to paper. Neither Prickett nor Bylot (whose answers are the only ones that survive to the Woodhouse questions) said they could they recognize his script; neither said they knew what he might have been writing about.

Despite the startling insinuations of the unrecorded questions, there was no trial for the survivors on the immediate horizon after Edward Wilson provided the final deposition of that second round of interrogations, in August 1617.

But Smythe's fortunes continued to shift in the trade and colonization business. Prospects for Virginia were discouraging. There were only four hundred colonists in early 1618, and the enterprise teetered on failure. Sandys and Southampton made a personal commitment to send more than three hundred new colonists that year. While their efforts to make a success of the colony were crucial to its survival, their action also precipitated a direct challenge to Smythe for control of the venture.

The case of the *Discovery* mutiny took another lurch forward. The admiralty court moved to bring most—but not all—of the survivors to trial. Evidently no earlier than January 1618, a grand jury produced an undated indictment naming Bylot, Prickett, Wilson, Moter, Bond and Sims. Mathew and Clement for some reason were excluded.

The depositions of Prickett and Bylot had left the court with the problem of what charge could be laid. It had been their carefully measured case that Greene and his cohorts had planned to turn to piracy with the *Discovery*, which made Greene's seizure of the *Discovery* an act of spoliation. If Prickett and Bylot were believed, only Greene and his "lusty" co-conspirators could be charged with spoliation and the associated murders of the castaways, but dead men could not be charged with anything. Prickett and Bylot were not believed. Spoliation was left aside entirely.

The men were charged with "having, on 22 June 9 James I, in a certain ship called The Discovery of the port of London, then being on the high sea near Hudson's Straits in the parts of America, pinioned the arms of Henry Hudson, late of the said precinct of St. Katherine, mariner, then master of the said ship The Discovery, and putting him thus bound, together with John Hudson, his son, Arnold Ladley, John Kinge, Michael Butt, Thomas Woodhouse, Philip Staffe, Adam Moore and Sidrach Fanner, mariners of the said ship, into a shallop, without food, drink, fire, clothing or any necessaries, and then maliciously abandoning them, so that they came thereby to their death and miserably perished." The indictment rejected the survivors' testimony that the men in the shallop had been provided with food, clothing, weapons, and other "necessaries."

On Friday, July 24, 1618, more than seven years after Henry Hudson and his eight companions were cast away in the shallop, the *Discovery* survivors went on trial in Southwark for murder.

Only two of the six men named in the undated indictment, Habakkuk Prickett and Edward Wilson, turned up to face the murder charge. Appearing with them were Francis Clement and Bennet Mathew, who had come to be charged through a separate indictment, since lost.

The accused turned up at the court on St. Margaret's Hill, a former church that was also home to Compter Prison. Court records indicate that the four men had been "called under a caution to appear on this day and at this place, and [with] their sureties." No note was made of the identities of these sureties, the men who posted bonds and pledged that the accused would appear for trial. The *Discovery* accused and their guarantors must have cut an impressive figure, compared to the unwashed and pallid rabble brought in from Marshalsea also to face justice that day. The officers of the court, and the pool of jurors, could not have helped but make a preliminary judgment of the four *Discovery* accused as a breed apart.

The others named in the surviving indictment—Silvanus Bond, Nicholas Sims, Adrian Moter, and Robert Bylot—did not appear. The accused who turned up, in entering their pleas, pointedly denied having fled, as if this should be noted in their favour.

Spoliation, or piracy, was the stock-in-trade of High Court of the Admiralty prosecutions, and it filled the docket of the Southwark court that Friday. Including the *Discovery* defendants, the whirlwind of justice would either condemn or free fourteen or more men facing death sentences, with their individual cases flashing through the docket in a matter of minutes.

Richard Fox, Richard Arloby, and Nicholas Scott were charged with the "capture and spoliation of a ship the *Herring Maid* of Enckhuisen, and slaughter of Peter Hanckes, Master of the same." They pleaded guilty to the piracy charge but not to murder, and said they had none of the goods. Robert Walsingham was charged with the spoliation of the *Susan Constance* of London, to which he said he was guilty but that he had none of the goods. William Mortimer, William Austen, and Thomas Cotgrave were charged with the spoliation of the *Angel of Norway*, while Austen and Cotgrave were further charged with the spoliation of an unknown ship from Salcombe in Devonshire. All three pleaded not guilty to their charges, although Mortimer's co-defendants apparently accused him of having committed the *Angel of Norway* spoliation.

The *Discovery*'s accused broke the pattern of the day, charged as they were with "the ejection of Henry Hudson and others from the ship the *Discovery* in a boat called a shallop, without food or drink and other necessities, and the murder of the same." The court records are incomplete, but Prickett and Wilson at least are shown to have pleaded not guilty ("nor have they fled"), and a not-guilty plea also survives for Clement. Mathew most certainly pleaded the same way.

Everyone who came before the bars that day chose a jury trial. A pool of twenty-four "honest and lawful men" from the county of Surrey were sworn in to hear their cases.

Defendants were not allowed to be represented in court by lawyers until the eighteenth century. Nothing is known of what the *Discovery* accused said in their defence, but it is not difficult to imagine. They had consistently maintained over the years that the ones who plotted and carried out the mutiny had all died on the voyage home, and through no fault of the survivors.

As the court records of July 24 affirm, it was common practice for juries to hear cases in a great batch, pause for deliberation, and then render verdicts for all of them. Entering a guilty plea was the equivalent of signing one's own death warrant. Every man who did so that day on the piracy charges was agreeably found guilty, although a not-guilty plea was hardly a guarantee of safe legal passage. Among the Marshalsea prisoners, only Austen and Cotgrave beat the piracy charges against them, for the spoliation of the *Angel of Norway* and the vessel out of Salcombe. The rest of the accused pirates were found guilty and asked what they could show to prevent a death sentence being pronounced. None could offer any grounds for mercy, and the men were duly convicted. They were to be returned to prison and then taken to Wapping, "and there to be hanged by the neck until they were dead." It was the custom to string up pirates along the riverbank at Wapping and leave their bodies rotting from the gibbet, as a warning to passing mariners who might consider spoliation as a career option.

As for the *Discovery* survivors, they had been charged with committing a crime for which no one could or would testify against them. The survivors stuck together, and their own stories, as rendered in depositions, must have been the only evidence to be weighed. And there was no time for the jury to consider the internal contradictions and inconsistencies within the record of events or to ask to examine the ship's log and journal. After a wait of more than seven years, the court could only manage this routine rush to judgment.

The jurors turned the *Discovery* defendants free. The mutiny case would never be reopened.

The four *Discovery* survivors emerged from the court on St. Margaret's Hill with their sureties. One can well imagine that Sir Dudley Digges, Sir John Wolstenholme, and especially Sir Thomas Smythe had been the ones to post bonds for them and gloss their innocence with their supportive presence. Rain or shine, this was still a day bright with possibility. The Thames was to the north: opportunity in perpetual motion for any seaman. Nothing more was ever heard of any of the survivors, as they vanished into obscurity.

Samuel Purchas had initially published an account of the Hudson voyage in 1617, based on the Gerritsz materials. When he published in 1625 the voyage's available documents— Hudson's truncated journal abstract, Prickett's narrative, Woodhouse's letter to Samuel Macham, and the account of Juet's hearing—he was aware that culpability for the mutiny remained far from clear and professed not to be interested in fingering guilty parties. "I take not on me to sentence, no not to examine. I have presented the evidence just as I had it; let the bench censure, hearing with both ears, that which they see in those and in these notes." Yet in Purchas's estimation, Habakkuk Prickett's narrative blamed Hudson for his own demise. And in 1626, in a new edition of another one of his works, *Purchas His Pilgrimage,* Purchas alleged that, shortly before the mutiny, Hudson "out of despair, [let] fall some words of setting some on shore." But there was no evidence for this in the primary documents, unless it had been edited out of Prickett's account before the haberdasher's narrative was published in *Purchas His Pilgrimes* in 1625.

Nevertheless, Prickett would go to an unknown grave with a black spot against his reputation. He avoided the noose, but not the broad and persistent condemnation of history. "Well, Prickett," Luke Foxe would write in 1635, after making his own voyage to the waters in which Henry Hudson was lost, "I am in great doubt of thy fidelity to Master Hudson."

But not even Prickett could be expected to explain what became of Henry Hudson and the rest of the castaways. It was certainly beyond Prickett's powers of recollection and persuasion to account for the ultimate fate of Hudson's son John. That responsibility rested with another narrator, working in another language.

Thirty-four

—

THROUGH THE CALUMET RAPIDS Samuel de Champlain traced, downbound in a party of forty Kichesipirini canoes. It was June 10, 1613, the day after the *tabagie* with Tessöuat and his people. The Ottawa River was still gorged on spring floodwaters as he shot through one set of rapids after another on the way to the foot of the Portage du Fort whitewater—to where, only three days earlier, his march through the country of the Kinounchepirini had begun en route to Tessöuat's village. Champlain's world since then had capsized, righted, then surged forward, with the explorer bailing furiously.

After Nicolas de Vignau fell to his knees before Champlain at Tessöuat's village, the young interpreter had admitted that what he had told him, both in France and while on this journey, "in respect to the sea in question was false; that he had never seen it, and that he had never gone farther than the village of Tessöuat; that he had said these things in order to return to Canada." Unable to stand the presence of the youth, Champlain had left it to Thomas to question de Vignau further. After Daniel Boyer's servant reported to Champlain on what he had learned, Champlain had taken the news to Tessöuat: "Very sorrowfully I went and informed the *sauvages* of the deceit of this liar, telling them that he had confessed the truth to me."

Tessöuat and the other Algonquin elders—chiefs who said they were "my friends, who always spoke the truth"—were pleased to hear this, and they chastised Champlain for his behaviour, for slighting their loyalty to him, for showing so little confidence in their word. "This very wicked liar must die," Champlain was told. "Do you not see that he wanted to kill you? Give him to us, and we promise you he will tell no more lies."

The Algonquin, Champlain recalled, "were all howling to get at him, and their children still more loudly." It was all Champlain could do not to have de Vignau torn to pieces. He could not allow de Vignau to be killed by Tessöuat's people. Natives could not be permitted to think that they could summarily inflict their own justice on a Frenchman. Champlain had to retain authority for his own people. And as much as he would have wished to see de Vignau strangled and decapitated, he had promised the youth that he would not be harmed if he told the truth.

Champlain ordered the Kichesipirini who were gathered with Tessöuat to leave de Vignau alone and to call off their children. Champlain needed for his own sake to take de Vignau back to the Great Rapid, so that his confession could be heard by the likes of the Sieur de L'Ange, respected nobles who could attest that the misadventure was entirely the fault of de Vignau. Only then, "I should consider what was to be done with him." To this, Tessöuat agreed.

Champlain had been forced to surrender all hope of reaching the Northern Sea or of retrieving the English boy from the Nebicerini. His efforts had left him with nothing "but the regret of not having made better use of my time, as well as the troubles and labours which nevertheless I had to tolerate patiently." Champlain now had "no other desire than to return" to the Great Rapid. But in the process, he might be able to salvage something from the deeply frustrating experience. He made presents to

Tessöuat and persuaded him to dispatch trade canoes there, where he promised ships were waiting, loaded with goods, "and where they would receive good treatment. This invitation they made known to all their neighbours." Tessöuat remained behind at his island redoubt, but ordered his own son to accompany Champlain, and agreed that next year they would go to war with the French against the Iroquois.

Before they departed the summer camp to begin the river's descent, Champlain erected another of his cedar crosses bearing the French shield. He placed it in a prominent place on the shore of the riverine lake upstream, and asked the Kichesipirini to take care of it, along with the others he had already erected, which they would find along the route he had followed to them. "I said to them that if they broke these down, harm would come to them, but if they preserved them, they would not be attacked by their enemies. They promised me to do this, and that I would find these again when I returned to them."

"They are killing me!" Champlain heard the young man scream in Algonquin as he dashed into the river. Champlain turned to see dozens of Kichesipirini plunging in after him, and could not help but share in the panic that gripped the terrified youth at the head of the human stampede.

The confusion and fear soon gave way to laughter. Thomas explained to Champlain that the Kichesipirini youth, dreaming of Iroquois attacking their camp, had sprung to his feet, fleeing into the Ottawa River and sweeping up his fellow Algonquin in his sleepwalking terror.

They could all manage to share laughter when the cause of the commotion was revealed. The previous midnight, two canoes of Algonquin, that had been fishing ahead of their downbound course on Lac Deschênes, had arrived at the island camp to report that they had seen four Iroquois canoes. The news, which had infested the young Algonquin's dreams, remained troubling. If true, it meant that the Iroquois had ventured above the Akikodjiwan rapids, which Champlain, on his way upriver, had been assured they never did.

Moving downriver, the number of canoes accompanying Champlain swelled from forty to sixty, and he would note approvingly that nine canoes joined them carrying "forty strong and powerful men" from the Ouaouechkarini, or Petite Nation, the Algonquin tribe that lived to the north of the Ottawa, below the Akikodjiwan rapids. Another twenty canoes were spotted, travelling as they were toward the Great Rapid, heavily laden with furs for trading. The restoration of Champlain's reputation gathered momentum with every pelt-laden canoe that joined his birchbark armada as it glided toward the shallops waiting at the height of navigation on the St. Lawrence.

On an island at the entrance to Lac des Deux-Montagnes, the Algonquin flotilla had its final disquiet of the journey, when word came in the night that Iroquois had been seen. The natives built large fires as a defensive measure, but Champlain had them doused, telling the Algonquin they would give away their position. The alarm passed, and the next day, their seventh on the river, they safely reached the broad cascade of the Great Rapid.

Champlain could see vessels at anchor downstream: more than the two shallops with which he had arrived. The Sieur de L'Ange, who had waited faithfully for his return, approached in a canoe and informed Champlain that three Malouin ships had come to trade, under the passport secured by the Sieur de Maisonneuve, who was with them. Champlain called the Algonquin together and asked them not to trade until he had given permission. In the meantime, he would deliver them provisions. The Algonquin agreed, "saying they were my friends."

And so Champlain was borne by the Algonquin to the French vessels. A salute of cannon fire delighted some of them, and alarmed others who had never witnessed such a pyrotechnic performance. The Algonquin went ashore, and de Maisonneuve came to Champlain, presenting the passport secured at Tadoussac. Satisfied that all was in order, Champlain extended to the Malouins the same rights as his own associates, and informed the Algonquin that they could begin trading the next day.

Champlain had left the Great Rapid on May 27 with just one reluctant Algonquin guide to assist him, and he had returned on June 17 with eighty canoes bearing not only pelts that would save the trading season but hundreds of Algonquin who did as he commanded. He had reversed the fortunes of a wasted trade, restored his esteem among the native peoples, and proved to the Malouins that he could single-handedly ensure access to the furs harvested beyond the Great Rapid.

Champlain had one last item of business from his journey to Tessöuat's summer camp: the fate of Nicolas de Vignau.

Before the trading began, he approached the chiefs who had made the journey downstream to trade. Tessöuat was not there to explain what had happened, and so Champlain did, through Thomas. The chiefs were "greatly amazed" by his story, but Champlain was not finished. He had the chiefs assemble, and ordered de Vignau to stand before them, to answer again for his behaviour.

There was some confusion among the chiefs. They seemed to think that de Vignau had in fact been to the Northern Sea and had erred by conspiring not to show Champlain the way to it. For as Champlain related, "they summoned him, and asked him, why he had not shown me the sea in the north, as he had promised me at his departure. He replied that he had promised something impossible for him, since he had never seen this sea, and that the desire of making the journey had led him to say what he did, also that he did not suppose that I would undertake it."

Thomas had already reported to Champlain that de Vignau "did not believe that I would undertake the journey on account of the dangers, thinking that some difficulty would present itself to prevent me from going on, as in the case of these *sauvages,* who were not disposed to lend me canoes; and accordingly that the journey would be put off until another year." If they were to return to France, having been unable to complete the journey, de Vignau had hoped to still collect a reward for the discovery of a route to the Northern Sea.

De Vignau was so captivated by the country that, even after the terror he had experienced at Tessöuat's village, he had asked Champlain to be left with the Algonquin, in order to attempt the journey north: "He would go until he found the sea in question, even if he should die in the attempt." Standing before the Algonquin chiefs at the Great Rapid, de Vignau repeated his extraordinary request. He begged the chiefs as well as Champlain to pardon him, "confessing that he had greatly offended, and if I would leave him in the country, he would by his efforts repair the offence, and see this sea, and bring back trustworthy intelligence concerning it the following year."

Champlain was both enraged and mystified by de Vignau. He would admit that the explanation de Vignau had provided through Thomas "did not give me much satisfaction, astounded as I was at the effrontery and maliciousness of this liar: and I cannot imagine how he could have devised this imposition, unless he had heard of the . . . voyage of the English, and in the hope of some reward, as he said, had the nerve to venture on it."

Even with the confession from de Vignau, Champlain was not convinced the youth had crafted his tale of an English wreck, English scalps, and an English boy out of thin air. And Champlain's comment that de Vignau had confessed to telling him lies "in respect to the sea" was telling: Champlain omitted all mention of the English boy being held by the Nebicerini, and would report nothing about what he might have learned of the inspiration for the story about the wrecked vessel, the scalps, and the boy. Champlain could not seem to shake the suspicion that de Vignau in fact knew something. He may not have been to the Northern Sea as he had claimed, but he somehow had gathered valuable intelligence. Perhaps some Nebicerini had visited Tessöuat, and de Vignau, who was living with the chief, had overheard their discussions of the boy and the scalps.

Nebicerini traders to James Bay could have seen, or been told of, broken pieces of an abandoned English shallop whose iron fittings had been scavenged by the Cree, and been shown the scalps of the English killed by them, as well as a young prisoner, the lone survivor of a desperate assault by Henry Hudson's starving castaways on a Cree camp. The Nebicerini would have traded with the Cree for the boy and the scalps, and planned to lever them to their own advantage with Champlain, the esteemed Frenchman they had heard of from the Arendarhonon but had not yet met. The Nebicerini had to find a way to bring the gift and Champlain together, without having to give in to any demand by Tessöuat, who blocked their route to the Great Rapid, that they turn over the boy to him, so that he could make his own grand presentation.

Champlain's anger was mollified by qualms over de Vignau's confession. He was not prepared to accept that the liar was an outright liar. Tessöuat had been behaving oddly during their visit: telling Champlain that the Nebicerini harmed his people through witchcraft while secretly preparing a canoe to visit them. Champlain never reflected in print on what he thought Tessöuat had been up to. Native tribes, manoeuvring to secure the best advantage with the French, were as adept at spreading disinformation as the independent French traders who had told them Champlain was dead. The single canoe Tessöuat despatched to the Nebicerini could have delivered a bleak message, alleging that Champlain was dead, or that he was not interested in collecting the boy. It must have been clear to Champlain that Tessöuat could have been engaging in some subterfuge that would keep the English boy out of the Frenchman's grasp, buying time until Tessöuat could arrange to hand the boy over himself. And so the English boy could in fact exist. Champlain might yet be able to collect him. And Champlain still believed the Northern Sea was within reach.

After all the pain Nicolas de Vignau had caused him, Champlain agreed to pardon the young man, on the condition that he would, as promised, return to the Algonquin and complete the journey he now denied ever having made.

Once he had returned to the Great Rapid, Champlain hoped to place two other Frenchmen, in addition to de Vignau, with the assembled Algonquin. The Algonquin balked at this request, made after trading was completed. They pointed to all the trouble de Vignau had caused, and expressed their fear that two more Frenchmen would only bring Champlain false reports and fuel further misunderstandings. "I replied that they were men of probity and truth," Champlain would write, "and that if they would not take them they were not my friends, whereupon they resolved to do so."

The identities of these two Frenchmen are unknown, although one of them could have been Thomas. None of the Algonquin tribes would agree to take de Vignau, despite Champlain's direct request. The interpreter was suspended between the worlds of the Algonquin and the French. Champlain would pardon him only if he agreed to make a journey that required an additional pardon from the Algonquin. Champlain may have saved de Vignau from an excruciating death by torture at Tessöuat's village, but he had brought the youth all the way back to the Great Rapid only to once more place his fate in the hands of the Algonquin.

Champlain had what he needed from the youth: a confession delivered to the chiefs at the Great Rapid, assuredly in front of senior members of Champlain's trading partners. A written confession might well have been secured, to satisfy the merchant investors in France. He had no further use for de Vignau. The Algonquin would accept the other Frenchmen, and from them Champlain might then learn more about the distance to the Northern Sea— and, perhaps, the truth about this English boy.

Champlain chose to depart the Great Rapid early, on June 27, leaving behind his own shallops and men, including de Vignau. The Sieur de Maisonneuve, duly impressed by Champlain's performance in bringing so many Algonquin traders to the rapids, and in commanding their respect and cooperation, had invited Champlain to make the passage home with him, to meet with the merchants of St-Malo.

Sailing downriver with the current in the company of the Malouin nobleman, Champlain could take considerable satisfaction in the way the events of the past year had concluded. Although he had not reached the Northern Sea, and had not recovered the English boy, he had parlayed Nicolas de Vignau's report on both matters into a powerful new monopoly. He had turned around the trade, convincing natives and merchants alike that he was the central figure in their relationship. Like the Great Rapid itself, all prosperity flowed through him.

Not everything in his life would unfold smoothly when he returned to France. His child bride, Hélène Boullé, would run away for a spell that October, causing such scandal that her parents would legally disown her in January 1614, citing her "disobedience and ingratitude." But Malouin merchants would agree to join the new company Champlain formed that autumn, "after recognizing the necessity of the regulations," he would observe, "without which it is impossible to hope for any profit from these lands."

On his return to France, Champlain would also publish an updated version of *Les Voyages,* describing the events of 1612–13 in an additional bound section, *Quatriesme Voyage,* and revising his map that blended his portrait of New France with Hessel Gerritsz's rendering of Hudson's discoveries to show his new insights into the upper Ottawa River. He would commit uncharacteristically egregious errors in latitude. After producing fairly exacting latitude results for Lac St-Louis and the Chaudière rapids, he would err by more than a full degree for the beginning of the overland portage at the foot of the rapids at Portage du Fort, as well as for the location of Tessöuat's summer camp. It strains credulity to think that a man so accomplished in dead reckoning would have accepted the idea that, in travelling from the Chaudière rapids to the base of Portage du Fort, struggling through the Rapides des Chats along the way, he had somehow gone northward some seventy miles, when his compass, the sun's westerly trajectory, and his own common sense told him he had gone westward about forty miles.

Champlain doubtless had inflated his northerly progress at this point so that he could claim he had come closer to the Northern Sea than he actually had, and so keep alive the possibility of proving the route, as well as preserving the monopoly. As he lamented in *Quatriesme Voyage,* in reaching Tessöuat's camp, "this northern sea cannot be farther off than one hundred leagues of latitude; for I was in latitude 47." He was actually still below latitude 46, and he surely knew it. He was also the only Frenchman who could confirm the latitudes of these places. De Vignau's credibility was destroyed, and Thomas was a merchant partner's translator, most certainly not a navigator. The third Frenchman on the journey was so inconsequential as to remain anonymous. And like Hudson in his final days, when he appointed an illiterate John King as his mate and forbade anyone other than himself to make navigation observations, Champlain alone knew precisely where he was. In Champlain's case, it worked to his advantage. He described the lands and drew the maps. The world was as he defined it, and he lived to get in the last word.

Champlain's associates, still minding Nicolas de Vignau, remained at the rapids after trading was finished, awaiting the return of a war party from a raid on the Iroquois. At last, on July 6, the canoes appeared downstream, the paddlers digging against the current, making for the shallops and the landing place Champlain called Place Royale. Before the French was the spectacle of the returning warriors, with their freshly harvested scalps and wretched prisoners. Behind them, beyond the Great Rapid, was a world they had scarcely penetrated. Nicolas de Vignau had seen more of this wilderness than all but a handful of Europeans, and he wished nothing more than to be in it.

As for what became of the young translator, Champlain would only write, "We left him to the mercy of God."

Afterword

—

AFTER THE TRIAL OF THE FOUR SURVIVORS of the 1610–11 *Discovery* voyage, Sir Thomas Smythe suffered a series of commercial setbacks. Sir Edwin Sandys' supporters seized power on a new ruling council for the residents of the Virginia colony in 1619. Back in England, Smythe wearied of the accusations orchestrated by Sandys regarding the company's books, and resigned as treasurer that year; Sandys was elected as his replacement. Though an apparent attempt by Sandys in 1619 to supplant Smythe as governor of the East India Company failed, Sandys did get himself elected as a director.

In the Bermuda venture, another Smythe adversary, Sir Robert Rich, Earl of Warwick, died in March 1618. The power struggle over the colony took a strange turn that November, when the Lord Chamberlain, William Herbert, 3rd Earl of Pembroke, and others engineered a marriage between Smythe's eighteen-year-old son, John, and the late Sir Robert's daughter, Isabella, without Smythe's knowledge. Smythe was able at least to then make an ally of his daughter-in-law's eldest brother, Robert, heir to the Warwick earldom, in the Bermuda struggle. In 1619 the new earl had Nathaniel Butler, his preferred nominee for governor of the Bermuda colony, installed over Sandys' candidate, his own brother,

George. Smythe held on to his governorship of the Bermuda colony's Somers Islands Company until 1621, when Sandys at last seized control. Two years later, however, Smythe would wrest back the position.

Smythe would have further satisfaction when the investigation into the Virginia Company's books reached its long-awaited conclusion with the exoneration of Smythe and the condemnation of Sandys. He had just retired to a home in Kent when he died in September 1625, around age sixty-seven, probably of the plague.

Robert Bylot was a meticulous explorer, methodical and productive. Like Hudson, he demonstrated a benign attitude toward the indigenous people. Whatever bloodshed Bylot might have witnessed from a safe distance at East Digges Island on the 1610–11 *Discovery* voyage and on the follow-up expedition under the privateer Thomas Button, he welcomed contact with the Inuit on his voyages with William Baffin, and he treated them humanely. Indeed, it was impressive that Bylot attempted to anchor the *Discovery* in 1615 while exploring with Baffin so that he could respond to gestures from Inuit on East Digges Island to meet with them. Bylot must not have faulted them for the previous clashes. And like Hudson, he took uncommonly good care of his men. No one died on the 1615 or 1616 voyages.

While no explorer probed more of the Canadian Arctic and subarctic before or after him, no journal or chart of his would survive. Bylot would be relegated by history to near anonymity. His only recorded words were his signed depositions from the mutiny interrogations. His legacy was further undermined by the editorial decision-making of Samuel Purchas. Baffin's journal from the 1615 voyage was reproduced in *Purchas His Pilgrimes,* but only a précis of his 1616 journal was included, even though

Purchas had the full journal as well as Baffin's chart of Baffin Bay. Both were discarded, with Purchas explaining that they were "somewhat troublesome and too costly to insert." The veracity of Baffin's and Bylot's 1616 explorations would be doubted until the nineteenth century.

Samuel de Champlain did not go to war with the Algonquin against the Iroquois, as he had promised Tessöuat, in 1614. He next travelled up the Ottawa River in 1615, this time to visit and overwinter with the Huron. He passed through the chokepoint held by the Kichesipirini, but did not mention the tribe or Tessöuat when he related the journey in *Voyages et Descouvertures,* published in 1619. He simply directed his readers to consult his previous volume if they wished to know anything about the river or its peoples on the portion of his journey to Tessöuat's stronghold.

When he reached the Nebicerini (whom he called the Nipisierinii), Champlain wrote, "There was a large number of them, who gave us a very welcome reception . . . During the time that I was with them the chief of this tribe and their most prominent men entertained us with many banquets according to their custom, and took the trouble to go fishing and hunting with me, in order to treat me with the greatest courtesy possible." Missionaries subsequently would avow that the Nebicerini had an unusually large number of sorcerers among them, but Champlain made no mention of sorcery, and he enjoyed their hospitality. The Nebicerini would offer to take him to the Northern Sea, but under pressure from the Huron, who wanted to limit Champlain's direct contact with more distant tribes, they did not fulfill the promise. Champlain wrote nothing about the English boy or the English scalps the Nebicerini were supposed to have been holding for him as a gift.

The 1615–16 journey to Huronia was Champlain's last exploration venture. He never reached the Northern Sea, and never found the English boy. He never built his envisioned settlement at present-day Montréal. And he never stopped promoting the idea that a route to the Orient lay somewhere upstream of the Great Rapid.

When Champlain died at his habitation in Quebec on Christmas Day, 1635, more than thirty-two years after first coming to the St. Lawrence, his vision of a colony was scarcely alive. A new settlement had just been established at Trois-Rivières, but there probably weren't many more than two hundred people at the main base at Quebec. The head of the Jesuit mission in Canada, Charles Lalement, was at his side when he died. His burial place has still not been found. Champlain willed all of his possessions to the Virgin Mary, or more pragmatically to the church of Notre-Dame-de-la-Recouvrance, which he had ordered built at Quebec in 1633. This did not sit well with his small circle of potential worldly heirs. However, his estranged wife, Hélène Boullé, who had not set foot in Quebec since 1624, was unwilling to pursue a legal struggle over his property. She had already been planning to join the Ursuline order while Champlain was still alive. Her parents' decision to revoke their disownership of her after Champlain's death may have been a factor in her disinterest in fighting over his estate. Champlain's shares in the colony's partnership ended up with his cousin, Marie Camarat, after his will was quashed. Boullé entered the Ursuline monastery in Paris in 1645, then founded her own Ursuline monastery in the town of Meaux. She died there in 1654.

Additional clues to the events surrounding the 1613 journey would have rested in Champlain's personal papers: his notebooks, his legal documents, his hand-drawn charts, which have never been found. In the four works he published after *Quatriesme Voyage*, Champlain had nothing more to say about what became of Nicolas de Vignau.

Bibliographic Essay

—

I HAVE STRIVEN WHERE POSSIBLE to work from original narratives, whether in published or in manuscript form—or, as is often the case, from scholarly annotated republications of those items, sometimes in translation. England's Hakluyt Society and Canada's Champlain Society have performed much yeoman's work over the years in the scholarly reprinting field. Where a physical copy of the work was not readily accessible, I was well served by the digital reproductions available online from such database sources as the Champlain Society's digital archives, Early Canadiana Online, the Robarts Library of the University of Toronto, the Virtual Jamestown Project, Yale Law School's The Avalon Project, and the Tufts Digital Collection and Archives.

Henry Hudson: the documentary record

Nothing is known about Henry Hudson's life before his first documented voyage, the 1607 expedition in the *Hopewell,* and I have not speculated on those years in this book. Previous authors have proposed that he sailed with John Davis in search of the Northwest Passage in the 1580s, or that he opposed the Spanish Armada in 1588. There's no evidence for any of it. The Hudson name (and spelling variants typical of the age) does appear repeatedly in the annals of the Muscovy Company, as preserved by Richard Hakluyt, and it's not unreasonable to think that Henry Hudson might have been a relative or descendant of some of them. (See below for the research published by Janvier.) I also have been struck by a number of similarities between Hudson's experiences and methods and those of Sir James Lancaster, who commanded the first East India Company expedition to the Orient, in 1601–03. John Davis also happened to be the pilot on that voyage, and Lancaster was greatly interested in the possibility of a viable Northwest Passage. I would not be surprised if Hudson sailed with Davis and Lancaster on that voyage, but there is no way to prove it.

The nature of the documentary record on Hudson's four known voyages of exploration is part of the narrative of this book, but I will review the accumulating knowledge base here as a way of explaining sources. Nothing was published under Hudson's name in his own lifetime. Only with his disappearance in 1611 did he become something of a publishing *cause célèbre,* and even then, only initially in Holland, largely because of state suppression of sensitive exploration accounts in England.

Hessel Gerritsz published the sensational map based on Hudson's own cartography as well as a brief discussion of the 1609 *Half Moon* and 1610–11 *Discovery* voyages in the small volume that became known as *Detectio Freti Hudsoni,* first issued in Dutch in 1612. I own an 1878 reprint of the original Dutch work (along with the map), which is contained in the volume *Arctic North-East and West Passage,* published in Amsterdam that year. It includes a transcription of the 1612 Dutch edition, that of a 1613 Latin edition, along with an English translation.

Emmanuel van Meteren, the Dutch consul in London who was involved in Hudson's 1609 voyage for the VOC, published (posthumously) an authoritative account of that third voyage in his *Historie der Nederlanden* in 1614. Van Meteren's account is complemented by that of Johannes de Laet's *Nieuwe Werelt* of 1625. De Laet was a cartographer and a director of the Dutch West India Company, which was formed in 1621 by independent traders who had begun exploiting Hudson's discoveries from New England to the Hudson River in 1610, and he acquired papers from Hudson's 1609 voyage in the process. After de Laet, a number of seventeenth-century Dutch writers tackled Hudson's 1609 voyage, but their accounts became increasingly derivative and less credible, as their assertions (for example, that Hudson was actually a Dutchman, or had spent many years in Holland) were coloured by increasing hostilities between England and the Dutch Republic.

Some of Hudson's papers came into the possession of the peerless historiographer Richard Hakluyt, but were not published by him. After Hakluyt's death in 1616, Samuel Purchas, chaplain to Archbishop George Abbot, who had ambitions to become Hakluyt's successor, bought Hakluyt's papers from his estate. He had already published in 1613 *Purchas His Pilgrimage, or Relations of the World and their Religions,* and in a 1617 edition of that work, he included an account of the Hudson mutiny based on Gerritsz. In 1625, Purchas brought out his four-volume *Purchas His Pilgrimes (Hakluytus Posthumus),* an edited reissue of Hakluyt's *Principal Navigations* that was expanded with fresh materials on voyages that had occurred since the final volume of *Principal Navigations* in 1600. He revisited the Hudson mutiny in an essay in a new edition of *Purchas His Pilgrimage* in 1626, which largely summarized Prickett's narrative but also included facts of unknown origin. He died that year, apparently in debtor's prison. Hereafter, and in chapter notes on sources, I will simply refer to "Purchas" when speaking of *Purchas His Pilgrimes.*

Purchas became a core source of primary materials on Hudson's voyages. He was the first to publish many critical documents, which do not otherwise survive. These included the journal of the 1607 *Hopewell* voyage, written in whole or in part by John Playse, although it is thought to substantially represent Hudson's own missing journal; Hudson's journal for the 1608 *Hopewell* voyage (with snippets of Robert Juet's journal preserved as margin notes); Robert Juet's journal for the 1609 *Half Moon* voyage; the papers Hudson had acquired from Petrus Plancius and Jodocus Hondius (Ivor Boty's sailing directions for east Greenland, a note by Willem Barentsz) and which had been in Hakluyt's possession; and all of the known 1610–11 *Discovery* voyage documents that were produced by its participants. Those documents included Habakkuk Prickett's written narrative, the letter home from Iceland by Thomas Woodhouse, Woodhouse's note relating the events of the September 1610 hearing into Robert Juet's conduct, and the heavily edited abstract of Hudson's journal, which stops on August 3, 1610.

Writers have routinely asserted that the mutineers destroyed the rest of Hudson's 1610 journal to eliminate incriminating evidence. But both Prickett, in his narrative, and Bylot, in his High Court of the Admiralty testimony, made references to entries in Hudson's journal concerning events after August 3 that they were confident could be consulted to support their statements. Far more likely is that the journal's subsequent entries were suppressed, to keep them from being read by foreign rivals as the English continued to search for the Northwest Passage. The entries would have revealed details of the *Discovery*'s explorations of Hudson Bay and James Bay, and there was still hope for success in that region. As Purchas was not given anything to publish beyond August 3, the entire journal disappeared altogether.

The next significant milestones in the Hudson documentary record came close upon each other in the mid-nineteenth century.

In 1859, Henry Cruise Murphy, U.S. ambassador to The Hague, produced a booklet, *Henry Hudson in Holland,* to mark the 250th anniversary of Hudson's discovery of the Hudson River. Murphy's work remains the reference for Dutch documents relating to Hudson's 1609 voyage for the VOC. Murphy published materials from the VOC archives in their original Dutch and in English translation.

In 1861, George Michael Asher produced *Henry Hudson the Navigator: The Original Documents in which His Career is Recorded,* for the Hakluyt Society, to mark the 250th anniversary of the navigator's disappearance. Asher gathered in one volume virtually everything previously published, including the materials in Purchas and translations of the Dutch authors' contributions from the seventeenth century. He also found room for the correspondence between Pierre Jeannin and Henry IV relating to the French attempt to hire Hudson in early 1609 through the Amsterdam merchant Isaac Lemaire. Asher was aware of the Murphy monograph but was unable to secure a copy, and he leaves the distinct impression that Murphy did not want him to have it.

Between them, Asher and Murphy produced two fundamental compilations of Hudson material that are still consulted by scholars. Murphy's privately published booklet was reprinted in 1909, with annotations, as the 300th anniversary of the Hudson River's discovery was marked. I have used a 1972 reissue of the 1909 edition (New York: Burt Franklin). Although I have also consulted *Purchas His Pilgrimes,* I have relied on Asher for his transcription of the voyage narratives that first appeared in print in 1625.

In the individual chapter source notes, I have omitted reference to the following primary narrative materials first published by Purchas: the 1607 and 1608 *Hopewell* voyage journals, the 1609

Half Moon journal by Robert Juet, Hudson's *Discovery* journal abstract, Habakkuk Prickett's *Discovery* narrative, and Thomas Woodhouse's letter to Samuel Macham and his note on the Juet hearing of September 10, 1610. They can all be found in Purchas or Asher.

After Asher and Murphy, the main outstanding documentary items with respect to Hudson's career were the Trinity House transaction of October 24, 1611, and the fragmentary records of the High Court of the Admiralty from 1612 and 1617–18, including the depositions of survivors, an undated indictment, and the uneven record of the 1618 trial. Historian Reginald Godfrey Marsden dredged up the HCA records for *English Ships in the Reign of James I*, published in 1905 as Vol. 19 in the New Series of the Transactions of the Royal Historical Society. Thomas Janvier followed his lead and attempted to find the cited items himself, but he couldn't locate all of them in the crumbling rolls of documents. Nevertheless he included an English translation of what he could find in a monograph, *Henry Hudson: A Brief Statement of his Aims and his Achievements,* published in 1909. Janvier also incorporated research by the late General John Meredith Read into the Hudson name, including possible ancestors within the Muscovy Company and passage search milieu, on which nothing concrete has further emerged. Janvier remains an important source, and I employed an electronic version of the text produced by Project Gutenberg. The 1928 biography *Henry Hudson,* by Llewelyn Powys (New York: Harper & Bros.), includes full transcriptions of the surviving 1618 trial documents in Latin and English in its appendix. C. L'Estrange Ewan also published transcriptions of the Latin originals along with English translations of HCA records in a 1938 monograph, *The Northwest Passage: Light on the Murder of Henry Hudson from Unpublished Depositions.* Dr. Conrad Heidenreich, who has lectured on the mutiny at the university level, very decently sent me copies of these different published versions of the admiralty case records.

The final noteworthy document is the October 30, 1609 (Julian date), letter from Thomas Holland to Sir Robert Cecil, Earl of Salisbury, relating his conversation with Henry Hudson on his appearance at Dartmouth with the *Half Moon*. It was unknown to the scholars previously cited. An American choirmaster named Linden J. Lundstrom, who was passionate about locating the *Discovery*'s overwintering location and scoured British archives for any Hudson evidence, located the letter. He published a paper on his theory of the location of the overwintering bay in 1980 ("The Bay where Hudson did winter," James Ford Bell Lecture, University of Minnesota), mentioning the Holland letter in passing but revealing little about it. Since Lundstrom's publication, the Cecil papers of which it is a part had been relocated from Cambridge University to Hatfield House. The librarian and archivist to the Marquess of Salisbury at Hatfield House agreed to provide me with a previously published abstract of the letter as well as a photocopy of the original letter. The abstract is close in language to the original, but the original has particular phrasing and additional information, and I have worked from it as a result.

Samuel de Champlain: the documentary record

Unlike Hudson, Champlain was a prolific author. His output began with *Brief Discours,* which purports to relate his adventurers in the Spanish Caribbean from 1599 to 1601. It survives in different manuscript versions, and they were most likely made after his death. Academics cannot agree whether they are real, corrupted, or fake. I corresponded with Italian scholar Luca Codignola, of the University of Genoa, who has proposed that the manuscripts are seventeenth-century fabrications, but nevertheless that their creator must have drawn on privileged information about Champlain, which he has suggested might have come from the Sieur de Monts. I am persuaded that essential biographical information is too good for this work not to have at least some basis in reality, and I have used it for essential facts with respect to his diversion to the Spanish Caribbean.

While all of Champlain's published works have some bearing on this story, three are fundamental: *Des Sauvages* (1603), *Les Voyages* (1612) and *Quatriesme Voyage* (1613).

The process of translating Champlain into English is a story in itself, and some of the most informative (and even entertaining) aspects are contained in *Champlain and The Champlain Society: An Early Expedition into Documentary Publishing* by Dr. Conrad Heidenreich (Toronto: Occasional Papers of The Champlain Society, Number 3, 2006). The first English translation of Champlain's entire works was a three-volume effort edited by Edmund Slafter and translated by Charles Pomeroy Otis for the Prince Society of Boston, which was published between 1878 and 1882. It suffers slightly from being based on Charles-Honoré Laverdière's *Œuvres de Champlain,* published by Quebec's Université de Laval in 1870, which was the first compilation of all of Champlain's writings as well as some contemporary documents. Although Laverdière's annotated effort was a landmark work, he produced it from transcriptions made for him in longhand of Champlain's works at the Bibliothèque nationale in Paris, and these were not always perfectly faithful to the published originals. The Otis translation of Laverdière nevertheless was a good effort, and Edmund Slafter's introductory essay, "Memoir of Samuel de Champlain," in Volume 1 is a fine work of scholarship. William Grant updated the Otis translation of Champlain's 1604–18 writings for a new translation published by Charles Scribner's Sons of New York in 1909.

The best-known translation may be *The Works of Samuel de Champlain,* published by the Champlain Society of Toronto in six volumes between 1922 and 1936 under the general editorship of Henry Percival Biggar. These are bilingual, and the scholars involved were meticulous in returning to Champlain's originally published works for the French text, once they began to recognize the problems with Laverdière's version. (The Grant update of Otis was a departure point for the English translation.) Biggar unfortunately overruled his translators on key occasions, for example preferring to preserve inaccurate decisions for *Des Sauvages* made by (or for) Richard Hakluyt before his death in 1616. (*Des Sauvages* was first published in English by Purchas in 1625, using the Hakluyt materials.) One can at least consult the original French on the very same page.

Dr. Heidenreich as I write is overseeing a new bilingual edition of Champlain's published works for the Champlain Society, for which Janet Ritch is producing the translations. It will assuredly be the most authoritative annotated English translation of Champlain, addressing any shortcomings of the previous translation by the Champlain Society (which nevertheless was a significant accomplishment).

The English translations of Champlain in this book are something of a hybrid, drawing on the Otis as well as the Champlain Society translations. In addition, a portion of the fresh translation of *Des Sauvages* by Janet Ritch was provided to me by Dr. Heidenreich. This advanced peek allowed me to avoid Biggar's earlier error of deferring to the Hakluyt translation published by Purchas, which proved to be so influential on later translations. I have relied on this much-improved translation of a portion of *Des Sauvages* where noted.

Although I am no scholar of early French, my grasp of the modern language is sufficient to have allowed me to reconsider past translations and tackle phrases and words on my own where earlier efforts now seem arch or prone to beautifying Champlain's coarse delivery. (As Heidenreich's monograph on the Champlain Society's translation effort records, translator George Wrong charged that editor H. P. Biggar, who had the last word on what was printed, made Champlain "a better writer [in English] than he was in French" in Volume 1. Biggar himself declared, "I never before in my life dealt with so disorderly a writer as Champlain," and further remarked that Champlain "often says what he does not really mean.") At times, past translations make Champlain sound like a late-nineteenth-century English schoolmaster, not a French mariner-soldier from three centuries earlier. I have where it seemed appropriate eased the stiffness in Champlain's delivery, without changing the meaning. In addition to punctuation changes, in some cases I have made what I think is a more appropriate word choice.

I have been on my own in translating the vast bulk of primary documents relating to Champlain's life and career, gathered in *Nouveaux documents sur Champlain et son époque, Volume 1 (1560–1622)*, compiled and annotated by Robert Le Blant and René Baudry, which was published in Ottawa in 1967 by the National Archives of Canada (hereafter *Nouveaux documents*). The archival documents are transcribed faithfully with their original spellings, and the explanatory footnotes are also in French. No one has translated this work into English. (And there has never been a Volume 2.) In many cases, the original phrasing in the documents is so difficult as to defy translated quotations of any length, and I have resorted to paraphrasing or to simply presenting the salient facts. But in a few instances, especially the Malouin factum of 1612–13, it was important to deliver the full venom of the remarks, and I have offered up my own quotations, in modern English. I also produced my own English translation of a French translation of an Italian edition of Francesco Giuseppe Bressani's *Relation abrégée de quelques missions des pères de la Compagnie de Jésus dans la Nouvelle-France* (Montréal: J. Lovell, 1852).

Major historical French works are often available in translated (sometimes bilingual) scholarly editions. I am indebted in particular to one standard reference work, *The Jesuit Relations and Allied Documents* by Reuben Gold Thwaites, which was published in seventy-three volumes between 1896 and 1901 (Cleveland: Burrow Bros.). Thwaites provided transcriptions in the original French, Italian, and Latin of Jesuit *Relations* from their missionary work in French North America between 1610 and 1791, as well as an English translation and notes. (Hereafter, my citations of materials from the *Relations* will refer to volumes in the Thwaites edition.) I also employed George Wrong's translation of Gabriel Sagard's *Le grand voyage du pays des Hurons* of 1632, published by the Champlain Society in 1939. Any minor variances from the original translations are my own efforts to bring the English into the early twenty-first century.

About the jacket

The jacket of this book displays portraits of Samuel de Champlain and Henry Hudson. Both are speculative. No authentic portrait survives for either man, although Champlain's *Les Voyages* did include an illustration of the author fighting the Iroquois in 1609. In it, Champlain is a small figure in a cavalier's armour; a full beard can be seen behind the butt of his harquebus.

In the mid-nineteenth century a Canadian government official dispatched to Paris to find a historic portrait of Champlain contrived to have a Paris artist, Louis César Joseph Ducornet, concoct one, based on a portrait by Balthasar Moncornet of

Signor Michel Particelli, France's Italian-born, scandal-plagued controlleur-général of finances in the mid-seventeenth century. The Champlain portrait's authenticity was questioned by Victor Paltsits in 1904. It was confirmed as a fake by H. P. Biggar while he was overseeing the Champlain Society's translations of Champlain's works, and he published to that effect in *Canadian Historical Review* in 1920. But by then, the Particelli deception had become a cultural fixture, the inspiration for a host of likenesses, and it has proved virtually unshakable in the absence of an authentic alternative. The portrait on this book's jacket, which followed the example of Ducornet, was created by Eugène Ronjat for François Guizot's *Histoire de France* of 1876. Ronjat's rendering of Champlain was somewhat corpulent, and has been narrowed slightly, as well as mirrored so that he faces to our right.

As for Henry Hudson, the jacket employs one of many speculative portraits that circulated in the nineteenth and early twentieth centuries. In his 1909 scholarly monograph *Henry Hudson: A Brief Statement of his Aims and his Achievements,* Thomas Janvier was adamant that no portraits, which featured "a dapper looking man wearing a ruffed collar," were authentic. "Who that man was is unknown. That he was not Hudson is certain." As with the Ducornet fiction of Champlain, this portrait and its many variants have become iconographic of Hudson.

Spelling and "translation" of English historical works

It might seem odd to speak of English documents from the sixteenth and seventeenth centuries in terms of "translation," but a writer must decide whether to reproduce such materials verbatim or to make an effort to clean up the spelling and punctuation for the sake of clarity and comprehension.

Like Champlain's French, the English written by Henry Hudson and his contemporaries was a work in progress. The first dictionary did not appear until 1606, and spelling often is somewhere just this side of phonetic. I decided that it was more important for the reader of a work of popular nonfiction to easily comprehend what a writer of this period was actually saying than it was to adhere to scholarly exactitude and turn quotations into head-scratching puzzles. In most instances, little more than the occasional "misspelled" word has been corrected, and I have not done any rephrasing. For example, the original text of William Baffin's letter to Sir John Wolstenholme on his return from the passage search of 1616 reads: "How many of the best sort of men haue set their whole endeauoures to prooue a passage that wayes?" I have rendered this as "How many of the best sort of men have set their whole endeavours to prove a passage that way?" And in quoting from *Diary of Nicholas Garry*, as published by the Royal Society of Canada, circa 1900, in which he relates his travels on the Ottawa River in 1821, I have decided to deny him his particular affectation of capitalizing what seems like every third word.

Spelling of names

The spelling of names was far from standardized in France or England during the times in which this story takes place. People spelled their own names any number of ways, and there are many examples of a name being spelled more than one way within a single document. One can easily argue that there is no single correct spelling for most of the contentious names. In consulting primary sources, you will find plenty of options to choose from, especially for the members of the *Discovery* crew. Names are reversed at times: Arnold Ludlow and Mathew

Bennet become Ludlow Arnold and Bennet Mathew, along with many variations in spelling. Some variations, it must be said, have been unnecessary complications. Robert Juet's last name has sometimes been rendered as Ivett in modern works, but that variation comes from Latin court records, which simply followed the language's strictures and used "I" for "J" and "v" for "u." Most important for this book was that I chose one variation for a particular name and stuck with it from start to finish.

In the case of Habakkuk Prickett, I have settled on a variation that no one until this date has employed, but I hope I have done so for good reason. The name of the *Discovery*'s supercargo on the 1610–11 voyage shifts considerably in contemporary records, so much so that there cannot be said to be a single "true" name. Purchas in 1625 rendered his name as Abacuk Prickett, which is the variant writers have tended to use. Prickett himself, however, signed his February 7, 1617, deposition before the High Court of the Admiralty as either Abacooke or Abacak Periket, depending on which transcription of the document you consider most correct. Periket could be a corruption of Periquet, which would suggest a Huguenot origin. But the Periquet/Periket name is not otherwise known in English genealogy, and his last name is accepted to be Prickett, as per Purchas. His first name is far less clear. Other versions of it in documents related to the voyage include Abacuck, Abacucke, Abackuk, and Obacuck. The name is that of an Old Testament prophet, the spelling for which was settled upon as Habakkuk in the King James Bible first published in 1611, around the very time of the *Discovery* mutiny, and remains so today in English-language bibles. As none of the many phonetic variants in the documentary record (including Prickett's own) can be said to be correct, I've opted to use the King James spelling.

Terminology

Ship's records

"Log" and "journal" can be confusing terms in this period. A ship's log by this time was becoming a sophisticated record, as navigation itself became more sophisticated and investors' expectations for proper reports increased. The Muscovy Company for one maintained high standards for shipboard records, and individual logs were kept by a ship's master, mate, and pilot. A log was generally organized into a series of columns that recorded navigation observations such as calculated latitude, course, wind direction, compass variation, and estimated distance covered in the last twenty-four hours. These items made up the "table of course." On the right-hand side was a column with room for comments, which was sometimes said to comprise the "journal." Baffin's log from his 1615 voyage was called his "brief journal," and it consisted of the table of course as well as the right-hand journal column. Baffin then wrote up a longer journal, or narrative, as a report to investors. A voyage of discovery typically produced such a separate journal, sometimes several, depending how many people on board set their mind to it. This journal more fully described the voyage and its events, on land and at sea, with reference to the table of course. A journal's writer might have to consult the logs maintained by all of the senior officers to get the full picture of the voyage, as the mate would be concerned with recording which sails were set or reefed, and the pilot with soundings and the like. The writer might be a senior officer of the voyage, but in some cases the task was turned over to someone aboard with a gift for prose.

It is not always clear which sort of voyage record is being referred to in events surrounding Henry Hudson's career. By "journal," someone like Petrus Plancius or Hessel Gerritsz probably had in mind something like Baffin's "brief journal," or a longer report that incorporated the table of course. The partial "abstract" of Hudson's journal for the *Discovery* voyage, published by Purchas in 1625, appears to have been a heavily edited version of the right-hand column from the "table of course."

Distance measures

I have used Imperial units for general distance measures, principally the statute mile (5,280 feet) and the nautical mile (6,076 feet), which is equal to one degree of longitude at the equator. Historic measures also appear in the story, and their use was neither consistent nor standardized. "Leagues" are routinely used for distances at sea. The English counted twenty leagues to a degree of longitude at the equator, making one league equal to three nautical miles. Samuel de Champlain's leagues are problematic. Their length varied, depending on where he was and how he was employing them. Conrad Heidenreich has analyzed his cartography and writings and concluded that Champlain probably used a variety of leagues, albeit inconsistently. The Spanish marine league, of 17.5 to the degree (about 3.4 nautical miles) was employed at sea. Two different French leagues, of between about 2.4 and 3 statute miles, were employed in coastal and inland surveys. For his overland journeys, such as the 1613 expedition, Champlain appears to have used still another league, of about two statute miles. See "An Analysis of Champlain's Maps in Terms of His Estimates of Distance, Latitude and Longitude," by Conrad Heidenreich, *University of Ottawa Quarterly*, Vol. 48, No. 2, 1978. A cogent overview of Champlain's methods can be found in the essay "Samuel de Champlain's Cartography," by Conrad Heidenreich and Edward Dahl, published in *Champlain: The Birth of French America* (Montréal: McGill-Queen's University Press, Septentrion, 2004).

Monetary units

So much currency is afloat in this story that it would require an entire chapter to explain it all, and I have striven to minimize the complexities. Where appropriate I have also attempted to provide a modern equivalent value, using conversion tools available through EH.Net and other sources, although relative purchasing values become fairly tenuous over the course of four centuries.

For England, the old system of pounds, shillings, and pence was in effect, with twelve pence to the shilling and twenty shillings to the pound. France was more complicated. French valuation employed the similar system of the livre, sol, and denier, with the same relative values. The livre coin, more properly the livre tournois, was colloquially known as the franc. Henry III in 1577 decreed that a gold coin called the écu would supplant the livre tournois as the kingdom's standard accounting unit, a reference point for the decreed conversion rates for domestic and foreign coins. One écu at that time was set at 60 sol (three livre), and in September 1602 Henry IV pegged the value of a gold écu at 65 sol. But Henry IV also brought back the livre tournois as the basis of accounting in 1602. Documents relating to Champlain consequently have a mix of uncertain references to actual coinage and accounting units. For example, the authors of the Malouin factum in Chapter 23, in alleging losses by the Sieur de Monts of 50,000 écus, were writing around January 1613, when the livre tournois was back as the standard accounting unit. The factum could have used écu to mean the old accounting unit or the actual gold coin.

Julian and Gregorian Calendars

The stories of Champlain and Hudson pose challenges in determining which calendar was in use in particular documents. To correct a flaw in leap years that was causing the Julian calendar to become progressively out of sync with celestial events, Catholic countries (including France) converted to the modern Gregorian calendar in 1582. The Dutch Republic followed suit in 1583, but England and Scotland continued to use the Julian calendar into the mid-eighteenth century. Consequently, at the time of this book's events, two rival calendars were in disagreement by ten days. A date of August 11 Julian was August 21 Gregorian. Knowing which calendar was in use in a particular document is not as simple as determining the country of origin. For English documents, it's clear that many ship's logs and journals were maintained to the Gregorian calendar, because leading celestial almanacs necessary for accurate navigation were produced to Gregorian dates. (This was nevertheless a source of major navigation problems, as English pilots maintaining Julian logs sometimes failed to appreciate that the tables in their almanac were Gregorian.) In the case of Robert Juet's 1609 *Half Moon* journal, he states at the outset that it has been kept *novo stilo,* or "new style," meaning Gregorian. In other cases the calendar type is not clear. Habakkuk Prickett's *Discovery* narrative is clearly Julian when relating the mutiny events, as he gives both dates and days of the week. That doesn't necessarily mean all of his voyage dates were Julian, especially if he consulted a ship's log in composing the account. But there is nothing in Hudson's surviving journal abstract to give a clue to the calendar type followed by the voyage's mariners.

I have used the celestial-observation software Skychart III to confirm the dates and times of some events in this story, and the program has helped in verifying which calendar was in use. I have also used the program to determine certain celestial events mentioned in the story, such as times of sunrise and sunset, and lunar phases, which are not found in the primary sources.

I have used calendar dates as I found them in the documentary record, not attempting to convert any Julian dates to Gregorian or worrying about which calendar might have been in use, unless it is necessary (or possible) to reconcile the timing of events in different accounts. I have noted in the chapter notes where specific dates have been adjusted. Otherwise, I have followed standard practice in adjusting the first day of the Julian New Year for England from March 25 (the Annunciation) to January 1, a change that did not actually occur until the Gregorian calendar was adopted in 1752.

Notes and Sources

—

PART I
Beyond the Furious Overfall

General historical sources
The surviving accounts of all of Hudson's known voyages, as first published
by Purchas, are best preserved in Asher. A digital facsimile of the four-
volume *Purchas His Pilgrimes (Hakluytus Posthumus)* is accessible online from
The Kraus Collection of Sir Francis Drake at the Library of Congress
(international.loc.gov/intldl/drakehtml/rbdkhome.html). All High Court of
the Admiralty records relating to the mutiny investigation and trial, and the
Trinity House record of October 1611, are found as previously noted in
Marsden, Janvier, Ewan, and Powys.

Documents and voyage accounts related to the history of the Muscovy
Company are found in Richard Hakluyt, *The Principal Navigations Voyages
Traffiques & Discoveries of the English Nation,* Vol. 1 (1598). (All references to
Principal Navigations in these notes refer to the three-volume second edition of
1598–1600.) See also D. W. Waters, *The Art of Navigation in England in
Elizabethan and Early Stuart Times* (New Haven: Yale University Press, 1958) for
a wealth of information on maritime activities as well as navigational methods.

First-hand accounts from the voyages of John Davis and Martin
Frobisher, and other northern passage-making efforts dating back to John
Cabot, are compiled in Hakluyt's Vol. 3 (1600). Various transcribed and
edited reissues of Hakluyt have been made over the years. The version by
Edmond Goldsmid (Edinburgh: E. & G. Goldsmid, 1885–90), which repack-
ages the content of the volumes (while omitting items that are not explicitly

English), is well known, as is the 1927 edition published by J. M. Dent & Son of London and H. P. Dutton of New York. An e-text transcription of the Goldsmid edition can be read online courtesy the University of Adelaide (etext.library.adelaide.edu.au).

An excellent guide to the histories of the Muscovy, East India, and other early English chartered companies is Sir Percival Griffiths' *A Licence to Trade: A History of the English Chartered Companies* (London and Tonbridge: Ernest Benn, 1974). See also Kenneth R. Andrews, *Trade, Plunder and Settlement: Maritime Enterprise and the Genesis of the British Empire 1480–1630* (Cambridge: Cambridge University Press, 1984).

Biographies have been sourced at three dictionaries of national biography, all via their online editions: the subscription-based Oxford Dictionary of National Biography (DNB) at www.oxforddnb.com, Dictionary of Canadian Biography (DCB) at www.biographi.ca, and Welsh Biography Online (WBO), at yba.llgc.org.uk. Where appropriate, individual authors are cited in the chapter notes.

General reading on the historical period and exploration activities, documentary sources, and specific chapter source references include: *Calendar of State Papers, Domestic Series, James I, Vol. 8, 1603–10*, and *Vol. 9, 1611–18* (Great Britain: Public Record Office, 1858); *Calendar of State Papers, Colonial Series, Vol. 7 (America & West Indies) 1574–1660* (Great Britain: Public Record Office, 1860); Kenneth R. Andrews, *Ships, Money and Politics: Seafaring and Naval Enterprise in the Reign of Charles I* (Cambridge: Cambridge University Press, 1991); Robert Ashton, *Reformation and Revolution 1558–1600* (London: Granada Publishing, 1984); Philip Barbour, editor, *The Jamestown Voyages Under the First Charter 1606–1609*, 2 vols. (London: The Hakluyt Society, Cambridge University Press, 1969); John Barrow, *A Chronological History of Voyages into the Arctic Regions* (London: John Murray, 1818); Nicholas Crane, *Mercator: The Man Who Mapped the Planet* (London: Weidenfeld & Nicolson, 2002); J. H. Elliot, *The Old World and the New 1492–1650* (Cambridge: Cambridge University Press, 1970); G. R. Elton, *England Under the Tudors*, 3rd edition (London: Routledge, 1991); Samuel Rawson Gardiner, *History of England, Vol. 1, 1603–06*, and *Vol. 2, 1607–16* (London, 1883; new impression, London: Longmans, Green, 1900); John Harris, *Navigantium atque itinerantium bibliotheca, Or, A Compleat Collection of Voyages and Travels* (London: 1705), Derek Hayes, *Historical Atlas of Canada* (Vancouver: Douglas & McIntyre, 2002); Elizabeth Jenkins, *Elizabeth the Great* (New York: Time, 1964); Donald S. Johnson, *Charting the Sea of Darkness: The Four Voyages of Henry Hudson* (Camden: International Marine, 1993); Robert W. Kenney, *Elizabeth's Admiral: The Political Career of Charles Howard, Earl of*

Nottingham 1536–1624 (Baltimore: The Johns Hopkins Press, 1970); Samuel Lewis, *A Topographical Dictionary of Ireland* (London: S. Lewis, 1837); Clements R. Markham, editor, *The Voyages of Sir James Lancaster, Knight, to the East Indies, with Abstracts of Journals of Voyages to the East Indies, during the Seventeenth Century, Preserved in the India Office; and the Voyage of Captain John Knight (1606), to Seek the Northwest Passage* (London: The Hakluyt Society, 1877); Samuel Eliot Morison, *The European Discovery of America: The Northern Voyages AD500–1600* (Oxford and New York: Oxford University Press, 1971); John Lothrop Motley, *History of the United Netherlands, from the Death of William the Silent to the Twelve Year Truce,* 4 vols. (New York: Harper & Bros., 1860–1867); John Nichols, *The Processions, and Magnificent Festivities of King James the First* (London: J. B. Nichols, 1828); David B. Quinn, *New American World: A Documentary History of North America to 1612,* 5 vols. (New York: Arno Press and Hector Bye, 1979); David B. Quinn, *England and the Discovery of America 1481–1620* (London: George Allen & Unwin, 1974); David B. Quinn, *North America from Earliest Discovery to First Settlements: The Norse Voyages to 1612* (New York: Harper & Row, 1977); David B. and Alison M. Quinn, editors, *The English New England Voyages 1602–1608* (London: The Hakluyt Society, 1983); John L. Ridley, *Flora of the Hudson Bay Lowland and Its Postglacial Origins* (Ottawa: NRC Research Press, 2003); Thomas Rundall, editor, *Narratives of Voyages towards the North-West, in Search of A Passage to Cathay and India, 1496 to 1631* (London: The Hakluyt Society, 1849); Alan Stewart, *The Cradle King: A Life of James VI and I* (London: Chatto & Windus, 2003); John Stow, *A Survey of London* (Charles Lethbridge Kingsford, editor; 1603 edition collated with the first edition of 1598. Oxford: Clarendon Press, 1908); Thomas H. B. Symons, editor, *Meta Incognita: A Discourse of Discovery—Martin Frobisher's Arctic Expeditions, 1576–78,* 2 vols. (Ottawa: Canadian Museum of Civilization, 1999); E. M. W. Tillyard, *The Elizabethan World Picture* (London: Chatto & Windus, 1943); Henry Benjamin Wheatley, *London, past and present; its history, associations, and traditions* (London: J. Murray, 1891); Robert Wilkinson, *Londina illustrata; graphic and historic memorials . . .* (London: R. Wilkinson, 1819–25); and John Winton, *An Illustrated History of the Royal Navy, in Association with the Royal Naval Museum, Portsmouth* (London: Salamander Books, 2000).

Chapter 1

For details on the Irish campaign of George Lord Carew and the local history of Bearhaven, I have relied on Carew's DNB entry by Ute Lotz-Heumann; Samuel Lewis, *A Topographical Dictionary of Ireland*; and Sean

Ryan's monograph "Spanish Wild Geese," as published online by the Wild Geese Heritage Museum and Library in Galway.

Chapter 3

I have used the term "merchant adventurers" broadly, in reference to men of commerce willing to risk capital on voyages of exploration in England, France, and the Dutch Republic at this time. There was an actual Company of Merchant Adventurers in England, chartered in 1579, which held the English right to operate abroad in market towns as traders, and members such as Sir Thomas Smythe participated in funding exploration voyages. See Griffiths' *A Licence to Trade.*

The instructions to Sir Henry Middleton's 1610 East India Company voyage are in Markham's *The Voyages of Sir James Lancaster.* The letter of Thomas Holland to Sir Robert Cecil is preserved in the library of Hatfield House (Cecil Papers, Letters and Documents, 1563–1610, Archon Code 2173), and has been transcribed here with the library's permission. I have converted the Julian calendar dates of the letter's writing and receipt to Gregorian.

Details about Hudson's family are from Powys's *Henry Hudson.* His date of birth is unknown; "perhaps forty" is a reasonable guess for his age. John Hudson's precise age is unknown. He was listed as the ship's boy in the 1607 *Hopewell* voyage journal published by Purchas. For the 1608 voyage, he was simply listed among the rest of the crew, but Hudson referred to John as "my boy" in his journal. An age somewhere in the teens was most likely. No crew list for the *Half Moon* voyage survives. Thomas Holland took note of three Englishmen, and we know that there was a fourth, John Colman, who had been killed. As Henry Hudson and Robert Juet were aboard, it is safe to assume that the third English expedition member was John Hudson, as he was along for every other recorded voyage by his father.

Hudson's discussions with Plancius are known second-hand from a letter written to Henry IV by Pierre Jeannin, French ambassador to The Hague during the negotiations for the 1609 truce between Spain and the Dutch Republic, which France and England brokered. The letter is reproduced in its original French and in English translation in Asher. A notation by Hudson on the Boty manuscript indicated that William Stere translated it for him in 1608, but as the year-end of the Julian calendar followed in England was March 24, he could have acquired the Boty translation in early 1609. He also received some notes that had been made by Barentsz that related directly to the Northeast Passage attempt. These items found their way to Richard Hakluyt. When Hakluyt died, they were acquired from his estate by Samuel Purchas, who published them for the first time. They appear in Asher.

Extracts relating to Hudson from the writings of Emmanuel van Meteren and Johannes de Laet are in Asher. For VOC documents relating to the *Half Moon* voyage, see Henry C. Murphy's *Henry Hudson in Holland.* For Hessel Gerritsz's repeatedly revised writings on Hudson's 1609 and 1610 voyages, I have used the annotated 1878 reproduction of *Detectio Freti Hudsoni,* as well as Asher and Murphy.

The surviving records of George Waymouth's 1602 voyage are transcribed in Rundall's *Narratives of Voyages towards the North-West.* James Rosier's *A True Relation,* recounting Waymouth's 1605 voyage, is reproduced in the Quinns' *The English New England Voyages 1602–1608.* The missing sentence from Rosier's manuscript with respect to the passage potential of the Georges River was included by Purchas, who was working from a Rosier manuscript in his own version of the Waymouth voyage narrative, and is noted by the Quinns.

Dates for the start of the voyage are confusing. Robert Juet wrote that the departure of March 25 followed the "old account" or Julian calender. Thus their Gregorian departure was April 4, and their clearing of The Texel was April 6. Juet then notes his switch to Gregorian thereafter.

There is some dispute over where Hudson made his New World landfall. Lahave, on Nova Scotia's South Shore, has often been cited; the alternative, of the Georges River area, has been more recently proposed, by Donald S. Johnson in *Charting the Sea of Darkness,* and I concur, based on Johnson's plotting of the *Half Moon*'s course and the evidence of Juet's journal, which is a better fit for the Georges River area.

Documents from the 1609 search-and-destroy mission of *La Asunción de Cristo* are reproduced in Vol. 2 of Barbour's *The Jamestown Voyages under the First Charter 1606–1609.* Gabriel Archer's letter of August 31, 1609, originally published by Purchas, is also in Vol. 2 of Barbour. I have adjusted the Julian dates he more than likely employs to their Gregorian equivalent. Archer wrote that his ship "fell into the Kings River [James River] happily the eleventh of August." That placed the first arrivals of the relief flotilla in the lower reaches of Chesapeake Bay on August 21, Gregorian. Juet, who was following the Gregorian calendar, has Hudson arriving in the bay on the eighteenth.

Sir Robert Cecil's life and career are discussed in Elizabeth Jenkins's *Elizabeth the Great* and Alan Stewart's *The Cradle King.* I also employed his DNB entry by Pauline Croft.

Chapter 4

With respect to the confidential English information Hudson carried, Robert Juet noted on August 6, 1609: "And this is that headland which Captain Bartholomew Gosnold discovered in the year 1602, and called Cape Cod, because of the store of cod-fish that he found thereabout." The official published account of the 1602 expedition by John Brereton had not named the cape, and was extremely vague about its location. No map had been published, either. Archer's unpublished manuscript was far more specific and evidently inspired Juet's observation. Wrote Archer: "Near this Cape we came to Anchor in fifteen fathom, where we took great store of Cod-fish, for which we altered the name, and called it Cape Cod." Archer's manuscript and Brereton's official account are in the Quinns' *The English New England Voyages 1602–1608*.

For Sir Walter Cope, see his DNB biography by Elizabeth Allen. See also the Institute of Historical Research: Office Holders in Modern Britain (www.history.ac.uk/office) for a comprehensive list of appointments, along with dates, during this period. Sir Thomas Challener (or Challoner) crops up in various works and primary documents related to the Virginia Company, in which he was an investor. See Chapter 3 for Virginia Company sources related to the Jamestown venture. See also the Virtual Jamestown Project (www.virtualjamestown.org) which offers e-text versions of documents from 1550 to 1749.

Published comments by Emmanuel van Meteren and Hessel Gerritsz on Hudson's 1609 voyage again are reproduced in Asher as well as Murphy.

The list of principal investors in the 1610 *Discovery* voyage are presented in the charter granted for the follow-up voyage of 1612. The charter's beginning and summary are reproduced by Asher. The full contents are reproduced by David B. Quinn in *New American World*. Cecil's involvement in 1610 is circumstantial but entirely persuasive. The original investor list for the 1610 voyage does not survive, but the charter for the 1612 follow-up voyage asserts that it was backed by the same group that funded Hudson. Hudson's decision to name Salisbury Island at the western end of Hudson Strait in 1610 indicates that Robert Cecil was part of his investment group. Mentioned in the 1612 charter is "William Earl of Salisbury." This was Robert Cecil's son, who succeeded him as earl after his death in 1612, before the Button expedition was mounted. And so we can safely conclude that Sir Robert Cecil backed the 1610 voyage, and his heir, William, then took his place for the succeeding one.

It is not absolutely certain that Waymouth's *Discovery* of 1602 and Hudson's *Discovery* of 1610 were one and the same ship, although circumstantial evidence argues strongly in favour of it. In September 1601, the East India Company had resolved with Waymouth that he would be equipped with two ships for the 1602 voyage, the larger of which should be about 50 tons burden. The *Discovery* used by Hudson was described on a later voyage as being about 55 tons burden. Waymouth's journal identified his *Discovery* as being of 70 tons burden. But the definition of tonnage (and tunnage), a volume measurement that indicated carrying capacity, was not yet fixed. Still, Hudson's crew complement of twenty-three is more in keeping with a ship of the larger tonnage, as the general manning rule of thumb was one crewmember for every three tons. Waymouth had thirty men for both of his vessels in 1602, according to pay records. (The record does not differentiate between the *Discovery* and the *Godspeed.*) One problem with the *Discovery* being considered one and the same command for Waymouth in 1602 and Hudson in 1610 is that in 1603, the East India Company resolved to sell both the *Discovery* and the *Godspeed,* although there is no firm proof that the *Discovery* was actually sold. But even if she was, the *Discovery* could have ended up in Arctic service with the Muscovy Company and then been provided to Hudson in 1610.

See Rundall, *A Narrative of Voyages towards the North-West,* for the documentary record on the Waymouth voyage. No documents survive specifying Hudson's 1607 and 1608 sponsors, but we can be certain that the Muscovy Company was prominent in backing him. A Muscovy master, Thomas Edge, would inspect the 1607 log of the *Hopewell* in 1610, as reported by Purchas. And in 1614 the company petitioned the High Court of the Admiralty to uphold its exclusive right (particularly over Dutch interlopers) to northern trade and the whale fishery, based in part on a 1608 voyage to Novaya Zemlya by "William [*sic*] Hudson" (see *Calendar of State Papers, Domestic Series, James I,* Vol. 9). As the East India Company was involved in the passage-seeking efforts immediately before and after the 1607 and 1608 Hudson voyages, the company was more than likely also involved in his *Hopewell* efforts.

Chapter 5

Sir Thomas Smythe's career is discussed in a variety of sources already cited, most importantly Griffiths' *A Licence to Trade.* See also Robert W. Kenney's *Elizabeth's Admiral.* For a concise, detailed biography, see Basil Morgan's DNB entry for him. Richard Hakluyt owed a great debt to Smythe because he set high standards for ship's logs, which he then made available to the historiographer. Hakluyt's praise of Smythe is in the dedication to *The Dialogues in the English and Malaiane Languages . . . by Augustus Spalding* (1614). The dedication was addressed to "the truly Honorable and right worthy Knight, Sir Thomas Smith, Governor of the East India, Muscovia, Northwest Passages, Sommer Islands Companies, and Treasurer for the first Colonie in Virginia." It is included by Waters in *The Art of Navigation.* That it fell to Smythe to choose Prickett as voyage supercargo is a reasonable assumption. Purchas would state that Sir Dudley Digges was Prickett's employer, but this service more than likely came after the *Discovery* voyage. Prickett reported directly to Smythe on the *Discovery*'s return, and his membership in the Haberdasher's Company logically aligned him with

Smythe, a member and former master. Sir Dudley Digges was the son of Sir Thomas Digges, the mathematician and publisher of the navigational almanac *Prognostication*. Sir Dudley was a sponsor of the 1610 voyage, and was also an investor in the Virginia Company. But he was a statesman in training at the time of the *Discovery* voyage, twenty-four years old and a graduate of Christ Church, Oxford, in 1601. In 1618 he would be named ambassador to Russia. Hudson's discovery of Hudson's Touches was first noted by a Muscovy Company master, Thomas Edge, who found the reference in the log of the *Hopewell* for 1607 while preparing for a Muscovy voyage to Spitsbergen. Edge's comments on his findings were published by Purchas and appear in Asher.

The evolution of onboard labour relations and the legal status of mutiny are thoroughly explored by Kenneth R. Andrews in *Ships, Money and Politics*. Details of Waymouth's 1602 voyage and the associated mutiny are in Rundall's *Narratives of Voyages towards the North-West*. Hessel Gerritsz asserted in 1612 that the *Discovery* had been provisioned for only eight months. The figure is consistent with the other aspects of the voyage planning.

Chapter 6

For the *Trades Increase* and the sailing of Sir Henry Middleton's East India Company flotilla, see Markham's *The Voyages of Sir James Lancaster*. See also biographical sources for Sir Thomas Smythe noted in Chapter 5. Edward Wilson gave his age as twenty-two in January 1612, and so he was around twenty in April 1610. For details on the 1602 Waymouth voyage with William Cobreth, see Rundall. Luke Foxe's comment about Cobreth and Hudson was made in *Northwest Fox* (1635); the quote, and a précis of Foxe's own 1631 voyage, appear in Rundall. Portions of Robert Juet's 1608 *Hopewell* journal survive as margin notes to Hudson's journal in Purchas. A great frustration for historians is the decision Purchas made not to include Juet's entire journal, even though he possessed it—and ultimately lost or discarded it. Instead he included an aggravating footnote: "I have Robert Juetts journal also, for brevitie omitted." William Gilbert's magnetic theories are explored in Waters' *The Art of Navigation*. Juet's possible sunspot observation led to this entry for his journal on May 19, 1609: "Then we observed the sun having a slake, and found our height to be 70 degrees, 30 minutes." Such an observation would have required a telescope, models of which had become commercially available in Holland in 1608. But Juet's observation also could have been inspired by a high-latitude atmospheric distortion of the sun's appearance.

Of the possible high-born young men aboard the *Hopewell* in 1608, Thomas Hilles could have been a relative of Peter Hill (or Hills/Hilles), the owner of a fleet of merchant ships who underwrote walrus-hunting expeditions to the St. Lawrence, and may have been part of a failed mission in 1597 to oust the Basques from the walrus-rich Magdalene Islands. Thomas Hilles's presence on the *Hopewell* would explain Hudson's particular determination to prove walrus resources at Novaya Zemlya. John Barnes could have been from the Barne/Barnes family, merchants who were prominent in the Muscovy Company's history. And Humfrey Gilby was a possible relation of the late Sir Humphrey Gilbert, perhaps his eldest son, about whom little is known, and brother of Ralegh Gilbert, who was active in English expeditions to eastern North America.

George Waymouth's *Jewell of Artes* is reproduced by the Quinns in *The English New England Voyages 1602–1608*. The letter of Thomas Woodhouse to Samuel Macham was published by Purchas and can be found in Asher. Biographical details on Macham appear in the DNB entry by James Knowles for Henry Hastings. The text of *Nova Britannia* (1609), by Sir Thomas Smythe's son-in-law, Robert Johnson, can be accessed at the Virtual Jamestown Project. Its title page states: "Printed for Samuel Macham, and are to be sold at his Shop in Pauls Churchyard, at the Signe of the Bul-head."

Ironically, Arngrimus Ionas must have been out of the country when composing his Hekla diatribe, despite dating it July 29, 1592, in Iceland. For despite his assurance of its lengthy dormancy, the volcano had erupted for six solid months in 1591. The dating problem is a curiosity. Ionas was firm in saying that the last eruption was in 1558, and that this was thirty-four years earlier. But records of Hekla eruptions indicate one having occurred in 1554, and the next in 1591. Perhaps Ionas was a concoction of Hakluyt, a voice through which he could render criticisms of other historiographers and cosmographers. In any event, Hekla did not erupt again until 1636.

Thomas Woodhouse's name has typically varying spellings in the surviving documents, including Widowse and Wydowse. A goldsmith named Richard Widdowes was a member of the 1609 Virginia Company, and may have been a relation. On balance, the Woodhouse connection as presented seems stronger. The family's involvement in the Virginia enterprise is well documented in primary sources—see Barbour's *The Jamestown Voyages Under the First Charter* and Virginia resources previously cited. For the family's admiralty appointments, see the Institute of Historical Research: Office Holders in Modern Britain, as cited in Chapter 4. Dionise Settle's account of the second voyage of Martin Frobisher appears in Hakluyt's *Principal Navigations*.

Chapter 7

Prickett cryptically related how at Iceland "the surgeon and [Greene] fell out in Dutch, and [Greene] beat him ashore in English." Prickett may have meant that the argument that led to the fight drew on a rich vocabulary of profanity that was migrating from Dutch to English. But this also may have been a suggestion that the fight originated as a gambling dispute. Dutch financiers who dominated the marine insurance business had invented what is still known as the Dutch book, a system of odds-making that proved portable to gambling and remains with us today. The mathematical proof of a particular Dutch book is known as an argument. The berthing assignments of *Discovery* crewmembers are discussed by Prickett in his voyage narrative.

The theory of the temperate Arctic, including materials from Gerhard Mercator and Dr. John Dee relating to Septentrion, is well documented in Hakluyt's *Principal Navigations.* See also Nicholas Crane's *Mercator* for the cartographer's credulous adoption of the Zeno fictions. With respect to the age's conviction that sea ice came from rivers, first-year Arctic ice is still noticeably salty, but the content drops significantly in multi-year ice. The idea that Arctic ice is formed by freshwater rivers was an enduring one. Captain James Cook still assumed this was the case when he sailed into Bering Strait in 1778. Waymouth's report of water flowing like black pudding is from his journal account in Rundall's *Narratives of Voyages towards the North-West.* Difficulties in high-latitude navigation have been explored by any number of authors, but Waters' *The Art of Navigation* is a particularly lucid source.

Chapter 8
The documents relating to John Knight's 1606 voyage, as well as the summary statements made by Purchas, are reproduced by Markham in *The Voyages of Sir James Lancaster.* Note that among the crew on Hudson's 1607 voyage was James Knight, who may have been a relative of the lost John and Gabriel Knight. The pleadings to turn back by John Davis's 1586 crew are recounted by Davis in his voyage narrative, which Hakluyt published in *Principal Navigations.* Lancaster's marooning on Mona Island in 1593 and his report of the location of the Northwest Passage are contained in Markham.

Chapter 9
The confused state of cartography with respect to Greenland and the Northwest Passage, obvious from an examination of historic cartography, has invited repeated commentary. An excellent source is "The Cartographic Lure of the Northwest Passage: Its Real and Imaginary Geography," by Richard I. Ruggles, in Vol. 1 of Symons's *Meta Incognita.* See also Hayes's *Historical Atlas of Canada.* The Frobisher voyage narratives, including that of George Best, which had already been published separately, as well as the accounts of John

Davis's voyages by Davis himself and John Janes, were all included by Hakluyt in *Principal Navigations*. For the story of Emery Molyneux's globe and related cartography, see Waters' *The Art of Navigation*, as well as the DNB entries for Jodocus Hondius (by Anita McConnell) and John Davis (by Michael Hicks).

Hudson's appearance at St. Ethelburga's Church to take communion with his crew before the start of the 1607 *Hopewell* voyage is stated at the beginning of the voyage journal first published by Purchas and found in Asher.

Sebastian Cabot's ordinances of 1553 were included in Hakluyt's *Principal Navigations*. The clothing worn aboard ship is drawn from the list of apparel purchased by the East India Company for Waymouth's 1602 voyage, as preserved in Rundall's *Narratives of Voyages towards the North-West*.

For my discussion of tides and general navigational challenges provided by the Furious Overfall and Hudson Strait, I have looked to the relevant *Sailing Directions* published by the Canadian Hydrographic Service. Note that Luke Foxe would doubt Waymouth's assertion that he sailed one hundred leagues of Hudson Strait in four days, after needing about three weeks to sail the strait himself in 1631. The harshest criticism waited until 1818, when John Barrow, second secretary of the Royal Navy, wrote *A Chronological History of Voyages into the Arctic Regions,* as he provoked a renewed English effort to find the Northwest Passage. Of Waymouth's claim to have sailed one hundred leagues southwest into the strait, "we now know must have been impossible," Barrow wrote. "Indeed the whole account of Weymouth's [*sic*] proceedings is so confused, that little or nothing can be drawn from it, except that he was among the islands to the northward of Hudson's Strait, and probably those of Cape Chidley."

Chapter 10

Of Prickett's possible allusion to Hudson's offering a reward to the crew for agreeing to press forward with the voyage, note that William Cobreth had made the entire Waymouth voyage of 1602 for six pounds as mate. Other crew were paid considerably less. See Rundall's *Narratives of Voyages towards the North-West* for a list of Waymouth's crew wages. See also Rundall for Baffin materials, which reveal that at the departure of William Baffin's 1615 voyage, sponsor Sir John Wolstenholme promised the crew a bonus of triple their wages if they proved the Northwest Passage. Note as well that Waymouth had agreed to a salary of 100 pounds if he proved the passage, nothing if he failed, which might explain his fury at being forced to turn back.

Important Bird Areas of Canada (www.ibacanada.com) gives the size of the thick-billed murre colony in Digges Sound as 287,000 breeding pairs, based on a 1992 survey, a population of global significance. A WWF report in 2004 (*Arctic Bulletin* No. 4.04) put the number of breeding pairs at 300,000. Note that the thick-billed murre is also known as Brünnich's guillemot. English sailors knew these birds as wellocks. Prickett's "scurvy grass" is common scurvy-grass, *Cochlearia officinalis,* a white flowering plant that grows in abundance on East Digges Island. William Baffin's comment on the abundance of seabirds (he calls them willocks) at East Digges Island is from his 1615 voyage journal, and is found in Rundall. Note as well that Baffin testified to the difficulty of anchoring in Digges Sound in 1615: "here the water is so deep, that it is hard to find a place to ride in, which we seeing, lay to and fro with our ship."

Sebastian Cabot's passage-making claims are in Hakluyt's *Principal Navigations.* Thomas Woodhouse's note regarding the Robert Juet hearing of September 10, 1610, was published by Purchas and appears in Asher. Edward Wright's 1599 world map, which shows the passage from the St. Lawrence, through Lake Tadouac, to the Northern Sea, was included in Vol. 3 of Hakluyt's *Principal Navigations* in 1600. William Gilbert's *De Magnete* is discussed by Waters in *The Art of Navigation.*

Chapter 11

I am grateful to Ken Abraham, a research scientist with Ontario's Ministry of Natural Resources, and Jean Iron, a member of his bird-count crew, for sharing with me their experiences of the southern James Bay lowlands. Jean provided me with evocative photographs and Ken described the sequence of species that pass through on annual spring migration. I have also consulted John L. Ridley's *Flora of the Hudson Bay Lowland and Its Postglacial Origins.* I have written in the past about isostatic (postglacial) rebound in the Laurentian Shield as it affects the Great Lakes; for its more pronounced impact on James Bay, I have used data from the Geological Survey of Canada (gsc.nrcan.gc.ca). See also "A Reappraisal of Postglacial Decay Times from Richmond Gulf and James Bay, Canada," by Mitrovica, Forte, and Simons in *Geophysics Journal International* (2000), No. 142.

Prickett's description of movements in the final days before the overwintering site was selected were vague, but the *Discovery* seems to have inspected Rupert Bay, whatever its contours then might have been, a broad tidal basin into which several major rivers flow from the south and east. It could have been the Bay of God's Mercies, where the *Discovery* went aground. The vicinity of Rupert Bay, at latitude 51 degrees, 30 minutes—and not at latitude 53, as Gerritsz's map suggested—remains the strongest candidate for the location of the overwintering. In 1668, Médard Chouart, Sieur des Groseilliers, led an English ship into James Bay to establish a fur-trading post, Charles Fort, at the mouth of the Rupert River. The expedition, a forerunner of the Hudson's Bay Company, reported finding an old cabin said to be sixty years old. This may well have been the cabin Philip Staffe built for the winter of 1610–11. Rupert Bay was also advanced as the wintering site by Linden J. Lundstrom, after he personally surveyed this remote locale, in "The Bay Where Hudson Did Winter" (James Ford Bell Lecture, University of Minnesota, 1980). Lundstrom argued that the entirety of Hudson/James Bay in the Gerritsz chart was actually Rupert Bay, mistakenly turned sideways and improperly scaled by Gerritsz. My thanks to Conrad Heidenreich for drawing my attention to this lecture paper and sending me a copy. My hunch is that the peculiar shape of Hudson Bay in the Gerritsz chart, with its "double" James Bay, is due to a mistaken scaling-up (by Gerritsz or his English source) of James Bay to represent the entirety of James and Hudson bays. Rupert and Hannah bays would then represent the double bay shown where James Bay should be.

Luke Foxe's suggestion of Hudson's reason for dismissing William Cobreth is in *North-West Fox* (1635). The 1553 voyage of Sir Hugh Willoughby is recounted by Hakluyt in *Principal Navigations*. The final entry in Willoughby's journal is reproduced by Waters in *The Art of Navigation*.

With respect to conventions for the treatment of a dead seaman's effects, the ordinances set down by Sebastian Cabot in 1553 for the first Muscovy expedition to the northeast had become the general rule of shipboard life of English merchant ships. In the event of a sailor's death, the ordinances prescribed how "apparel, and other goods, as he shall have at the time of his death," were to be treated. On order of the ship's commanding officer, the dead man's possessions were to be "kept"—in other words, an inventory was to be taken, and the possessions were to be "conserved to the use of his wife, and children, or otherwise according to his mind, and will." The ordinances appear in Hakluyt's *Principal Navigations*. By the time the *Discovery* sailed under Hudson, elaborations had crept into this time-honoured routine. They are preserved in the commission issued to Sir Henry Middleton for the East India Company's voyage of 1610: Middleton, the merchants along on the voyage, and the ships' companies were "to draw up an agreement in writing relative to the disposal of possessions of such of their number as may die on the voyage, such goods either to be stored away until the ships' return, or sold at the mast, in which case no man to be allowed to spend more than one-third of his pay." Middleton's commission appears in Markham's *The Voyages of Sir James Lancaster*.

The story of the final voyage of Willem Barentsz was told by survivor Gerrit de Veer in a generously illustrated book, *Waerachtighe beschryvinghe van drie seylagien,* relating all three of Barentsz's Arctic voyages. University College London's Department of Dutch (www.ucl.ac.uk/dutch) maintains a database on historical Dutch works, giving their dates of publication and translation. It was first published in Dutch by Cornelis Claesz in 1598, and authorized (and unauthorized) editions quickly followed in French, Latin, German, and Italian. The first English translation as noted appeared in 1609. An annotated English translation of de Veer, *The Three Voyages of William Barents to the Arctic Regions,* was published by the Hakluyt Society in 1876. A thorough overview of Barentsz's explorations (and Dutch interest in a northern passage to the Orient) can be found in "In Search of Het Behouden Huys," by Louwrens Hacquebord, *Arctic,* September 1995.

Chapter 12
Prickett's mention of fishing through the winter could only have been possible if the crew chopped a "fire hole" in the ice, from which water could be accessed to fight any shipboard fire. The expedition of Thomas James to James Bay in 1631–32 chopped such a hole when they overwintered at Charlton Island. Rundall offers a detailed précis of James's expedition account; the full account appears as Chapter 34 in John Harris's *Navigantium,* from which I have drawn James's comment about the difficulty of hunting waterfowl. Lancaster's antiscorbutic knowledge and strategies are found in Markham's *The Voyages of Sir James Lancaster.* Cartier's experience with the lifesaving "anneda" remedy appear in his 1535–36 voyage account; see *The Voyages of Jacques Cartier* (see Part II sources). Purchas complicated the issue of the *Discovery* voyage's scurvy remedy by asserting facts of unknown origin in his essay ("Of Hudson's Discovery and Death") in his 1626 edition of *Purchas His Pilgrimage.* He described "a tree, which in December blossomed, with leaves green and yellow, of an aromatical savour, and being boiled yielded an oily substance, which proved an excellent salve, and the decoction being drunk proved as wholesome a potion, whereby they were cured on the scorbute, sciaticas, cramps, convulsions, and other diseases, which the coldness of the climate bred in them."

While we don't know the specific nation of the visitor to the *Discovery,* the time of year suggests that he was a local Cree, as the rivers were frozen solid and it seems highly unlikely that traders from the south would have been visiting the area. I discussed the Cree's knowledge of scurvy with Conrad Heidenreich, who has published on historic scurvy treatments as well as in the area of First Nations ethnography, and he indicated to me that the Cree's diet saved them from the disease. Traditional Cree medicine has long been of interest to science and ethnographers. E. M. Holmes wrote on medicinal plants used by the Cree of Hudson Bay in the *American Journal of Pharmacy,* December 1884, and he makes no mention of a scurvy treatment at that time. Health Canada is currently supporting research into the medicinal benefits of some 400 species of plants known to the Cree. For Saami knowledge of scurvy treatment, see the Encyclopedia of Saami Culture maintained by the University of Helsinki (www.helsinki.fi). The Canadian Museum of Civilization (www.civilization.ca) maintains an extensive digital collection of historic native clothing. Extensive resources on Cree culture, past and present, are accessible through www.native-languages.org. Attitudes of East India Company sailors to indigenous peoples can be gathered from reading the voyage accounts reproduced by Markham in *The Voyages of Sir James Lancaster.*

Chapter 13
See Chapter 11 for my notes on de Veer's account of the Barentsz expeditions.

Chapter 14
Prickett's account of the departure from the overwintering bay is confused, perhaps because of heavy-handed editing by Samuel Purchas, and it cannot be said precisely when each event occurred. I have settled on the most reasonable timeline of events: that Hudson left the overwintering bay with Robert Bylot still as his mate, after providing the crew with the bill of return; he then replaced Bylot with John King. The nature of the bill of return is a mystery, and historians and Hudson biographers previously have not commented on it. A "bill" was a written set of orders, and I have concluded that it was like the quarter bill issued by captains on British warships, which set down the command structure for different quarters, or areas, of the ship in battle. The bill of return thus outlined the command structure for the return voyage, with an order of succession as well. Prickett's description of Hudson handing it over, "willing them to have that to show, if it pleased God that they came home; and he wept when he gave it to them," suggests that it was also meant to protect the crew from any accusations that they had forced Hudson to return to England against his will, particularly if he did not survive the voyage. It must have contained language similar to the note he gave his 1608 *Hopewell* crew, in which he stated that he had decided to return to London on his own volition. Note that in dividing the remaining foodstores, Hudson chose to follow the strategy used by James Lancaster on his 1591–93 voyage to the East Indies, when food began to run short on the return: "every man had his share of his victuals . . . in his own custody, that we might be sure what to trust to, and to husband it more thriftily." See Markham's *The Voyages of Sir James Lancaster.*

Chapter 15
I obtained a copy of *The Offences at Sea Act* of 1536 from a seemingly unlikely source: the Australian Capital Territory Parliamentary Council's Office. The act

arrived in Australian law through legislative heritage, and was last amended in 1986. I have modernized the spelling in the quotes.

Chapter 16

Documents relating to the case of Sir Edward Maria Wingfield can be found in Barbour's *The Jamestown Voyages Under the First Charter*, Vol. 1. It is purely speculative as to who among the key mutineers and their accomplices would have thought to frame strategy, evidence, and testimony along the lines of the Wingfield overthrow. But Prickett was by far the most likely man. And it may have been the case that the survivors fine-tuned their recollections to best fit the Wingfield model. Their evidence was further revised (sometimes significantly altered) between 1612 and 1617, when the second round of interrogations occurred.

The details of the mutiny experienced by George Waymouth aboard the *Discovery* in 1602, including his journal account, are found in Rundall's *Narratives of Voyages towards the North-West.*

A few additional points with respect to the court depositions by the *Discovery* survivors are worth making. In his February 1617 deposition, Robert Bylot named five ringleaders. His list agreed with the roll call of oath-takers in Prickett's narrative, except that he left out Adrian Moter. The court transcription mistakenly called Staffe the master's mate in Wilson's 1612 deposition. Edward Wilson's 1612 testimony that Greene and Wilson planned from the beginning to keep Staffe aboard contradicted Prickett's case that he persuaded Greene and William Wilson to keep Staffe, when they initially wanted to get rid of him. But Wilson's deposition may have conveyed the results of Prickett's lobbying, without acknowledging it. Edward Wilson also avowed in his 1617 deposition that he was asleep when the mutiny began, and that the instructions given to him by the mutineers when he appeared at his cabin door to see them manhandling Hudson were that he "be quiet & keep himself well if he were well." The barber-surgeon also claimed in his 1617 deposition to have no idea of who led the mutiny, and he never identified the men who were pinioning Hudson. This despite having already described for the court in 1612 how William Wilson had confronted Staffe about favouritism in the rationing, and had then taken his answer to Greene, leading directly to their plan to cast away Hudson, King, and others.

Chapter 17

George Waymouth's kidnapping of five natives from the Georges River area is related by Rosier and reproduced by the Quinns in *The English New England Voyages 1602–1608*. See Champlain's *Les Voyages* as translated by the

Champlain Society in Vol. 1 for his perspective on the event in the summer of 1605. Champlain met a chief named Annasou at the Georges River. "He told us that there was a ship, ten leagues off the harbour, which was engaged in fishing, and that those on her had killed five savages of this river, under cover of friendship," Champlain wrote. "From his description of the men on the vessel, we concluded that they were English." No natives were actually killed, and Waymouth was long gone, but at the time of the kidnappings, Champlain had been, geographically speaking, right next door, probing Penobscot Bay. Van Meteren's paraphrasing of Hudson's *Half Moon* journal is in Asher. Hudson's comments on the native propensity to steal is quoted by de Laet and appears in Asher.

Chapter 18
The allegations made against Wingfield at Jamestown in 1607 appear in the associated materials reproduced by Barbour in *The Jamestown Voyages Under the First Charter*, Vol. 1. Coincidentally, Wingfield had recalled that while he was imprisoned in the pinnace at Jamestown, "the president and council had sent for the keys of my coffers, supposing that I had some writings concerning the colony." It thus seems possible that Thomas Woodhouse offered the *Discovery* mutineers the keys to his chest so they could gather and destroy his writings, in hope of being allowed to come back aboard from the shallop.

PART II
Beyond the Great Rapid

As discussed in the bibliographic essay, the main sources for this part of the story are Samuel de Champlain's writings and the primary documents transcribed and annotated in *Nouveaux documents*. A page facsimile version of all six volumes of the Champlain Society's bilingual edition of Champlain's "works," issued between 1922 and 1936, is available online from the society's digital archives at www.champlainsociety.ca. The three volumes of the Prince Society translation (issued from 1878 to 1882) can be read in e-text format via Project Gutenberg (www.gutenberg.org). The relevant works for this story, as previously stated, are *Brief Discours*, *Des Sauvages*, *Les Voyages*, and *Quartriesme Voyage*. For the Champlain Society, Vol. 1 contains *Brief Discours*, *Des Sauvages*, and *Les Voyages* through to 1607. Vol. 2 contains the rest of *Les Voyages* to 1612, and the *Quatriesme Voyage* of 1612–1613. I will not provide references to these volumes for Champlain's narrative in the individual chapter notes.

I have read several Champlain biographies over the years, but none have figured in this work as a source. Samuel Eliot Morison's *Samuel de Champlain: Father of New France* (New York: Little, Brown, 1972) is the most accessible and reliable of recent efforts, although it suffers from its rather dated attitude toward native peoples.

Nouveaux documents is a principal reference for primary sources preserved in French archives. Item numbers for source material are provided in the individual chapter notes.

English translations of quotations from Jacques Cartier's voyage accounts are from *The Voyages of Jacques Cartier* (Toronto: University of Toronto Press, 1993). This is an amended version of the 1924 translation by Henry Percival Biggar, with updated footnotes and an introductory essay by Ramsay Cook. Wherever you find a Cartier account quoted, this translation is the source.

Regarding words and phrases in Algonquin, we cannot know precisely which Algonquin dialect was spoken on the Ottawa River circa 1613. Seventeenth-century Jesuit missionaries concentrated on producing an Iroquoian lexicon because of their outpost in Huronia. Dialects also change over time. Early explorers of eastern North America composed very short Algonquin lexicons, and John Long in 1791 published his memoir, *Voyages and travels of an Indian interpreter and trader,* which included a very basic "list of words in the Iroquois, Mohegan, Shawanee, and Esquimeaux tongues, and a table, shewing the analogy between the Algonkin and Chippeway languages." Sacrificing distance in time in favour of sheer detail, I have opted to use the most complete historic linguistic reference available: Jean André Cuoq's *Lexique de la langue algonquine,* published in Montréal by J. Chapleau in 1886. A digital page facsimile of the Jesuit linguist's work can be found at Early Canadiana Online. (Cuoq also produced an Iroquoian lexicon, which I have consulted more casually, as well as *grammaires* for both language groups.) The *Lexique* is an Algonquin-French dictionary, and so I have had to move through three languages to get at the words and phrases that occasionally appear in this book. I beg forgiveness from modern speakers of Algonquin if any nuances have been trampled in the process. Spelling systems also differ between Cuoq's dictionary and modern Algonquin dialects. For consistency I have stayed with Cuoq. Within the text I have used the term "Algonquian" for the language group, to distinguish from the historic Algonquin people of the Ottawa River watershed. See notes to Chapter 19.

For quotations from the Jesuit *Relations,* I have employed the standard reference, *The Jesuit Relations and Allied Documents,* the multivolume annotated multilingual edition produced by Reuben Gold Thwaites, mentioned in the bibliographic essay.

Listings in biographical dictionaries follow the style in Part I.

General historical sources

In addition to general sources mentioned in Part I that apply to the events in Part II, the following have been read or consulted, and some are referenced in the chapter notes: Denys Delâge, *Bitter Feast: Amerindians and Europeans in Northeastern North America, 1600–64*, translated by Jane Brierley (Vancouver: UBC Press, 1993); Nicholas Garry, *Diary of Nicholas Garry, Deputy-Governor of the Hudson's Bay Company from 1822–1835: A Detailed Narrative of His Travels in the Northwest Territories of British North America in 1821* (Ottawa: Royal Society of Canada, 1900); George Grant (aka George Munro), *Picturesque Canada: The Country as It Was and Is* (Toronto: Belden, c. 1882); Conrad Heidenreich, *Huronia: A History and Geography of the Huron Indians 1600–1650* (Toronto: McClelland & Stewart, 1971); Raymonde Litalien and Denis Vaugeois, editors, *Champlain: The Birth of French America* (Montréal: McGill-Queen's University Press/Septentrion, 2004); Alexander Mackenzie, *A General History of the Fur Trade from Canada to the North-west*, aka *Voyages from Montreal through the Continent of North America* (London and Edinburgh: c. 1801); Roger Schlesinger and Arthur P. Stabler, *André Thevet's North America: A Sixteenth-century View* (Montréal: McGill-Queen's University Press, 1986); Don W. Thomson, *Men and Meridians: The History of Surveying and Mapping in Canada, Vol. 1: Prior to 1867* (Ottawa: Department of Mines and Technical Surveys, 1966); Bruce Trigger, *Natives and Newcomers: Canada's "Heroic Age" Reconsidered* (Montréal: McGill-Queen's University Press, 1985), and *The Children of Aataentsic: A History of the Huron People to 1660* (Montréal: McGill-Queen's University Press, 1976).

Chapter 19

I have used *Algonquin* (sometimes spelled *Algonkin*) to refer to all of the Algonquian/Algonkian-speaking tribes who lived along the Ottawa River, distinct from the northern Algonquin group that included the Nebicerini. (I have used an early spelling for this northern Algonquin tribe. It has also been spelled as Nipisirini, and Nipissing, among other variants.) Champlain initially referred to only the Ouaouechkarini (Petite Nation) of the tribes along the river as *Algommequin,* and *Algonquin* for a time was applied only to this particular tribe. The name may have been acquired by Champlain from the Montagnais, in whose Algonquian dialect the term has been said to be roughly equivalent with "red skin," a reference apparently to the body paint the Algonquin of the Ottawa River applied when going to war. However, I cannot find the term in Cuoq, who gives *miskwaje* for *avoir le peau rouge*—to have red skin—and there is nothing at all to translate for *Algonquin*. Today, the Algonquin call themselves the Anishinabe. *Kitci sipi* is also sometimes spelled *kitsi sipi*. According to Cuoq, *kitci* is an adjective or adverb meaning "grande," *sipi* a noun meaning "rivière." *Kitci sipi* he specifically translates as *la grande rivière, l'Ottawa*. Cuoq gives *kitcikami* as a single word, rather than *kitci kami*, and translates it as "le grand liquide, la mer, l'océan," and further defines the suffix *kami* as connoting "eau, étendue d'eau." While the word most properly applies to an ocean, it was generally acknowledged to be an Algonquin term for the St. Lawrence River.

Chapter 20

For a concise biography of Sieur de Monts, see his DCB entry by George MacBeath. Spelling of his name varies (including du Mons, which is used by the editors of *Nouveaux documents*), and I have chosen to follow the DCB example.

I have maintained the historic French term for the Iroquois confederacy, as much as it may have been a pejorative label of their enemies (a common situation with historic names of tribes and nations). Some have proposed that their Huron enemies gave them the name, meaning "rattlesnakes" or "black snakes." The Iroquois called their confederacy the Haudenosaunee, and in the early seventeenth century it comprised five nations located in what is now Upstate New York, known today by the names Cayuga, Seneca, Oneida, Onondaga, and Mohawk. "Iroquois" is not to be confused with "Iroquoian," the language group that was also spoken by the Huron—hence the French label of "good Iroquois" for the Huron. The name "Huron" was not in use at this time. Its exact origin is disputed, although it came into use in print in the 1620s in works by Champlain, the Jesuit order, and Récollet missionary Gabriel Sagard. It refers to the confederacy of Iroquoian-speaking tribes living at the southern end of Georgian Bay in what became known as Huronia. The people identified themselves more with their individual tribes than a collective group name. In time, they would come to be known as the Wendat (or Oüendat, or Wyandot), although this term historically seemed to apply to their territory rather than the people. For consistency I have retained the use of the historic term Huron. See Heidenreich's *Huronia*, and Trigger's *The Children of Aataentsic*.

With respect to Champlain's size and appearance, we have no real idea of what he looked like, beyond the basic sketch of him fighting the Iroquois in 1609 that appears in *Les Voyages*, which tells us he had a beard. The average

European male at this time was five feet, five inches tall. Biographers of Champlain have speculated that he was even shorter, based on the fact that after being wounded in the knee by an Iroquois arrow in 1616, he was carried in a basket on the back of a Huron warrior for several days.

For sources on the Hessel Gerritsz material, see the notes for Part I. Note that the main item in his little volume was a report by Isaac Massa, a Haarlem native who had travelled to Russia around 1600 to peruse its business opportunities. Massa had come away persuaded of the viability of a Northeast Passage that employed a route at the Waigats; he had also come away with a map of Russia's north coast, drawn around 1609, which Gerritsz reproduced. Champlain did not understand Gerritsz perfectly. He would assert in *Quatriesme Voyage* that the English had lost "some vessels, as their report proves." Evidently, Gerritsz's reference to a "sloop or boat" (*Sloep ofte Schuit*) had been misread by Champlain's translator as two vessels. Champlain would also erroneously, and impossibly, move the Hudson voyage into 1612 in his published recollections. Champlain's error could have been caused by the Latin label on Gerritsz's map, which said it revealed explorations of 1612 (*indagata Anno 1612*)—which may have referred to the fact that the new geography depicted in the northwest was being explored at the time of publication by the follow-up expedition of Thomas Button.

In the ensuing Latin edition, Gerritsz's details in the introductory essay about Hudson's 1609 voyage in the *Half Moon* also were much improved. He must have been set straight by someone within the VOC, even Petrus Plancius, for he was able to make the connection between Hudson, Plancius, and the logs of George Waymouth, who in the Dutch edition Gerritsz had mistakenly been called Winwood (the name of the English ambassador at The Hague during the negotiations to secure the Twelve Year Truce between the Dutch Republic and Spain). Gerritsz was also able to correct the essay to agree with the account on the back of the map, stating that Hudson and his companions had been cast adrift in a sloop or boat, not set on shore.

Edward Wilson's deposition before the High Court of the Admiralty can be found in the HCA sources cited in notes for Part I.

The leading role of Dutch financiers in the French fur trade can be gleaned from contracts in *Nouveaux documents*. See also Cornelius Jaenen's essay "Champlain and the Dutch" in Litalien and Vaugeois' *Champlain: The Birth of French America*.

Chapter 21

Champlain's age is unknowable. Baptismal records in his hometown of Brouage were destroyed by fire in 1614. Educated guesses for his date of birth have ranged from 1567 to 1580, and I have chosen to more or less split the difference. His level of formal education is debated, but his writing lacks the classical allusions of contemporary Marc Lescarbot, who was a trained lawyer, and he struggled to express himself clearly in the official *francien* French. See Conrad Heidenreich's *Champlain and The Champlain Society* for comments made by his frustrated translators. His *Traitte de Navire,* or treaty on seamanship, appended to his final work of 1632, provides a window into his skill set. His advice on what pilots and navigators should know conspicuously lacks any reference to the higher mathematics of spherical trigonometry. Conrad Heidenreich and Edward Dahl provide an excellent tour of his skills and methods in their essay "Samuel de Champlain's Cartography, 1603–32," in Litalien and Vaugeois' *Champlain: The Birth of French America.* His lack of ship commands, despite his title of *capitaine ordinaire* in the royal navy, is plain from his own account of his life. See also Litalien and Vaugeois for Étienne Taillemite's "The Royal Navy in Champlain's Time."

As for his name and social standing, the title page of *Des Sauvages* and his hand-drawn map of the Bay of Fundy and New England region of 1607 identified him as "Samuel Champlain," which is also how the status-conscious Marc Lescarbot, who was with him at Port Royal in 1606–07, referred to him in his *Histoire de la Nouvelle France* when it was first published in 1609. (The third edition [1618] of Lescarbot's work is reproduced in its original French along with an annotated English translation, as the three-volume *History of New France,* edited by H. P. Biggar, published by the Champlain Society between 1907 and 1914.) But Champlain otherwise was de Champlain, and he was already being referred to that way in his military pay records of the 1590s. He seems to have been the one to standardize his family's name as Champlain. A Brouage pilot named Antoine Chappelain who is recorded selling interest in a ship in 1573 (*Nouveaux documents,* item 5) has been suggested as his father; his father was identified in Champlain's own marriage contract as "the late Anthoine de Complain, in his lifetime captain in the Navy." (The contract is an appendix to Vol. 2 of the Champlain Society translation of his works.)

For his military pay records, see item 9 in *Nouveaux documents.* The introductory "Memoir of Samuel de Champlain" in Vol. 1 of the Prince Society translation, by editor Edmund Slafter, in particular provides a detailed overview of the turbulent history in which Champlain came of age. The circumstantial evidence for Champlain's Protestant birth hinges mainly on the fact that the name Samuel was a typical Protestant appellation. He was probably born during Brouage's years as a Huguenot (Protestant) stronghold. In

Champlain's military career in the 1590s, he was associated with Catholic officers from Brouage loyal to Henry IV.

While Champlain's 1603 commission has never been found, that of Admiral Aymar de Chaste has turned up, and it mentions seeking proof of a route to the Orient. Champlain would write in 1632 that de Chaste recruited him for the expedition.

With respect to the Cartier voyage accounts, a manuscript version of Cartier's first two voyages existed in France at the time, but not even the sixteenth-century royal cosmographer, André Thevet, was aware of it. It would not be found until 1867. While the fragmentary and sole surviving account of Cartier's third voyage had been published only in English, by Hakluyt, when Champlain began exploring the St. Lawrence, he may have been familiar with some of Cartier's findings, at least second-hand, from that voyage. Hakluyt had related how Cartier informed the Sieur de Roberval that there were diamonds in the country. Champlain then wrote in *Des Sauvages:* "Along the shore of Quebec, there are diamonds in some slate-rocks, which are better than those of Alençon."

I first proposed Champlain's indebtedness to the midcontinental passage theories of Edward Hayes in "Was New France Born in England?" *The Beaver,* Vol. 86, No. 6 (December 2006/January 2007). A more complete presentation of the evidence is available there. I suspect that Champlain was dispatched in 1603 specifically to investigate evidence for a route to the Orient beyond the Great Rapid as assembled by Hayes and published in late 1602. As for the influence of *Des Sauvages,* there is an unmistakable echo of Champlain's fact-finding results in the instructions given by the London wing of the Virginia Company to leaders of the English flotilla that set out to found the Jamestown colony in the Chesapeake in December 1606, in Captain John Smith's *Map of Virginia,* published in 1612, and in George Popham's letter to James I in December 1607. The accuracy of Champlain's latitude fixes has been subjected to exhaustive statistical analysis by Conrad Heidenreich. Of his many publications in this regard, see his *Cartographica* monograph (No. 17/1976), "Explorations and Mapping of Samuel de Champlain."

Chapter 22
See Edmund Slafter's "Memoir of Samuel de Champlain" in Vol. 1 of the Prince Society translation of Champlain for a good overview of de Sillery, de Cosse-Brissac, and Jeannin. Details of the hiring of *Saint-Julien* for the Spanish relief flotilla are in Champlain's disputed *Brief Discours,* but I believe the essential facts are reliable.

The two-ship expedition of Jan Cornelisz May is discussed by Frederik Muller in the introductory essay of the 1878 reprinting of Gerritsz's volume. For the surviving record of Button's voyage, see Rundall's *Narratives of Voyages towards the North-West,* which republished everything gathered by Luke Foxe for *North-West Fox* (1635).

The chief of the Kichesipirini is cause for some historical confusion. In *Des Sauvages,* Champlain called the chief he met at Tadoussac "Besouat." Laverdière, the first modern editor of Champlain's published works, proposed that he was one and the same as the Tessöuat Champlain later dealt with, and this has been generally accepted by historians. But there were several successive chiefs called Tessöuat, which evidently was an inherited title. The one Champlain dealt with in 1629, for example, appears to have been a successor to the Tessöuat of 1613. Champlain would call this chief *Le Borgne:* The One-Eyed.

Charles Lalement's 1626 letter to his brother, Jérôme, is in Vol. 4 of *The Jesuit Relations and Allied Documents.*

The historic ethnography is not always clear, but the Maliséet people apparently were an Algonquin-speaking nation whose territory centred on the St. John River valley in what is now New Brunswick; Champlain called them the Étechemin. "Maliséet" may have been a Mi'kmaq pejorative meaning "poor talkers." Today they call themselves the Wolastoqiyik, although Maliséet is still in use.

The 1632 *relation* by Paul le Jeune is in Vol. 5 of *The Jesuit Relations and Allied Documents.* Champlain's description of Tessöuat planting poles which suspended Iroquois heads has invited differing translations. Champlain specifically referred to heads, with which the Otis translation for the Prince Society agreed. This was instead translated as "scalps" in the Champlain Society's Vol. 1, but Jesuit missionaries would also specifically mention trophy heads in other circumstances. Champlain freely admitted to his poverty of skills in native languages, and by *matachiats,* he could have meant *Mikis-apikan,* which Cuoq defines as a wampum necklace employed for diplomatic messages; this would be consistent with the ceremonial renewal of peace treaties at Tadoussac in 1603. For the role of the Macain-Georges alliance in the affairs of de Monts and de Poutrincourt, see numerous contracts and legal actions in *Nouveaux documents,* indexed under the name of Samuel Georges.

Chapter 23

For the Prince de Condé's letters patent, see item 122 in *Nouveaux documents.* For the notice for the admiralty officers, see item 123. For the undated Malouin factum, see item 125. For the judgment of the Conseil d'État throwing the

Canada trade open in October 1609, with 6,000 livres in compensation to be paid to the Sieur de Monts, see item 104.

In their mention of an atlas published at Douai, the Malouins seemed to be referring to a French edition of Cornelius Wytfliet's *Descriptionis Ptolemaicae augmentum,* first published at Louvain in 1597. It was the first atlas devoted to the New World, and included nineteen regional maps of the Americas. The factum refers in particular to a 1542 map contained in it.

Some historians (beginning apparently with Marcel Trudel) continue to identify the youth Thomas, who was employed by Daniel Boyer, as Thomas Godefroy, Sieur de Normanville, but this is most certainly wrong. Godefroy did work as an interpreter with the Algonquin but was not born until 1610 and went to New France in 1626.

In *Les Voyages,* Champlain scoffed at the idea that the Malouins were entitled to profit from lands beyond where Cartier had explored. He advised that the Malouins "can only take cognizance of the fact that [Cartier] was a citizen of theirs, and render him accordingly the praise which is his due." He insisted that Cartier had been no farther upriver than Trois-Rivières: "For had he made further explorations, he would not have omitted to speak of them." Champlain then declared that Cartier "left all the upper part of the St. Lawrence, from Tadoussac to the great rapid, being a territory difficult to explore, and that he was unwilling to expose himself or let his barks engage in the venture. So that what he did has borne no fruit until four years ago, when we made our settlement at Quebec, after which I ventured to pass the fall to help the savages in their wars, and send among them men to make the acquaintance of the people, to learn their mode of living, and the character and extent of their territory."

The biographies of the notaries Germain Tronson and Claude Dauvergne appear in the online database of Etanot (Etat de notaires de Paris du XVe au XXIe siècle; www.chan.archivesnationales.culture.gouv.fr/sdx/etanot/). Tronson's biography indicates he married Claude Dauvergne's mother in 1603. Dauvergne had begun working as a notary only in November 1612.

The January 16, 1613, accord with Mathieu Georges is item 126 in *Nouveaux documents.* Note that while Champlain identified himself as a captain-in-ordinary of the royal navy on his new map of New France, the January 16 agreement described him as an *escuyer*—an *écuyer,* or cavalier. The succeeding agreement of February 5 is item 127 in *Nouveaux documents.* For the 1611 Pont-Gravé voyage backed by Dutch interests, see Cornelius Jaenen's essay "Champlain and the Dutch" in Litalien and Vaugeois' *Champlain: The Birth of French America.*

A possible factor in the uncertainty surrounding the participation of a La Rochelle ship for the new partnership's 1613 season was an ongoing lawsuit filed by de Monts and other Rouen merchants against Georges and Macain over profits from the Canada trade during de Monts' monopoly years, which would not be settled until September 1613. (The settlement is item 137 in *Nouveaux documents*.) The trade was extremely litigious, having inspired de Monts to launch earlier suits against Legendre, de Bellois, Boyer, and Pont-Gravé over its spoils, and these actions litter *Nouveaux documents*. While the unresolved suit involving Georges and Macain was a par-for-the-course complication, it may have become a particular issue for Champlain, because he was rushing toward an early departure for the St. Lawrence before money arguments between de Monts and the Rochelais could be resolved.

For the Sieur de Monts' hiring of the surgeon and sailors in 1604, see item 53 in *Nouveaux documents*. The *parlement* of Rouen's ruling in favour of the Malouin factum is item 129. Louis XIII's instructions to the *parlement* to recognize the Prince de Condé's monopoly is item 130. The *parlement's* order of March 4 registering the letters patent is item 131.

As Champlain described in *Les Voyages,* the standoff with Darache was resolved when Champlain and Pont-Gravé agreed to make no further effort to drive Darache from Tadoussac. Any legal issues regarding what had transpired or who had what rights, Champlain pledged, would be left for the courts in France to resolve—as Champlain put it, "justice should be done in France, and their differences should be settled there." In return, Darache promised to "undertake nothing against Pont-Gravé, or what would be prejudicial to the King and Sieur de Monts." Darache and the wounded Pont-Gravé signed the agreement, and Pont-Gravé and his ship were rescued.

Chapter 24
The Spanish strategy for converting and settling natives in Florida and levying a corn tax is described in Quinn's *North America from Earliest Discovery to First Settlements*. The 1606 contract between de Monts and the locksmith Duval is item 67 in *Nouveaux documents*.

Chapter 25
The importance of dreams to native peoples in Champlain's time is described by Conrad Heidenreich in his entry for the Huron people in *The Handbook of North American Indians, Vol. 15*, published by the Smithsonian Institution in Washington, D.C., in 1978 (Bruce Trigger, volume editor). Charles Lalement's comments on native dreams are in Vol. 4 of *The Jesuit Relations and Allied Documents*. The illustration of the 1609 battle in *Les Voyages* by engraver David Pelletier should not be taken as a documentary record of what Champlain wore or how the conflict unfolded. Pelletier was an inventive illustrator, and

erroneously included some palm trees in the Lake Champlain foliage. The correspondence from Pierre Jeannin to Henry IV relating Isaac Lemaire's efforts to have the French king hire Henry Hudson in January 1609 appears in Asher.

Chapter 26

Edward Wright's instructions to the 1612 Button expedition appear in Rundall's *Narratives of Voyages to the North-West*. Wright actually wrote that the eclipse would occur on May 20. Days at sea began at noon, not midnight, with the taking of the noon sun sight, and this meant that sailors lived a half-day ahead of landsmen. Thus an eclipse on the early afternoon of May 19 took place in the first hours of May 20, according to a ship's timekeeping. I have used the program Skychart III to determine the convergence of sun and moon for that time when observed from the positions of Champlain and Button, as well as from latitude 80 along a similar longitude.

Bressani's observations on language are in *Relation abrégée*. Despite Father Bressani's assurances that the natives could not master French, it must be noted that when English expeditions reached what became New England in the first decade of the seventeenth century, they found natives who spoke French. Robert Juet's 1609 *Half Moon* journal made such an observation when Hudson reached the Georges River area.

Yroquet's Onontchataronon people had a complex history with the Huron, which Champlain most certainly did not yet understand, if anyone ever did fully. The Arendarhonon for their part were latecomers to the Huron confederacy, settling the farthest east of any of its tribe, in the desirable agricultural lands to the west of Lake Couchiching. According to the Jesuit missionary Jean de Brébeuf (who would live—and die—in Huronia, suffering a horrific martyrdom at the hands of Iroquois captors), the Arendarhonon had only arrived in 1590 from the Trent River valley, where they were neighbours of Yroquet's Onontchataronon. The Arendarhonon dialect distinguished them from the other Huron tribes, and like the Onontchataronon, they may have absorbed members of the Hochelaga diaspora before moving west. See Bruce Trigger's *The Children of Aataentsic* and Conrad Heidenreich's *Huronia*.

Champlain initially referred to all Hurons in his writings as Ochateguin, then changed to the curious Charioquois in 1611. I have used the term Huron to refer to the confederacy, and Arendarhonon specifically for Yroquet's people. Negotiating with the Huron involved complexities Champlain may not yet have understood. There was no single chief of a Huron tribe such as the Arendarhonon. Each clan within the tribe had a war chief and a civil chief, and Champlain left behind no impression of which positions were held by the chiefs (or "captains") he met at this time. The Huron also entered into military alliances as a confederacy, but trade was a right that belonged to particular clans and their individual tribe. Having been the first Huron tribe to establish contact with Champlain, trade with the French was the exclusive purview of the Arendarhonon, and most likely of the clans of Ochateguin and the brothers Savignon and Tregouaroti. Again, see Trigger and Heidenreich, for clan rights and politics.

With respect to Brûlé's overwintering of 1610–11, Champlain was somewhat confused about where the youth had been. He wrote that the territory of the Onontchataronon was eighty leagues away from the Great Rapid, when in fact it was just beyond Lac des Deux-Montagnes. His impression of a great distance must have been based on the fact that they overwintered with the Arendarhonon in Huronia.

The finance rates of twenty-five to thirty percent interest for fur traders appear in contracts in *Nouveaux documents*. In January 1608, for example, Matthijs Duysterloo, acting for Hontom, Jabach & Co., the most powerful financiers in Europe, provided Pont-Gravé with 1,290 livres tournois, 5 sols, for a trading voyage to Tadoussac and Canso at a guaranteed twenty-five percent return (Item 83, *Nouveaux documents*). Duysterloo, who was financier Evrard Jabach's son-in-law, personally controlled the supply of finished beaver pelts to Parisian hatmakers.

Chapter 27
Charles Lalement's itemizing of trade goods is in Vol. 4 of *The Jesuit Relations and Allied Documents*.

With respect to the changes to the historic Ottawa River, along the route followed by Champlain, hydroelectric dams would be installed at Rapides des Chats in 1931–32, at Portage du Fort (Chéneaux) in 1950, and at Long Sault (Carillon) in 1959–63. At the Chaudière, the river was initially dammed in 1868, with hydroelectric generation added in 1891 and 1900. Damming information has been gathered from Hydro Québec and Ontario Power Generation. The Deschênes rapids, a few miles upstream from Ottawa at the entrance to Lac Deschênes, are considered the only whitewater unchanged from Champlain's time along the route he followed. Damming has not only altered or obliterated the historic rapids but has increased the size of some of the riverine lakes, flooding shorelines and islands. See Ottawa Riverkeeper's *River Report, Issue No. 1, Ecology and Impacts,* May 2006. Father Bressani's description of river travel is from *Relation abrégée*.

Champlain called the Kinounchepirini the Quenongebin. He erroneously rendered the Algonquin name of the Akikodjiwan rapids as Asticou, which was the name of a chief who lived in the Penobscot area when Champlain was surveying what is now the coast of Maine in 1605. Alexander Mackenzie's description of the rapids is from *A General History of the Fur Trade*. Nicholas Garry's description is from *Diary of Nicholas Garry.*

Chapter 28

Rapides des Chats may be a misnomer, as the French who followed in Champlain's wake and so named it were probably thinking of the raccoon, an animal they believed was some kind of cat. For Garry's and Mackenzie's descriptions in this chapter, see Chapter 27 source notes. The description of Rapides des Chats by George Grant (aka George Munro) is from *Picturesque Canada*. While there is some evidence that later fur traders used the overland portage route followed by Champlain when the main passage around the east side of Grand Calumet was considered too dangerous, the route seemed to be scarcely known, if at all, in the decades after Champlain's 1613 visit. A landmark 1657 map of New France attributed to Bressani would show only the portages along the east side of Grand Calumet, nothing at all of the route on which Champlain was led by his Algonquin guides. Bressani's description of a makeshift bark shelter is from *Relation abrégée;* the translation is mine. Note that Champlain is famously thought to have lost an astrolabe at Green (Astrolabe) Lake along this portage. The instrument is in the collection of the Canadian Museum of Civilization. But the provenance is, to say the least, tenuous, and I am more persuaded that it was lost at a later date by Jesuit missionaries. See my article "The Mystery of Champlain's Astrolabe," *The Beaver,* Vol. 84, No. 6 (December 2004/January 2005).

Chapter 29

Regarding his initial meeting with Algonquin elders at Tessöuat's village and his proposals to them, Champlain's plans were increasingly echoing the Spanish model in Florida. He had pledged to spread the Roman Catholic faith among the native people as a condition of the new monopoly. They could be converted, and settled next to French habitations, which would provide them with security against their enemies in exchange for food they cultivated. (At the village of Nibachis, Champlain even noted that the Kinounchepirini "plant their maïze, grain by grain, as do those of Florida.") And as with Spanish Florida, chains of forts could be built deeper into the country in support of trade, and to extend the French military presence. Champlain's marriage contract of December 27, 1610, is in Vol. 2 of the Champlain Society's translation of his works, and identifies Nicolas Boullé as "secretary of the King's Chamber." An addendum, acknowledging Champlain's receipt of the balance of the dowry from Hélène's parents on January 14, 1619, is an appendix to Vol. 4. As for their married life, Boullé lived with Champlain at Quebec from 1620 to 1624, but thereafter never set foot in the colony. See her DCB entry by Marie-Emmanuel Chabot.

Chapter 30
Champlain did not say who served as his interpreter at the *tabagie,* but by this point in the journey he was plainly relying on Thomas, not de Vignau.

PART III
The Returning

Chapter 31
Regarding the hunting of birds at East Digges Island, according to Prickett, the Inuit used a long pole with a snare fitted on the end to snag birds. Prickett could not have been present for this demonstration, having most certainly misunderstood the device. The looped snare was probably a lanyard that secured the pole to the hunter's wrist. Inuit who hunted birds in this area were known to use poles to knock flying birds out of the air. No device with a snare loop on the end has ever been encountered.

John Davis's experiences with the Inuit are preserved in his voyage accounts, which are gathered in Hakluyt's *Principal Navigations.* For a textbook case of a trading encounter between English and Inuit that nearly ended in tragedy, see Sir John Franklin's experience when he reached the Beaufort Sea on an overland expedition. The Inuit were so gripped with desire to have Franklin's trade goods that they cut buttons from the coats of his men and tried to take goods even while the English attempted to drive them off with blows from rifle butts. The two parties were at dangerous odds for several hours, but in the end serious violence was avoided. Even at that, after the encounter, some of Franklin's men found stab marks in their coats, the knives having failed to reach their skin. The incident is described by Franklin in *Narrative of a Second Expedition to the Shore of the Polar Sea, in the Years 1825, 1826, and 1827* (Philadelphia: Carey, Lea, and Carey, 1828).

The survivors aboard the *Discovery* had no idea that a year-round English colony had been established at Cupers Cove in Conception Bay in 1610. Had they sailed for Newfoundland, help would have been remarkably close at hand.

Chapter 32

The 1611 Trinity House case in which men were docked wages for a mutiny is cited by Kenneth Andrews in *Ships, Money and Politics*. John Chamberlain's letter of December 4, 1611, to Sir Dudley Carleton is abstracted in the *Calendar of State Papers, Domestic Series, James I*, Vol. 9. The East India Company's commitment to three years of funding the passage search in late 1611 is established by the fact that in December 1614, Sir Thomas Smythe reminded the company's Court of Committees that it had been "three years since this Company did adventure £300 per annum for three years towards the discovery of the Norwest Passage." See Rundall, *Narratives of Voyages towards the North-West.*

For the life of Charles Howard, Lord High Admiral, as well as the functionings of the Court of the High Admiralty, see the Kenney biography noted in Chapter 5. Further information on courts appears in Sir William Blackstone's four-volume *Commentaries on the Laws of England* (Oxford: Clarendon Press, 1765–1769). For the Trevor family of Trevalyn, see the record of office-holders (Vice Admirals of the Coasts) at the Institute of Historical Research, as cited in Chapter 4; the family and individual biographies in the WBO; and the biographical history attached to the Plas Teg manuscripts held by the Flintshire Record Office. See also Virginia Company records cited in Chapter 3. For Sir Robert Mansell, see his listing by Andrew Thrush in the DNB, Kenney's biography of Charles Howard, Virginia Company records cited in Chapter 3, and his listing in the WBO. Sir John Coke's complaint about the corruption in the Royal Navy is quoted by Winton in *An Illustrated History of the Royal Navy.* For Sir Thomas Button, see his listing in the WBO as well as his entry by Aled Eames in the DCB. For all surviving materials related to the Button voyage of 1612–13, the Gibbons voyage of 1614, the North-West Company under Sir Thomas Smythe, including the surviving materials related to the 1615 and 1616 voyages of Bylot and Baffin, see Rundall. For the 1612 voyage of James Hall, see Rundall. See also Elizabeth Baigent's separate entries for Bylot and Baffin in the DNB.

Note that when Sir John Wolstenholme came to the dock to see off Bylot and Baffin in March 1615, Baffin wrote that the company director was accompanied by "Mr. Allwin Carye (husband for the voyage)." This was assuredly the same "Allin Cary" whom Edward Wilson testified took charge of the effects of the men lost with Henry Hudson in 1611 and ensured that their wages were paid to their beneficiaries. As "husband," it was likely that he was similarly providing fiscal oversight for the 1615 voyage back on shore. His relationship, if any, to Catherine Carey, first wife of the Lord High Admiral, is unknown. He was presumably the inspiration for Cary's Swan's-Nest (now Coats Island, although the name still applies to its southeast point) at the northern end of Hudson Bay, which was named by the Button expedition in 1612, and possibly for Carey's Islands in northern Baffin Bay, named by Baffin in 1616.

Sir Edward William Parry pays his compliment to Baffin in *Three Voyages for the Discovery of a Northwest Passage from the Atlantic to the Pacific, and Narrative of an Attempt to Reach the North Pole*, Vol. 1 (New York: Harper & Bros., 1844). For the 1616 and 1617 letters of Carew to Roe, see the abstracts in *Calendar of State Papers, Domestic Series, James 1*, Vol. 9. For Baffin's letter to Wolstenholme, see Rundall. Note that three of the "sounds" that Baffin and Bylot found in Baffin Bay in 1616 were actually straits, albeit choked with ice. Their northernmost progress, into what they named Smith's Sound (for Sir Thomas Smythe), was actually the entrance to the gap between Greenland and Ellesmere Island. Nearby Jones Sound, leading west, divides Ellesmere Island from North Devon Island. Lancaster Sound, to the south, was proven to be a navigable strait by Parry in 1819, and in time to be the entrance to the Northwest Passage.

Chapter 33
The feud between Sir Thomas Smythe and Sir Edwin Sandys (as well as Henry Wriothesley, Earl of Southampton) is covered well by Griffiths in *A Licence to Trade*. See also Smythe's DNB listing as cited in Chapter 5, as well as the DNB listing for Sandys by Theodore K. Rabb. See also Virginia Company sources as cited in Chapter 3. The January 1616 Carew letter to Roe is abstracted in the *Calendar of State Papers, Domestic Series, James I*, Vol. 9. Sebastian Cabot's 1553 ordinances were published by Hakluyt in *Principal Navigations*. The careers of Richard and Katherine Hudson are related by Llewelyn Powys in *Henry Hudson*.

Note that while the undated indictment has been tentatively placed in 1617 by past authors, to align with the second round of interrogations, I suspect it was created in early 1618. County courts generally heard Admiralty Oyer and Terminer cases twice annually. As the Hudson mutiny accused appeared at court in Surrey on July 24, 1618, the indictment must have been sworn out some time after the last batch of admiralty cases would have been heard around January 1618. Note in any case that this period was still "1617" at the time, as year-end was March 24 under the Julian calendar. As to the charge, the 1618 verdicts for their case further stated that they had stood trial for "feloniously pinning and putting Henry Hudson, master of the *Discovery*, out of the same ship with eight more of his company into a shallop in the Isle in [the parts of] America without meat, drink, clothes or other provision, whereby they died."

Chapter 34

There was one clue that de Vignau's knowledge of the English boy and a wrecked vessel in the Northern Sea came from eavesdropping, and it was a clue that befits an eavesdropper whose mastery of Algonquin was less than perfect, according to Champlain. Champlain would write that he had understood from de Vignau that eighty men ("80 hommes") had come ashore and been killed, when the true number of the Hudson castaways who would have been slain if John Hudson were the lone survivor was eight. Although the mistake may have been a typesetting error (there were others involving numbers in the pertinent chapter in *Les Voyages,* one in which "3" was used instead of "30"), Champlain's recollection could have been genuine, as well as informative. The difference phonetically between eight and eighty in French—*huit* and *quatre-vingt*—is great, but not so much in Algonquin—*nishwaswi* and *nishwaswomidana*—especially when a speaker is new to the tongue. And *midana,* the ten multiplier in the Algonquin numerical system, is very close to *mite* (sorcerer) and *mitek* (sorcerers). Had de Vignau, with his limited Algonquin, confused eight with eighty in a discussion that involved slaughtered English and a lone survivor being held prisoner by the Nebicerini, the sorcerer people?

Note that Champlain may have had another motivation for placing his last two latitude fixes of the 1613 journey so far north of their true location. His result for the beginning of the overland march, opposite Portage du Fort, was 46 2/3 degrees, which happened to be his exact value for the habitation at Quebec. His value for Tessöuat's summer camp was "around" 47 degrees. These measurements lifted Tessöuat's territory, and the watershed beyond it, above the latitude of the Quebec habitation, and above the old upper limit of the de Monts monopoly, of latitude 46. If need be, Champlain might have been able to lay claim to a new area of trading activity, separate from a monopoly covering the upper St. Lawrence. I have discussed the navigational aspects of Champlain's 1613 journey in far more detail in "The Mystery of Champlain's Astrolabe."

Hélène Boullé's disappearance in the autumn of 1613 is detailed in the disinheritance by her parents of January 10, 1614; see Item 149 in *Nouveaux documents.*

Afterword

For Sir Thomas Smythe's battles with his political and commercial adversaries, see the sources cited in Chapter 33. With respect to his son's marriage, see the *Calendar of State Papers, Domestic Series, James I,* Vol. 9, for abstracts of two key letters from John Chamberlain to Sir Dudley Carleton. On

November 26, 1618, Chamberlain wrote: "The Lord Chamberlain and others forwarded the marriage of Sir Thomas Smythe's son, of eighteen, to Lady Isabella Rich, without knowledge of his father, who, at their entreaty, has consented to receive her." Chamberlain followed up on December 12 with: "Sir Thomas Smythe has agreed to allow his new daughter-in-law 800£ a year jointure, and 800£ a year to his son and her for maintenance." For Smythe's death, see his DNB entry by Basil Morgan. Bylot's and Baffin's explorations, and Samuel Purchas's careless treatment of their results, can be found in Rundall's *Narratives of Voyages towards the North-West*. A useful timeline of Champlain's final years appears in Litalien and Vaugeois' *Champlain: The Birth of French America*. For Hélène Boullé, and facts concerning Champlain's estate, see her DCB listing by Marie-Emmanuel Chabot. For her parents' revocation of her 1614 disinheritance, dated May 23, 1636, see Item 149 in *Nouveaux documents*.

Acknowledgements

—

MANY PEOPLE WERE BADGERED OR OTHERWISE engaged by me in the course of writing this book, which went on for a good three years, and I have striven to acknowledge them in the source notes. But I must give particular thanks to Dr. Conrad Heidenreich, a gentleman of a scholar whom I first encountered while researching the provenance of the so-called Champlain's astrolabe. We corresponded by e-mail for almost a year before finally meeting in person. I hope I have been as helpful to him in his own researches on Champlain as he has been to mine on Hudson and Champlain, although I suspect I got the better end of the bargain.

I redrafted this book about six times, and produced (and discarded) enough material for at least two additional books. I am thankful to Maya Mavjee, Doubleday Canada's publisher, for her patience. I am especially grateful to my agent, Dean Cooke, and my editor, Martha Kanya-Forstner, for laying out the orange pylons I needed to steer this story through, and having the confidence that I would finally negotiate them without knocking any down. Copy editor Shaun Oakey then gave the final manuscript a careful and crucial review, and I am grateful for the lucid queries he attached, above and beyond his finesse with grammar and punctuation.

Index

—

Southampton, Earl of—see:
Wriothesley, Henry
Southampton I., *xv*, 321
Spitsbergen, 4, 17, 18, 37, 39, 43,
62–64, 208, 316, 374
Spoliation—See: piracy
Stadacona, 193
Staffe, Philip, 46, 60–61, 82, 83, 85, 88,
89, 97, 100, 106–09, 110, 116, 119,
125, 143–47, 149, 159, 162–64,
166, 171, 325, 327, 379, 382
Stere, William, 17
Supercargo, role of, 40–41
Swallow, 24

T
Tadouac, Lake, 91–93, 124, 129, 198,
378
Tadoussac, *xv*, 115, 192, 198–99,
210–11, 216, 218, 224, 226–27,
228–31, 232, 248, 251, 280, 282,
305, 336, 390, 391, 392, 394
Temperate Arctic theory, 17, 62–63
Tessöuat, 179, 184, 195, 209, 211–16,
254, 255–56, 262, 266, 270, 271,
273–74, 275–78, 280–81,
282–91, 305, 332–41, 345, 390,
395, 399
Thomas—(interpreter, servant of
Daniel Boyer), 220–21, 224, 231,
254, 259, 270–71, 273, 277–78,
281, 284, 286–88, 290, 332, 334,
336–37, 339, 342, 391, 396
Thomas, John, 142, 149, 163–64, 297,
298, 299–302
Tilbury Hope, 47
Torres Strait, 185
Torture of native prisoners, 184,
242–43, 247, 250, 280, 283. 340
Tower of London, 35, 37, 45
Trade goods (French), 257, 283

Trade and colonization monopolies,
in New France, 183, 190–92,
198–200
Trade's Increase, 45
Tregouaroti, 252–54, 394
Trevor, Sir John, 311–12, 314, 397
Trevor, Dr. Richard, 173. 311–12, 322,
397
Trinity House (Deptford Strand), 14,
40, 161, 165, 295, 297, 308–09,
323, 325, 353, 367, 397
Trois-Rivières, 222, 346, 391
Tronson, Germain, 223, 226
Truce, Twelve Year (Spain and Dutch
Republic, 1609), 22, 244

U
Ungava Bay, *xv*, 79, 81–82, 86, 89,
102
United Netherlands Chartered East
India Company—see: VOC

V
Vaches, Pointe au, 210, 228
van Meteren, Emmanuel, 25, 30–33,
152, 349–50, 371, 372, 383
Varsina River, 102
Veer, Gerrit de, 106
Vermeulen, Ludowica, 188, 224, 225
Vervins, Treaty of (Spain and France,
1598), 207
Vignau, Nicolas de, 177–80, 181,
184–85, 188, 195, 204, 205–07,
209, 213–16, 217, 221, 224, 226,
231, 236, 256, 259, 265, 270–71,
274, 277–78, 280, 287–91, 305,
332–33, 336–41, 347, 396, 399
Virginia Company 21, 23–24, 28–30,
33, 36, 38, 56–57, 139, 198, 311,
320–22, 326, 343–44, 372, 373,
374, 375, 389, 397, 398